TORONTO'S
MANY FACES

TORONTO'S
MANY FACES Fifth Edition

Tony Ruprecht

DUNDURN PRESS
TORONTO

Page Layout: Beth Crane, WeMakeBooks.ca
Printer: Marquis
Pullout map by Christopher Pandolfi
Interior maps by John Mardon

Library and Archives Canada Cataloguing in Publication

Ruprecht, Tony, 1942-
   Toronto's many faces / Tony Ruprecht. -- 5th ed.

Includes bibliographical references and index.
Issued also in electronic format.
ISBN 978-1-55488-885-6

1. Toronto (Ont.)--Guidebooks. 2. Minorities--Ontario--Toronto. I. Title.

FC3097.18.R86 2010   917.13'541045'08693   C2010-905987-5

1   2   3   4   5   15   14   13   12   11

We acknowledge the support of the **Canada Council for the Arts** and the **Ontario Arts Council** for our publishing program. We also acknowledge the financial support of the **Government of Canada** through the **Canada Book Fund** and **Livres Canada Books,** and the **Government of Ontario** through the **Ontario Book Publishers Tax Credit** program, and the **Ontario Media Development Corporation.**

Care has been taken to trace the ownership of copyright material used in this book. The author and the publisher welcome any information enabling them to rectify any references or credits in subsequent editions.

J. Kirk Howard, President

Printed and bound in Canada.
www.dundurn.com

Dundurn Press	Gazelle Book Services Limited	Dundurn Press
3 Church Street, Suite 500	White Cross Mills	2250 Military Road
Toronto, Ontario, Canada	High Town, Lancaster, England	Tonawanda, NY
M5E 1M2	LA1 4XS	U.S.A. 14150

Contents

INTRODUCTION VI

ACKNOWLEDGMENTS VIII

THE (NATIVE) ABORIGINAL COMMUNITY . . 1

THE AFGHAN COMMUNITY 8

THE AFRICAN COMMUNITIES 11

THE AHMADI MUSLIM COMMUNITY . . . 19

THE ALBANIAN COMMUNITY 22

THE ARAB COMMUNITIES 25

THE ARMENIAN COMMUNITY 34

THE AUSTRALIAN & NEW ZEALANDER
COMMUNITIES 41

THE AUSTRIAN COMMUNITY 45

THE BELARUSAN COMMUNITY 49

THE BELGIAN COMMUNITY 52

THE BENGALI COMMUNITY 55

THE BLACK CANADIAN COMMUNITY . . 58

THE BRAZILIAN COMMUNITY 63

THE BULGARIAN COMMUNITY 66

THE CAMBODIAN COMMUNITY 71

THE CARIBBEAN COMMUNITIES 75

THE CHINESE COMMUNITIES 86

THE CROATIAN COMMUNITY 102

THE CZECH COMMUNITY 107

THE DANISH COMMUNITY 113

THE DANUBE SWABIAN COMMUNITY . 118

THE DUTCH COMMUNITY 122

THE ENGLISH COMMUNITY 127

THE ERITREAN COMMUNITY 135

THE ESTONIAN COMMUNITY 137

THE FILIPINO COMMUNITY 143

THE FINNISH COMMUNITY 149

THE FRENCH COMMUNITY 156

THE GERMAN COMMUNITY 164

THE GREEK COMMUNITY 172

THE GUJARTI COMMUNITY 183

THE HUNGARIAN COMMUNITY 189

THE ICELANDIC COMMUNITY 196

THE INDO-CANADIAN COMMUNITIES . 200

THE INDONESIAN COMMUNITY 209

THE IRANIAN COMMUNITY 212

THE IRISH COMMUNITY 216

THE ISMAILI MUSLIM COMMUNITY . . 223

THE ITALIAN COMMUNITY 226

THE JAPANESE COMMUNITY 238

THE JEWISH COMMUNITY 247

THE KOREAN COMMUNITY 261

THE LAOTIAN COMMUNITY 268

THE LATVIAN COMMUNITY 272

THE LITHUANIAN COMMUNITY 278

THE MACEDONIAN COMMUNITY 283

THE MALAYSIAN COMMUNITY 288

THE MALTESE COMMUNITY 291

THE NORWEGIAN COMMUNITY 297

THE PAKISTANI COMMUNITY 301

THE POLISH COMMUNITY 307

THE PORTUGUESE COMMUNITY 316

THE ROMANIAN COMMUNITY 328

THE RUSSIAN COMMUNITY 333

THE SCOTTISH COMMUNITY 340

THE SERBIAN COMMUNITY 345

THE SIKH COMMUNITY 353

THE SLOVAK COMMUNITY 357

THE SLOVENIAN COMMUNITY 361

THE SOMALI COMMUNITY 372

THE SPANISH AND LATIN AMERICAN
COMMUNITIES 375

THE SWEDISH COMMUNITY 385

THE SWISS COMMUNITY 390

THE TAMIL COMMUNITY 393

THE THAI COMMUNITY 397

THE TURKISH COMMUNITY 401

THE UKRAINIAN COMMUNITY 406

THE VIETNAMESE COMMUNITY 419

THE WELSH COMMUNITY 424

GLOSSARY OF HOLIDAYS &
CELEBRATIONS 427

ORGANIZATIONS SERVING
MULTICULTURALISM 431

BIBLIOGRAPHY 434

Maps

ARABTOWN 28

DOWNTOWN CHINATOWN 92

GREEKTOWN 176

CORSO ITALIA 236

JEWISH NEIGHBOURHOOD 258

KOREATOWN 266

LITTLE POLAND 309

PORTUGAL VILLAGE 319

UKRAINIAN VILLAGE 417

Introduction

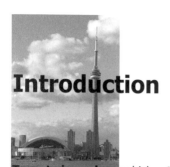

Toronto is a mirror which reflects a world of many faces. Since its beginning, the city has been shaped by the cultural diversity of its people—from the Native people who first named the site *Taronto* to the newest arrivals who have travelled across oceans to call the city home. Whether they came seeking new opportunities or fleeing persecution in their homeland, the people of Toronto brought to the city their skills and enthusiasm for work. Yonge Street, built in the 18th century, the subway system, constructed in the 1950s, and the engineering feats of modern-day landmarks such as SkyDome (now the Rogers Centre) stand as testimonies of how, together, cultural communities have contributed to building Toronto. People from across the globe have infused the city with a cosmopolitan character, creating neighbourhoods to explore, and introducing new cultures and cuisines to discover. In 1989, Toronto was named the world's most multicultural city by the United Nations. Today, its citizens include more than 168 different cultural groups, speaking over 100 different languages.

Many Faces pays tribute to the contributions of old and new Torontonians. It is a guide for tourists, a source book for newcomers, a directory for businesses and organizations, and for Torontonians it is a passport to the many cultures that exist at their doorstep.

The book provides a brief synopsis of the settlement and development of more than 70 of Toronto's communities, including neighbourhoods, commercial districts, landmarks, and significant and colourful events in their history.

The section entitled "Places to Go" is a handy guide for taking you inside the communities to explore cultural centres, museums, art galleries, and monuments. A brief introduction to the traditions of each group will assist you in sampling foods from the many restaurants, specialty shops, and bakeries that add adventure to shopping and dining.

The spirit of Toronto's cultural communities can be found in the religious centres listed in the book, while a calendar of local celebrations and festivals highlights how each community expresses its cultural heritage. Other helpful information includes the names, addresses, and contact information for institutions, media, major organizations, and cultural groups.

Finally, each section includes a list of prominent Torontonians who have excelled in the fields of business, politics, arts and sciences, or sports.

Almost every day, I receive requests for information on cultural communities from various individuals, organizations, media, and other politicians. *Many Faces*, now in its fifth edition, is an attempt to group together in one book information on the history, businesses, institutions, and organizations of Toronto cultural communities. An effort was made to include as many communities as possible, although some were so small or of such recent origin that they were difficult to locate and could not be included.

The problem with any directory is that it runs the risk of being outdated the day it goes to press. I have striven to provide updated information and have included phone numbers that can be used to verify places and organizations of interest.

The criteria for highlighting particular businesses was very often based on the authenticity of the foods and products sold, the establishment's popularity, and its place in the history of the community. I was guided by recommendations from members of the communities, and in many cases I made my selections arbitrarily, the way the reader may discover a new place by exploring a neighbourhood. To assist this process of discovery, we have provided rough maps of some neighbourhoods, though we advise the reader unfamiliar with Toronto to pick up a detailed street map at a tourist bureau or local store.

The lists of prominent Torontonians are only a sampling of names that came to mind and are in no way meant to reflect all those who have contributed to their community and the city. In general up to 10 people from each community were listed, while up to 20 names were included for the larger communities.

As new groups emerge, future editions of *Many Faces* will provide information on Toronto's constantly changing make-up. It may be that there are communities in the city that I have not discovered. I welcome your comments and suggestions. If you have updated information on any of the communities in this book, please write to:

Tony Ruprecht
71 Springhurst Avenue
Toronto, Ontario
M6K 1B5

I hope this book will foster an appreciation for the diversity of cultural expression that characterizes this city. I invite you to take *Many Faces* in hand and discover the world of Toronto.

—Tony Ruprecht

Acknowledgments

A book of this scope could not have been completed without the help of a number of people. I would like to give special thanks to Vida Radovanovic and Gail Hanney; without them this book would not have been possible. To the contributors of each chapter, I am indebted for the countless hours spent in gathering information lending assistance in the preparation of this volume. I am grateful to Janet Cangiano and David Hehn for their editorial suggestions, and John Mardon, who illustrated the maps.

In the preparation of this publication, many books and other resource materials were consulted. The Toronto Historical Board was helpful in providing us with information on historical plaques and monuments in the city. The primary source for history on Toronto's multicultural communities came from *Toronto's People* published by the Multicultural History Society of Ontario, an organization which enhances both academic and community understanding of multiculturalism.

The royalties from the sale of *Many Faces* will go to assist non-profit multicultural or charitable organizations.

Telephone Numbers

To place calls in the Greater Toronto Area, you must use 10-digit dialing—for example, 416-555-1212, 905-555-1212 or 647-555-1212.

The (Native) Aboriginal Community

Toronto owes its name and origin to the Huron, Iroquois, and Ojibwa nations who first used the area as a shortcut for trail and canoe routes between Lakes Ontario and Huron. The Humber River was then named Taronto, first by the Huron Indians who once populated the area, and later by the Seneca nation (an Iroquois tribe) who settled on the banks of the river in the area now occupied by Toronto.

This area remained a Seneca domain until the mid-17th century. In the early 18th century, the Ojibwa began moving into southern Ontario, and the Mississauga Indians (an Ojibwa tribe) gradually replaced the Iroquois along the north shore of Lake Ontario. Their most important village was located on what is now Baby Point. By 1805, all of the lands surrounding present-day Toronto were appropriated (The Toronto Purchase) from the Mississauga Indians. Native people remained in the area, but lived primarily on their own territories.

Today, Toronto is home to approximately 25,000–30,000 Native people, and a large number of Métis. The Ojibwa and members of the Iroquois Six Nations Confederacy make up the largest group in the community. One-third of the province's Native reserves are located within 200 miles of Toronto, and the city's Native community has grown significantly in the last three decades, as people leave the reserves for job opportunities in the city.

Toronto is the headquarters for the federal regional offices of the **Department of Indian Affairs**, and is home to a number of political, cultural, and service organizations representing reserve and non-reserve Natives. One of the many organizations is the **Native Canadian Centre of Toronto**. The centre offers services to help bridge the transition from life on the reserves to the city, and provides facilities for cultural groups, and social gatherings.

Native culture is exhibited by groups who perform ceremonial dances and by theatre groups such as the **Native Earth Performing Arts**, which stages plays articulating the views and concerns of Native people. The first Native Canadian ballet was staged in 1989. Toronto is also one of the major distribution centres in Canada for First Nations and Inuit art, sculpture, and crafts.

Native people have contributed to the city in the fields of art, sports, education, and politics. Lacrosse, the national sport of Canada, was first played as a game-ritual between villages of Native people. A downtown Toronto street bears the name of Tom Longboat, a renowned long distance runner who won the 11th annual marathon race in Toronto in 1907 and was later elected into the **Canadian Sports Hall of Fame**. Brant Avenue as well as Brantford, Ontario—the home of the Six Nations Indian territory—were named after the Mohawk leader Joseph Brant (Thayendonegea). The Grand River reserve is now the home of the Six Nations Iroquois but was originally purchased for them from the Mississaugas when they came to Canada from their traditional territory in New York, following the American Revolution.

Other notable Toronto Native individuals include Orenhyatekha, a medical doctor and prominent businessman in the 1890s, and O.M. Martin, a brigadier during the Second World War who was appointed a magistrate for the county of York. Symphony conductor John Kim Bell composed *In the Land of the Spirits*, the first Native ballet, and playwright and producer Tomson Highway is a Dora award winner. George Armstrong, former coach of the Toronto Maple Leafs hockey team, is a past recipient of the Charlie Conacher Memorial Trophy for his humanitarian contributions.

Places to Go

The mezzanine level of the fourth **Toronto Dominion Tower**, located on the south side of Wellington Street, features a permanent display of Native Canadian art. Located on the **Canadian National Exhibition** park grounds are statues of animals and mythical creatures. The shapes and details are taken from Native mythology and religious beliefs.

A large totem pole adorns the lawns of the **Native Canadian Centre of Toronto**, (Tel. 416-964-9087, www.ncct.on.ca, 16 Spadina Rd.) The centre hosts Native theatre, readings, art exhibits, and conferences. It also operates the **Native Craft Shop**.

The **Algonquians Sweet Grass Gallery**, (Tel. 416-703-1336, www.tasggi.com, 668 Queen St. W.,) specializes in authentic Canadian Native arts and crafts such as moccasins, pottery, beadwork, and various works of art.

Toronto art galleries that carry works by Native artists include: **Gallery Phillip**, (Tel. 416-447-1301, www.gevik.com, 75 The Donway W., Suite 202,) and **Armen Art Gallery**, (Tel. 416-924-5375, www.ravenspirit.ca, 16 Wellesley Street W), which displays contemporary Native art. The **Royal Ontario Museum**, (Tel. 416-586-5549, www.rom.on.ca, 100 Queen's Park) exhibits works by Toronto artist Paul Kane who traveled around the Great Lakes in the 1840s sketching Native people in their homelands.

Native people have contributed to the domestication of grapes, berries, pecans, and other nuts, and the cultivation of tobacco, corn, potatoes,

The Native Canadian Centre of Toronto features a totem pole in its courtyard.

peanuts, squash, melons, tomatoes, and maple syrup. Native cooking includes many versions of nabos (soups made from available vegetables and meats). Pakwejigan (a quickbread based on corn or wheat flour) accompanies most traditional meals. Sagamite (a thick mixture of meats, beans, and corn simmered in a cast-iron kettle) is often the central dish at any Iroquois occasion.

The largest concentration of Iroquois in Canada can be found at the Six Nations of the Grand River First Nation near Brantford, Ontario—a two-hour drive from Toronto. The territory is the largest in Canada, and features the **Woodland Culture Centre**, (Tel. (519) 759-2650, www.woodland-centre.on.ca, 184 Mohawk Street, Brantford). **Her Majesty's Chapel of the Mohawks**, (Tel. (519) 756-0240, www.mohawkchapel.ca, 301 Mohawk St, Brantford) was the home of Emily Pauline Johnson, (1861–1913). Johnson, the daughter of a Mohawk Chief and an English woman, is best known for her poetry celebrating her Native heritage. To the east are the territories at Tyendinaga and Akwesasne. All the territories have retail outlets that sell Native Indian arts and crafts.

Religious Centres, Schools and Other Institutions

Native people practise a number of religions, including Amerindian religions. Many members of the Six Nation Territory follow the Longhouse way of life. In Toronto, a Native religion closely related to traditional Algonkian practices is observed. The First Nations in North America at the time of contact with Europeans had their own forms of spirituality. This spirituality forms the basis of the manner in which they live their lives. In their systems, spirituality is the basis of social, economic, and political systems.

The creation stories of each of the Nations provides the framework for understanding the elements of life, such as land, water, and air. These stories determined laws to live by, the laws of nature, and the laws of human and non-human relationships. The belief is that all aspects of the Earth are alive—each with their own responsibilities to ensure that all life continues and that all life forms are connected, each one needing the other to survive.

For all of these gifts that are provided on Mother Earth by the Creator, it is humanity's responsibility to show gratitude. This gratitude is demonstrated in ceremonies, which are a key element in the lives of the Iroquois people. It is believed that tobacco, sage, sweetgrass, and cedar are sacred gifts from the four directions. Burning these in ceremonies and giving thanksgiving prayers are ways of purification and communication to the Creator. Gratitude is also demonstrated in daily thanksgiving each morning, as well as in various gatherings, such as Pow Wows.

Many Native people today practice one of the many Christian religions that were brought into their territories by European settlers. There are several different denominations that have established themselves. Some Native people have assumed leadership roles in the churches, such as Rev. Stan McKay from Northern Ontario who served as the first Aboriginal Moderator of the United Church of Canada.

Native ceremonies often include the burning of sacred herbs, such as cedar (Ojibwa), sweetgrass, sage and tobacco. The smoke is meant to purify the environment and cleanse the participants. The smoking of the pipe creates a communion between the spirits to whom it is offered and those who smoke the pipe. Feasts are held to offer food to the spirits, and a bowl of water symbolizing the life-blood of Mother Earth is shared. Dancing and healing rituals are often part of the ceremonies.

♦ FIRST NATIONS SCHOOL OF TORONTO, (Tel. 416-393-0555, 935 Dundas St. E), teaches Native ways based on traditional beliefs and ancestral practices. Its aim is to carry on the spirituality passed on to a select few who believe and practise the old ways.

Holidays and Celebrations

Throughout the year, celebrations are held marking the seasonal changes in nature.

♦ **NEW YEAR'S MORNING.** On January 1, children of the Six Nations Reserve go from home to home to collect gifts of homemade pastries, candy, and other treats.

♦ **BREAD AND CHEESE DAY,** is celebrated on Victoria Day, May 24. Residents of the Six Nations Reserve form a line outside the community centre, and band councillors distribute offerings of bread and cheese. There are also cultural displays, horse racing, and ball games.

♦ **THANKSGIVING DAY** celebrations are held in Autumn to give thanks for the beauty of nature and the rich harvest of food.

♦ **PIPE OF PEACE SMOKING CEREMONY** is the most important ceremony. These Pow Wows are held from time to time for the development of friendships and the promotion of culture, featuring foods, crafts displays, singing, dancing, and drumming.

♦ **HARVEST CEREMONIES** for corn, strawberries, and other foods are regulated by the seasons, the moon, and the growth of plants.

♦ **CHRISTIAN HOLIDAYS AND EUROPEAN DAYS,** such as New Year's Eve and Christmas, are often celebrated. Natives have incorporated their own traditions into these celebrations.

♦ **TREATY DAYS** are observed (though not always celebrated).

♦ **POW WOWS** are now annual events, and include: International Pow Wow, held at the **Rogers Centre** in Toronto; Pow Wow at Six Nations, usually held in July in Toronto; and in August in Mississauga. Most of the larger First Nations also hold events in their own communities. Pow Wows traditionally bring together people from various communities for social gathering and thanksgiving. People wear their finest outfits and participated in feasting, dancing, and singing.

See Holidays and Celebrations in Glossary.

Media

♦ **ABORIGINAL VOICES RADIO,** 106.5 FM. (Tel. 416-703-1287, www.aboriginalvoices.com, P.O. Box 87, Station E) Radio station which plays Native Canadian and Native American music.

Organizations

- **ASSOCIATION FOR NATIVE DEVELOPMENT IN THE PERFORMING & VISUAL ARTS**, (Tel. 416-972-0871, www.andpva.com, 60 Atlantic Ave., Suite 111), assists in the development of programs that encourage persons of Aboriginal ancestry to become involved in the performing and visual arts, including theatre, music, dance, literature, and film.

- **NATIVE CANADIAN CENTRE OF TORONTO**, (Tel. 416-964-9087, www.ncct.on.ca, 16 Spadina Rd). One of the first organizations established to help Native people in the city. Services offered include individual counselling and referral, and the provision of social, recreational, and cultural programs. The centre publishes the monthly *The Native Canadian* and sponsors Native theatre, readings, art exhibits, and conferences. Executive Director: Larry Frost.

- **NATIVE EARTH PERFORMING ARTS INC.**, (Tel. 416-531-6377, www.nativeearth.ca, 55 Mill St., #74, Suite 300 & 305), is a not-for-profit Native theatre company dedicated to the development of a theatre that articulates the concerns and viewpoint of this country's Native people. The company performs at various theatres throughout the city. Managing Artistic Director: Yvette Nolan.

- **ONTARIO FEDERATION OF INDIAN FRIENDSHIP CENTRES**, (Tel. 416-956-7575, Fax 416-956-7577, www.ofifc.org, 219 Front St. E), is an umbrella organization for Aboriginal centres. Executive Director: Sylvia Maracle.

- **NATIONAL ABORIGINAL ACHIEVEMENT FOUNDATION**, (Tel. 416-926-0775, Fax 416-926-7554, www.naaf.ca, 215 Spadina Ave., Suite 450), is a non-profit organization that arranges assistance, grants, and scholarships for Native youth to study in the arts and business. They also sponsor fundraising events, including Canada's first Native ballet, *In the Land of the Spirits*, and hold an annual achievement event, televised on CBC TV. Chief Executive Officer: Roberta Jamieson.

- **INDIAN AND NORTHERN AFFAIRS CANADA**, (Tel. 416-973-6234, Fax 416-954-6329, www.ainc-inac.gc.ca, Toronto office: 25 St. Clair Ave. E., 8th floor).

- **INDIAN COMMISSION OF ONTARIO**, A mediation body between the First Nations in Ontario and the federal and provincial governments.

- **MÉTIS NATION OF ONTARIO**, (Tel. 416-977-9881, Fax 416-977-9911, www.metisnation.org, 103 Richmond St. E., Suit 404).

- **NATIVE WOMEN'S RESOURCE CENTRE**, (Tel. 416-963-9963, Fax 416-963-9573, www.nativewomenscentre.org, 191 Gerrard St. E), provides support services, including family court, life skills, and job training. Run by and for Native women. Executive Director: Linda Ense.

♦ **WIGWAMEN INC.**, (Tel. 416-481-4451, www.wigwamen.com, 25 Imperial St., Suite 310), is a non-profit housing corporation established in 1972 and managed by Native people. General Manager: Angus Palmer.

Prominent Torontonians

Allen (Ahmoo) Angeconeb, artist; Roberta Jamieson, Chief of Six Nations, Former Ontario Ombudsperson and first Native woman lawyer in Canada; Harry Laforme, judge, Ontario Indian Commission.

Sources: Larry Frost (Native Canadian Centre), Ron Robert, Sylvia Thompson.

The Afghan Community

Toronto's Afghan community made its presence known on February 15, 1989, when members paraded down Yonge Street to celebrate the withdrawal of Soviet troops from Afghanistan. The rich culture of the Afghans can be discovered during the community's religious and cultural celebrations throughout the year.

Most of Toronto's Afghans are political refugees who were displaced in the late 1970s during the Soviet invasion of Afghanistan, a republic in Central Asia. Afghans began arriving in Canada in 1982, and today there are 45,000 Afghani Canadians scattered throughout Toronto, with a concentration in the Keele and Sheppard area.

Members of the community speak Pushto and Dari. Many Afghans have been highly educated in their homeland in such disciplines as engineering and journalism, and have established themselves in the professions. Others have started their own businesses, which range from grocery stores to carpet stores and auto repair shops.

Afghan House, in North York, is the community's main cultural institution, where Afghans celebrate their cultural values with festivals and political events. The organization, which publishes a newspaper and a magazine, aims to educate Canadians about the culture, history, and politics of Afghanistan.

Places to Go

Afghan carpets, ceramics, gifts, and figurines are available at a number of carpet stores in the city including **Mohammad Yousof Rug Co.**, (Tel. 416-359-1690, 163 Queen St. E). **Saleem Caravan & Barakat Foods**, (Tel. 416-269-6600, 565 Markham Rd).

Religious Centres, Schools and Other Institutions

Ninety-nine percent of the community is Muslim and most of the rest is Hindu. The mosque frequented by Afghans is the **Afghan Association Mosque and Cultural House**.

- AFGHAN ASSOCIATION OF ONTARIO MOSQUE, (Tel. 416-744-9289, Fax 416-744-6671, 29 Pemican Court, Unit 6).
- AFGHAN ASSOCIATION MOSQUE AND CULTURAL HOUSE, (29 Pemican Court, Unit 5).

Holidays and Celebrations

- NEW YEAR'S DAY is celebrated on March 21, when members of the community gather together for musical events and cultural activities.
- EIDS are the major Muslim religious celebrations. The first Eid is at the end of a month of fasting, followed two months later by a second celebration. During this time Afghans visit each other, offering best wishes over a cup of tea.

See Holidays and Celebrations in Glossary.

Media

- NAYAB MAGAZINE, (Tel. 416-803-2353, 85 Emmett Ave, Suite 305). Newspaper for the Afgani community. Editor: Mr. Ghafar Hamid.
- THE AFGHAN MONTHLY, (Tel. 416-744-9289, 100 Tempo Ave, Suite 305). A monthly publication by the Afghan Association of Ontario.
- VOICE OF AFGHAN SOLIDARITY RADIO, AM 1430, (Tel. 416-937-1414, 6 Radcliffe Rd). Producer: Halim Amini.
- ZARNEGAAR, (Tel. 416-438-7784, 2376 Eglinton Ave. E., P.O. Box 44504), is published bi-weekly. Editor: Mrs. Mahboob.

Organizations

- AFGHAN ASSOCIATION OF ONTARIO (CANADA), (Tel. 416-744-9289, Fax 416-744-6671, 100 Tempo Ave. Suite 305). Provides counselling services in orientation, interpretation, translation, immigration, assistance filling out forms, and employment and housing information. Heritage language classes are also held. The organization sponsors Afghan refugees from Pakistan, Iran, India, and other countries.
- AFGHAN WOMEN'S COUNSELLING & INTEGRATION COMMUNITY SUPPORT ORGANIZATION, (Tel. 416-588-3585, Fax 416-588-4552, www.afghanwomen.org, 789 Don Mills Rd. Suite 312), provides free

services to Afghan women such as English classes along with a daycare during classes for their children.

◆ SABAWOON AFGHAN FAMILY EDUCATION AND COUNSELLING CENTRE, (Tel. 416-293-4100, www.safecc.org, 1200 Markham Rd., Suite 219), is a non-profit organization that provides counselling and awareness education. President: Wassay Shefa.

◆ CONSULATE GENERAL OF AFGHANISTAN, (477 Richmond St. W. Suite 901).

◆ AFGHAN CANADIAN CHAMBER OF COMMERCE, (Tel. 416-409-4928).

◆ AFGHAN SENIOR ASSOCIATION, (Tel. 416-741-6633).

Prominent Torontonians

Dr. Saira Markovic, physician and surgeon; Elder M. Akram Lodin; and Elder Hadi Wafi.

Contributors: Jan Alekozai, former Executive Director, The Afghan Association of Ontario (Canada); Mr. Ghulam Ferotan, Mr. Khaled Akbar.

Source: Nasrin Hotaki, Amini Halim.

The African Communities

African art and culture can be found in city arts and crafts stores, restaurants, and in performances by African theatre and musical groups such as the 1988 **World Drums Musical Festival** held at **Roy Thomson Hall**. Writers, including Wole Soyinka, Nigeria's Nobel Prize winner for literature, have lectured at the city's universities, where African studies programs are offered.

Toronto's African communities represent a diversity of cultures, races, religions, and linguistic groups from the second largest continent in the world. African Blacks, Whites, Asian Indians, and other ethnocultural groups who are viewed as African after several generations of settlement on the continent are represented. Among these later groups are Asian Indians of Muslim, Hindu, and Goan Christian religious-cultural backgrounds, Europeans of British, Portuguese, Afrikaner-Dutch, and Jewish ethnocultural origins, and people of mixed descent.

The first Africans to come to Canada were brought as slaves as early as 1628. From 1791 to 1792 many returned to Africa from Nova Scotia. Immigration to Canada before 1950 was sparse, increasing between 1968 and 1970 when many Africans from Ethiopia, Kenya, Ghana, Nigeria, Zimbabwe, Zambia, the Republic of South Africa, Tanzania, Uganda, and Zaire arrived in Toronto. In the 1970s, a large number of Ugandan Asians immigrated to Canada after they were expelled by President Idi Amin. The city also gained new citizens of Portuguese descent who left newly independent African nations such as Angola and Mozambique.

Immigration continued throughout the 1980s and 1990s with the return of many African students of the 1960s. The African communities are spread throughout the city and are largely represented by the countries of Cape Verde, Ethiopia, Nigeria, Uganda, Angola, Mozambique, Sierre Leone, Somalia, South Africa, and Zimbabwe.

Many African Torontonians share cultures with European and British communities in the city. The Cape Verde community, which numbers around 500, originates from the African island nation ruled by Portugal from the 15th century until achieving independence in 1975. For the most part, the community associates with Toronto's Portuguese, sharing a common language, religion, cuisine, and the celebration of festivals and holidays. The **Cape Verde Community Centre** of Toronto was the community's first organization in the city.

Other Northern African nations represented in the city include Algeria, Morocco, Egypt, Tunisia, and the Western Sahara.

People from Ethiopia, Uganda, Tanzania, Somalia, and Kenya represent a large majority of Toronto's Eastern Africans.

Amharic-speaking Ethiopian students began arriving in Canada in the 1960s and 1970s. Following the 1974 Ethiopian revolutions, refugees fled to neighbouring African countries and eventually immigrated to Canada, many settling in Parkdale and downtown Toronto. The **Ethiopian Association** in Toronto was formed to assist newcomers to the community.

Italian and Tigrinya are spoken by Toronto's Eritreans who represent nine different cultural groups. Eritrea, independent from Ethiopia, was occupied by Italy during the Second World War. In the late 1980s, refugees from Eritrea arrived in the city, often immigrating indirectly from countries such as Sudan, Italy, and Greece.

In 1972, with the "Africanization" of Uganda by Idi Amin, some 50,000 Ugandan Asians were expelled from the country. Approximately 7,000 arrived in Canada, with about 40 percent settling in Toronto. Included in this group were the Gujarati Hindus, traditionally a business caste in India and East Africa, and Goan Indians.

The majority of West Africans in the city are from the countries of Ghana, Sierra Leone, Gambia, Liberia, and Toronto's largest West African community, Nigeria. Representatives from these West African nations who studied in Toronto in the early 1960s later returned and settled in the city.

A few Nigerian students came to study in Canada as early as the 1930s and 1940s, but the largest groups to settle in the city arrived in the late 1960s and in the early 1970s following the Nigerian Civil War. Nigeria is a country with over 200 ethnic groups and languages. There are a large number of Yoruba, and some 2,000 Ibo-speaking peoples in the city. The Nigerian community's religious activities centre around St. Bartholomew's Church on Dundas Street. There are also several Nigerian soccer clubs active in the city.

New settlers from the Central African nations of Zaire, Rwanda, and Burundi have also made Toronto their home.

The largest African communities in the city are represented primarily by the Republic of South Africa, Ghana, Nigeria and Angola. There are 50,000 South Africans living throughout the area, with concentrations in Thornhill, Mississauga, and Oakville. From 1973 to 1983, some 16,000 South Africans, mainly of non-Black ethnic origins, entered Canada. These

Traditional African costumes

included English-speaking South Africans of British and Jewish descent, and smaller groups of Afrikaners (Dutch-French Huguenot), mixed descent, Asian Indians, Chinese, and a small number of Black Africans.

Members of Southern African communities in Toronto have organized social clubs and newsletters. English-speaking South Africans of British, Jewish, and Afrikaner origins hold rugby matches, and braai (barbecues) where delicacies such as boerewors (spicy farmers' sausages) are grilled on a wood fire.

Places to Go

A number of shops selling African art, crafts, and other imports are found throughout the city. **Volta Records**, (1921 Eglinton Ave. E., and 16 Arrow Rd.), carries African music.

There are several Ethiopian restaurants in the city. On weekends, Ethiopian musicians perform. Popular dishes include kitfo (spicy steak tartar) and injera or enjera (a pancake-like leavened bread). Teff flour (fermented wheat), traditionally used to make injera, is found only in Ethiopia, but Toronto's chefs use suitable substitutes. Popular accompaniments to a meal are wat (spicy lamb or goat) and tej (a fermented honey drink). You can experience Ethiopian cuisine and culture in Little Ethiopia on the Danforth between Greenwood and Coxwell. **Kantamanto Food Market**, (Tel. 416-235-1470, 1288 Wilson Ave.) offers African and Caribbean Foods; **Makola Tropical Foods, African and Caribbean Foods**, (Tel. 416-789-3908, 3035 Dufferin St.); **East End Tropical Market**, (Tel. 416-286-0516, 287 Morningside Ave.), Wholesale and West Indian Foods. Manager: Kingsley Marfo; **Soma International Foods**, (Tel. 416-747-6500, 246 Eddystone Ave). Wholesale prices, exeter corned beef, vegetable salads, tiitus sardines, original quaker oats, ghana cerlac, original tinapa.

A strip of restaurants is located on the west end of Bloor Street, **Queen of Sheba**, (Tel. 416-536-4162, 1198 Bloor St. W), features Ethiopian cooking, including injera and wats (chicken, lamb, and beef) seasoned with berbere (a hot red-pepper sauce); **Abyssinia Restaurant**, (Tel. 416-588-1666, 933 Bloor St. W); **Selam Restaurant**, (Tel. 416-588-5496, 875 Bloor St. W) Another restaurant is: **Addis Ababa Restaurant**, (Tel. 416-538-0059, 1184 Queen St. W) Several Toronto stores carry African, and East and West Indian foods, such as kokonte, cassava (tropical plant with starchy roots), gari (fermented cassava), abe (palm nut soup) yams, cocoyam, and hot kenkey. These include: **India Africa Grocers**, (Tel. 416-241-5435, 2121 Jane St.); and **Ray's Tropical Foods**, (Tel. 416-248-9690, 1640 Jane St).

Somali Halaal Food Market, (Tel. 416-244-8248, 2371 Weston Rd.), carries halal meat (slaughtered in a ritual manner fulfilling the special dietary requirements of Muslim law) and food products for Somali cooking.

South African meat delicacies such as wors (sausage), sosaties, kingklip, salmon, and beef biltong (similar to beef jerky) are available at **Florence Meat Supply**, (Tel. 905-842-2066, 81 Florence Dr. in Oakville).

Religious Centres, Schools and Other Institutions

Most African Torontonians are followers of Christianity, Islam, or Judaism. Many Ethiopians belong to the Ethiopian Coptic church, while Falashas (Black Jews), an Ethiopian subgroup, practise an ancient form of Judaism.

- ◆ ALL NATIONS FULL GOSPEL CHURCH, (Tel. 416-665-9964, 4401 Steeles Ave. W).
- ◆ ANGLICAN CHURCH OF CANADA AND CARE CANADA, (Tel. 416-924-9192, 600 Jarvis St).
- ◆ BRITISH METHODIST EPISCOPALIAN CHURCH, (Tel. 416-534-3831, 460 Shaw St).
- ◆ CROATIAN ISLAMIC CENTRE, (Tel. 416-255-8338, 75 Birmingham St).

- ♦ FIRST BAPTIST CHURCH, (Tel. 416-977-3508, 101 Huron St).
- ♦ ISLAMIC FOUNDATION OF TORONTO INC., (Tel. 416-321-0909, 441 Nugget Avenue).
- ♦ JAMI MOSQUE, (Tel. 416-769-1192, 56 Boustead Ave).
- ♦ MEDINAH MOSQUE, (Tel. 416-465-7833, 1015 Danforth Ave).
- ♦ ST. BARTHOLOMEW ANGLICAN CHURCH, (Tel. 416-368-9180, 509 Dundas St. E).

Holidays and Celebrations

Members of more than a dozen African nations represented in the city celebrate their respective liberation or republic days with cultural displays, dancing and dinners.

- ♦ GHANA NATIONAL DAY is celebrated by the community on March 6.
- ♦ REPUBLIC DAY. On April 19, the Sierra Leone community celebrates Republic Day.
- ♦ SOUTH AFRICAN REPUBLIC DAY is commemorated on May 31, with a reception held at the South African Consulate.
- ♦ MOZAMBIQUE INDEPENDENCE DAY is celebrated by the community on June 25.
- ♦ SOMALI UNION AND INDEPENDENCE DAY, July 1, sees more than 1,000 Somali Torontonians gather to celebrate. The event commemorates the independence of Northern Somalia from Britain, which took place on June 26, 1960. Celebrations include singing, dancing, food, and film presentations.
- ♦ CAPE VERDE NATIONAL DAY is celebrated on July 5.
- ♦ NEW YEAR'S DAY is celebrated by members of the Ethiopian community with festivities on September 11.
- ♦ ETHIOPIAN NATIONAL DAY is celebrated on September 12.
- ♦ NIGERIAN INDEPENDENCE DAY is celebrated by the Toronto community on October 1.
- ♦ UGANDAN NATIONAL DAY is commemorated on October 9.
- ♦ CHRISTMAS AND EASTER are celebrated by Ethiopian Orthodox Christians according to the Julian calendar. The faithful fast the day before Christmas and attend an evening church service. At 2:00 a.m., a big breakfast that includes meat, dairy products, and injera is eaten.
- ♦ BURUNDIAN INDEPENDENCE DAY is celebrated on July 1, to commemorate Burundi's independence from Belgium in 1962.

See Holidays and Celebrations in Glossary.

Media

- ◆ AFRICA TODAY, CHRY 105.5 FM, York University Community Radio, (Tel. 416-736-5293, www.yorku.ca/chry, 4700 Keele St., Sunday, 12:00 p.m. to 1:00 p.m.).
- ◆ BLACK PAGES, (Tel. 416-784-3002, Fax 416-784-5719, www.blackpages.ca, 1390 Eglinton Ave. W)
- ◆ CRESCENT INTERNATIONAL, (Tel. 905-474-9292, 300 Steelcase Rd. W., Unit 8, Markham). A bi-monthly news magazine of the Islamic Movement.
- ◆ PRIDE (AFRICAN AND CARIBBEAN NEWSPAPER), (Tel. 416-335-1719, 5200 Finch Ave. E., Suite 200A). Publisher: Michael Van Cooten.
- ◆ SOUNDS OF AFRICA, CKLN 88.1 FM, (Tel. 416-595-1477, www.ckln.com, 380 Victoria St). Saturday, 6:00 p.m. to 8:00 p.m. Features the latest rhythms from the African continent along with concert listings and information.
- ◆ AFRICAN WOMEN AND FAMILY, CIUT 89.5 FM, (Tel. 416-978-0909 ext. 203, Fax 416-946-7004, www.ciut.fm), Saturday, 12:00 p.m. to 1:00 p.m. Station Director: Bryan Burchell.

Organizations

Almost every group, nation, or tribe of African descent is represented by clubs or cultural groups in the city, including:

- ◆ AFRICAN COMMUNITY HEALTH SERVICES, (Tel. 416-591-7600, 76 Gerrard St. E., 2nd floor).
- ◆ AFRICAN WOMEN RESOURCE AND INFORMATION CENTRE, (Tel. 416-214-4823, 203 Sackville Green).
- ◆ CANADIAN-AFRICAN NEWCOMER AID CENTRE OF TORONTO (CANACT), (Tel. 416-658-8030, 21B Vaughan Rd., Unit 114). Assists refugees and African immigrants with the immigration process, problems, and government agencies. Organizes workshops, educational programs, and the **All African Conference**.
- ◆ ERITREAN CULTURAL AND CIVIC CENTRE, (Tel. 416-516-1246, 120 Carlton St., # 309).
- ◆ ERITREA RELIEF ASSOCIATION OF CANADA, ℅ Eritrean Cultural and Civic Centre. A developmental and educational organization with 10 branches. Assists the people of Eritrea and offers an educational program that includes lectures.

- **ERITREAN CANADIAN COMMUNITY CENTRE**, (Tel. 416-658-8580, Fax 416-658-7442, 50 Euston Ave).
- **ETHIOPIAN ASSOCIATION IN TORONTO INC.**, (Tel. 416-694-1522, 2064 Danforth Ave., 3rd floor). Provides assistance to newcomers, sponsors refugees, and offers heritage programs and computer training courses. Publishes a newsletter.
- **FRIENDS OF THE SPRINGBOKS**, (Tel. 416-920-5466, 1491 Yonge St., Suite 300). A South African travel club which helps organize reunions and provides special low air fares and insurance plans. The organization publishes a bi-monthly newsletter and organizes wine and cheese parties where more than 500 members attend. President: Lucille Sive.
- **ORGANIZATION OF BLACK TRADESMEN AND TRADESWOMEN OF ONTARIO**, (Tel. 416-921-5120, 22 College St., Suite 104).
- **SOMALI CANADIAN ASSOCIATION**, (Tel. 416-742-4601, 925 Albion Rd). President: Osman Ali.
- **SOUTH AFRICAN NETWORK**, (P.O. Box 112, Port Credit Postal Station, Mississauga). This social club, established in 1987, organizes an annual dinner dance in November, country hikes, a picnic in May, a prawn evening, and a braai (barbecue) in September. It also publishes a newsletter. Contact: Mr. Debbo.

Consulates, Trade Commissions and Tourist Bureaus

- **CONSULATE OF THE GAMBIA**, (Tel. 416-923-2935, 102 Bloor St. W., Suite 510). Honorary Consul General: Irving Gould
- **CONSULATE OF SOUTH AFRICA**, (Tel. 416-364-0314, 2 First Canadian Place, Suite 2300). Consul: Patrick Evans.
- **AFRICAN CHAMBER OF COMMERCE**, (Tel. 416-265-8603, 6 Chevron Cres).

Prominent Torontonians

Mr. Shimeles Asseffa, President, Ethiopian Canadian Association; John Nana Opoku Boahene, Consular General of Ghana; Wilson Lagunju, President and CEO, 1st Capital Financial Corporation; Emmanuel Ayiku, Publisher, Ghanaian News; Rev. Paulette Brown, Pastor, Presbyterian Church, Canada; Ms. Fatma Khalid, President, Tanzania Canadian Association; Sam Kabu Asante, President and CEO, D&S Personnel Services; Joseph Kobina Annan, President and CEO, Canada Africa Business Council Inc.; Mrs. Agnes Summers, CEO, Makola Tropical Foods-Toronto; Nana Asare Bediako, Ashanti Chief of Toronto; Prof. George

Dei, President, Ghanian Canadian Association; Ms. Hawa Jilao, President, Somali Canadian Association; Dr. John Kitakufe, President, Uganda Canadian Association; Prof. Njoki Wane, President, Kenya Canadian Association; Kojo Atuahene, President, Gloryland Shipping Enterprise; Festus Bayden, Executive Director, Bankay Financial Services; Bruce Shapiro, Chair, Canada-South Africa Chamber of Business; Tunde Olagundoye, Director, Canada Nigeria Chamber of Commerce; Edmund Kwaw, Barrister and Solicitor; Paul L. Tiago, CEO, Global Systems Analysis Inc.; Charles Agyei-Amoama, Deputy High Commissioner of Ghana; Dr. Otto, Medical Doctor, Family Physician Clinic; Richard Emode, President, Geomatic Inc.; Dr. Charles Edebiri, Executive Director, All Nations Development Agency; Dr. Sylvester Osamusali, President, Delta State Cultural Association.

Contributors: Momoh Kakulatombo, consultant, Race Relations Directorate; Ferdinand Odeligbo, Program Director, African Resource Communications Centre; Francis A. Omoruyi, Commissioner, Parking Authority of Toronto; Mahad Ali Yusuf, public relations officer, Somali Immigration Aid Organization (Toronto).

Sources: Stanley Ansong, Adrian Melville-Richards, Francis Omoruyi, Lucille Sive, Maria Teixeira, Bridget Ubochi, Joseph Annan.

The Ahmadi Muslim Community

In the fall of 1992, members of the Ahmadiyya community in Toronto began to attend prayers at **Bai'tul Islam**, the largest specially designed mosque with a minaret in Canada, located north of Canada's Wonderland. The mosque features two large prayer halls, and other facilities that make it the cultural and religious centre for the Ahmadiyya community.

Close to 40,000 Canadian Ahmadi Muslims live in Ontario. Ahmadiyyat is a missionary movement that was founded in 1889 by Hazrat Mirza Ghulma Ahmad of Qadian (1835–1908). He proclaimed himself to be the Messiah, in fulfilment of the prophecies found in the Bible, Mahdi, and Quran, and as foretold in the Holy Quran and sayings of Prophet Mohammed. The movement has a membership of more than 200 million followers around the world. Ahmadi Muslims are well established in Pakistan, India, Indonesia, Bangladesh, the Caribbean, East and West Africa, Europe, and North America.

The first Ahmadis in Canada came in the 1950s, but the majority arrived in the 1980s and 1990s, composed primarily of refugees from Pakistan. The centre for community activity is **Bai'tul Islam**. The **Mission House**, located on a 25-acre property in Maple, Ontario, holds published translations of the Holy Quran in 54 languages and selected verses in 118 languages. Affiliated with it are newspapers, women's and youth groups, and sports teams, which hold various events.

Throughout the year the Ahmadiyya Movement and its different auxiliary organizations hold several events. One of the most significant events for Canadian Ahmadis is their **Annual Gathering** in the first week of July. 20,000 Ahmadis attend this three-day event from different parts of Canada, USA and other countries. The **Annual Convention** is occasionally attended by the Supreme Head of the Ahmadiyya Movement in Islam, His Holiness, Mirza Maskoor Ahmad Caliph IV. When His Holiness is present, the attendance at the Annual Convention is increased substantially.

Muslim Television Ahmadiyya International (MTA Int.) is a unique network which is owned and operated by the Ahmadiyya Muslim Community and is fully financed by its worldwide members. It is the first 24-hour Worldwide Muslim Television direct to home channel. Programs are produced by communities in over 150 countries.

Places to Go

♦ AHMADIYYA MOVEMENT IN ISLAM, (Tel. 905-832-2669, 10610 Jane St, Maple). The national headquarters of the movement.

For restaurants and specialty stores, see the chapters on Pakistani and East Indian communities.

Religious Centres, Schools and Other Institutions

The Ahmadiyya movement in Islam has 30 "Namaz Centres" (prayer centres) and 4 large mosques in Toronto.

♦ BAI'TUL ISLAM MOSQUE, (Tel. 905-832-2669, 10610 Jane Street, Maple).

Holidays and Celebrations

♦ JUMA'T-UL-WIDA, last Friday of Muslim Holy Month Ramadhan.

♦ EIDUL FITR, at the end of Ramadhan, on 1st day of Shawal (according to Muslim Lunar Calendar).

♦ EIDUL ADHIYA, on 10th of Zil-Hajj.

♦ MUSLEH MAUOOD DAY, held on February 20, celebrates the prophecy about the second Caliph, Hadrat Mirza Bashirudin Mahmood Ahmad.

♦ SEERATUN NABI DAY is dedicated to discuss the life and teaching of the Prophet of Islam.

♦ KHILAFAT DAY, on May 27, is held to educate the public about the institution of Caliphate, ("Khilafat") the supreme head of the Ahmadiyya Movement. A symposium with lectures is held on this day.

See Holidays and Celebrations in Glossary.

Media

♦ AHMADIYYA GAZETTE CANADA, (Tel. 905-303-4000, 10610 Jane St., Maple). A national monthly magazine published in Urdu, English and French.

♦ MUSLIM TELEVISION AHMADIYYA, (Tel. 905-303-4000 / 416-748-1231, www.alislam.org/mta). Canada Jama'at launched the world's first Muslim television station to broadcast programs on Islam 24 hours a day throughout the world.

♦ MUSLIM TELEVISION AHMADIYYA INTERNATIONAL (MTA INT.), (Tel. 905-832-2669, www.mta.tv), is a unique network which is owned and operated by the Ahmadiyya Muslims.

♦ NEW CANADA (URDU-ENGLISH), (Tel. 416-481-7793, P.O. Box 994, Station Q). Leading voice of south Asians.

Organizations

◆ AHMADIYYA MOVEMENT IN ISLAM, CANADA, (Tel. 416-425-1951, www.ahmadiya.ca, 63 Baker St). President and Missionary in Charge: Malik Lal Khan. At the same address: **Khuddam ul Ahmadiyya** (youth wing), **Ansarullah** (senior wing), **Lajna Amaullah** (women's wing), **Nasi'rat ul Ahmdiyya** (young ladies' wing), and **Atfalul Ahmadiyya** (children under 16 wing).

◆ HUMAN RIGHTS AND RACE RELATIONS CENTRE, (Tel. 416-481-7793, 1-888-No Slurs, www.race-relations.ca, 120 Eglinton Ave. E., Suite 500). Community based resource centre dealing with issues of equity, multiculturism, racism, and immigration. President: Hasanat Ahmad Syed.

Prominent Torontonians

Lal Khan Malik, President of the Ahamdiyya Community; Khalifa Abdul Aziz, lawyer; Hasanat Ahmad Syed, President, Human Rights Race Relations Centre; Abdul Aziz Khalifa, Vice President of Ahmadiyya Community in Canada; Mubarak Ahmad Nazir, Vice President of Ahmadiyya Community in Canada; Kaleem Ahmad Malik, Vice President of Ahmadiyya Community in Canada.

Community members at prayer on the eve of Ramadan (the Muslim holy month)

The Albanian Community

Among the first Albanians to settle in Toronto was a businessman, Mr. Shamata, who arrived around 1902. He owned and operated his shoe store on Bloor Street West for more than 50 years.

Albanians, known as "Shqipetare" (Sons of the Eagle), are direct descendants of the Illyrians, the oldest inhabitants of Southeastern Europe. The first wave of Albanians to arrive in Canada arrived between 1904 and 1906. They settled in the greater Toronto area, working in factories and restaurants. Early cultural activities centred around konaks (boarding houses), religious organizations, and nationalist clubs. The second wave of immigrants came to Canada after the First World War. Among the new settlers was Sejdali Qerim, a prominent businessman who helped found the first mosque in Toronto.

Following the Second World War, many families immigrated to Canada from Albania, some settling in Ontario. Others entered Canada from countries such as Greece, Yugoslavia, Italy, and Turkey. The early 1990s saw another wave of Albanians immigrating to Canada, many settling in Toronto. Many of these recent settlers include professionals such as engineers, doctors, teachers, and accountants.

Toronto's Albanian community currently numbers around 20,000. There are several Albanian social and sports clubs and organizations in the Toronto area, including: two soccer teams (Illyria and Kosovo-Albania), the **Albanian-Canadian Community Association**, and the **Canadian Albanian Relief Effort**, which carries out charitable work for Albanians in need.

Albanian emigrants in Canada after the Cold War

Most of the Albanians who live in Toronto came after 1990 when Albania opened its doors at the end of the Cold War and the collapse of Yugoslavia. The first Albanians who arrived in Canada after the Communist era of Eastern Europe were those who claimed refugee status. Obviously Canada hosted a number of Albanian emigrants as permanent residents as well. According to Canadian immigration consulting firms approximately another 1,000 Albanians came to Canada after immigration increased dramatically due to the economic crisis in Albania in 1997 and the 1998

The Albanian community on Flag Day, exhibiting their pride in their national symbol—the double headed eagle.

conflict in Kosova. Around 1,000 Albanians came to Canada every year after 1997 and around 7,000 Albanians from Kosova arrived after 1998. There are no very well defined statistics, but there are around 25,000 Albanians in Canada and among them 14,000 are from their home country, 7,000 from Kosova and 4,000 from Macedonia. Almost 90 percent of the Albanian Community in Canada lives in the GTA and surrounding areas.

Places to Go

Albanian-owned delicatessens in the city include: The **Cheese Boutique and Delicatessen**, (Tel. 416-762-6292, 45 Ripley Ave.) **Via Egnatia Restaurant**, (Tel. 416-766-2332, 395 Keele St.) serves delicious Albanian food. Contact: Gashi Ness. **Zemra Caffe**, (Tel. 416-651-3123, 778 St. Clair Ave. W) **College Fallafel**, (Tel. 416-532-8698, 450 Ossington Ave.) **Silver City Bar & Cafe**, (Tel. 416-461-1504, 780 Danforth Ave.)

Religious Centres, Schools and Other Institutions

The majority of Albanian-Canadians are Sunni (Orthodox) Muslims, or belong to the Bektashi sectarians. Most of the rest are Christians who belong to the Orthodox or Roman Catholic churches.

Holidays and Celebrations

◆ INDEPENDENCE DAY is celebrated on November 28, in honour of the day in 1912 that Albania proclaimed its independence from the

Ottoman Empire. The community celebrates with a program of speeches and cultural performances.

◆ KOSOVA'S INDEPENDENCE DAY, celebrates the July 2, 1990, declation by the Parliament of Kosova of an independent republic, equal to the other republics of the Yugoslav Federation. The Albanian Community celebrates on the second day of July with a program of speeches and cultural performances.

◆ SEPTEMBER 7 is the day the community celebrates the adoption of Kosova's new constitution on September 7, 1990.

◆ ALBANIA NATIONAL INDEPENDANCE DAY (FLAG DAY), is celebrated on November 28, in honour of day in 1912 when Albania proclaimed its independant from the Ottoman Empire. The community celebrates it with the Albanian flag being raised in front of the Ontario Legislative Building (started 2009), speeches, cultural performance and banquets organized all over the province.

Organizations

◆ ALBANIAN CANADIAN ASSOCIATION OF TORONTO, (Tel. 416-504-4704, 26 Sixpoint Rd). President: Samir Loua.

◆ ALBANIAN MUSLIM SOCIETY, (Tel. 416-763-0612, 564 Annette St).

◆ KOSOVA COMMUNITY AND INFORMATION CENTRE, (Tel. 416-760-0172, Fax 416-760-7902, 3416 Dundas St. W., Suite 202). President: Mr. Murat Binaku.

Prominent Torontonians

Stephanie Teuta Haxhillari, realtor; Jani Papadhimitri, composer; Anton Brunga, Brunga Law Offices; Neritan Ciraku, Ciraku Law Offices; Meri Verli, Vice-President of Financing and Corporate Control, Lake Shore Gold Corporation; Agako Nouch, Vice-President of Ingersoll Rand Canada; Dr. Adriana Peci, respiratory epidemiologist at Ontario Agency for Health Protection and Promotion; Ferzi Bekiri, businessman; Kristaq Turtulli, writer; Ilir Lena, TV producer.

Contributors: Frank Bekirovski, President, Albanian Canadian Association of Toronto; Agim Hadri, President, Kosova Community and Information Centre.

Source: Aferdita Beqiri.

The Arab Communities

Far from the pyramids of Egypt, the warm waters of the Mediterranean on the shores of North Africa, the hot deserts of the Arabian Peninsula, the ancient cities of the Middle East, and Yemen, the birthplace of civilization, Arab Canadians are adjusting to Toronto's frigid winters. In January and February, many members of the city's Arab community warm themselves with the fires of outdoor barbecues and hot Arab coffee at social gatherings called snow picnics. Others, through societies or organizations, meet once a month to discuss Arab-Canadian economic, political, and cultural issues. Involved in all facets of the cultural, political, and economic life of Toronto, Arab Canadians are making their contributions to the development of the the city's future.

Throughout the year, social evenings of music and dance called haflahs and participation in various cultural events have become a means of preserving the heritage of Toronto's Arab community. In addition, Arabic language schools and courses in religious studies flourish in all districts of the city.

Toronto's Arab-speaking immigrants from 22 countries are represented by diverse coloration and a good number of the world's religions. Immigration to Canada began with Syrian-Lebanese immigrants who arrived in 1882. Among these pioneers was Salim Shaykh, a Syrian-Lebanese immigrant who became Toronto's first Arab settler.

An early Syrian enclave formed around St. Patrick's Church on McCaul Street, the community's first religious centre. At the turn of the century, St. Vincent de Paul Hall on Shuter Street became the unofficial Syrian church. In the neighbourhood surrounding the hall, Arab businesses, such as confectionery shops and grocery stores, and, later on, clothing factories, flourished and the area became known as "Little Syria."

In 1913, the Melkites (Byzantine rite Catholics) bought a property on Jarvis Street and formed **Our Lady of the Assumption Parish**, while the Maronites worshipped at **Our Lady of Mt. Carmel Church**. In the 1930s, youth groups, ratepayers associations, and political and cultural organizations were formed.

Immigration remained slow until the end of the Second World War, when immigrants began arriving from Algeria, Bahrain, Egypt, Iraq, Jordan, Lebanon, Libya, Mauritania, Morocco, Palestine, Somalia, Sudan, Syria,

Tunisia, and Yemen. These post-war newcomers included a broader mix of religious, social, and cultural groups and included an educated and financially secure core who formed numerous organizations according to the ideology, religious sect, or nationalism of the state from which each hailed. The largest post-war group, the Egyptians, established the Coptic Orthodox Church in 1965, while Assyrian-speaking people from Iraq, Syria, and Lebanon established two Eastern Apostolic churches in the city. Today, half of Arab-Canadians are of Syrian-Lebanese origin, a quarter are Egyptian and Palestinian, and the rest are from other Arab states. In the past few decades, events in the Arab world such as the Arab-Israeli conflict, civil wars in Somalia and Lebanon, and more recently the conflict in the Gulf have forced many Arabs to immigrate to Canada in ever increasing numbers. Today, Canada is home to about 400,000 Arab Canadians. Of these, nearly half reside in Ontario, with the majority living in and around Toronto.

The great majority of Arabs are Muslim, but there is also a sizable group of Christian Arabs who belong to a variety of denominations. Though there is no exclusive Arab mosque, there are 18 houses of worship which serve the Muslim community and many other churches that cater to constituents from all the Arab Middle East and other lands.

Several Arab social, cultural, and political organizations have emerged, representing various national groups of the Arab community. In 1960, the **Canadian Arab Friendship Society** was organized to promote social, cultural, and educational interests such as multicultural events, conferences, special lectures, and special briefs concerning educational curricula about the Arabs. The society helped raise money for the establishment of the **Arab Community Centre of Toronto (ACCT)** in 1972, which assists newcomers in acclimatizing to life in Canada.

The Arab influx continued in the 1980s with the arrival of Somalis in the wake of the strife in Somalia. Their numbers have increased dramatically from the early 1980s. Please note that almost all Somalis are Muslims. In the 1990s Arab immigrants, specifically Iraqis, also made their way to Canada. Others, too, came from the Arabian Gulf area as it degenerated and became a hotbed of political turmoil and strife. These immigrants again were predominantly Muslim.

The **Canadian-Arab Federation**, established in 1967, is a national organization which represents Arab-Canadian societies throughout Canada. In 1993, **Educational Advising Services**, an educational consulting service specifically created to assist visa students, primarily from the Arab world, was established. This agency serves the needs of post-secondary students from the Arab world who have made or intend to make Toronto their home.

Places to Go

The sweet smells of Arab almond pastries and the fragrant aroma of cardamom and saffron can be enjoyed at a number of Toronto restaurants, bake shops, and specialty stores.

Arab cuisine begins with maza (a course of appetizers) that may include hot peppers, olives, cheese, and numerous cooked tidbits. The basic diet is lamb, rice, chickpeas, lentils, broad beans, bulgur (cracked wheat), yogurt, vegetables, nuts, and fruit flavoured with a mixture of healthy herbs and exquisite spices. Baba ghannouj (eggplant and tahini), falafel (deep-fried patties of chickpea or broad beans with spices and parsley), hommos or hummus (chick pea-tahini dip), shish kebab (skewered meat), tabbouleh (salad of parsley, mint, bulgur, tomatoes, onions, and lemon juice), bisteela (filo dough stuffed with onions, chicken, and spices), couscous (steamed semolina with vegetable and meat stew), and kibbee (ground lamb or beef combined with bulgur wheat) are popular dishes available at most of the city's Arab restaurants.

There is a large Middle Eastern community living in Scarborough, and a good sized concentration of shops and restaurants along Lawrence Ave. East between Pharmacy Ave. and Warden Ave.

Arab music plays in the background of **Jerusalem Restaurant**, (Tel. 416-783-6494, 955 Eglinton Ave. W). The menu includes chicken, beef, lamb and tender liver shish kebab, spicy fish, kafta (a mixture of meat, parsley, onions, and spices), foule (fava beans), hummus, tabbouleh, labaneh (yogurt cream cheese), falafel, and shawarma (slowly roasted chicken or beef marinated and sliced into bite-size pieces).

Family-owned **Tarboosh Restaurant**, (Tel. 905-949-0222, 3050 Confederation Pkwy., Mississauga), serves home-cooked meals. The aromas of Middle Eastern vegetarian and non-vegetarian stews and buffets fill the air. Waraq Areesh (stuffed vegetarian or non-vegetarian grape leaves), varieties of shish kabab, and shawarma are also on the menu. Catering available.

Ameer Family Restaurant, (Tel. 416-757-2727, 2034 Lawrence Ave. E); **Nasib's Shwarma and Falafel**, (1867 Lawrence Ave. E., Tel. 416-285-7223).

Fast food restaurants specializing in falafel and shawarma sandwiches include **Lotus Catering & Fine Foods**, (Tel. 416-757-8315, 1960 Lawrence Ave. E), serving Egyptian-style cuisine, kabab and shish kabab, beef and

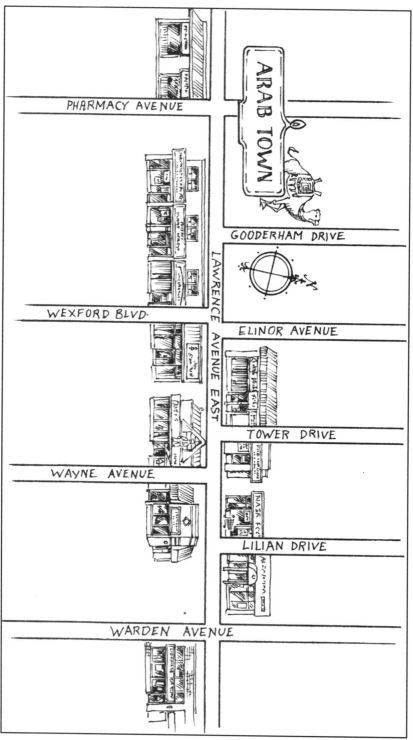

chicken shawarma, and falafel sandwiches; **Falafel Express**, (Tel. 416-665-2552, 1300 Finch Ave. W., Unit 6), featuring falafel, chicken and shawarma sandwiches served in a dining room or as take-out; and **Falafel World**, (Tel. 416-769-9336, 2396 Bloor St. W).

Middle Eastern products such as dates, dried fruits, figs, raisins, pistachios, lentil, chickpeas, pita, tahina, broad beans, olives, olive oil, imported canned goods, walnuts, cream cheese, bulgur wheat, scented Arab coffee, and mint tea are available at: **Babil Middle East Market**, (Tel. 416-755-0244, 1987 Lawrence Ave. E); **NASR Foods Inc.**, (Tel. 416-757-1611, 1996 Lawrence Ave. E); **Rabba Fine Foods**, (Tel. 416-234-0609, 4869 Dundas St. W); **Samiramis Arabic Supermarket**, (Tel. 416-741-4729, 977 Albion Rd.); **Town and Country Market**, (Tel. 905-275-2781, 3355 Hurontario St., Fairview Ten Plaza); **Challal Pasteries**, (Tel. 416-752-4684, 1960 Lawrence Ave. E); **Patisserie Royale, Fine Lebanese and Syrian Pastries**, (Tel. 416-755-6323, 1801 Lawrence Ave. E).

Some of these stores also carry newspapers, magazines, videos, and recordings by Umm Kalthum, considered the greatest Arab singer of this century, and Sabah Fakhri who sings muwashshahaat, a thousand-year-old tradition in Arab music.

Stores that provide halal meats cleaned and prepared according to Muslim dietary laws include: **Hadad Bakery**, (Tel. 416-661-8998, 4610 Dufferin St.); **Ghadir Halal Butcher Shop**, (Tel. 416-750-7404, 1821 Lawrence Ave. E); **Nadir Halal Meat and Grocery**, (Tel. 905-949-6895, 48 Dundas St. W, Mississauga); **Hassan & Bros. Meat Market**, (Tel. 416-285-9446, 1887 Lawrence Ave. E).

Toronto's Middle Eastern bakeries carry pita (Arabic bread), marqooq (very thin Arabic bread), filo pastries with nuts or custards, kul wasushkur (cashew and almond filled pastries), and baklava. These items are available at: **Golden Dough**, (Tel. 905-949-6521, 800 Dundas St. E., Mississauga); **Ararat Bakery**, (Tel. 416-782-5722, 1800 Avenue Rd.); **Breadko National Bakery**, (Tel. 905-670-4949, 6476 Kestral Rd., Mississauga); and **Mr. Pita**, (Tel. 416-743-6634, 190 Norelco Dr.); **Lebanese Bakery**, (Tel. 416-441-2450, 1790 Birchmount Rd).

Arabic to English translation is done by: **AMM Arabic Translation Service**, (Tel. 416-759-4334, 1919 Lawrence Ave. E., Suite 301A).

Religious Centres, Schools and Other Institutions

The Arab community consists of diverse religious groups. Christian groups include Antiochian Orthodox, Coptic Orthodox, Melkite, Syrian Orthodox,

Anglican, and Maronite Catholic churches; Muslim groups include the Sunni, Shi`ah, and Druze.

- ◆ JAFARI ISLAMIC CENTRE, (Tel. 905-881-1763, 7340 Bayview Ave., Thornhill).
- ◆ IMDADUL ISLAMIC CENTRE, (Tel. 416-636-0044, 26 LePage Ct).
- ◆ MADRESATUL-BANAAT AL-MUSLIMAAT, (Tel. 416-244-8600, 10 Vulcan St).
- ◆ TARIC ISLAMIC CENTRE, (Tel. 416-245-5675, 99 Beverly Hills Dr).
- ◆ JAMI MOSQUE, (Tel. 416-769-1192, 55 Boustead Ave).
- ◆ JESUS THE KING MELKITE CATHOLIC CHURCH, (Tel. 905-886-0566, www.jesustheking.com, 1 Lyndhurst Dr., Thornhill).
- ◆ OUR LADY OF LEBANON CATHOLIC CHURCH, (Tel. 416-534-7070, 1515 Queen St. W).
- ◆ ST. GEORGE'S ANTIOCHIAN ORTHODOX CHURCH, (Tel. 905-731-7210, 9116 Bayview Ave., Richmond Hill).
- ◆ ST. MAR BARSAUMO SYRIAN ORTHODOX CHURCH, (Tel. 416-694-4500, 72 Birchmount Rd).
- ◆ ST. MARK'S COPTIC ORTHODOX CHURCH, (Tel. 416-494-4449, 4 Glendinning Ave).
- ◆ ASSYRIAN CHURCH OF THE EAST, (Tel. 416-744-9311, 19 Hibiscus Ct).
- ◆ MADINAH MASJID, (Tel. 416-465-7833, 1015 Danforth Ave).
- ◆ ISLAMIC INFORMATION & DAWAH CENTRE INTERNATIONAL, (Tel. 416-536-8433, 1168 Bloor St. W).
- ◆ ISLAMIC FOUNDATION (SCARBOROUGH), (Tel. 416-321-0909, 441 Nugget Ave).
- ◆ MADINATUL-ULOOM ACADEMY, (Tel. 416-332-1810, 676 Progress Ave).
- ◆ ISSRA (ISLAMIC SOCIAL SERVICES & RESOURCES ASSOCIATION), (Tel. 416-767-1531, 2375 St. Clair Ave. W).

Holidays and Celebrations

Some members of the Arab community celebrate their former Homeland's national day along with a series of religious holidays. Religious events include, for example for Muslims, Ramadan, a month of fasting, when Muslims abstain from eating, drinking, sex, smoking and cursing from sunrise to sunset. During Ramadan (even more than during the rest of the year), Muslims cultivate their moderation, willpower, patience and unselfishness. The month of Ramadan originates in people the real spirit of social belonging, of caring for the less fortunate, and of equality before God. Also, the month of Ramadan is a happy time for most Muslims, as family and friends gather around at sunset to break their fast together. On the first day of the lunar month after Ramadan, Eid Al-Fitr (the festival of the breaking of the fast) is celebrated.

◆ EID AL-ADHA (THE FESTIVAL OF SACRIFICE) is celebrated throughout the Muslim world over a period of three days. Each of the Eid days begins with prayers (Salat) and is spent in alms-giving, visiting friends and relatives, and exchanging greetings and gifts. Eid Al-Adha celebrates the completion of the Hajj, or pilgrimage to Mecca, which is one of the five pillars of Islam, and represents to Muslims immense spiritual and emotional significance.

◆ EID AL-FITR (THE FESTIVAL OF THE BREAKING). A religious celebration is observed on the day following the last day of fasting (Ramadan).

◆ THE FEAST OF ST. MARON celebrated on February 9, honours the patron saint of Maronite Christians.

◆ THE DAY OF THE LAND, celebrated on March 30, represents the commitment of Palestinians to hold on to their lands in Occupied Palestine. Lectures and discussions about Palestine are held on this day.

◆ NEW YEAR'S DAY is celebrated by Assyrians in early April with a weekend of cultural and social festivities.

◆ ST. MARK'S DAY is celebrated on May 8, with commemorative church services held in honour of the patron saint of the Coptic Orthodox Church.

◆ THE FEAST OF ST. PETER AND ST. PAUL on June 29, is celebrated by the Antiochian Orthodox community to commemorate the two founders of the Church of Antioch. Church services are held on this date.

◆ COPTIC NEW YEAR begins on September 11, and is celebrated with a Divine Liturgy. The colour red is found throughout the church and in homes red dates are eaten in memory of the church martyrs.

◆ DECLARATION OF THE PALESTINIAN STATE is celebrated on November 15. Celebrations are marked by lectures and discussions about Palestine.

◆ ARAB HERITAGE DAY, held on November 21, is a celebration of the Arab community in Canada. A reception, with speeches followed by a dance, is sponsored by the Canadian Arab Federation.

See Holidays and Celebrations in Glossary.

Media

◆ KAN YA MAKAN, CKLN Ryerson Radio (88.1 FM, Tue. 8–10 PM), (Tel. 416-595-1477), contact: Manager: Mike Philip.

◆ ARAB NEWS INTERNATIONAL, (Tel. 416-362-0304, Fax 416-861-0238, www.arabnews.ca, 368 Queen St. E), Middle East Consultants. Publisher: Sal Allam.

◆ ARAB NEWS OF TORONTO, (Tel. 416-362-0304, 368 Queen St. E). Publisher: Frank Ahmad.

◆ LISAN AL-ARAB (ARAB NEWS OF TORONTO), (Tel. 416-231-7746, 555 Burnhamthorpe Rd. Suite 209), Published by the **Arab Community Centre of Toronto**. Contact: Laila Bondugjie.

◆ THE NECEF REPORT (NEWSLETTER), (Tel. 416-301-5019, Fax 416-483-5732, 20 Bloor St. E. P.O. Box 73090), **Near East Cultural and Educational Foundation of Canada**.(106 Duplex Ave), Publisher: Jonnes Graff.

◆ MIDDLE EAST REPORT, (Tel. 416-362-0304, 368 Queen St. E).

Organizations

◆ ARAB COMMUNITY CENTRE OF TORONTO, (Tel. 416-231-7746, 555 Burnhamthorpe Rd). Established in 1972, provides social, cultural, recreational and educational programs and publishes a newsletter in Arabic and English.

◆ ARABESQUE ACADEMY, (Tel. 416-920-5593, 1 Gloucester St., Suite 107), teaches Middle Eastern dance and music. President: Yasmina Ramzy.

◆ ASSYRIAN COMMUNITY OF CANADA WELFARE COMMITTEE, (Tel. 416-741-8836, 964 Albion Rd., Suite 102, Rexdale). President: M. Shmoil.

◆ ASSYRIAN SOCIETY OF CANADA, (Tel. 905-624-0636, www.assyriansocietycanada.org, 1150 Crestlawn Dr., Mississauga). Annual events such as evenings of entertainment featuring traditional music and dance are held in the club hall. President: Nano Ganja.

◆ CANADIAN ARAB FEDERATION, (Tel. 416-493-8635, Fax 416-493-9239, www.caf.ca, 1057 McNicoll Ave). Acts as the official voice of the community, coordinates activities of Arab organizations in Canada, and arranges annually for a national convention of members. Also publishes a weekly e-bulletin. Executive Director: Audrey Jamal.

◆ DRUZE SOCIETY, (Tel. 416-439-3976, 898 Markham Rd).

◆ PALESTINE HOUSE, (Tel. 905-270-3622, 3195 Erindale Station Rd., Mississauga).

◆ EGYPTIAN CANADIAN CLUB, (Tel. 416-410-0763, 31 Snowball Cres). President: Sam Mina

- **NILE ASSOCIATION OF ONTARIO**, (Tel. 905-842-8333, www.nileclub.org, 1293 McCraney St. E., Oakville). Contact: Mahmoud El Farnawani, President.
- **AL-HUDA CENTRE & LEBANESE MUSLIM SOCIETY**. (Tel. 416-446-0935, Fax 416-446-0931, www.hlms.com, 10 Codeco Court, Don Mills). Contact: Khaled Kefel.
- **ARAB HERITAGE CENTRE**. (Tel. 416-493-8635, 1057 McNicoll Ave), Contact: Khaled Homaidan.
- **ARAB CANADIAN MEDIA ASSOCIATION**. (Tel. 416-493-8635, 1057 McNicoll Ave) Contact: Kamal Al Gindy.
- **IRAQI CANADIAN SOCIETY OF ONTARIO**. (Tel. 416-494-1435, www.icsociety.org, 1057 McNicoll Ave), lower level.
- **CANADIAN ARABIC MEDICAL ASSOCIATION**. (Tel. 416-962-5545, 1366 Yonge St., #306). President: Dr. A. Elzawi (MD FRCPC ABIM).

Consulates, Trade Commissions and Tourist Bureaus

- **CONSULATE OF THE LEBANESE REPUBLIC**, (Tel. 416-530-2121, 2224 Dundas St W). Honorary Consul General: Mr. Nazem El Kadri
- **CONSULATE OF THE SYRIAN ARAB REPUBLIC**, (Tel. 905-564-0955, 7370 Bramalea Rd, Suite 14, Mississauga). Honorary Consul General: Mr. Yaser Kherdaji

Prominent Torontonians

Johnny Essaw, sports commentator; Habeeb Salloum, author and freelance writer.

Contributors: Muna Salloum, M.A. Middle East and Islamic Studies; Dr. Ibrahim Hayani, Professor of Economics at Seneca College, and a writer and activist; Nadia Abu-Zahra, Canadian Arab Federation.

The Armenian Community

The 25,000-member Armenian community is among the city's most active in preserving its culture and heritage. Armenians have clung tenaciously to their rich traditions, organizing language classes, youth groups, theatrical and choral endeavours, churches, and political, cultural and benevolent organizations.

Two striking monuments in Toronto are dedicated to the Armenian people whose existence was once threatened throughout the First World War by Turkey. At the **Armenian Community Centre** in Willowdale, **Revival**, a poignant sculpture by Armenian artist Arto, depicts the survival and rebirth of the Armenian people. A second memorial depicting the tragic past of the Armenian people is located at the **Alex Manoogian Cultural Centre** in Scarborough. Designed by Dick Dakessian, the monument's two arches join at their peak to form a cross, while the base holds an eternal flame, symbolizing peace.

Armenian students were among the first members of the community to come to Canada, sponsored by Protestant missionaries in the late nineteenth century. One student, Mesrob Baghdasarian, and his family were allowed to stay permanently. Early Armenians in Ontario worked on construction of the Canadian Pacific Railroad, and others who intended to work only temporarily as labourers in Southwestern Ontario became permanent residents due to the outbreak of the Balkan Wars in 1912.

In 1915, during the First World War, Armenians sought refuge from the genocide that was taking place in their homeland in South Caucasus. A group of successful Canadian businessmen formed an association that helped in the adoption of a group of 109 orphaned Armenian children. Set up and cared for on a farm training school in Georgetown, Ontario, the children became affectionately known as the Georgetown Boys.

By 1923, some Armenians that had settled in Canada were living near Church Street. Many were involved in the rug business—including the selling, repairing, and cleaning of rugs. At this time, Armenians began to organize cultural, political, and religious activities.

In the 1930s, the upstairs chapel of the landmark **Holy Trinity Anglican Church** in Eaton Square became the site of Armenian religious services.

The first community-owned religious building was the **Holy Trinity Armenian Church** on Woodlawn Avenue, consecrated in 1953.

Armenians who came to Toronto in the late 1950s were largely from the Middle East and outside Turkey, where Armenians had settled after fleeing their country. In the 1960s, thousands of Armenian business men, craftsmen and professionals from the Middle East, Europe, and Soviet Armenia moved to Toronto and Montreal. In the 1970s and 1980s, during the Lebanese Civil War and the Iran-Iraq war, more Armenians from the Middle East came to Canada.

Armenian Torontonians have excelled in the arts. Personalities include comedian and actress Andrea Martin, children's songwriter Raffi, and film director Atom Egoyan.

In 1988, Toronto's Armenians, along with other Torontonians, worked day and night in a compassionate effort to send supplies and money to the victims of the major earthquake in Armenia. The generosity of the community is also extended to their fellow Canadians and their new homeland. Every year, the Armenian community hosts an awards dinner in honour of an outstanding Canadian. Proceeds from the event are placed in a university scholarship fund to encourage interest in Armenian studies. Past recipients include former Ontario premier Bill Davis, Prime Minister Jean Chretien, former U.N. Ambassador Stephen Lewis, labour leader Bob White, and author Margaret Atwood.

Places to Go

Founded in 1981 and named in honour of its lifetime president, The **Alex Manoogian Cultural Centre**, (Tel. 416-431-2428, 930 Progress Ave.), houses the **Gulbenkian Library**, as well as athletic, social, scouting, and art centres. On Sundays, the women's guild operates a cafeteria serving Armenian dishes such as shish kebab.

The **Armenian Community Centre**, (Tel. 416-491-2900, 45 Hallcrown Pl.), was opened in 1979. The centre's brown brick interior reflects the harshness of the Armenian homeland's landscape, while works of art by local artists adorn the walls. The **Hamazakain Cultural Association** maintains a library and a bookstore at the centre.

Other Armenian specialties are hoom kufteh (steak tartar kneaded with cracked wheat and spices), and herriseh (thick stew made from oats, chicken or lamb). Armenian Christmas specialties include anooshaboor (a pudding made with wheat, apricots, raisins, walnuts, pistachios and almonds).

Armenian wines and brandies are widely appreciated—in particular, Duin, a noted favourite of Sir Winston Churchill.

Several bakeries in the city carry a variety of Middle Eastern foods and Armenian favourites, including fresh lahmajoon, soujoukh (Armenian sausage), basterma, sinee keofta, keofta, beureg, as well as various pastries, such as nut and syrup pakhlava.

These delicacies are found at **Ararat Fine Foods**, (Tel. 416-782-5722, 1800 Avenue Rd.); **Araz Bakery**, (Tel. 416-757-1559, 1646 Victoria Park Ave.); and **Arz Bakery**, (Tel. 416-755-5084, 1909 Lawrence Ave. E).

Armenian delicatessens include: **Arax Meat Products**, (Tel. 416-636-6143, 3905 Chesswood Dr.); **Grande Cheese Co. Ltd.**, (Tel. 416-787-7670, 22 Orfus Rd.), which produces white Armenian stretch cheese; and **Shirak Delicatessen & Meat Products**, (Tel. 416-266-7519, 1375 Danforth Rd).

The following art galleries occasionally display works by Armenian artists: **Armen Art Gallery**, (Tel. 416-924-5375, 16 Wellesley St. W); and **Sevan Art Gallery**, (Tel. 416-920-8809, 480 Yonge St).

Armenians were among the first people to practice the art of rug weaving. Designs reflect Chinese influences, as well as Christianity, with crosses, stars, and snakes that symbolize wisdom.

Stores that carry Armenian rugs include: **Adourian's Rug Galleries Ltd.**, (Tel. 416-362-6713, 89 King St. E); **Alexanian Carpet**, (Tel. 905-624-0844, 1855 Dundas St. E., Mississauga); **Armenian Rug Company**, (Tel. 416-483-3300, 476 Davisville Ave); **Karakashian Rug Gallery**, (Tel. 416-964-1995, 1257 Bay St.); **Selyan's Oriental Rugs**, (Tel. 416-781-2030, 1783 Avenue Rd.); and **Indo-Iranian Rugs Ltd.**, (Tel. 905-886-7400, 165 East Beaver Creek Rd, Richmond Hill).

Religious Centres, Schools and Other Institutions

Armenia was the first nation to adopt Christianity as its official religion, in 301 A.D. St. Gregory the Illuminator is recognized as the patron saint of the Armenian Apostolic Church. Nearly 90 percent of Armenians belong to the Armenian Apostolic Church; the rest are divided between the Armenian Catholic and Evangelical churches.

Armenian churches located in Toronto are:

◆ ARMENIAN EMANUEL CHURCH OF THE NAZARENE, (Tel. 416-385-9874, 2537 Bayview Ave., North York).

◆ ARMENIAN HOLY TRINITY CHURCH, (Tel. 416-431-3001, Fax 416-431-0269, 920 Progress Ave., Scarborough).

- ST. MARY'S ARMENIAN APOSTOLIC CHURCH, (Tel. 493-8122, 45 Hallcrown Place, North York).
- ARMENIAN EVANGELICAL CHURCH, (Tel. 905-305-8144, Fax 905-305-8125, 2600 14th Ave., Markham).
- ARMENIAN BROTHERHOOD BIBLE CHURCH, (Tel. 416-492-3300, 2755 Victoria Park Ave., Scarborough).

Armenian is an Indo-European language with a 36-letter alphabet that was devised by St. Mesrob Mashtots in 404 A.D. The language is taught at Armenian day schools. Armenian schools include:

- THE A.G.B.U. ZAROUKIAN DAY SCHOOL, THE ALEX MANOOGIAN CULTURAL CENTRE, (Tel. 416-439-3900, 930 Progress Ave), teaches Armenian, English, and French to students from nursery to grade 6.
- ARMENIAN RELIEF SOCIETY DAY SCHOOL, BABAYAN KINDERGARTEN AND KOLOLIAN ELEMENTARY SCHOOL, (Tel. 416-491-2675, 50 Hallcrown Pl), was inaugurated in 1982 and has an attendance of 350 students. It offers trilingual education in English, French, and Armenian from kindergarten to grade 8.
- HOLY CROSS ARMENIAN DAY SCHOOL, (Tel. 416-759-7222, 505 Ellesmere Rd). The trilingual school has approximately 100 students.
- ST. SAHAG & ST. MESROB ARMENIAN SATURDAY SCHOOL, ℅ HOLY TRINITY ARMENIAN CHURCH, (Tel. 416-431-3001, 920 Progress Ave, Scarborough).

Holidays and Celebrations

- VARTAN'S DAY (VARTANANTZ), in February or March, honours the battle of Avarair, 451 A.D., between Zoroastrian Persians and Armenians. The Armenians fought to retain their Christianity, and although they lost the battle and General Vartan Mamikonian was killed, they still maintained their faith. Thirty years later, under Vartan's nephew, Vahan Mamokonian, the Armenians were victorious.
- MEMORIAL DAY or MARTYR'S DAY, April 24, is the most significant day of the year for Armenians. It commemorates the day in 1915 that Armenian intellectuals and religious leaders were put to death by the Turkish government. The day is commemorated worldwide with memorial services and political rallies. Members of the community pay their respects by visiting the two monuments located at the Armenian cultural centres.

- **SARDARABAD DAY**, held in May, celebrates a victory over the Turkish army and remembers Armenians who died in the great battle at Sardarabad, Armenia from May 22 to 26, 1918.
- **INDEPENDENCE DAY OF THE FIRST REPUBLIC**, May 28, commemorates the proclamation in 1918 of Armenia as an independent republic. The republic lasted two years.
- **INDEPENDANCE DAY** September 21, 1991, following the collapse of the USSR, Armenia became an independent republic and elected its first parliament and president, Levon Der Bedrossian. The embassy of the republic of Armenia opened on March 19, 1995.
- **CHRISTMAS** is celebrated by Armenian Catholics and Armenian Protestants on December 25. January 6 is Epiphany in the Armenian Orthodox Church, and on this day, the birth and baptism of Jesus Christ are celebrated simultaneously.

Every year a Christmas bazaar, offering handicrafts, sweaters and other items, is held by the **Armenian Relief Society** at the community centre. October is a cultural month at the **Alex Manoogian Cultural Centre**, with several activities, including drama and dance performances, recitals, and exhibits of art by artists from Armenia.

Media

- **CANADA ARMENIAN PRESS**, (Tel. 905-305-8144, Fax 905-305-8125, 2600 14th Ave., Markham). Published quarterly by the **Armenian Evangelical Church**. Editor: Rev. Y. Sarmazian.
- **KHOSNAG**, (Tel. 416-431-2428, 930 Progress Ave). A newsletter published four times a year by the **A.G.B.U.** Editor: Salpi Derghazarian.
- **LOUSSAPATZ (THE DAWN)**, (Tel. 416-285-6982, 174 Shropshire Dr). A periodical published by the **Nor Serount Cultural Association**. Editor: Bedros Mouchian.
- **NOR SEROUNT (NEW GENERATION)**, (Tel. 416-431-3001, 920 Progress Ave). A periodical published by the **Armenian Holy Trinity Church**.
- **ZANK (BELL)**, (Tel. 416-491-2675, 50 Hallcrown Pl). A periodical published by the **ARS Day School**.

Organizations

◆ THE ARMENIAN COMMUNITY CENTRE, (Tel. 416-491-2900, Fax 416-491-2211, 45 Hallcrown Pl). The centre houses several organizations. The **Homenetmen General Armenian Sports Union** oversees basketball, volleyball, soccer, ping-pong, martial arts and tennis teams and other activities. The Scout wing includes Scouts, Cubs and Girl Guides, who participate in world jamborees as part of the Canadian delegation. Every two years in July, the **Athletic Association** hosts the annual **Armenian Olympics** in Toronto. Over 600 participants engage in three days of activities and celebrations.

Several other organizations are housed at the centre:

◆ ARMENIAN RELIEF SOCIETY, a chapter of the worldwide women's organization established in 1924, is dedicated to charitable and educational pursuits.

◆ ARMENIAN SENIOR CITIZENS CLUB raises funds for various community projects and also runs day trips and gatherings.

◆ ARMENIAN NATIONAL COMMITTEE OF TORONTO is a political organization that acts as a voice for the community.

◆ ARMENIAN YOUTH FEDERATION sponsors seminars and social activities for their members.

◆ HAMAZKAIN CULTURAL ASSOCIATION, has a choir of over 130 members, theatre group, arts exhibits committee, literary group, social group, music group and dance ensemble, the Hamazkain Dance Group.

◆ ARMENIAN GENERAL BENEVOLENT UNION (AGBU), (Tel. 416-431-2428, 930 Progress Ave), is a cultural and charitable organization. It operates the **Zaroukian Day School**, ladies auxiliary, youth committee which includes sports teams, the **Hrachia Nercessian drama group**, **Sanouts Alumni**, **A.M.C.C. Musical Society**, choir, the **Grounk dance group**, art committee, women's guild, and Scouts.

◆ ARMENIAN FOLK DANCE ENSEMBLE, (Tel. 416-781-1620, 3180 Bathurst St). The ensemble has been performing at various multicultural functions held in the city for nearly 30 years. Director: Arpi Meras.

◆ HAYASTAN FOUNDATION CANADA, (Tel. 416-332-0787, 5005 Steeles Ave. E., Suite 208), President: Mig Migirdicyan.

◆ NOR SEROUNT ARMENIAN CULTURAL ASSOCIATION AND SOCIAL DEMOCRAT HENTCHAG PARTY, (Tel. 416-285-6982, 174 Shropshire Dr.) Contact: Bedros Mouchian.

◆ TEKEYAN ARMENIAN CULTURAL ASSOCIATION, (Tel. 416-293-7173, 2105 Midland Ave).

Prominent Torontonians

Hrant Alyanak, theatre producer; Varoujan Ayvazian, economics professor, University of Toronto; Diane Babayan, painter; Ara Baliozian, writer; Dr. Keresteci, Chief Urologist, Wellesley Hospital; Dr. Solo Nigosian, professor, University of Toronto; Gerard Paraghamian, artist; Edward Safarian, economics professor, University of Toronto and advisor to former prime minister Pierre Trudeau; Khazaros Surmeyan, ballet dancer; Arto Yuzbasiyan, internationally renowned painter and gallery owner; Izabelle Bayrakdarian, opera singer; Cavolikian Onnig, portrait photographer; Ann Cavoukian, infromation and privacy commissioner of Ontario; Arsinee Khanjian, actress; David Alpay, actor; Peter Oundjian, musical director of the Toronto symphony orchestra.

Contributors: Aris Babikian, Canadian citizenship judge; Sarkis Tchilingirian, executive secretary, Armenian General Benevolent Union, Armenian Folk Dance Esembly, Shahen Mirakian.

The Australian & New Zealander Communities

If you hear "Kiwi" or "Aussie" being called out around Brunswick Avenue and Bloor Street, it's probably a member of Toronto's Australian or New Zealand community greeting a fellow national. The neighbourhood is home to the **TRANZAC Club**, a large building that has served as a gathering place for the community's clubs and cultural organizations since 1961. The mandate of the club is to foster friendly relations between Canadians, Australians, and New Zealanders through social and recreational activities.

Improved transportation, as well as accessible work permits, made Canada a prime destination for those working their way around the world in the 1950s and '60s. Following the Second World War, close to 30,000 Australians and New Zealanders came to Canada, many arriving from England.

On April 25, 1948, New Zealanders and Australians gathered together to celebrate Anzac Day, a national holiday commemorating the landing of Australian and New Zealand forces at Gallipoli in 1915. The organizers of the event formed the **ANZAC (Australia and New Zealand Army Corps) Association**, which later became the **TRANZAC (Toronto ANZAC Club)**.

Popular movies have sparked an interest in Australian and New Zealand culture. New Zealand spring lamb is available in most supermarkets; Foster's Australian beer, brewed by Molson Breweries, is a Canadian favourite; and outback fashions are sold in clothing stores.

Australians and New Zealanders have contributed to the city's professional, business, and sports sectors. New Zealander Eric Ross Arthur (1898–1982), a professor of architecture at the University of Toronto, founded the **Architectural Conservancy of Ontario** in 1932. Named a companion to the Order of Canada, Arthur's restoration projects included St. Lawrence Hall. He was the author of several authoritative books on the city's architecture, including *Toronto: No Mean City*.

Places to Go

The British and Irish ancestry of most Australians is reflected by their cuisine. Steak and eggs are eaten any time of the day, and fruits are common desserts. Popular beverages are tea and beer. Sheep farming, an integral part of the New Zealand economy, has made oven-roasted lamb a national dish.

The **Australian New Zealand Club (TRANZAC)**, (Tel. 416-923-8137, www.tranzac.org, 292 Brunswick Ave), welcomes visitors at the club's two licensed lounges and hall, which are open daily from 5:00 p.m. to 2:00 a.m. Bar snacks include meat pies and shepherds' pie. Every Sunday afternoon the club features folk music from such groups as the Flying Cloud, who perform Celtic and Irish melodies.

Australian Clothing and Gift Imports and Downunder Travel, (Tel. 416-322-5826, 374 Brookdale Ave). Owner John Keating sells oilskin coats, outback hats (as seen in the movie *The Man from Snowy River*), saddles, blundstone boots, paua shell jewelry, opals, lambskins, boomerangs, koala bear and kangaroo toys, and foods such as ginger, vegemite, and eucalyptus oil products.

The Australian Boot Company, (Tel. 416-504-2411, 791 Queen St. W), carries clothes and boots from Australia.

Religious Centres, Schools and Other Institutions

Among community members are Catholics, Church of England followers, and other Protestants.

Holidays and Celebrations

◆ AUSTRALIA DAY, January 26, marks the arrival and settlement of Governor Phillip at Sydney Cove in 1788. It has been a public holiday since 1838, and is also known as Anniversary Day and Foundation Day. Receptions and other social gatherings are held on this day.

◆ WAITANGI (NEW ZEALAND DAY), February 6, commemorates the signing of the Treaty of Waitangi in 1840. The treaty guaranteed protection of Maori lands, forests, and fisheries, and was an agreement between the Maori (Natives) and the Pakeha (Europeans) to form a peaceful and cooperative nation. The TRANZAC Club sponsors sporting events and a party with traditional spring lamb, desserts, and New Zealand wines.

◆ ANZAC DAY, on April 25, was first observed in 1916 in memory of those who served in Gallipoli and later for those who died during both world wars and other conflicts. The day is observed by the Toronto community on the Sunday nearest to April 25, with a wreath-laying ceremony at City Hall, followed by a dinner-dance.

See Holidays and Celebrations in Glossary.

Media

◆ TRANZACTION, (Tel. 416-923-8137, 292 Brunswick Ave). An announcement sheet distributed by the Australian New Zealand Club.

Organizations

◆ THE AUSTRALIA NEW ZEALAND CLUB (TRANZAC), (Tel. 416-923-8137, www.tranzac.org, 292 Brunswick Ave).

Sub-groups at the same address: **The Maori Dancers**, (Tel. 416-321-3134), made up of 30 dancers of all nationalities as well as Maori (New Zealand Natives), perform Native dances at various functions and exhibitions, including the International Caravan. Contact: Rob Macey. **NAGs (Nomad Acting Group)**, (Tel. 416-391-4692, www.nagsplayers.com). A theatre troupe which has performed in plays in Toronto since 1976. It stages three productions a year, usually a comedy/farce for the Fall and Spring and an annual English-style pantomime each February. Contact: Chairman Dave Harris. **NOMAD Rugby Club**, (Tel. 416-410-3655 or 416-410-FOLK, www.torontonomads.com), was formed in 1951 and is joint owner of Fletcher's Fields, just north of Toronto. The club runs four men's teams, a woman's team, and two colts teams, under 19 and under 17. The **Nomad's 1st XV** plays in the "A" Division of the **Ontario Rugby Union League**. The **Flying Cloud Folk Club** is centrally located at the **TRANZAC Club**. Regular concerts are held most Sunday evenings from September to May, as well as dances and special events throughout the season. While the club focuses on traditional folk music from Ireland and Scotland, it also tries to book acts that reflect the ethnic diversity of Toronto.

Consulates, Trade Commissions and Tourist Bureaus

◆ AUSTRALIAN CONSULATE GENERAL, (Tel. 416-323-1155, 175 Bloor St. E., Suite 1100, South Tower). Consul General: Mr. Stefan Trofimovs.
◆ AUSTRALIAN TRADE COMMISSION, (Tel. 416-323-3909, 175 Bloor St. E., Suite 1100, South Tower).

Prominent Torontonians

Jack Cahill, former author and newspaper reporter; Dr. Foley, Psychology Department, University of Toronto; John Kruger, advisor to former-Premier David Peterson; Adam Vaughan, Toronto city councillor.

Contributor: Professor Cecil Houston, professor of geography, University of Toronto.

Source: TRANZAC Club.

The Austrian Community

The first Austrians to come to Canada were among the German-speaking agricultural workers from Galicia, who arrived from Austria-Hungary in the 1880s and settled in the Canadian West. With the dissolution of the multi-ethnic Hapsburg empire and the creation of the German-speaking Republic of Austria in 1918, Austrians fled the country's turbulent political situation to find opportunities in other countries. Some came to Canada in the late 1920s. Other refugees followed in 1938 after the "Anschluss," the incorporation of their homeland into Hitler's Germany.

In 1949, **Austrian Club Edelweiss** grew out of the **Society for Austrian Relief**, organized to help Austrians struggling with post-war economic problems. Members of the club were part of a large wave of immigration to Canada that occurred between 1946 and 1955 as Austrians left a homeland occupied by Great Britain, France, the United States, and the USSR. The Club celebrated its 60th anniversary in the year 2010.

As Austria recovered from its economic and political problems, immigration to Canada slowed down in the 1960s and '70s. Today, there are approximately 10,000 Canadians of Austrian origin living in Toronto, and members of the community have contributed to the city in the fields of music, decorative arts, and recreation.

Places to Go

Austrians are known for their soups, schnitzels, and pastries. Dumpling-garnished broths include rindsuppe with leberknodl (a combination of meat stock and liver). Other dishes feature knodl (dumplings made of flour, breadcrumbs, onions, and smoked bacon). Among meat dishes, veal ranks highest and is the basis of wiener schnitzel (veal pounded thin, breaded and sautéed to crispness). Backhendl (fried chicken), spicy stuffed peppers and cabbages, and tafelspitz (a boiled beef dish) served with horseradish are among the zestier dishes. Austrian pastries found in Toronto restaurants and pastry shops include cakes, cream puffs, fruit tarts and sachertorte (chocolate cake with apricot jam filling).

The Musket, (Tel. 416-231-6488, 40 Advance Rd). Serving Austrian-style cuisine and pastries.

The Old Country Inn, (Tel. 905-477-2715, www.oldcountryinn.ca, 198 Main St., Unionville), resembles an Austrian country inn. The family-style restaurant was opened in 1978 by Hans Klebesitz and is located in a converted century-old house decorated with flowers, stained-glass windows with Austrian crests, and a brightly lit wintergarten. Hearty meals include various schnitzels, goulash, sausages, and steaks, and the Schachtplatte—which includes schnitzel, pork loin, sausages, home fries, and sauerkraut. The dessert menu offers Viennese-style ice cream along with Black Forest cake and homemade strudel.

Cafe Konditor, (Tel. 416-693-7997, 1856 Queen St.), owned by Austrian pastry chef Burgi Riegler, who makes Austrian specialties such as sachertorte, apfelstrudel (apple strudel).

Religious Centres, Schools and Other Institutions

The majority of Austrians are Roman Catholic. A small group is Protestant.

Holidays and Celebrations

♦ AUSTRIAN NATIONAL DAY on October 26, is one of the most important holidays for the community, celebrated with a reception held by the Austrian Consulate. It commemorates Austria's declaration of neutrality and the restoration of Austria's sovereignty and independence on October 26, 1955.

See Holidays and Celebrations in Glossary.

Media

♦ NEUE WELT, German language bi-weekly newspaper, (Tel. 416-237-0591, Fax 416-237-9590, www.neueweltonline.com, 2 Billingham Rd., Suite 203). Publisher & Editor-in-chief: Karsten Mertens

♦ DEUTSCHE PRESSE, German language weekly newspaper, (Tel. 416-595-9714, Fax 416-595-9716, 87 Judge Rd., 3rd Floor).

Organizations

♦ CANADIAN-AUSTRIAN SOCIETY OF TORONTO, (Tel. 416-928-1400, 55 Erskine Ave., Suite 1702). President: Christine Meyer.

- BURGENLAENDISCHE GEMEINSCHAFT, (10 Royal Orchard Blvd., Box 53032, Thornhill). President: Helmut Jandrisits.
- STEIRER KLUB-INC., (Tel. 416-621-4384, Fax 905-238-6122, 56 Hagersville Court). President: Karl Vogl.

Consulates, Trade Commissions and Tourist Bureaus

- AUSTRIAN CONSULATE GENERAL, (Tel. 416-967-3348, 2 Bloor St. W., Suite 400). Consul General: Dr. Karl Schmidt.
- AUSTRIAN NATIONAL TOURIST OFFICE, (Tel. 416-967-4867, Fax 416-967-4101, 2 Bloor St. W., Suite 400).
- AUSTRIAN TRADE COMMISSION, (Tel. 416-967-3348, www.austriantrade.ca, 2 Bloor St. W., Suite 400).

Vienna's Spanish riding school visiting Toronto

Prominent Torontonians

Agnes Grossman, conductor; Frank Stronach, Chair of the Board, President and CEO of Magna International; Dr. Bernard Cinader, medical research scientist; Professor Eli Kassner, musician, artist and scientist; Helga Plumb-Dubois, architect; Mayumi Seiler, concert violinist; Ernestine Tahedl, landscape painter; Josef Ebner, Regional Vice-President of Delta Chelsea Hotel Toronto; Dr. Helfried Seliger, Chair, German Department of University of Toronto; Dr. Henry Bartel, senior full professor and area coordinator; Anton Kuerti, concert pianist and composer; Karl Kaiser,

Inniskillin Wines; Alfred Wirth; Fred Braida, President, Carlton Hotels International; Belinda Stronach, former MP, recipient of Canada's Confederation Medal, executive vice-chairman of Magna International; Fredrick Istl, Business Executive and Consul General Emeritus of Austria and recipient of the Decoration of Merit in Gold of the Republic of Austria, recipient of the ACC Award from the Austrian Canadian Council and many other achievements; Joe Stritzl, President and Owner of Crown Food Service Equipment in Toronto who supports many projects of Austrian interest and also the Austrian community; Attila and Marion

Frank Stronach
Philanthropist and Canada's most famous entrepeneur.

Glatz, Impresarios of Salute to Vienna and the Vienna New Years Concert in 38 North American cities; Karl Gyaki, Pioneer of Austrian Wine Imports to Canada, recipient of the Decoration of Merit of the Republic of Austria; Josl and Elfriede Huter, Ski Pioneers and developers and owners of Mr. St. Louis Ski Resort; Ing. Felix Heller, Architect; Dr. Gerald Schorn, Architect; Dr. Jutta Szep Kroath, Consul of Austria, recipient of the Decoration of Merit in Gold of the Republic of Austria; John Raschke, Banker and longest serving President of the Canadian Austrian Society of Toronto, recipient of the Decoration of Merit in Gold of the Republic of Austria, ACC Award; Christine Meyer, Business Executive and President of the Canadian Austrian Society of Toronto, recipient of the Decoration of Merit in Gold of the Republic of Austria representative of all matters Austrian, hostess of the annual Austrian National Holiday celebration at her residence for members of the Society.

Contributors: Dr. I. K. Altermann; Dr. Hartmut Froeschle, Professor of German, University of Toronto; History Society of Mecklenberg Upper Canada; Christine Meyer, Business Executive and President of the Canadian Austrian Society of Toronto.

The Belarusan Community

Toronto's Belarusan community numbers 3,000 people. Until the breakup of the Soviet Union in 1991, Belarusans in the Western world were called Byelorussians and Belarus was known as the Byelorussian Soviet Socialist Republic.

Belarus is a country located between Poland, Lithuania, Latvia, the Russian Federation, and the Ukraine. Belarus fell under the Russian Empire from the latter part of the 18th century until 1918, when the Belarusan Democratic Republic was declared. It was conquered in 1920 by the Russo-Bolshevik armies and was divided between Poland and Soviet Russia.

Belarusans began settling in Canada as early as 1817. Most early immigrants were classified as Russians. Between the First and Second World Wars, Western Belarus was under Polish rule, and immigrants coming to Canada were classified as Polish.

Following the Second World War, a large number of political refugees came to Canada and began to establish cultural organizations to preserve the heritage of Belarusans. Among them was Kastus Akula, who helped other Belarusans settle into the Canadian way of life. In 1947, while working on a farm near Toronto, he started publishing *Bielaruski Emihrant*, a bulletin that evolved into a monthly newspaper and lasted until 1954. Also in 1947, a group of Belarusan veterans laid the foundation for the **Belorussian Alliance of Canada**, later renamed **Belarusan Canadian Alliance**. It now belongs to the umbrella organization of **Belarusan Canadian Co-ordinating Committee**.

In 1950, a parish was formed. At first, parishioners worshipped at premises rented from the Anglican Church on College Street, later moving to a Ukrainian building on Bathurst Street. The congregation eventually split in two; half went to the Russian Orthodox Church and then later to **St. Euphrasinia of Polatzak**; the other half formed the independent **Belarusan Autocephalous Orthodox Church** in Canada. Both parishes acquired their own buildings and are still practising churches.

In 1969, a 47-acre farm on the shore of Lake Manitowabing was purchased and converted into a community resort called **Slutzak**. Every six years, Toronto is the site of the **Biennial Convention of Belarusans** in

North America, a cultural, business, and social gathering. The last convention held in Toronto was in 2004.

Religious Centres, Schools and Other Institutions

The majority of Belarusans belong to the Roman Catholic or Greek Orthodox churches, but some follow the United, Anglican, and Baptist faiths.

♦ BELARUSAN ORTHODOX CHURCH, (Tel. 416-530-1025, 524 St. Clarens Ave).
♦ BELARUSAN GREEK ORTHODOX CHURCH OF ST. EUPHRASINIA, (Tel. 416-536-4449, 1008 Dovercourt Rd).

The Belarusan Canadian Alliance sponsors a festive youth festival every year.

Holidays and Celebrations

♦ INDEPENDENCE DAY commemorates March 25, 1918, the day of the proclamation of the Independence of the Belarusan Democratic Republic. Church services, meetings, and festivals are held each year on the nearest Sunday.
♦ EASTER is celebrated by most Belarusans according to the Julian calendar, in March, April, or May.
♦ ST. KRYLA (CYRIL), the bishop of the Eastern Orthodox Church who lived in the city of Turow in 1169, is honoured on May 11. He became

known for his missionary work and sermons. On the Sunday nearest May 11, church services and dinners are held in his memory.

◆ ST. EUPHRASINIA OF POLATZAK DAY, June 5, is observed in honour of the patron saint who was a member of the ruling family of the Polatzak principality in the 12th century. Euphrasinia devoted her life to God and to her country. She established two monasteries that became centres of education, and two churches that were monuments to art. Special church services are held in her memory.

◆ BELARUSAN MEMORIAL DAY, November 27 (or the first Sunday following), is recognized in remembrance of the anniversary of the Slutzak (Slucak) Uprising. The anniversary commemorates the heroic stand that was taken by the forces of the Belarusan Democratic Republic against the Communist forces near the city of Slutzak in 1920. It is celebrated with recitals and a traditional meal.

◆ CHRISTMAS is celebrated by Belarusan Catholics and Protestants on December 25, while members of the Orthodox Church (the largest group) celebrate on January 7. The Christmas Eve celebration, known as Kalady and Kucia, consists of a meal of 12 meatless dishes eaten in honour of the apostles.

See Holidays and Celebrations in the Glossary.

Organizations

◆ BELARUSIAN CANADIAN ALLIANCE, (Tel. 416-530-1025, 524 St. Clarens Ave), Established in 1948.

Prominent Torontonians

Madeline Ziniak, National Vice-President of OMNI Television, and Chair of the Canadian Ethnic Media Association.

Contributor: Dzmitry Elyashevich, Belarusian Canadian Alliance.

The Belgian Community

For well over half a century the **Belgo-Canadian Association** has met on the second Saturday of each month to swap stories about life in Belgium and their new homeland, Canada. First started in 1948 by a group of Toronto war brides, the club became a meeting place for new settlers. Today, members of the association celebrate their heritage with monthly dances and cultural events.

The 250-member club makes up more than a quarter of Toronto's Belgian community. Like the citizens of Belgium who are divided linguistically, members of the club speak the official languages of Dutch and French and a variety of Flemish (Dutch) and Walloon (French) dialects. Also a small group of Belgian Torontonians are German speaking.

One of the first Belgians in the country was Father Louis Hennepin, a Recollet missionary who accompanied French explorer Cavelier de La Salle on his explorations through Canada in 1676. Belgian soldiers, servants, artisans, and missionaries came to New France in the 17th and early 18th centuries.

Immigration to Canada began in 1880 and became more active between the two World Wars. In agricultural areas of Ontario, such as Delhi, Chatham, and Leamington, Belgian labourers worked on sugar-beet and tobacco farms. Early settlers in Toronto started small businesses and found employment as teachers and musicians; Belgian financiers invested in real estate and the paper and mining industries.

During the Second World War, the armament factories attracted workers to the city, and many Belgian youths supported the war by joining the **Canadian Armed Forces**. A monument at **Queen's Park**, dedicated to those who fought for freedom in the two World Wars, bears the names of several Belgian towns.

Immigration continued in the 1950s and '60s, when many professionals came to Canada. Although the Toronto Belgian community is small, its members have contributed to the city in the fields of fashion design, business and industry, the arts, and as diamond cutters and chocolatiers.

Following the war, the **Belgo-Canadian Association** began holding meetings in rented halls on Church Street, Isabella Street, and at **Little**

Lou's restaurant on Danforth Avenue. A new generation of Belgian Canadians, children of the first settlers, have continued to show an interest in their heritage. They've added new themes to monthly gatherings and formed the **B.C.A. (Belgian-style) Archery Club** in 1979, which has hosted and won two international competitions.

Places to Go

Cafe Brussel, (Tel. 416-465-7363, 124 Danforth Ave.), specializes in light snacks and desserts popular in Belgium and France. Owner Roger Wils' homemade desserts include frangipan (almond tarts), mousse soufflés, swans, éclairs, truffles, waffles, marzipan, streusel, and apple almond cake. Café au lait is served in a bowl, and a checkerboard ledge adorned with lacy curtains adds to the look of a Belgian café. On a rack displaying 40 brands of international beer are Belgian favourites, including Duvel (Devil), containing 8.5 percent alcohol, Chimay (Monk Beer), Mort Subite (Sudden Death), and Gueuze (a sweet dark beer).

Belgian Chocolate Shop, (Tel. 416-691-1424, 2455 Queen St. E). Eric Smets and Patricia Cohrs import callebaut chocolate from Belgium, like many other shops, to make semi-sweet and milk chocolates.

Other chocolate shops: **Leonidas Famous Belgian Chocolates**, (Tel. 416-944-8822, 200–50 Bloor St. W); **Simone Marie Belgian Chocolate**, (Tel. 416-968-7777, www.simonemarie.net, 126A Cumberland St).

Bier Market, (Tel. 416-862-7575, Fax 416-862-0879, 58 The Esplanade). Belgian style brasserie featuring 18 different styles of moules and an authentic style steak and fries, with over 150 different beers from 24 countries.

Rahier Patisserie, (Tel. 416-482-0917, Fax 416-882-6291, 1586 Bayview Ave). Belgian style bakery and patisserie.

Religious Centres, Schools and Other Institutions

The community is predominantly Roman Catholic. There are several Belgian bishops within the Canadian Roman Catholic Church.

Holidays and Celebrations

◆ NATIONAL DAY, July 21, marks the day in 1831 that King Leopold I took the oath of allegiance for a new constitution. The consulate in Toronto holds a reception celebrating the birth of Belgium as an independent nation.

◆ KING'S DAY, celebrated on November 15, Kings Day or St. Leopold's Day, pays tribute to Belgium's monarchy. Members of the Belgo-

Canadian Association gather for a dinner and dance. On December 31, an annual New Year's Eve dinner and dance is organized by the Belgo-Canadian Association.

See Holidays and Celebrations in Glossary.

Organizations

◆ BELGIAN CANADIAN BUSINESS ASSOCIATION, (Tel. 416-572-2345, Fax 416-572-2201, www.belgium-canada.ca, 161 Bay St., 27th floor, P.O. Box 508). President: Pierre Boutquin. Treasurer: Elly De Winne.

◆ THE BELGO-CANADIAN ASSOCIATION, (Tel. 416-261-4603, 121 Chillery Ave). The club gathers at **CEP Hall**, (975 Kennedy Rd). Activities include an annual carnival dance and cultural events at Harbourfront. The association also has a folk-dance group, a bicycle club, and an archery club. President: Yvonne Kennedy.

Consulates, Trade Commissions and Tourist Bureaus

◆ BELGIAN CHAMBER OF COMMERCE IN TORONTO, (Tel. 416-863-2472, Fax 416-863-2653, 199 Bay St., Suite 2800). President: Craig Thorburn.

◆ CONSULATE GENERAL OF BELGIUM, (Tel. 416-944-1422, Fax 416-944-1421, 2 Bloor St. W., Suite 2006, Box 88). Consul General: Mr. Paul De Vos.

◆ THE OFFICE OF THE TRADE COMMISSIONER FOR THE FLEMISH REGION, (Tel. 416-944-8005, Fax 416-944-3131, 2 Bloor St. W., Suite 2008, Box 94). Trade Commissioner: Mrs. Liliance Vermeersch.

◆ WALLON REGION OF BELGIUM, (Tel. 416-515-7777, Fax 416-515-7774, 2 Bloor St. W., Suite 2508, P.O. Box 86). Trade Commissioner: André Mathieu.

Prominent Torontonians

Roger DeBacker, artist; John F. Kennedy, community worker; Yvonne Kennedy, community worker and recipient of "Knight of the Order of King Leopold II of Belgium"; Claire Kerwin, graphic artist; Allan Usher, community worker.

Contributor: Yvonne Kennedy, President, The Belgo-Canadian Association.

The Bengali Community

Every year, the Bengali community of Toronto holds a festival to celebrate the birthday of Rabindranath Tagore, the great Nobel-laureate poet (1913) of India. Poet Rabindranath wrote songs, novels, dramas, and short stories, and two of his works became the national anthems of India and Bangladesh. The Bengalis also celebrate the birthday of revolutionary poet Nazrul Islam (born in 1899) every year. His charismatic writings and songs energized the efforts of the people of India during their struggle for independence. Even today his works influence them greatly. He wrote patriotic, devotional and classical songs, stories and dramas. Much of Bengali cultural life in Toronto centres around Tagore and his teachings of universal humanism and poet Nazrul for generating self-energy in every day life and for musical recreation.

From the perspectives of culture and heritage language, the Toronto Bengali community is comprised of people from West Bengal, India, and Bangladesh. Politically, India and Bangladesh are two nations. In 1947, British India was divided into India and Pakistan. That division created East Pakistan out of the eastern part of Bengal, while the western part of Bengal became the State of West Bengel in the Indian Union. In 1971, East Pakistan separated itself from Pakistan and became the sovereign nation of Bangladesh. Bengali is the only language spoken in Bangladesh, whereas in India, it is one of 14 languages spoken.

From a very modest group of approximately 100 in the mid-1960s, the Bengali community in Toronto has grown to almost 5,000. Until 1975, most Bengalees came to Canada after spending a number of years in Europe (in particular England and Germany), where they obtained higher education or acquired new skills. Now in the new millennium, many second generation Bengalees are pursuing academic disciplines or performing various professional activities.

Bengalees are known for their cultural leanings to music, literature, drama, and social celebrations. In 1968, Bengali Torontonians staged the first Bengali drama in Canada. Gradually, the theatre troupe evolved into **Prabasi**. Another organization, **Bengali Cultural Association**, was formed in 1974. For many years, both organizations catered to the social and cultural needs of the community by organizing a number of regular events featuring vocal and instrumental music, dance dramas, theatrical performances and religious festivities. Both organizations invited many prominent personalities of the cultural circle of West Bengal for special presentations or shows in Toronto.

The two organizations united in 1987 to become the **Prabasi Bengali Cultural Association (PBCA)**, and a year later, the PBCA purchased an old warehouse on Millwick Drive in North York and remodelled it into a community centre. In 1989, the **Tagore Centre** was inaugurated as a community building. Today, the Tagore Centre is the focus for the community's cultural and educational activities.

In 1992, the PBCA hosted, with active participation of the **Bengladesh Association of Canada** (Toronto), the **XII North American Bengali Conference** in Toronto—an annual event that is held in various cities of North America under the auspices of the **Cultural Association of Bengal** (New York). The three-day event, held for the first time in Canada, attracted more than 4,000 visitors from all parts of North America. Distinguished personalities from the cultural sphere of West Bengal and Bangladesh were invited to present seminars, workshops, and musical recitals.

Religious Centres, Schools and Other Institutions

Bengali is taught as a heritage language both in general and credit course levels at six schools supported by various boards of education. The **Bramalea Bengali school** has published a textbook for teaching Bengali at the elementary level. A number of schools have also been established by community members to promote vocal and instrumental music and to preserve their heritage among second generation Bengalees.

See chapter on East Indian communities for religious institutions.

Holidays and Celebrations

Bengalees are well-known for grasping the opportunity to celebrate any happy occasion—social or religious. Bengali Torontonians are no exception. However, because of many other priorities, the celebration of religious festivals is limited.

♦ CELEBRATION OF SARASWATI, GODDESS OF KNOWLEDGE, occurs in January or February.

- **DURGA PUJA** (DUSSEHRA), **LAKSHMI PUJA**, and **KALI PUJA** (DIWALI), involve worship of dieties depicting harmony, wealth, and strength. They are celebrated in October or November. Most of the festivities are held at the Tagore Centre on Millwick Drive.

See Holidays and Celebrations in Glossary.

Media

- **BENGALI RADIO AUHWAN**, CJMR 1320 AM, (Tel. 905-271-1320, 284 Church St., Oakville). Airs Sunday, 7:30 p.m. to 8:00 p.m.
- **BENGALI RADIO**, CHIN 1540 AM, (Tel. 416-531-9991, 622 College St.), 91.9 FM, Sunday, 6:30 a.m. to 7:30 a.m. Producer: Sujoy Kanunzo.

Organizations

- **PRABASI BENGALI CULTURAL ASSOCIATION** (PBCA), **Tagore Centre**, (Tel. 416-740-PBCA / 7222, 140 Millwick Dr).
- **CANADA BANGLADESH BUSINESS COUNCIL**, (Tel. 416-833-5206,1110A Wilson Avenue, Suite # 203).

Prominent Torontonians

Gora Aditya, businessman; Himani Banerjee, writer; Dr. Prasanta Kumar Basu, recipient of the Order of Canada; Prabhubandhu Das, poet; Shambhu Das, sitar maestro; Ramen Ganguly, social worker; Dr. Kanti Hore, community leader; Mrs. Sudhira Roy Chowdhury, social worker; Khitish Dutt, social worker; Bejoy Pan, social worker; Jugal Ghosh, community leader; Mr. Samir De, owner of Auhwan Rucho St.

Contributor: Dr. Kanti Hore.

Sources: Riten Ray, Kanti Hore, Samirk Mahajan.

The Black Canadian Community

Outside of 660 Broadview Avenue, a commemorative plaque and park bear the name of William Peyton Hubbard, called a "champion of various minorities" for his significant contributions to human rights and equal opportunity legislation. He was also a pioneer founder of Toronto Hydro and Toronto's first Black politician. In 1893, Hubbard, the son of freed slaves, entered politics as an alderman. He was re-elected in 13 consecutive elections and served as acting mayor on several occasions. He was among the early Black residents who enhanced the city's business, professional, and political life.

The history of Canada's Black community dates back to the fur traders in the 1500s; however, by the early 19th century Toronto saw a steady increase in the city's African-Canadian population. The 1830s saw the first wave of Black immigration from the United States when Toronto became a major haven for runaway slaves. Black Torontonians were trained as waiters, barbers, cooks, blacksmiths, carpenters, painters, and shoe makers. By 1847, there were more than 50 Black families in Toronto. Many had settled in the city's west end.

During the mid-nineteenth century, the **Underground Railroad** assisted in the escape of thousands of Blacks to Southern Ontario. In the 1840s, Emancipation Day was organized by White and Black Torontonians to celebrate the abolition of slavery. There were between 35,000 to 50,000 Blacks in Upper Canada from 1850 to the beginning of the American Civil War.

By the 1860s, Toronto's Black population was 1,400 and included a number of prominent citizens. There were a number of churches, a business community, associations such as the **Queen Victoria Benevolent Society** (established to assist refugees), and an active Black press.

The *Provincial Freeman*, established in 1853, was initially published in Windsor but later moved its offices to Toronto. The newspaper, published and edited by Blacks, gave expression to the problems and accomplishments of the southwestern Ontario Black community. Its official founder, Samuel Ringgold Ward, was a prominent spokesman for the **Anti-Slavery Society of Canada**, formed in Toronto in 1851. Its editor, Mary Ann Shadd Cary, is acknowledged as the first Black woman journalist in North

America and was the actual founder of the *Provincial Freeman*. She had to use Ward's name to establish the paper—since women at that time could not do so. She was also an educator, and later a lawyer.

The first Black businessmen in the city were contractors Jack Mosee and William Willis, who opened a road in 1799 westward from Yonge Street. James Mink, reputed to be one of the city's wealthiest Blacks in the 1840s, operated an inn, livery stable, and stage-coach service. Another successful business man, Wilson Ruffin Abbott, prospered as a real estate agent and owned over 75 properties in Toronto in 1875. His son Anderson became the first Canadian-born Black doctor.

Following the outbreak of the American Civil War, the common belief is that many Blacks returned to the U.S.; by the end of the 19th century only a few hundred lived in Toronto.

During the first two decades of the 20th century, American Blacks settled in Toronto, seeking employment in construction, industry, and railroads. Early Black organizations consisted of self-help leagues and other groups formed to help fight against discrimination. Many lived in the area surrounded by Front, Bloor, Dovercourt, and Sherbourne streets. By 1950, the community numbered 4,000. Canadian Blacks from Nova Scotia and Southwestern Ontario were recent additions to the city.

Today, there are approximately 300,000 Canadian-born Blacks (of non-West Indian origin) living in Toronto. Black organizations focus on the social, educational, and cultural needs of the community.

Every year in February Black History Month is celebrated by the Ontario Black History Society, the formal initiators locally, provincially and nationally of this celebration. It features movies, music, cooking, art, and readings that serve as reminders of the role the Black community plays in Canada.

Places to Go

"Discover Black History in Toronto" guided bus tour, contact **Ontario Black History Society**, (Tel. 416-867-9420, 10 Adelaide St. E., Suite 202).

Religious Centres, Schools and Other Institutions

There are three principal, long-established Black churches in Toronto the **British Methodist Episcopal Church**, the **African Methodist Episcopal Church**, and the **First Baptist Church**. The Seventh Day Adventist congregations, however, claim the largest Black membership. In addition, there are Anglican, Roman Catholic, Pentacostal, and United Church congregations that are predominantly Black.

◆ **FIRST BAPTIST CHURCH**, (Tel. 416-977-3508, 101 Huron St). The oldest Black institution in Toronto, it was founded in 1826 by a group of fugitive slaves. Before this, Toronto's Black Baptists worshipped outdoors near the waterfront. Several other churches were founded between 1838 and 1847.

◆ **AFRICAN METHODIST EPISCOPAL CHURCH**, (Tel. 416-690-5169, 2029 Gerrard St. E).

◆ **BRITISH METHODIST EPISCOPAL CHURCH** (BME), (Tel. 416-534-3831, 1828 Eglinton Ave).

Holidays and Celebrations

◆ **BLACK HISTORY MONTH** is celebrated every year, in February, and includes cultural shows, dances, dinners, and poetry readings.

◆ **KWANZA**, December Festival of Africal family values.

See Holidays and Celebrations in Glossary.

Media

◆ **SHARE**, (Tel. 416-656-3400, Fax 416-656-0691, www.sharenews.com, 658 Vaughan Rd). A weekly newspaper serving Black and West Indian communities. Publisher: Arnold A. Auguste.

◆ **PRIDE**, (Tel. 905-665-2892, Fax 416-335-1723, 5200 Finch Ave. E., Suite 200A). A weekly publication serving the Black and Caribbean communities. Publisher: Michael Van Cooten.

Organizations

◆ **ONTARIO BLACK HISTORY SOCIETY**, Ontario Heritage Centre, (Tel. 416-867-9420, www.blackhistorysociety.ca, 10 Adelaide St. E., Suite 402), is a charitable organization dedicated to the study of Black history in Ontario. Established in 1978, it co-sponsors a travelling exhibit, **Black History in Early Toronto**, which educates the public on the role played by Blacks in the building of the province for the last 200 years. The society is committed to promoting interest in Black history by way of exhibitions, speeches, slide shows, research, and tape recordings of senior citizens in the Black community speaking about their experiences growing up in Toronto.

◆ ASSOCIATION FOR THE ADVANCEMENT OF BLACKS IN HEALTH SCIENCES, (1 King's College Circle, Medical Sciences Building, Room 2304). A community service organization primarily composed of people in health sciences. President: Trevor Bon.

A musical presentation by students from the new TDSB Afrocentric School at the launch of February as Black History Month.

◆ BLACK BUSINESS & PROFESSIONAL ASSOCIATION, (Tel. 416-504-4097, www.bbpa.org, 675 King St. W., Suite 210). Presents the annual **Harry Jerome Awards** for Black achievements in business, community involvement, academics, arts, and athletics. The awards are a tribute to late track star Harry Jerome, who is regarded as a role model and symbol of excellence by Canadians. Contact: Hugh Graham.

◆ THE BLACK SECRETARIAT, (Tel. 416-924-1104, 511 Richmond St. W), provides information on services for the Black community and publishes a directory of Black services, organizations, churches, and media in the city.

◆ URBAN ALLIANCE ON RACE RELATIONS, (Tel. 416-703-6607, www.urbanalliance.ca, 302 Spadina Ave., Suite 505), serves the Black community on all spheres of race relations.

♦ AFRICAN CANADIAN LEGAL CLINIC, (Tel. 416-214-4747, www.aclc.net, 111 Richmond St. W., Suite 503). Executive Director: Ms. Margaret Parsons.

Prominent Torontonians

Salomey Bey, singer and actress; Leonard Braithwaite, lawyer and former MPP; Beverly Mascoll, business woman; Daniel G. Hill, former Ombudsman of Ontario, first Director of the Ontario Human Rights Commission and Commission Chair, and author of The Freedom-Seekers; Robert Payne, broadcaster and Chair of the Ontario Census Board; Sylvia Searles, former Manager, Multiculturalism and Race Relations, Metro Toronto; Deborah Cox, singer; Maestro Fresh West, singer; Dr. J. Carey, optometrist; Rosemary Sadlier, President Ontario Black History Society, member Ontario Heritage Alliance; Judge Stanley Grizzle, Judge; Jean Augustine, Former MP; Alvin Curling, Former Speaker Ontario Legislature; Hope Sealy, broadcaster, former bencher of the Law Society of Upper Canada, member of Hu IRB; Philomen Wright, member of the Board of Directors of United Way; Sandra Whiting, Storyteller and Former President Black Business and Professional Assoc; Superintendent Jay Hope, Chief Superintendent, Traffic Review; David R. Mitchell, Officer with the Ontario Provincial Police; Selwyn Pieters, B.A., LL.B., Refugee Protection Officer, Immigration and Refugee Board of Canada, member of the Canadian Bar Association, member of the Canadian Association of Black Lawyers, member of the Association of Black Law Enforcers; Margarett Best, MPP and Minister of Health Promotion.

Contributors: Selwyn Pieters, Rosemary Saddler.

The Brazilian Community

The excitement of Rio's Carnival, with its spectacular costumes and pulsating samba music, is re-enacted every February by Toronto's Brazilian community in two charity balls, attracting a large crowd of Brazilians, Canadians, and other ethnic groups. The festivities coincide with the celebrations held in every state of Brazil, with lots of music, dances, food, and folklore.

The Brazilian community has grown in numbers over the last few years and has established itself mostly in Toronto's downtown area, known as Little Portugal. Brazilians first arrived in the city in the late 1980s as economic refugees, taking jobs in construction and the blue-collar trades. Today, the community has approximately 4,500 people and includes people working in many occupations and professions.

Places to Go

Brazilian goods, such as groceries, CDs, clothes, and crafts, can be found in most Portuguese or Brazilian-owned establishments, including **Brazilian Star Bar & Grill**, (Tel. 416-588-2967, 1242 Dundas St. W). **Caju**, (Tel. 416-532-2550, 922 Queen St. W). **Brazil Bakery and Pastry Ltd**, (Tel. 416-531-2888, 1566 Dundas St. W).

Escola de Samba de Toronto, (Tel. 416-532-7923, www.sambatoronto.ca, Contact: Alan). Is a steadily growing group of drummers, instrumentalists, singers and dancers who share a passion for Brazilian music, Samba above all. **Mistura Fina**, (Tel. 416-532-7923), features the delicate blending of violao, percussion and vocals, creating an exquisite sense of musical intimacy. **Sounds of Wave**, (Tel. 416-532-7923), is a musical ensemble of six talented musicians combing different elements to create a delicious blend of Brazilian popular music. **Sambacana**, (Tel. 416-532-7923), is a creation of powerful melodies and rhythms provided by a battery of drums and percussion, guitar, bass, keyboard, and vocals.

The excitement of Brazil Day is abundantly obvious. It is held annually at Dundas Square.

Religious Centres, Schools and Other Institutions

Roman Catholicism is the predominant religion. Many Brazilians attend city churches where services are held in Portuguese.

◆ REGINA MUNDI, (Tel. 416-393-5362, 70 Playfair Ave.), teaches children Portuguese on weekends.

◆ ST. ANTHONY'S CHURCH, (Tel. 416-536-3333, Fax 416-532-7091, 1041 Bloor St. W), Pastor: Ezio Marchetto.

Holidays and Celebrations

◆ INDEPENDENCE DAY. On September 7th, Brazilians celebrate their National Day (Independence Day).

See Holidays and Celebrations in Glossary.

Media

◆ BRASIL NEWS, (Tel. 416-538-4298, brasilnews@brasilnews.ca, 877 College St., Suite 201); contact: Tania Nuttall.

◆ THE BRAZILIANIST MAGAZINE, (Tel. 416-826-1455, Fax 416-533-8658, www.brazilianist.com); contact: Teresa Botelho.

◆ INTERLISTA DE NEGÓCIOS, (Tel. 416-201-1009, Fax 416-927-9530, www.interlista.com); contact: Teresa Botelho.

◆ SOTAQUE BRASILERO MAGASIN, (Tel. 416-533-1376, Fax 416-533-8658, www.sotaquebrasilero.com, 828 Bloor St. W., Unit C); Quartely Magazine, editor: Teresa Botelho.

Organizations

◆ PORTUGUESE (BRAZILIAN) LANGUAGE SERVICES, (Tel. 416-593-1444, 277 Wellington St. W).

◆ GRUPO BRAZIZ OF ONTARIO INC, (Tel. 416-201-1009, www.grupobrazil.ca, PO Box 451, Station E). President: Regina Felieov.

◆ CENTRO DE INFORMACIO BRAZIL ANGOLA, (Tel. 416-760-2665, 248 Ossington Ave). President: Eugenia Gardim

Consulates, Trade Commissions and Tourist Bureaus

◆ CONSULATE GENERAL OF BRAZIL, (Tel. 416-922-2503, Fax 416-922-1832, 77 Bloor St. W., Suite 1105). Consul General: Mr. Américo Dyott Fontenelle.

◆ BRAZIL CANADA CHAMBER OF COMMERCE, (Tel. 416-364-3555, www.ccacanada.com/bccc, 438 University Ave., Suite 1618, Box 60).

Prominent Torontonians

Dr. Tirone David, Head of the Cardiology Dept. of Toronto General Hospital; Dr. Tomas Antonio Salerno, Former Head Division of Cardio-vascular Surgery–University Health Network; Ana Maria de Souza, Founder and President of the Brazilian Carnival Ball.

The Bulgarian Community

One of the pioneers of the Toronto Bulgarian community was Dr. D.M. Malin whose benevolent deeds included free treatment for his patients. Dr. Malin helped establish the community's first church in 1910; for more than 100 years, **Saints Cyril and Methodius Macedono-Bulgarian Eastern Orthodox Church** has been a centre of cultural and social life for the Toronto Bulgarian community. A language school was established in 1915, and theatrical performances, concerts, lectures, and horos (round dances) have highlighted parish events since the church's early days.

The first wave of Bulgarian immigration took place between 1908 and 1913 in the years surrounding the Balkan Wars. More Bulgarians arrived in Canada between 1920 and 1930, but the largest influx followed the Second World War, when Communists seized control of Bulgaria. Many Bulgarians living and studying in Western European countries chose not to return to Bulgaria.

Bulgarians came from a country with an impressive political and cultural history. The Southeast European state was founded as early as 681 and even then it was not a new phenomenon but rather an outgrowth of several centuries old political entity developed to the northeast on the Black Sea. Bulgarians managed to establish a small but independent state striving to achieve modernization and progress. Yet many Bulgarians were still under the repressive five-century long rule of the Ottoman empire. It was the Bulgarians from these regions, mainly Macedonia, who after the failure to achieve liberty through an uprising in 1903 decided to search for it in the New World.

Thus around 1905–1907 the first Bulgarian settlements in Toronto took shape, in the southeast part of the city along King and Trinity streets. It was here on the junction of Trinity Street and Eastern Avenue that the community's first church was established in 1910—**Saints Cyril and Methodius Macedono-Bulgarian Eastern Orthodox Church**.

The earliest Bulgarians in Canada were men from small towns who helped build railroads and canals in Welland and the Trent Valley. Others worked in the nickel mines of Sudbury or as labourers on tobacco farms in the Niagara Peninsula. Following the Second World War, political refugees from Bulgaria included professionals, such as engineers, architects, and doctors.

The early Toronto community settled in the Church and Parliament streets area and along Queen and Dundas streets. With the influx of new immigrants, joint Macedonian-Bulgarian organizations were formed. Churches, benevolent societies, and cultural and sports clubs were established by settlers from the Pirin region of Bulgaria, Northern Greece, and Macedonia.

In the 1950s, avenues of cultural expression included performances of Bulgarian traditional music by church choirs and the **Christo Boteff Orchestra** led by Christo Dafeff, a violinist and teacher at the **Royal Conservatory of Music**.

Today, there are approximately 15,000 Bulgarians living in Toronto. Prominent members of the community include self-made millionaire, builder, and developer Ignat Kaneff. Kaneff, who chairs the **I. Kaneff Charity Foundation**, has contributed financially to worthwhile causes, including hospitals in Mississauga, Brampton, and Oakville.

Canadian-Bulgarian Association was established in 1992 to promote cultural and economic cooperation between Bulgaria and Canada. Contact: Alex Kovatchev.

Contributing to the Toronto arts scene are Peter Daminoff, a first violinist with the **Toronto Symphony Orchestra** for more than 30 years, sculptor Marian Kantaroff, pianist Marian Grudeff, and art history professor Bogomila Welsh-Ovcharov.

Places to Go

Bulgarian meals are based on whole-grain cereals, particularly bulghur and kasha, which are often cooked with side dishes of vegetables and cheeses. Yoghurt is a specialty, and popular meals include thick vegetable stews and kebabches (broiled meat rolls on skewers). Fruit compotes are often served for dessert.

Karlovo Bulgarian Store, (Tel. 416-421-5207, 469 Cosburn Ave). provides Bulgarian food and fresh meat products.

Bulgarian jams and other products are available in European delicatessens and grocery stores around the city.

Religious Centres, Schools and Other Institutions

◆ HOLY TRINITY MACEDONO-BULGARIAN EASTERN ORTHODOX CHURCH, (Tel. 416-461-2214, 201 Monarch Park Ave). The church has a choir and Sunday school.

◆ SAINTS CYRIL & METHODIUS MACEDONO-BULGARIAN ORTHODOX CATHEDRAL, (Tel. 416-368-2828, 237 Sackville St). The church has a religious school and a choir.

◆ ST. GEORGE'S MACEDONO-BULGARIAN EASTERN ORTHODOX CHURCH, (Tel. 416-366-1810, 17 Regent St). Established in 1941, the church has a choir and school.

◆ CHESTER PUBLIC SCHOOL, (Tel. 416-396-2325, 115 Gowan Ave). The school has Bulgarian language classes.

Holidays and Celebrations

◆ NATIONAL LIBERATION DAY, March 3, honours the day in 1878 that Bulgaria became an autonomous principality after five centuries of Turkish rule. Church services, speeches, and cultural programs are held on this day.

◆ ST. GEORGE'S DAY, the weekend closest to May 6, is celebrated in honour of the saint, once a Roman soldier who advanced to high military rank under the Emperor Diocletian. He was arrested and was executed for protecting his new-found Christian faith and converting many people to Christianity.

◆ SAINTS CYRIL AND METHODIUS DAY, May 24, is celebrated in honour of the two ninth-century missionaries who created a new Slavonic alphabet.

◆ LLINDEN DAY The Bulgarian community also celebrates the Llinden day —August 2—as a crucial date during 1903 uprising for national self-determination of Bulgarians in Macedonia and Thrace, then under the rule of the Ottoman Empire. In fact the participants of the uprising, persecuted by the Ottoman authorities were the first settlers to form the Bulgarian-Macedonian community in Toronto at the turn of the century.

See Holidays and Celebrations in Glossary.

Media

- ◆ BULGARIAN RADIO PROGRAM CHIN FM 100.7, (Tel. 416-531-9991, www.chinradio.com, 622 College St). Saturdays, 6 p.m. to 7 p.m.
- ◆ BULGARIAN HORIZONS, (Tel. 416-962-7100, 648A Yonge St., Suite 7). Editor: Maxim Bozhilov. Weekly publication.
- ◆ MACEDONO-BULGARIAN REVIEW 'VARDAR,' (Tel. 416-431-1163, 37 Marcella St), biannual journal of history and contemporary problems of the Bulgarian people.

Organizations

- ◆ BULGARIAN CULTURAL CENTRE, 125 Neptune Dr., Suite 901, was established in 1994.
- ◆ BULGARIAN NATIONAL FRONT (BNF), Canada Inc., (Tel. 416-449-8649, 55 Wynford Heights Cres., Suite 2015). Established in 1951 for the purpose of providing moral, material, social, and charitable assistance to its members and their friends and relatives. It also promotes the traditions of the democratic National Bulgarian culture and cooperates with groups and organizations with a similar mandate. The BNF helps its members adapt to Canadian life and institutions, and organizes meetings and speakers for congresses. President: Peter Peltekoff.

St. George's Macedono-Bulgarian Eastern Orthodox Church

- ◆ CANADIAN BULGARIAN ASSOCIATION, (Tel. 905-454-0221, 8501 Mississauga Rd).
- ◆ THE BULGARIAN CANADIAN SOCIETY OF TORONTO, (1092 Islington Ave., Suite 201), is a registered charitable and cultural organization. Since March 7, 1957, the Bulgarian Canadian Society has been the authoritative representative of Bulgarians in Canada. The society's main aims are to organize conferences and cultural festivities, to meet with and

assist expatriates, and to award scholarships and plaques in recognition of community work. President: Boris Ivanov.

◆ MACEDONIAN PATRIOTIC ORGANIZATION—TORONTO. (Tel. 416-483-5366). Established in 1920s as the chief social and political organization of Macedonian Bulgarians in Toronto. Chairman: Fred Meanchoff.

Consulates, Trade Commissions and Tourist Bureaus

Saints Cyril & Methodius Macedono-Bulgarian Orthodox Cathedral

◆ CONSULATE GENERAL OF BULGARIA, (Tel. 416-696-2778, 65 Overlea Blvd., Suite 406). Consul General: Tchavdar Nikolov.

Prominent Torontonians

Boris Ivanov, P.Eng., Honourary President of the Bulgarian Canadian Society; Sylvia Ivanov, Honourary President of the Bulgarian Canadian Society and Ladies' Auxiliary Section; Ignat Kaneff, builder and developer, Chair of the Kaneff Charity Foundation, one of the founders of the Canadian Bulgarian Association, Inc., and Honourary Consul of the Republic of Bulgaria; Maryon Kantaroff, the famous sculptor; Dr. Bogomila Welsh-Orcharoff, art historian and professor at the University of Toronto; Katerina Atanassova, art historian, author, and Chief Curator of the McMichael Canadian Art Collection; Bill Evanov, President and CEO of Evanov Radio Group; Veneta Ilieva, philantrhopist and founder of Bulgarian Voice Radio; Voislav Loukanov, President of D&V Electronics and philantrhopist.

Contributors: Boris Ivanov, President, Bulgarian Canadian Society; and Naoum Kaytchev.

The Cambodian Community

Toronto's Cambodians have an impressive cultural tradition, which is displayed through their dance and music performances at festivals throughout the year. Cambodians speak Khmer and French and share a culture closely affiliated with East Indians. The Toronto community has two soccer teams, a volleyball team, and a number of bands that perform at various functions.

Cambodians come from the The Kingdom of Cambodia (formerly Kampuchea), located in Southeast Asia between the countries of Laos, Vietnam, and Thailand. One of Toronto's newest cultural groups, they first arrived in Canada when approximately 20 Cambodian families came in 1975, comprised mainly of professionals. A second wave of immigration came in the 1980s bringing many blue-collar workers to Canada after the invasion of Kampuchea by the Vietnamese army.

Some 6,000 Cambodians live in Toronto, many in the areas of Gerrard Street and Broadview Avenue, Jane Street and Woolner Avenue, Jane Street and Finch Avenue, Regent Park, London Green, Driftwood Avenue, and Gosford Boulevard.

Places to Go

Angkor, (Tel. 416-778-6383, 614 Gerrard St. E). The First Cambodian restaurant in Toronto, catering for all occasions.

Tai Kong Supermarket, (310 Spadina Ave.; and Lawrence Supermarket, 1635 Lawrence Ave. W), is a shop in Chinatown that carries products for Cambodian cooking.

Religious Centres, Schools and Other Institutions

The majority of Cambodians are Buddhists with a smaller percentage of Protestants, Catholics, and Seventh Day Adventists.

◆ KHMER BUDDHIST TEMPLE, (Tel. 905-303-0077, 9575 Keele St, Maple). A Buddhist Society and a cultural group are affiliated with the temple. Heritage language courses are taught in the temple by the monk.

◆ CAMBODIAN CHRISTIAN CENTRE, (Tel. 416-740-6729, 15 Lund Ave).

♦ **TORONTO CAMBODIAN ALLIANCE CHURCH**, (Tel. 416-741-1110, 2459 Islington Ave).

Holidays and Celebrations

Most Cambodian holidays are celebrated with a show of traditional dance and music and parties where popular music is enjoyed.

♦ **NEW YEAR'S DAY** is celebrated from April 13–15 with processions and prayers. Homes are swept and ritual cleansing ceremonies clear away evil spirits. It is customary to sprinkle one's friends with water to help wash away their sins. Cambodians celebrate the day with an evening of entertainment by a Cambodian live band at a local hall.

♦ **PCHUM BEN** is an annual celebration similar to Thanksgiving.

♦ **BON PHKA AND KATHEN** is an annual festival held to raise money for the Buddhist temple. A show of traditional

Cambodian holidays are celebrated with a show of traditional dance and costumes.

dance and music and also a party with contemporary popular music accompany most Cambodian holidays.

See Holidays and Celebrations in Glossary.

Media

◆ CAMBODIAN NEWSLETTER, (Tel. 416-736-0138, Fax 416-736-9454, www.khmer-ontario.org, 1111 Finch Ave. W., Suite 308). Published four times a year by the Canadian Cambodian Association of Canada.

◆ CAMBODIAN TV PROGRAM: The only television program in the Khmer language in Ontario.

Organizations

◆ AID FOR VICTIMS OF CAMBODIAN LANDMINES, (Tel. 416-778-6383, 614 Gerrard St. E). Educates the Cambodian public about the prevention and treatment of landmines injuries. President: Candaramony, Eang.

◆ CANADIAN CAMBODIAN ASSOCIATION OF ONTARIO, (Tel. 416-736-0138, Fax 416-736-9454, www.khmer-ontario.org, 1111 Finch Ave. W., Suite 308). This incorporated non-profit organization was formed by a group of Cambodian immigrants who came to Canada in 1975. It received charitable status in 1980. Its main purpose is to unite and assist all Canadian Cambodians, immigrants, and refugees and to encourage a cultural exchange between Canadians, Cambodians, and other ethnic groups. The Canadian Cambodian Association of Ontario also works to promote higher education among Cambodian-Canadian students and helps integrate Cambodian youths into Canadian society. President: Jack Chang.

◆ THE UNITED CAMBODIAN YOUTH OF ONTARIO (same address as above). Principal objectives: to promote higher education among Cambodian-Canadian students; to provide opportunities for the development of organizational, educational and leadership skills; and to foster and strengthen friendship, mutual trust and unity among Cambodian youth. President: Mr. Sambath Chhom.

Prominent Torontonians

Thong Pheang Chang, President, Board of Directors of the Canadian Cambodian Association of Ontario; Sophat Allan Kao, founder of the Canadian Cambodian Association of Ontario; Kim Huot Sreng, Treasurer, Board of Directors of the Canadian Cambodian Association of Ontario; Chhim Ly Hour, businessperson; Tom Lam, businessperson.

Contributor: Lee Ung, Co-ordinator, Canadian Cambodian Association of Ontario.

Sources: Wihbol Lay, Jou-Lee Ung, and Sothy Long, Canadian Cambodian Association.

New Year's celebrations at the Canadian-Cambodian Association, Downsview.

The Caribbean Communities

For one weekend **every** summer, Toronto's downtown streets are filled with demons and devils, flowers and insects—costumed, energetic dancers gyrating to the sounds of calypso and steel bands. Caribana, Toronto's parade of people and colourful floats, is a celebration of the city's 400,000-member Caribbean community.

The West Indian community represents more than half of Toronto's Black population. They come from all of the 25 separate islands and countries that are washed by the Caribbean Sea, including Antigua and Barbuda, Barbados, Dominica and Haiti, Grenada, Jamaica, Montserrat, St. Lucia, St. Vincent, St. Kitts, and Trinidad and Tobago, and mainland territories like Guyana and Belize. The population of the territories is multicultural—a mixture of British, Chinese, Dutch, East Indian, French, Lebanese, Portuguese, Spanish and Syrian, combined with a long African legacy.

While West Indians have been in Canada for generations, the first large-scale immigration began in the 1960s. Previous to the 1960s, West Indian students, largely from Trinidad, arrived to study at local universities. Other early newcomers included young women from Jamaica, Trinidad, and Barbados who were sponsored as domestic workers. Those with higher levels of education and work experience were hired as stenographers, bookkeepers, hairdressers, nurses, nursing assistants, and teachers. After 1962 and through the 1970s, a great number of West Indians began entering Canada, and Toronto's Caribbean population increased dramatically.

An early area of settlement for the community was around Bloor and Bathurst streets, and later in the area around Eglinton Avenue and Dufferin Street. The community has gradually moved out to the suburbs, with identifiable areas along Jane Street and Finch Avenue, Lawrence Avenue and Markham Road, and Birchmount and Finch Avenue.

Approximately half the population of Guyana and Trinidad are of East Indian descent. Immigration records reveal that over 200,000 people of Indo-Caribbean background live in the Greater Toronto Area. In 1988, the Indo-Caribbean community celebrated the 150th anniversary of its presence in the Caribbean with a six-day conference at York University. The University also houses a centre for Indo-Caribbean studies.

In recent years, the community has come together to send relief to those Caribbean islands ravaged by hurricanes.

Caribbean Torontonians celebrate their heritage with distinctive foods and a passion for sports and music. Sports clubs are very popular, offering activities such as cricket, soccer and netball, and a popular pastime—dominoes. John Brooks, a Toronto West Indian, founded the National Domino League of Canada. Outstanding Caribbean-Canadian athletes include members of the 1996 Olympic gold medal relay team, sprinter Donovan Bailey, 1996 Olympic gold medalist in the 100 metre dash, and Mark McCoy, 1992 Olympic gold medalist in the 110 metre hurdles.

Places to Go

Throughout the city, at corner stores and in suburban shopping malls, the popular West Indian pattie (pastry turnovers filled with spicy ground beef) and roti (soft flat bread rolled around a filling of meat, fish, or vegetables) can be found. The prime shopping neighbourhood is Eglinton Avenue between Oakwood Avenue and Keele Street, followed by Bathurst Street north of Bloor Street, once the heart of the community's commercial district.

Various restaurants in these neighbourhoods serve cuisine that reflects the diversity of the Caribbean community—with strong undercurrents of Chinese, East Indian, and American influences.

Some say the best West Indian food is found in take-out places like those along Eglinton Avenue West, which sell Trinidadian rotis and Jamaican patties: **Rap's Express**, (1541A Eglinton Ave. W); **Randy's Take-out**, (Tel. 416-781-5313, 1569 Eglinton Ave. W); **Roti-King West Indian Restaurant and Dining Lounge**, (Tel. 416-781-8432, 1688 Eglinton Ave. W); **Mr. Jerk**, (Tel. 416-783-1367, 1552 Eglinton Ave. W); **ACR Hot Roti & Doubles**, (Tel. 416-755-7806, 2680 Lawrence Ave. E); Offers Caribbean entertainment, in addition to its island cooking. In the downtown area, on Dundas (between University Ave. and Elizabeth St.) is **Coconut Grove Restaurant**, (Tel. 416-348-8887, 183 Dundas St. W). It serves dishes from Jamaica, Trinidad and Guyana. Their specialties are fast lunch dishes.

While there is still a congregation of West Indian restaurants, especially Jamaican, on Eglinton Avenue, the past decade has seen the dramatic rise of posh Caribbean restaurants throughout the city. The pre-eminent dining place is **Tropical Nights**, (Tel. 416-693-9000, 3114 Danforth Ave), on Danforth Avenue at Victoria Park. Then there is **Club Sandos**, (Tel. 416-293-0050, on 5780 Sheppard Ave. E) (east of Markham Road). Another popular dining spot is **Benab II Restaurant**, (Tel. 905-277-2483, located at 169 Dundas Street E), in Mississauga. These three establishments serve unique Caribbean Chinese dishes, in addition to the regular Caribbean fare. **Island Brew Coffee**, (Tel. 416-267-6081), provides a unique blend of coffee from five Caribbean islands including the Jamaica Blue Mountain. Delroy Taffe, owner of **Spence's Three Star Bakery**, (Tel. 416-782-7850), a restaurant and food store at 1539 Eglinton Ave. W., give Toronto's Jamaicans a taste of home with homemade breads and popular foods, including bammis, cow foot, mackerel, ackee and salt fish, Shim's fruit-flavoured syrups, Montego ginger beer, plantation chips, Blue Mountain coffee, the famous pickapeppa sauce, curry goat, oxtail, patties, and cocoa bread. Spence's popular breakfast may consist of callaloo (soup made from callaloo leaves, fish, and okra), liver, green bananas, dumplings, and plantain.

There are also a number of Caribbean import specialty stores in the area, such as **Gus' Tropical Foods and Delicatessen**, (Tel. 416-789-2387, 1582 Eglinton Ave. W). **Play de Record**, (Tel. 416-586-0380, www.playderecord.com, 357A Yonge St). **The Real Jerk**, (Tel. 416-463-6055, 709 Queen St. E), reflects its Jamaican identity with non-stop reggae music and house specialties such as jerk (cured meat) dishes accompanied by pickapeppa hot sauce. Roti, rice, and plantain are served along with Jamaica's famous beer, Red Stripe.

Cutty's Hideaway Restaurant, (Tel. 416-463-5380, 538 Danforth Ave), is a restaurant and nightclub that combines West Indian music with Island cuisine, such as black pudding, pepper pot, fish cakes, and bora pork. Fresh roti and pastries are available at **Ali's West Indian Roti Shop**, (Tel. 416-532-7701, 1446 Queen St. W).

Other specialty stores include: **Joyce's West Indies Food Store**, (Tel. 416-533-4872, 854 Bathurst St); and **V&S West Indies Grocery**, (Tel. 416-267-0921, 1360 Danforth Rd).

Religious Centres, Schools and Other Institutions

Religion is an extremely important institution in Caribbean society. People of the Caribbean belong to many faiths, with the majority belonging to Roman Catholic, Protestant, and Pentecostal churches. Hindus and Muslims from the Caribbean frequent the city's mosques and temples.

♦ KINGSVIEW VILLAGE SDA CHURCH, (Tel. 416-245-6863, 70 Kingsview Blvd).

♦ APPLE CREEK 7TH DAY ADVENTIST CHURCH, (Tel. 905-946-8751, 700 Apple Creek Blvd., Markham).

♦ TRUTH TABERNACLE UPC, (Tel. 905-477-5324, 333 Denison St., Markham).

- MEADOWALE SDA CHURCH, (Tel. 905-821-9149, 16 Falconer Dr., Mississauga).
- MISSISSAUGA SDA CHURCH, (Tel. 905-608-0013, 2250 Credit Valley Rd).
- ABBA COMMUNITY FELLOWSHIP, (Tel. 416-438-9500, 1085 Bellamy N).
- PEOPLE'S WORSHIP CENTRE, (Tel. 416-261-5420, 215 Kennedy Rd).
- PERFECT LOVE TABERNACLE, (Tel. 416-438-7437, 727 Progress Ave).
- SHOUTERS N.E. SPIRITUAL BAPTIST FAITH, (Tel. 416-264-5153, 559 Kennedy Rd).
- B.M.E. CHURCH, (Tel. 416-534-3831, 1828 Eglinton Ave. W).
- BIBLEWAY CHURCH OF JESUS CHRIST, (Tel. 416-658-5600, 24 Innes Ave).
- CORNERSTONE BAPTIST TABERNACLE, (Tel. 416-658-3300, 833 St. Clair Ave. W).
- DOWNSVIEW PENTECOSTAL CHURCH (PAOC), (Tel. 416-633-1886, 80 Regent Rd).
- NEW LIFE PENTECOSTAL CHURCH, (Tel. 416-744-4107, 65 Irondale Dr).
- REVIVAL TIME TABERNACLE, (Tel. 416-630-9346, 4340 Dufferin St).
- ST. GEORGE THE MARTYR ANGLICAN CHURCH, (Tel. 416-598-4366, 205 John St).
- TORONTO LIVING WORLD TABERNACLE, (Tel. 416-264-3024, 22 Fishleigh).
- TORONTO EAST SDA CHURCH, (Tel. 416-696-5784, 170 Weswood Ave).
- YORK CHURCH OF GOD, (Tel. 416-604-2775, 325 Weston Rd).
- UNITED MUSLIM ASSOCIATION, (Tel. 416-675-3254, 4 Woodlot Crescent).
- SHOUTER SPIRITUAL BAPTIST, (Tel. 416-686-1433, www.shouterbaptist.org, 447 Birchmount Rd).
- ST. THERESA WELL OF LIFE SPIRITUAL BAPTIST, (Tel. 416-288-1728, 90 Northline Rd., Scarborough).
- SATYA JYOTI CULTURAL SABHA, (Tel. 905-564-6723, 6731 Columbus Rd., Units 7 & 8, Mississauga).
- DEVI MANDIR, (Tel. 905-686-8534, 2590 Brock Rd., Pickering).
- PRANAV HINDU MANDIR AND CULTURAL CENTRE, (Tel. 905-686-8534, 102 Rivalda Rd). (North of Sheppard, east of Weston).
- ANGLICAN CHURCH OF CANADA AND CARE CANADA, (Tel. 416-924-9192, 80 Hayden St.)
- BRITISH METHODIST EPISCOPALIAN CHURCH, (Tel. 416-534-3831, 1828 Eglinton Ave. W).
- CARIBBEAN CANADIAN CATHOLIC CHURCH AND CENTRE, (Tel. 416-534-1145, 867 College St).
- CHRISTIAN CENTRE CHURCH, (Tel. 416-661-6770, 4545 Jane St).
- CHURCH OF GOD OF PROPHECY, (Tel. 416-465-6321, 114 Pape Ave).

- **DONWAY UNITED CHURCH**, (Tel. 416-444-8444, 230 Donway Ave W).
- **FIRST BAPTIST CHURCH**, (Tel. 416-977-3508, 101 Huron St).
- **PERTH AVENUE SEVENTH DAY ADVENTIST CHURCH**, (Tel. 416-535-1909, 243 Perth Ave).
- **ST. DAVID'S PRESBYTERIAN CHURCH**, (Tel. 416-267-7897, 1300 Danforth Rd).
- **ST. GEORGE THE MARTYR ANGLICAN CHURCH**, (Tel. 416-598-4366, 197 John St).
- **ST. MATTHEW'S UNITED CHURCH**, (Tel. 416-653-5711, 729 St. Clair Ave. W).
- **ST. MICHAEL'S AND ALL ANGELS ANGLICAN CHURCH**, (Tel. 416-653-3593, 611 St. Clair Ave. W).

Holidays and Celebrations

- **CARIBANA**, held in late July or early August each year, is modelled after **Carnival** in Trinidad, which began as a celebration of freedom from slavery. The first parade took place along Yonge Street in conjunction with Montreal's **Expo '67**. Today, more than 1 million people show up for the parade that winds along the lakeshore. Caribana's masqueraders depict a specific theme which reflects history, current events, film, social commentary, and carnival tradition. Participants can be seen doing the Wine, a gyrating movement of the torso, characteristic of West Indian dance. Every year, the **Miss Black Ontario** Pageant is held.

  An annual summer music festival featuring steel bands, calypso and reggae music is held at **Ontario Place**, under the patronage of the Jamaican and Trinidad High Commissions in Canada.

Each island community in the city celebrates its own independence day with festivities:

- **GUYANA'S REPUBLIC DAY**, February 23, celebrates the day in 1970 that Guyana became the Co-operative Republic of Guyana within the Commonwealth of Nations. This event is celebrated with a dinner and dance.
- **CARNIVAL** is celebrated with dances and parties by the Trinidadian and Tobago community during the weekend and the Monday and Tuesday prior to Lent.
- **GRENADIAN CULTURAL DAY** is May 21. The Grenada Association of Toronto sponsors a cultural program including displays, food, and dancing.

◆ **JAMAICA'S INDEPENDENCE DAY** is celebrated on August 6 with a dinner, speeches and a cultural program. It commemorates the day in 1962 when Jamaica became an independent nation within the Commonwealth.

◆ **INDEPENDENCE DAY FOR TRINIDADIANS AND TOBAGONIANS** is August 31. It celebrates their Independence Day within the Commonwealth, which took place in 1962.

◆ **TRINIDAD AND TOBAGO REPUBLIC DAY** is celebrated on the last Saturday in September with awards, presentations, speeches, dinner, and a dance, followed by a cultural presentation.

◆ **BARBADOS INDEPENDENCE DAY**, November 30, commemorates the day in 1966 that Barbados became an independent nation within the Commonwealth. The community celebrates with a dinner, speeches, special church services, and a cultural program.

◆ **ANTIGUA AND BARBUDA INDEPENDENCE DAY**, November 1. Celebrated with a special service of Thanksgiving dinner and dance, it commemorates independence from Britain in 1981.

See Holidays and Celebrations in Glossary.

Media

◆ **BLACK PAGES**, (Tel. 416-364-1900, 6021 Yonge St., Suite 306).

◆ **CARIBBEAN CAMERA**, (Tel. 416-412-3605, 55 Nugget Ave., Suite 212). A weekly newspaper. Editor: Rayner Maharaj.

◆ **CARIBBEAN CONNECTION**, CHIN 1540 AM, (Tel. 416-531-9991, 622 College St). Saturday, 9:00 p.m. to 12:00 a.m. Host: Jai Maharaj.

◆ **CARIBBEAN CONNECTION**, CHIN 100.7 FM, (Tel. 416-531-9991, 622 College St). Tuesday to Thursday, 12:00 a.m. to 1:00 a.m.; Saturday, 12:00 a.m. to 2:00 a.m. Host: Jai Maharaj.

◆ **CKLN RADIO**, 88.1 FM, (Tel. 416-595-1477, 380 Victoria St), features Caribbean programs. Sunday, 4:00 p.m. to 6:00 p.m.; Friday, 8:00 p.m. to 12:00 a.m.; Saturday, 1:00 p.m. to 4:00 p.m.; and Sunday, 1:00 p.m. to 4:00 p.m.

◆ **INDO-CARIBBEAN WORLD**, (Tel. 905-738-5005, 312 Brownridge Dr., Thornhill). A Toronto publication aimed at West Indians in general, with an emphasis on the Indo-Caribbean population. Contact: Harry Ramkhelawan.

◆ INDO-CARIBBEAN VISIONS, CITYTV, channel 57, (Tel. 416-591-5757, 299 Queen St. W). Saturdays, 9:00 a.m. to 9:30 a.m. Producer: Ken Singh.
◆ PRIDE, (Tel. 416-335-1719, 5200 Finch Ave. E., Suite 200A). A weekly newspaper. Publisher: Michael Van Cooten.
◆ SHARE, (Tel. 416-656-3400, www.sharenews.com, 658 Vaughan Rd). A national weekly newspaper serving Canada's Black and Caribbean community. With a circulation of more than 130,500 it is Canada's largest ethnic newspaper. Publisher: Arnold A. Auguste. Editor: Jules Elder.

Organizations

◆ AFRICANS IN PARTNERSHIP AGAINST AIDS, (Tel. 416-924-5256,517 College St., Suite 338). Educational & Support Network for Continental Africans in Canada.
◆ AFRICAN WOMAN RESOURCE & INFORMATION CENTRE, (Tel. 416-214-4823, 203 Sackville Green, Suite 6).
◆ ONTARIO BLACK HISTORY SOCIETY, (Tel. 416-867-9420, 10 Adelaide St. E., Suite 202), is a registered non-profit organization working to present and promote the contributions of Black people and their history in Canada through education and research.
◆ BLACK BUSINESS & PROFESSIONAL ASSOCIATION, (Tel. 416-504-4097, 675 King St. W., Suite 210). Presents the annual Harry Jerome Awards for achievements in business, community involvement, academics, arts, and athletics. The awards are a tribute to the late track star Harry Jerome who is regarded as a role model and a symbol of excellence by Canadians. President: Hugh Graham.
◆ CARIBBEAN CULTURAL COMMITTEE, (Tel. 416-465-4884, 138 Hamilton St). Organizes Caribana parade.
◆ CARIBBEAN CANADIAN SENIORS CLUB, (Tel. 416-746-5772, 995 Arrow Rd.)
◆ CATHOLIC CARIBBEAN CENTRE, (Tel. 416-534-1145, 867 College St).
◆ WEST INDIAN SOCIAL AND CULTURAL SOCIETY, (Tel. 416-493-1292, 62 Ladner Dr., P.O. Box 298, Station E). Youth educational project and counselling. Contact: Karl Oliver.
◆ WEST INDIAN VOLUNTEER, (248 Jamestown Cres). Provides individual and family counselling and social activities.
◆ YORK COMMUNITY SERVICES, (Tel. 416-653-5400, 1651 Keele St). Provides free health care, legal advice and counselling.

Other Organizations include:

- ◆ BERMUDA SOCIAL CLUB, (Tel. 416-493-3512, 61 Palmdale Dr).
  Organizes social and cultural events. Contact: Mavis Simmon.
- ◆ CARIBBEAN CANADIAN BUSINESS AND PROFESSIONALS ASSOCIATION,
  (Tel. 416-690-3913, 2558 Danforth Ave., Suite 203).

Caribana Parade Participants

- **CARIBBEAN YOUTH AND FAMILY SERVICES**, (Tel. 416-740-1558, 995 Arrow Rd). Provides therapeutic counselling, support counselling, and advocacy to youths and families.
- **JAMAICAN CANADIAN ASSOCIATION (JCA)**, (Tel. 416-746-5772, 995 Arrow Rd). A non-profit organization formed in 1962 on the occasion of Jamaica's independence from Britain. Organizes the festivities every Independence Day and helps new immigrants with housing and employment, provides youth educational programs and a Black cultural arts project. It provides a Credit Union for its members and publishes INFOCUS, a newsletter of community information. Annual events include dances, musical evenings, picnics, a Walk-A-Thon, and an outstanding achievement award, presented to a member of the community in honour of Marcus Garvey, a Jamaican activist in the early 1900s.
- **NEVCAN**, (Tel. 416-239-2648, % 1529 Islington Ave). The association of Nevisians, established in 1978 to help newly arrived Nevisians settle in Toronto. Also assists in the development of health and education, helps maintain cultural links with Nevis, and informs young Canadians on the traditions of their ancestors.
- **TROPICANA COMMUNITY SERVICES ORGANIZATION**, (Tel. 416-439-9009, 670 Progress Rd., Suite 14). Offers individual and family counselling to African and Caribbean individuals.
- **YOUTH PROGRAMS**, (Tel. 416-656-8025, Davenport Perth Neighbourhood Centre, 1900 Davenport Rd).

Consulates, Trade Commissions and Tourist Bureaus

- **ANTIGUA AND BARBUDA GOVERNMENT DEPARTMENT OF TOURISM AND TRADE**, (Tel. 416-961-3085, 60 St. Clair Ave. E., Suite 601).
- **CONSULATE GENERAL OF ANTIGUA AND BARBUDA**, (Tel. 416-961-3143, 60 St. Claire Ave. E., Suite 601). Consul General: Ms. Madeline Blackman.
- **CONSULATE GENERAL OF BARBADOS**, (Tel. 416-214-9805, 105 Adelaide St. W). Consul General: Mr. Leroy McClean.
- **BERMUDA DEPARTMENT OF TOURISM**, (Tel. 416-923-9600, 1200 Bay St., Suite 1004).
- **CONSULATE OF THE REPUBLIC OF GUYANA**, (Tel. 416-494-6040, 505 Consumers Rd., Suite 206). Consul General: Mr. Danny Thakur Doobay.
- **CONSULATE GENERAL OF JAMAICA**, (Tel. 416-598-3008, 303 Eglinton Ave. E., Suite 402). Consul General: Mr. Seth George Ramocan.

- ◆ JAMAICA TOURIST BOARD, (Tel. 416-482-7850, 1 Eglinton Ave. E).
- ◆ CONSULATE OF ST. VINCENT AND THE GRENADINES, (Tel. 416-398-4199, 333 Wilson Ave., #601). Consul General: Mr. Steve O. Phillips.
- ◆ CONSULATE GENERAL OF THE REPUBLIC OF TRINIDAD AND TOBAGO, (Tel. 416-495-9443, 2005 Sheppard Ave. E., Suite 303, Willowdale). Consul General: Mr. Michael Glenn-Art Lashley.
- ◆ CARIBBEAN AND AFRICAN CHAMBER OF COMMERCE, (Tel. 416-265-8603, 6 Sherbourne Cres).

Prominent Torontonians

Bromley Armstrong, labour relations officer and former Human Rights Commissioner; Jean Augustine, Ontario Fairness Commissioner, former Metro Housing Chair and former MP; Austin Clarke, award-winning author; Alvin Curling, former speaker Ontario Legislative Assembly; Stan Grizzel, retired citizenship court judge; Charles Roach, attorney; Sherene Shaw, Former Councillor; Tom Sosa, former Deputy Minister, Ministry of Skills Development; Marry Anne Chambers, former Minister of Training, colleges and universities; Margarett Best, MPP and Minister of Health Promotion; Bas Balkissoon, MPP.

Celebrating at Caribana.

Contributor: Emmanuel J. Dick, President, the Federation of Trinidad and Tobago Organizations in Canada. Geri-Anne Seaforth, Acting Consul General of Antigua and Barbuda.

Sources: Sheila Bello, Jules Elder, Karl Fuller, Lincoln Depradine.

The Chinese Communities

Not far from the towers of Toronto's business and banking community, a sampling of the bustling commerce of the streets of the Far East can be found. Much like a street scene in Hong Kong, throngs of people crowd the neighbourhood on weekends to patronize restaurants that offer traditional Chinese dishes including Beijing, Cantonese and Szechuan dishes, and stores that sell everything from live crabs to decorative fans, jade jewelry, Chinese herbs and medicine, and chopsticks.

With over 435,000 members, the Toronto region is home to the largest Chinese community in North America and consists of six Chinese neighbourhoods: the vicinity of Spadina Avenue and Dundas Street West, Broadview Avenue and Gerrard Street, Scarborough, Richmond Hill, Markham, and Mississauga.

Early Chinese settlers arrived in British Columbia from the United States and Hong Kong during the Cariboo and Fraser gold rushes of the 1850s and '60s. Later, some 17,000 men came from rural areas of the South China Sea region to help construct the **Canadian Pacific Railway**. Chinese labourers settled in towns and cities along the railway tracks and eventually opened restaurants and laundry businesses.

The seeds of Toronto's Chinese community were planted at the turn of the century in the area of York Street, between Queen and King streets. The Ward, as it was called, was primarily a Jewish neighbourhood when Sam Ching, the first Chinese person to be listed in the city directory, opened a hand laundry.

"Old Chinatown" evolved from laundries, restaurants, and small tea, herb, and vegetable shops that sprang up behind City Hall along Elizabeth and Dundas streets. An early community institution was the Presbyterian Church on University Avenue, purchased in 1919. It maintained a school and was a meeting place for social and cultural groups. The Shing Wah Daily News began publishing in 1922; later the **Chinese Benevolent Association** was formed to provide legal and social assistance. By 1935, there were 300 Chinese hand laundries located in the area behind Toronto City Hall, operated by Chinese railway workers who had come to the city from Western Canada.

Toronto's Chinese population grew considerably between 1947 and 1960. Beginning in the 1950s, students from Hong Kong, Singapore, and Taiwan entered Canadian universities and upon graduation stayed and worked in the country. In the 1960s, the political and social instability of the Southeast Asian countries prompted more students, skilled workers, business men, and entrepreneurs of Chinese origin to immigrate to Canada. Early settlers were mainly from China's northern provinces; the later group came from Hong Kong and Chinese communities in Southeast Asia, South Africa, Peru, and the West Indies. In recent years, many more Chinese immigrants have come from mainland China; most of them are skilled and highly educated professionals, such as computer programmers, engineers, medical doctors, scholars, financial professionals, entrepreneurs and other high tech professionals who are needed in Canada. There are now over 200,000 (mainland) Mandarin speaking people living in the Toronto region.

The building of the new City Hall in the 1950s pushed the neighbourhood north. The new settlers, many more skilled and educated, concentrated on opening businesses and offices on Dundas Street West and along Spadina Avenue, giving rise to "New Chinatown."

As well as a large number of Chinese professionals who practise in the city, numerous Chinese-owned import and export companies, construction firms, electronics companies, and banks have been established. In the 1980s, and the start of the new century, real estate investments by Chinese, especially Hong Kong entrepreneurs, not only changed the look of the old neighbourhoods, but also sparked the creation of new Chinatowns across the city and modern Greater Toronto. But while only one-fourth of the community lives in downtown Chinatown, it remains a major commercial and meeting place for the community. Around Chinese New Year, the streets come alive with the lantern festival, highlighted by the lion and dragon dance. Lucky red envelopes for gifts of money and firecrackers for driving away evil spirits appear in the windows, in anticipation of the event. The image of the Chinese lion weaves its way through the streets as jesters swing colourful lanterns to rouse the powerful beast into a dance amid the sounds of drums and firecrackers.

Places to Go

Shops and restaurants in downtown Chinatown, along Dundas Street from Yonge Street to Spadina Avenue, are major tourist attractions, operating seven days a week and conducting millions of dollars worth of business.

Street signs are written both in English and Chinese, and a commemorative plaque acknowledging the historical importance of Chinatown is found on the pathway outside City Hall. Along Dundas Street West and Spadina Avenue, barbecued pork and duck hang in the windows of grocery stores, wind chimes tinkle in the breeze outside gift stores, and crates are constantly being replenished with Chinese melons, cabbage, and salted dried fish.

Apart from the sweet and sour dishes created to appeal to North American tastes, Chinatown's restaurants serve traditional cuisine. The plentiful amounts of seafood and meat served in dishes from the coast of southern China reflect an abundance of natural seafood, meat products, and produce. In the inland of northern China, where winters are cold, more preservatives are used and the food is more salty and spicy. In Northeastern China, garlic, brown-bean paste, and noodles are popular. In Southwestern China, the food is more spicy and peppery, and wild game with herbal additives are the favourite dishes. In Mongolia, roasted beef or lamb over an open fire is a celebrated meal, and in Northeast China, fire pot delicacies are cooked in the winter.

Popular Chinese dishes include wonton soup (minced pork, shrimp, bamboo sprout, and water chestnuts wrapped in pasta); Beijing roast duck (crisp-skinned duck eaten with a special sweet sauce); and Dim Sum ("little sweetheart" dishes of meat or mixed meat and vegetables, usually served piping hot in bamboo steamers). In some restaurants, Dim Sum is brought to the table on trolleys carrying dishes under glass such as barbecue pork and chicken's feet.

Two of Toronto's first Chinese restaurants were **Kwong Chow**, at 126 Elizabeth Street, owned originally by Jean Lumb, the first Chinese woman to receive the Order of Canada; and **Great China**, operated by Joseph Kong Ng, who was the first Toronto restaurateur to employ a famous Dim Sum chef directly from Hong Kong. In 1975, Ng opened and brought over expert chefs from Hong Kong. His restaurant offered the sophisticated service of the top Hong Kong restaurants. Many of his staff now own or manage Chinese restaurants in the city.

One of Toronto's most celebrated Chinese restaurants has been operating for more than 50 years. Located in the original Chinatown behind City Hall: **Sai Woo**, (Tel. 416-977-4988, 130 Dundas St. W).

Hong Fatt BBQ Restaurant, (Tel. 416-977-3945, 443 Dundas St. W), **Market Villiage Mall**, (Tel. 905-940-2243, 4350 Steeles Ave. E), serves BBQ pork skewers, jiaozi (steamed dumplings usually pork-filled), sliced ham, watermelon, beer, cola, tea.

Popular Chinatown restaurants include **Lee Garden**, (Tel. 416-593-9524, 331 Spadina Ave), which is known for its Mongolian hot pots.

An upscale restaurant is **Dynasty Chinese Cuisine**, (Tel. 416-923-3323, 131 Bloor St. W., Suite 211). The restaurant uses no MSG (monosodium glutamate) in their barbecue and seafood specialties. Mr. Li specializes in seafood chinese-style, including lobster, salmon and pickerel, steamed or pan-fried.

Like most Chinatown businessmen, Howard Wong chose the name of his bakery, **Kim Moon**, (Tel. 416-977-1933, 438 Dundas St. W), after an established chain in Hong Kong. The Chinese bakery is the largest in Toronto and ships its baked goods across Canada and to the United States. The 300 varieties of pastries include buns filled with barbecue pork, green beans, black beans, and curry beef. Popular desserts are egg tarts, sponge cakes, and almond and peanut butter cookies. The bakery makes traditional Chinese wedding cakes that are served individually to each guest.

The windows of the **Yung Sing Pastry Shop**, (Tel. 416-979-2832, 22 Baldwin St), tempt passersbys to sample the homemade goodies of the Ko family, who have been in the business since 1968. The oldest remaining Chinese bakery in the city sells popular Dim Sum desserts and red bean shortcake to its mostly student clientele.

Far East Products Ltd., (Tel. 416-977-2482, 273 Enford Rd., Richmond Hill), has been churning out fortune cookies since 1966, first by hand in Chinatown, and now by a fully automated process in their Richmond Hill factory. The company, owned by Edmond and Raymond Lee, makes 10,000 cookies per hour and an average 100,000 cookies a day that are sold across Ontario. A tradition in the West, fortune cookies are based on a 13th century Chinese invention for sending secret messages. Large cookies in gift packages are available and customers can write their own messages when 100 or more cookies are ordered.

Advertising a free sampling of China's national drink is **Ten Ren Tea Co. (Toronto) Ltd.**, (Tel. 416-598-7872, 454 Dundas St. W). The store offers more than 60 varieties from the semi-fermented green tea, jasmine tea, and oolong tea, to the non-fermented long chin and gunpowder tea, and the fermented black tea. The tiny, methodically laid out store with verdant hanging tea leaves and glimmering tea packets is part of a Taiwan chain. It sells non-caffeinated teas, herbal teas, and ginseng roots, as well as porcelain and clay tea sets.

The first shopping mall in Chinatown was The **Chinese Court**, built in 1974 by craftsmen from Hong Kong. It was a replica of the **Imperial Palace Garden** in China and featured bridges, ponds, and ceremonial arches. The

Lion dance eye dotting ceromonies are normally performed at special events.

mall was torn down to make way for **Chinatown Centre**, (222 Spadina Avenue), a commercial-residential development with boutiques, a super-market, and a department store. The Centre features one of the largest Chinese restaurants in North America.

With the symbol of a dragon, meaning "the power," the $18 million **Dragon City Complex**, (280 Spadina Ave), contains two-and-a-half levels of Chinese shops and boutiques. Chinese herbs, preserved mango, lemon snacks, records, books, porcelain vases, and many other interesting items are sold. Exotic Hong Kong fish, such as black and red orandas, shark tails, and black angels, are available at Spadina Aquarium. Wing Cheung (which means "forever good") carries jade jewelry and sculpture from mainland China and Burma. A self-serve eatery decorated with shrubs and a fountain is located on the lower level and offers Chinese, Japanese, Indonesian, Vietnamese, and Taiwanese cuisine.

Works by Chinese artists are exhibited at the **Ontario Gallery of Chinese Arts**, (Tel. 416-586-9837, 150 Beverley St). (Founder: Jeffery Lo,); and the **Karwah Art Gallery**, (Tel. 416-598-0043, ww.karwahgallery.com, 289 Dundas St. W), carries silk-screen prints, art books, calligraphy brushes, porcelain jars, and miniature sculptures.

Chinatown has many book stores including **Modern Books and Records**, (Tel. 416-979-1365, 494 Dundas St. W).

A memorial honouring the 17,000 Chinese recruited by the Canadian Pacific Railway to help build Canada's unifying rail system in the 1800s has been erected at the west entrance of Toronto's **Rogers Centre**. The 40-foot-high memorial depicts two Chinese workers building a railroad trestle, and pays tribute to the 4,000 Chinese who lost their lives during the construction. A scholarship fund was also set up by the Foundation to Commemorate Chinese Railroad Workers in Canada to assist students studying Canadian history and the history of Chinese in Canada.

At the gateway to East Toronto's Chinatown, a monument to Chinese revolutionary leader Dr. Sun Yat-Sen (1866–1925) is found overlooking Riverdale Park. **Riverdale Library**, (Tel. 416-393-7720, 370 Broadview Ave), contains a Chinese section with books, daily newspapers, and magazines. Along with markets, herb stores, and gift stores, the neighbourhood has several restaurants, including **Pearl Court Restaurant**, (Tel. 416-463-8778, 633 Gerrard St. E); and The **Grand Restaurant**, (Tel. 416-778-8888, 615 Gerrard St. E). Other downtown restaurants serving Chinese cuisine in elegant surroundings include **House of Pink Pearl**, (Tel. 416-966-3631, 120 Avenue Rd).

In Scarborough, the **Dragon Centre** contains more than 140 stores for the convenience of Chinese residents. The stores of the **Mandarin Shopping Centre**, (4386 Sheppard Ave. E), carry Chinese wares. The Hong Kong bazaar architecture of the **Milliken Shopping Centre** reflects the Chinese presence in Northeast Toronto.

Chinese restaurants in Scarborough include **New World Oriental Cuisine**, (Tel. 416-498-1818, 3600 Victoria Park Ave), which features a 20-foot-high ceiling and an impressive fountain.

Some other restaurants include **Dragon House**, (Tel. 416-762-1271, 1019 Weston Rd); **E-On Restaurant**, (Tel. 416-977-9737, 124 Chestnut St.); **East Gate Restaurant**, (Tel. 416-264-2531, 2268 Kingston Rd., Scarborough); **East York Restaurant Ltd.**, (Tel. 416-421-1686, 1039 Pape Ave); **Eating Court**, (Tel. 416-323-0171, 1560 Yonge St); **Eating Garden**, (Tel. 416-595-5525, 41 Baldwin St); **Eden Chinese Food**, (Tel. 416-461-0813, 1025 Coxwell Ave, Scarborough); **Excellent Peking House**, (Tel. 416-979-7598, 263 Spadina Ave.); **Fireplace Restaurant**, (Tel. 416-968-0071, 340 Jarvis St); **Frederick Restaurant**, (Tel. 416-439-9234, 1920 Ellesmere Rd., Scarborough); **Fu Chou Restaurant**, (Tel. 416-929-1212, 376 College St); **Laolee Restaurant**, (Tel. 905-731-3288, 100 Steeles Ave. W., Unit 18, Thornhill); **Garden Gate Restaurant**, (Tel. 416-694-3605, 2379 Queen St. E); **Garden Restaurant**, (Tel. 416-596-0818, 153 Dundas St. W); **Su Good Restaurant**, (Tel. 416-691-8828, 2626 Danforth Ave); **Royal Chinese Restaurant**, (Tel. 416-292-8888, 735 Middlefield Rd., Unit 4-5).

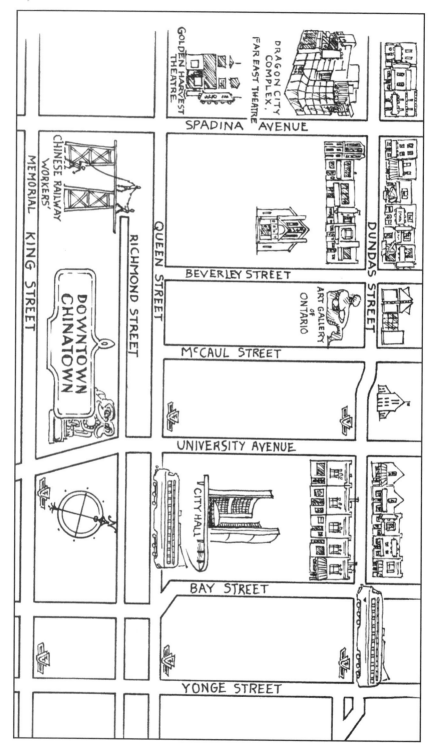

Religious Centres, Schools and Other Institutions

For Toronto's early Chinese settlers, the church was an important institution that served as a recreational club and meeting place. There are more than 30 churches in the city with Chinese congregations. Among Chinese Christians there are Catholics, as well as Protestant denominations such as Presbyterian and United. Others practise religions brought from China, such as Buddhism and Taoism.

- ◆ CHINESE GOSPEL CHURCH, (Tel. 416-977-2530, 450 Dundas St. W).
- ◆ OUR LADY OF MOUNT CARMEL, (Tel. 416-598-3920, 202 St. Patrick St).
  In the heart of Chinatown, this church has been a place of worship for the Chinese community for more than 20 years.
- ◆ TORONTO CHINESE BAPTIST CHURCH, (Tel. 416-596-8376, 78 Beverly St).
  Other churches with large Chinese congregations include:
- ◆ CHINESE GRACE BAPTIST CHURCH, (Tel. 416-603-3403, 20 Claremont St).
- ◆ CHINESE UNITED CHURCH, (Tel. 416-754-7147, 3300 Kennedy Rd).
- ◆ TORONTO MANDARIN CHINESE COMMUNITY CHURCH, (Tel. 416-299-3399, 2230 Birchmount Rd).
- ◆ TORONTO CHINESE LOGOS BAPTIST CHURCH, (Tel. 416-690-8306, 8 Amroth Ave).
- ◆ TORONTO CHINESE MENNONITE CHURCH, (Tel. 416-424-2078, 1038 Woodbine Ave).
- ◆ TORONTO CHINESE METHODIST CHURCH, (Tel. 416-754-8119, 8 Metropolitan Rd).
- ◆ ST. GEORGE THE MARTYR CHURCH, (Tel. 416-598-4366, 205 John St).
  Buddhist temples include:
- ◆ TORONTO BUDDHIST CHURCH, (Tel. 416-534-4302, 1011 Sheppard Ave W).
- ◆ TENRIKYO CHURCH, (Tel. 416-247-9791, 160 Gracefield Ave), is attended by Shintos.

There are many Chinese alumni and student associations in the city. Chinese schools include:

- ◆ CHINESE SCHOOL, (Tel. 416-977-1204, 177 Beverley St). (Call only on Saturdays)

Institutions for the elderly include:

- ◆ MON SHEONG HOME FOR THE AGED, (Tel. 416-977-3762, 36 D'Arcy St).
  The home is operated by the **Mon Sheong Foundation** which was formed in 1965. It was the first Chinese senior citizen residence built in North America and features a pleasant Chinese decor.

- ◆ YEE HONG CENTRE, (Tel. 416-321-6333, 2311 McNicoll Ave., Scarborough).

The community's financial institutions include:
- ◆ INTERNATIONAL COMMERCIAL BANK OF CATHAY (CANADA), (Tel. 416-947-2800, 4950 Yonge St., 10th Floor, #1002, and Tel. 416-597-8545, 2415 Spadina Ave).
- ◆ HONG KONG BANK OF CANADA, (Tel. 416-868-8000, 70 York St.; Tel. 416-348-8888, 222 Spadina Ave).
- ◆ BANK OF CHINA, (Tel. 416-362-2991, 130 King St. W., Suite 2730, and Tel. 416-971-8806, 396 Dundas St. W).

Holidays and Celebrations

- ◆ NEW YEAR'S DAY. Between January 20 and February 19, the Chinese greet each other with "Kung Hei Fat Choy," meaning "good fortune for the new year." The Chinese calendar is both lunar and solar. The year comprises 12 new moons and a thirteenth one is added every 12 years. Chinese legend says that Buddha once summoned all the animals to his court and promised them a reward if they came. Only 12 animals showed up and a year was named after each of them. It is believed that a person's character is dependent on the animal sign under which they are born.

New Year's celebrations last over 15 days and are primarily a family affair. Prior to the celebration, the house must be cleaned, debts are settled, and it is customary to wear new clothes and shoes. It is believed what happens on New Year's Day will repeat itself throughout the year. Special foods, tarts, and cakes symbolizing luck and fortune are prepared. The words "always full" are attached to the rice bin in hopes there will never be a shortage of rice. Houses are decorated with poems written on red paper—the colour that symbolizes wealth and prosperity—and no one sweeps the floor during the first day of the holiday for fear of sweeping away wealth. Chinese anticipate that long holidays and large family gatherings may result in heated discussions. The third day of the New Year is designated as one of argument—it is not customary to go visiting on this day. The seventh day of the New Year (corresponding to the day of creation) is the birthday for mankind.

- **THE FESTIVAL OF CH'ING MING**, in March or April, 106 days after the winter solstice, is an occasion to visit family graves and pay respect. The Chinese allot special days to remember the dead.
- **THE DRAGON BOAT FESTIVAL**, held annually by the Toronto Chinese Business Association of Greater Toronto, is celebrated on the fifth day of the fifth moon, and is commemorated by a boat race made up of 12 distinctive dragon boats fuelled by the power of more than a dozen rowers. Toronto Harbour plays host to the event in May or June each year. The festival honours Wut Yuen, a virtuous statesman who, it is believed, showed his disapproval of a corrupt government in 295 B.C., by drowning himself. His friends were unsuccessful in finding his body, but prepared rice wrapped in leaves and dropped it in the river to provide nourishment for Wut Yuen's spirit. In Toronto, the day is celebrated by eating joong (rice wrapped in bamboo leaves), which is sold in bakeries and food shops during the season.
- **ALL SOULS DAY**, in July or August, on the 15th day of the Seventh Moon, is a day for compassion for those spirits who have no descendants or resting place.
- **MID-AUTUMN MOON FESTIVAL** is held in August or September on the day the moon is at its fullest and brightest. Moon cakes symbolizing good luck are plentiful in Chinatown during this mid-autumn celebration. Similar to Thanksgiving, it is marked by outside dances, poetry readings, hymns, and prayers for a bountiful harvest.
- **THE FESTIVAL OF THE TOMBS**, held in September or October, honours deceased ancestors.
- **THE FESTIVAL OF THE WINTER SOLSTICE** occurs on the longest night of the year.
- **LION DANCE FESTIVAL** is a traditional Chinese Festival, and is also one of Toronto's most spectacular celebrations. The festival promoting Asian arts and culture, inaugurated in 1997, is organized annually by Scadding Court Community Centre. The Lion Dance is said to evoke good fortune and benevolent spirit. The year 2006 Lion Dance Festival from June 2–9th was celebrated with the **Lion Dance Film Festival, "Visit of the Lion" Show, Family Day Festival, Friday Night at the ROM, Children's Cross-cultural Adventure and International Drumming Festival**. Lion Dance is also performed during Chinese New Year celebration. **Lion Dance Festival**, (hotline 416-338-Lion (5466), www.liondancefest.com)

◆ THE KITCHEN GOD FESTIVAL, the preparatory festival for the New Year, occurs during the last days of the Twelfth Moon in December. One week before the New Year, the Kitchen God ascends to heaven to report on the behaviour of the household. Special foods are prepared in the hope that he will give a favourable report and offer his generosity and goodness in the New Year.

◆ NATIONAL DAY OF THE PEOPLE'S REPUBLIC OF CHINA, October 1st. Toronto's Chinese Community traditionally celebrates this day by holding a big banquet or parade in Chinatown and on important anniversary occasions, having a People's Republic of China flag-raising ceremony at the Ontario Legislature.

See Holidays and Celebrations in Glossary.

Media

◆ CHINESE CANADIAN POST, (Tel. 416-599-8633, Fax 416-288-0259, 746 Warden Ave Unit 18). Editor: David Lim.

◆ PEOPLE'S DAILY OVERSEAS EDITION, (Tel. 416-599-8633, 72 Huron St., B/F).

◆ A1, CHIN 1540 AM, (Tel. 416-531-9991, 622 College St). Monday to Friday, 3:00 p.m. to 8:00 p.m., and Sunday, 12:00 a.m. to 2:00 a.m. Host: Catherine Miu.

◆ CHINESE RADIO PROGRAM, CHIN 100.7 FM, (Tel. 416-531-9991, 622 College St, 2nd floor, Rm 205). Monday to Friday, 7:00 a.m. to 9:00 a.m. Host: Catherine Miu.

◆ CHINESE GOSPEL BROADCASTING CENTRE OF CANADA, (Tel. 416-466-4303, 4421 Sheppard Ave. E).

◆ MANDARIN PROGRAMMING, CFMT Channel 47, Cable 4, (Tel. 416-260-3620, ext. 467; Fax 416-260-3621), Sunday 11:00 to 12:00 p.m., 545 Lakeshore Blvd. W)

◆ CANADIAN CHINESE BROADCASTING CORPORATION, (Tel. 416-759-9502, 700 Gordon Baker Rd).

◆ CHANNEL 47, (Tel. 416-260-0047, Fax 416-260-3621, 545 Lakeshore Blvd. W).

◆ FAIRCHILD RADIO, (AM 1430 & FM 88.9), (Tel. 905-889-1430, 135 East Beaver Creek Rd., Unit 788, Richmond Hill).

◆ MING PAO DAILY NEWS, (Tel. 416-321-0088, Fax 416-321-3499, 1355 Huntingwood Dr). Executive Director: Ka Ming Liu.

- SING TAO DAILY, (Tel. 416-596-8140, Fax 416-599-6688, 417 Dundas St. W. The largest Chinese daily). Contact: Peter Lee.
- THE EPOCH TIMES, (Tel. 416-298-1933, Fax 416-298-1299, www.epochtimes.com, en.epochtimes.com, 201 Consumers Rd, Suite 103), President: Cindy Gu.
- WORLD JOURNAL DAILY, (Tel. 416-778-0888, 415 Eastern Ave), Contact: May Liu.

Organizations

- CHINESE CANADIAN NATIONAL COUNCIL, (Tel. 416-977-9871, Fax 416-977-1630, 302 Spadina Ave., Suite 507). Executive Director: Victor Wont, President: Colleen Hua.
- CHINESE CANADIAN NATIONAL COUNCIL (TORONTO) CHAPTER, (Tel. 416-596-0833, Fax 416-596-7248, 302 Spadina Ave., Suite 507). President: Philip Tsui.
- THE FEDERATION OF CHINESE CANADIAN ORGANIZATIONS (Tel. 416-443-8600, Fax 416-443-8688, 1315 Lawrence Ave., Suite 506). President: Mr. Ping Tan.
- THE FEDERATION OF CHINESE CANADIAN PROFESSIONALS (ONTARIO), (Tel. 905-890-3235, 55 Glenn Hawthorne Blvd, Mississauga). President: Elliot Tse.
- TORONTO CHINESE BUSINESS ASSOCIATION, (Tel. 416-595-0313, Fax 416-595-7334, 1220 Ellesmere Rd, Suite 13). President: Ralph Heu.
- CANADIAN CHINESE GENERAL CHAMBER OF INDUSTRY AND COMMERCE, (Tel. 416-502-9199, Fax 416-502-1566, 200 Consumers Rd, Suite 402). Chair: Shu Xin

Family and clan organizations offer assistance and provide welfare to members. Chinese regional associations hold picnics and functions throughout the year. There are a number of martial arts groups and Tai Chi societies in the city.

- CECIL COMMUNITY CENTRE, (Tel. 416-292-7510, Fax 416-292-9120, 3850 Finch Ave. E., Rm 403). Centre for information and community service.
- GANG WU LAW FIRM, (Tel. 416-225-4901, Fax 416-225-9535, 5799 Yonge St., Suite 409). Contact: Gang Wu.
- CHINESE COMMUNITY CENTRE OF ONTARIO INC., (Tel. 416-603-1917, 84 Augusta Ave). (Formerly the Chinese Benevolent Association.)
- CHINESE FREEMASONS, (Tel. 416-977-2467, 436 Dundas St. W., 3rd Floor). The oldest Chinese fraternal organization, established in 1905.

Dragon boat races are a popular attraction for the whole community. Toronto's are hosted by Centre Island every summer.

- ◆ CHINESE KUNG-FU INSTITUTE OF CANADA, (Tel. 416-321-6222 or Fax 416-321-9355, 70 Silver Star Blvd., Unit 107). President: Jimmy Chan.
- ◆ CARE FIRST SENIORS COMMUNITY SERVICES ASSOCIATION, (Tel. 416-585-2013, 479 Dundas St W).
- ◆ CHINESE TRANSLATION & INFORMATION SERVICE, (Tel. 416-598-2022, 58 Cecil St).
- ◆ METRO TORONTO CHINESE GOLDEN AGE SOCIETY, (Tel. 416-598-3562, 58 Cecil St).
- ◆ ONTARIO CHINESE RESTAURANT ASSOCIATION, (Tel. 416-340-7850, 260 Spadina Ave., Suite 305).
- ◆ ONTARIO SOCIETY FOR CHINESE EDUCATION, (Tel. 416-512-7315, Fax 416-229-2033, www.osce.ca, 11 Steeles Ave. E). Contact: Warren Ko, Vice President.
- ◆ SHIP TOY YEN SOCIETY, (Tel. 416-593-6518, 108 Beverly St). Performs ancient Chinese sword and spear dancing.
- ◆ TAOIST TAI CHI SOCIETY OF CANADA, (Tel. 416-656-2110, www.toronto.taoist-tai-chi.org, 1376 Bathurst St).
- ◆ TORONTO CHINESE COMMUNITY SERVICES ASSOCIATION, (Tel. 416-977-4026, 134 D'Arcy St).
- ◆ THE CROSS-CULTURAL COMMUNITY SERVICES ASSOCIATION, (Tel. 416-977-4026, Fax 416-351-0510, www.tccca.on.ca, 310 Spadina Ave, 3/F, Suite 301). Executive Director: Eliot Yip.

- WOODGREEN COMMUNITY CENTRE CHINESE SERVICES, (Tel. 416-469-5211, 835 Queen St. E).
  Community Services in Chinese:
- ASIAN COMMUNITY AIDS SERVICES, (Tel. 416-963-4300, 33 Isabella St., Suite 107).
- CECIL COMMUNITY CENTRE, (Tel. 416-392-1090, 58 Cecil St).
- CHINESE FAMILY LIFE SERVICES OF METRO TORONTO, (Tel. 416-979-8299, 3330 Midland Ave, Suite 229).
- CHINESE INFORMATION AND COMMUNITY SERVICES, (Tel. 416-292-7510, 3850 Finch Ave. E., Suite 403).
- EASTVIEW NEIGHBOURHOOD COMMUNITY CENTRE, (Tel. 416-392-1750, 86 Blake St).
- CHINESE CHAMBER OF COMMERCE IN MARKHAM, (Tel. 905-946-1137, Fax 905-946-9618, 4350 Steeles Ave. E., 2nd floor, Unit 207 (Market Village).
- HONG FOOK MENTAL HEALTH ASSOCIATION, (Fax 416-595-1103, 260 Spadina Ave., Suite 408).
- IMMIGRANT WOMEN'S HEALTH CENTRE, (Tel. 416-323-9986, 489 College St., Suite 200).
- TORONTO COMMUNITY EMPLOYMENT SERVICES, (Tel. 416-488-0084, 2221 Yonge St., Suite 403).
- METRO TORONTO CHINESE & SOUTHEAST ASIAN LEGAL CLINIC, (Tel. 416-971-9674, 180 Dundas St. W., Suite 1701).
- MON SHEONG HOME FOR THE AGED, (Tel. 416-977-3762, 36 D'Arcy St).
- MT. SINAI HOSPITAL (CHINESE OUTREACH PROGRAM), (Tel. 416-586-5206, Fax 416-586-5211, 600 University Ave., Rm 303).
- RIVERDALE IMMIGRANT WOMAN'S CENTRE, (Tel. 416-465-6021, 1326 Gerrard St. E).
- SCADDING COURT COMMUNITY CENTRE, (Tel. 416-392-0335, 707 Dundas St. W).
- SUPPORT AND ENHANCE ACCESS SERVICE CENTRE, (Tel. 416-362-1375, 603 Whiteside Place).
- ST. CHRISTOPHER HOUSE, (Tel. 416-532-4828, 248 Ossington Ave).
- ST. STEPHEN'S COMMUNITY HOUSE, (Tel. 416-925-2103, 91 Bellevue Ave).
- TORONTO CHINESE COMMUNITY SERVICES ASSOCIATION, (Tel. 416-977-4026, 310 Spadina Ave., Suite 301).
- YEE HONG CENTRE FOR GERIATRIC CARE, (Tel. 416-321-6333, Fax 416-321-6313, 2311 McNicoll Ave).
- WOODGREEN COMMUNITY CENTRE OF TORONTO, (Tel. 416-605-6000, 815 Danforth Ave, Suite 402).

Tony Luk
President of Canada-China
Association for the Promotion of
International Trade.

Shiu King Kong Ph.D.
President of the Sino-Canadian
Cultural Exchange Association and
honourary president and executive
director of Global Union of Hakka
and Tsung Tsin Associations of
Hong Kong.

- ◆ WORLD UNITED FORMOSANS FOR INDEPENDENCE CANADA HEADQUARTERS, (Tel. 416-512-7771, 35 Santa Barbara Rd).
- ◆ VOLUNTEER CENTRE FOR THE CITY OF TORONTO, (Tel. 416-961-6888, 344 Bloor St. W., Suite 207; Tel. 416-439-1919, 525 Markham Rd).
- ◆ UNIVERSITY SETTLEMENT RECREATION CENTRE, (Tel. 416-598-3444, 23 Grange Rd). Executive Director: Ms. Cassandra Wong.
- ◆ CHINESE CULTURAL CENTRE OF GREATER TORONTO (CCC), (Tel. 416-292-9293, Fax 416-292-9215, www.cccgt.org, 5183 Sheppard Ave. E). President: Mr. Ming Tat Chung.

Consulates, Trade Commissions and Tourist Bureaus

- ◆ CONSULATE GENERAL OF THE PEOPLE'S REPUBLIC OF CHINA, (Tel. 416-964-7260, 240 St. George St). Consul General: Mr. Chen Ligang.
- ◆ CHINESE CHAMBER OF COMMERCE, (Tel. 905-946-1272, 4350 Steeles Ave. E).
- ◆ HONG KONG ECONOMIC & TRADE OFFICE, (Tel. 416-924-5544, Fax 416-924-3599, 174 St. George St). Manager: Daniel Kwong.

Prominent Torontonians

Adrienne Clarkson, first Chinese Canadian
Governor General; Vivienne Poy, first Chinese
Canadian Senator; Jick-Kong Chan, architect,
designer of Scarborough's Dragon Centre; Gordon
Chong, former Toronto Councillor; Susan Eng,
Vice President of Advocacy for CARP, former
Police Commissioner; Kwong Kgok, artist; Jeffrey
Lo, founder of Ontario Gallery of Chinese Art; Dr.
Ken Ng, first Chinese President of Ontario Medical
Association, Scarborough Branch; Jim Pon, engi-
neer, founded Pons Technologies International,
winner of the Governor General's Medal for
increasing production during Canada's war effort;
Irene So, Chair, Canadian Foundation for the Preser-
vation of Chinese Cultural and Historical Treasures,
philanthropist; Ping Tan, President, Federation of
Chinese Canadian Organizations; Joseph Wong,
physician and community organizer; Dr. Michael
Tam, President of the Anti-Aging Society; Dr John
Hui, CEO, Knexx Medical Management & Trading
Ltd., Recipient of the Jubilee Medal; Tony Luk,
Recipient of the Jubilee Medal; Michael Chan, MPP
and Minister of Tourism and Culture.

Dr. John Hui, CEO, Knexx Medical Manage-ment & Trading Ltd., Recipient of the Jubilee Medal.

Dr. Michael Tam President of the Anti-Aging Society.

Sources: Steve Ang, Thomas Lam, Allen Leung,
Ken Ng, Wendy Sung, Dr. Michael Tam, King
Wong, Frank Chui, Tony Luk; Zhu Liu, consul, Wei
Wei Li, Vice-Consul, the Consulate General of the
P.R. China; David Lim, the Chinese Canadian Post;
Peter Li, Simon Chung.

Guangyu Wang Founder of Chinese Medicine Clinic: Camesin International Inc.

The Croatian Community

A plaque dedicated to the Croatian community's contributions to business, culture, and sports in Toronto is exhibited at the corner of Brock Avenue and Croatia Street. George Chuvalo, the former Canadian heavyweight boxing champion, Val and Sandra Bezic, former Olympic figure skaters, and Frank and Peter Mahovlich, former Toronto Maple Leaf hockey greats, are legends in Canadian sports and the Toronto Croatian community.

Croats come from what is today the Republic of Croatia and other republics in the former Yugoslavia. They have shared in the making of Canada's history, and were among the first explorers; it is believed that two sailors from Dalmatia served as crew on the voyages of Jacques Cartier and that a Croatian miner accompanied explorer Samuel de Champlain. Croats also served in the Austrian military sent by the French government to help defend New France in 1758, and some sought their fortunes in the Cariboo and Yukon gold rushes of the late 1800s. Attracted to Toronto's growing industries at the turn of the 20th century, the early Croatian settlers left farms in Southern Ontario to find work in the city.

During the Communist occupation following the Second World War, thousands of Croation refugees left Yugoslavia. Those who came to Canada generally settled in Toronto, finding work in industries, mining, and construction. Others worked in hospitals and public service, while some started their own businesses. From the 1950s to the 1970s, political and economic refugees continued to immigrate to Canada.

By 1951, the Croatian community had established its first parish and school, along with a number of social, business, and cultural organizations. Skilled Croatian construction workers were instrumental in building Toronto's subway system and developing Mississauga and Woodbridge. The **Metros-Croatia** soccer team proudly represented Canada by winning the 1976 **North American Soccer League** Championship.

In 1981, many of Toronto's 25,000 Croats enthusiastically poured into the streets of Parkdale to celebrate the renaming of Awde Street to Croatia Street. **Our Lady Queen of Croatia Roman Catholic Church**, at the top of Croatia Street, has been the religious, cultural, and educational pulse of the community for more than 50 years.

Places to Go

Our Lady Queen of Croatia, (Tel. 416-536-3669, 7 Croatia St), contains an attractive display of Croatian arts and crafts, as well as a library. In the parish hall, works of art by Toronto Croatian artists depict important events in Croatian history, such as the flourishing 19th-century Renaissance and the dramatic exodus following the Second World War. There are also landscape paintings of cities—Dubrovnik, Zagreb, Jajce, and the picturesque city of Mostar. The church features a statue and dedication to Aloysius Cardinal Stepinac, the Archbishop of Zagreb (1898–1960) and the man often called the Father of Croatia.

Every summer, the **Father Kamber Parish Recreational Park** in Mississauga is the site for colourful Croatian picnics and gatherings. Father Charles Kamber was a community leader and a pastor of the first Croatian parish.

Popular dishes among Croats include generous portions of meat, potatoes, and onions. Cevapcici (spicy ground barbecued veal or beef fingers), raznjici (barbecued veal or pork on a skewer), and pljeskavica (mixed ground meat) are found in Toronto's Croatian restaurants. Popular drinks include white Riesling and the favourite sljivovica (plum brandy). Desserts such as lemon krempite (custard squares) or rolati (sponge cake rolls) are often enjoyed with a cup of thick black coffee.

Croatia Restaurant, (Tel. 905-624-4111, 1989A Dundas St. E); **Joso's Restaurant**, (Tel. 416-925-1903, 202 Davenport Rd).

Croatia Meats & Deli, (Tel. 905-858-1357, 918 Dundas St. E), offers a complete selection of Croatian-style smoked and fresh meats, sausages, lamb, and roast pork.

Religious Centres, Schools and Other Institutions

The majority of Croats are Roman Catholic but there are also Croats of Islamic faith who have a mosque in the city.

- OUR LADY QUEEN OF CROATIA, (Tel. 416-536-3669, 7 Croatia St). Contact: Father Josipkos.
- HOLY TRINITY CROATIAN PARISH, (Tel. 905-842-2386, 2110 Trafalgar Rd., Oakville). Father: Illja Petrovic.
- CROATIAN ISLAMIC CENTRE, (Tel. 416-255-8338, 75 Birmingham St., Mimico). The mosque holds Arabic language classes and maintains a library of Croatian Islamic newspapers, books, and brochures.

- CROATIAN (TORONTO) CREDIT UNION (HRVATSKA KREDITNA ZADRUGA), (Tel. 416-532-4006, 1165 Bloor St. W.; Tel. 905-276-1962, 19 Dundas St. W), is the community's financial institution.
- QUEEN OF PEACE CROATIAN FRANCISCAN CENTRE, (Tel. 905-456-3203, 9118 Winston Churchhill Blvd). Father: Stjepan Pandzie.

Holidays and Celebrations

- THE DEATH OF ALOISIUS CARDINAL STEPINAC, a Croatian spiritual leader who died in 1960 while imprisoned in Yugoslavia, is commemorated on February 10. Commemorative masses are held on the Sunday nearest to the date. He was beatified by the Pope in 1998.
- THE NAMES OF PETAR ZRINSKI AND FRANC KRSTO FRANKOPAN are remembered in mass on April 30. They were 17th-century military heroes who fought bravely for the liberation of the Croatian People.
- CROATIAN INDEPENDENCE DAY is recognized by the Croatian community on October 8 with religious masses and banquets.
- A MEMORIAL DAY FOR THE BLEIBURG MASSACRE in 1945 occurs on the Victoria Day weekend in May. The day includes the joyous occasion of the annual **Croatian Folklore Festival**. When Toronto plays host to the events, Croatians from across Canada can be spotted wearing their traditional costumes in a parade down Dufferin Street to the **Canadian National Exhibition**.
- REMEMBERANCE OF THE DEATH OF RADIC STJEPAN, the leader of the Croatian Peasant Movement, killed in 1928, is held on August 8. Speeches by the Croatian Peasant Political Party are held in honour of the Croatian leader who promoted unity through non-violence.
- THE FOUNDATION OF THE CROATIAN PARISH is celebrated on October 22.
- THE DAY OF ALL SOULS, November 2, sees the community visit a Croatian cemetery in Malton to honour deceased friends, relatives, and those who were killed in Croatia.

See Holidays and Celebrations in Glossary.

Media

- DOMOBRAN RADIO STATION, (Tel. 905-828-1350, 4021 Rolling Valley Drive., Mississauga). Contact: Mr. Jerko Granic.

◆ HRVATSKA STRAZA, religious programs, CJMR Radio 1320. Sunday 3:00 pm to 4:00 pm. Has been on the air for over 15 years, delivering sermons from Ontario Croatian Catholic priests.

◆ SOUNDS OF CROATIA RADIO, CHIN Radio 100.7, (Tel. 905-602-8900, 3045 Southcreek Rd, Unit 1, Mississauga). On the air for 43 years. Contact: Mr John Loncaric.

Organizations

The churches are also centres for a number of cultural organizations.

◆ OUR LADY QUEEN OF CROATIA, (Tel. 416-536-3669, 7 Croatia St), houses junior and senior Croatian Catholic Youth groups; two church choirs; a benevolent society set up for funeral expenses; and the Tamburitza Orchestra, a group that performs using a traditional instrument similar to the mandolin. Publishes a weekly bulletin called *Zupni Vjesnik*.

◆ PARISH OF THE CROATIAN MARTYRS, (Tel. 905-826-8844, 4605 Mississauga Rd), houses the headquarters for the church choir; the **Zupna Kolo Grupa Sljeme dance group**; and **Croatian Tamburitza**.

◆ CANADIAN CROATIAN ARTISTS SOCIETY INC., (380 Kribs St, Cambridge, Ont.)

◆ CROATIAN CANADIAN STUDIES FOUNDATION, (Tel. 416-787-0303, Fax 416-787-8953, 168 Bridgeland Ave). President: Anton Kikas.

◆ UNITED CROATS OF CANADA GENERAL COMMITTEE, (P.O. Box 1631, Station B, Mississauga). President: Anthony Markovic.

◆ CROATIAN NATIONAL SOCCER FEDERATION, (Tel. 416-604-4477, 3009 Dundas St. W).

◆ ZAGREB CROATIAN SOCCER CLUB OF TORONTO, (Tel. 416-766-5569, 3725 Dundas St. W., Suite 615). Contact: Mr. Martin Latincic.

◆ CROATIAN CLUB "MEDJIMURJE," Tel. 416-744-3955, 377 Burnamthorpe Rd. E., Unit 39, P.O. Box 29568, Mississauga). Contact: Franjo Gavez.

◆ ALMAE MATRIS CROATICAE ALUMNI, (Tel. 416-487-9336, 4936 Yonge St., Suite 109, M2N 6S3). Contact: Mr. Nick Demarin.

◆ CROATA INTERNATIONAL CROATIAN BUSINESS ASSOCIATION, (Tel. 905-629-8415, 3045 Southcreek Rd., Unit 4, Mississauga.) Contact: Mr. Kresimir Mayer.

◆ DORA FOUNDATION, (Tel. 905-891-7115, 2192 Shawanaga Tr., Mississauga). Contact: Mr. Stanko Trtanj.

◆ CANADIAN CROATIAN FOLKLORE ASSOCIATION, (Tel. 905-508-9344, 44 Woodstone Ave., Richmond Hill). Contact: Mr. Nikola Vrdoljak.

◆ CROATIAN CLUB KARLOVAC, (Tel. 905-625-1229, 128 Queen St. S., P.O. Box 42286, Mississauga). Contact: Mr. Zvonko Dobrovoljac.

Our Lady Queen of Croatia Church, 7 Croatia St, Toronto

Consulates, Trade Commissions and Tourist Bureaus

◆ CONSULATE GENERAL OF THE REPUBLIC OF CROATIA, (Tel. 905-277-9051, Fax 905-277-5432, 918 Dundas St. E., Suite 302, Mississauga). Consul General: Mr. Ljubinko Matešic.

Prominent Torontonians

Anton Cetin, artist, winner of the Canadian–Croatian Artist of the Year Award; Ante Sardellic, artist; Vinko Grubisic, Professor, University of Waterloo; Anton Kikas, entrepreneur, consulting engineer and philanthropist; John Puhalo, community organizer; Ivica Zdunic, real estate and construction entrepreneur; Nik Vrdoljak, President, Croatian Folklore Federation of Canada.

Contributors: Father Josip Gjuran, Our Lady Queen of Croatia; Nik Vrdoljak; Millie Skrtich, Croatian Community Services.

The Czech Community

Every June on Czech and Slovak Day, Sokol Exercises take place at Masaryktown, a Czech and Slovak cultural and social centre in Scarborough. Sokol Exercises are designed to emulate the qualities of the Sokol (falcon), a bird admired for its strength, intelligence, and self-discipline. Young Czechs and Slovaks engage in physically challenging calisthenics, gymnastics, and track and field events, while the older generation displays its patriotism by watching soccer games or attending memorial services. The first Toronto Sokol unit was established in 1931. Jan Waldauf, a member of the unit and one-time president of the world-wide organization, made significant contributions to the development of physical fitness in Ontario.

The first Czechs in Canada were Moravians from the United States, who settled Ontario's Moraviatown around 1791. A wave of Czech immigration began in the 1880s as farmers, miners, artisans, and labourers came seeking opportunities in the Canadian West. In the 1920s, Czechs who had arrived in Ontario moved into farming communities and cities such as Hamilton, Windsor, and Oshawa, where many found work as auto mechanics and skilled tradesmen. In Toronto, the community settled in Parkdale around Queen Street West. Prior to the Second World War, Czech entrepreneur Thomas Bata established his world-renowned shoe company, helping many Czechs skilled in the shoe trade to immigrate to Canada. Political refugees fled Czechoslovakia after the Munich Surrender in 1938 and again in 1948 following the Communist takeover. A third wave left with the Soviet invasion of 1968.

One of the first organizations of Czechs and Slovaks was the **Czechoslovak National Association of Canada**, formed in response to the Nazi occupation of Czechoslovakia. The organization, now called the **Czech and Slovak Association of Canada**, promotes Czech and Slovak culture and assists newcomers. In 1988, the organization arranged a celebration to mark the 70th anniversary of the proclamation of the Independent Republic of Czechoslovakia. In 1992, it co-sponsored a celebration of the 400th anniversary of the birth of Jan Amos Komensky, a great theologian and scholar, proclaimed by **UNESCO** as a "world person."

In the 1940s, **Masaryk Hall** in Parkdale became a gathering place for community cultural and social events. The building was later sold to the City of Toronto. The **Masaryk Memorial Institute** transformed farm property it owned in Scarborough into a park called **Masaryktown**; a portion of the lands are protected by the conservation authority. Children of Czech and Slovak origin have spent many summers at camp at Masaryktown. On Czech and Slovak day, celebrations at Masaryktown honour the founders of the Republic of Czechoslovakia and pay tribute to the community's new homeland.

Toronto's Czech community is the largest in the country and has made important contributions to the city's cultural life. The rich musical and literary traditions of Czech and Slovak culture are exemplified by artists such as opera singer Jan Rubes; composer and pianist Oskar Morawetz; pianist Antonin Kubalek; Walter Susskind and Karel Ancerl, former conductors of the **Toronto Symphony Orchestra**; Milan Ichniovsky, interpreter of Slovak folk songs; Professor Josef Vaclav Skvorecky, winner of the Governor General's Award and the City of Toronto Book Award.

Places to Go

At Masaryktown, two monuments have been erected by members of the Czech and Slovak community. One monument bears the names of the founders of the Republic of Czechoslovakia: Masaryk, Stefanik, and Benes; the other, designed by Czechoslovakian Canadian artist Josef Randa, is dedicated to the victims persecuted during the Communist domination of Czechoslovakia in 1948. It was sponsored by the **K-231**, a club of former political prisoners. The grounds are maintained by The **Masaryk Memorial Institute**, (Tel. 416-439-4354, 450 Scarborough Golf Club Rd). The Institute operates a library, the largest of its kind in Canada, and the **Prague Restaurant**, (Tel. 416-289-0283), which serves Czech specialties. Favorite foods include snitzel with potato salad, roast pork, cabbage and flour dumplings, spanish birds, and roasted goose or duckling. Deserts include "Kolace"—pastry filled with poppy seeds, sweet cottage cheese or plum marmalade. Pilsner beer and slivovitz are popular drinks before or after a good meal.

Czechoslovakian-born artist Lea Vivot's sculptures can be found around the city, including **The Endless Bench**, outside the **Hospital for Sick Children**; and **Mother and Child**, outside **St. Joseph's Health Centre**.

New Czech Theatre and Slovak Young Scene perform classic and contemporary plays of Czech, Slovak and international play writers.

Religious Centres, Schools and Other Institutions

Many Czech Torontonians are Roman Catholic or Baptist and frequent the two Czech and some of the Slovak churches in Toronto.

♦ ROMAN CATHOLIC CHURCH OF ST. WENCESLAUS, (Tel. 416-532-5272, 496 Gladstone Ave). The first parish in the community was organized in 1951 and the church was built in 1963. Rev. Libor Svorcik.

♦ SLOVAK EVANGELICAL LUTHERAN CHURCH OF ST. PAUL, (Tel. 416-658-9793, 1424 Davenport Rd). Rev. Ladislav Kozak.

♦ SLOVAK GREEK CATHOLIC CHURCH OF ST. MARY, (Tel. 416-531-4836, 257 Shaw St).

♦ MASARYK MEMORIAL INSTITUTE, (Tel. 416-439-4354, 450 Scarborough Golf Club Rd). Publishes the newspaper **Novy Domov**, runs a library, a Czech school on Saturdays, organizes Czech and Slovak Day and concerts and used book sales throughout the year.

♦ PACE CREDIT UNION, (Tel. 416-925-0557, 740 Spadina Ave), is the community's financial institution.

Holidays and Celebrations

♦ BIRTHDAY OF TOMAS G. MASARYK (1850–1937), March 7, celebrates the renowned philosopher and founding president of the Czechoslovak Republic, established in 1918. The Masaryk Memorial Institute organizes speeches and concerts on the nearest weekend to the day.

♦ MEMORIAL DAY, on the third weekend in April, sees a commemorative service in honour of those who died fighting for freedom in Czechoslovakia.

♦ DEATH OF GENERAL MILAN STEFANIK, May 4, commemorates the Slovak astronomer and soldier who was one of the founders of the Independent Democratic Republic of Czechoslovakia. The former minister of defence was killed in an airplane crash in 1919.

♦ ST. CYRIL AND ST. METHODIUS are honoured on July 5. Czechs hold church services to remember the Apostles of the Slavs who influenced the religious and cultural development of the Slavic people in the ninth century. The two were responsible for creating a new Slavonic alphabet and were named saints of the Roman Catholic Church.

♦ DAY OF SHAME. On August 20 and 21, the invasion of Czechoslovakia in 1968 by military forces under Soviet leadership is commemorated. Prior to the fall of communism, this day was held in conjunction with Black Ribbon Day on August 23.

◆ **INDEPENDENCE DAY**, held on the nearest weekend to October 28, celebrates the day Czechoslovakia attained independence in 1918. The Masaryk Institute and the Czech and Slovak Association of Canada organize speeches, seminars, and concerts with dancing and singing.

See Holidays and Celebrations in Glossary.

Teaching children gymnastics is part of Czech tradition.

Media

◆ **GATEWAY TO EUROPEAN MARKETS** (quarterly), (Tel. 416-929-3432, 909 Bay St., Suite 1006). Editor: Lubomir Novotny.

◆ **KANADSKÉ LISTY (CANADIAN LETTERS)**, (Tel. 905-278-4116, 388 Atwater Ave., Mississauga). Published monthly in Czech and English. Editor/Publisher: M. Janecek. Mike Janecek & Jana Janeckova-Bayerova.

◆ **NOVY DOMOV (NEW HOMELAND)**, (Tel. 416-439-9557, 450 Scarborough Golf Club Rd). A bi-weekly newspaper. President: Gerry Formanek. Editor: Vera M. Roller.

◆ **NOVA VIZE CZECH**, television program on OMNI 1 every Saturday at 10 a.m., repeated on Tuesday at 7:30 a.m. Producer: Marketa Slepcik.

◆ **SLOVENSKY SVET SLOVAK**, television program on OMNI 1.

♦ SATELLITE, (P.O. Box 176, Station E). Publisher and Editor: Ales Brezina.

Organizations

♦ CZECH AND SLOVAK ASSOCIATION OF CANADA, (Tel. 416-925-2241, 3044 Bloor St. W., P.O. Box 564). Formerly the **Czechoslovak National Alliance**, it was established in 1939 to promote Czech and Slovak culture, language, history, and educational activities. Also helps refugees integrate into Canadian society. President: Milos Slichma. Toronto Branch President: Ms. Radmila Locher.

♦ CANADIAN FUND FOR CZECH AND SLOVAK UNIVERSITIES, (Tel. 416-446-2168, fax 416-446-2187, 59 Wynford Dr). President: Tibor Gregor.

♦ CANADA-CZECH REPUBLIC CHAMBER OF COMMERCE, (Tel. 416-929-3432, 909 Bay St., Suite 1006). President: Lubomir Novotny.

♦ CZECHOSLOVAK LEGION, (Tel. 416-964-7030, 30 Hillsboro, #1807). An organization of Czechs and Slovaks who served in the two World Wars. President: B.J. Moravec.

♦ MASARYK MEMORIAL INSTITUTE, (Tel. 416-439-4354, 450 Scarborough Golf Club Rd). Holds dances and bazaars throughout the year. President: Frantisek Jecmen.

♦ SOKOL GYMNASTICS ASSOCIATION OF TORONTO, (Tel. 416-762-6846, 24 Vanda Ave). Promotes physical fitness and moral education. Member of gymnastics in the province. Has weekly exercise and volleyball classes, organizes bazaars and dances and participates at slets, which are gymnastic festivals. Participants are aged 3 to 80+. President: Ms. Hana Jurasek.

♦ WOMEN'S COUNCIL OF THE CZECH AND SLOVAK ASSOCIATION OF CANADA, (Tel. 416-239-2456, 22 Reid Manor). Formed in 1960; performs charitable work and assists newcomers. Published a cookbook of national dishes in 1965. President: Blanca Rohn.

Prominent Torontonians

Josef R. C. Cermak, Q.C., retired lawyer and author of several books; Susan Douglas-Rubes, actress and radio and television personality; Hana Gartner, CBC-TV; Chavlva Milada Hosek, former MPP, one time advisor to the federal government; Eva Kushner, professor of French and Comparative Literature at U of T; Zdena Salivarova, writer; Helen Sinclair, former

President of Canadian Bankers Association; Josef Skvorecky, writer, professor emeritus of English at U of T; Marie Gabankova, artist-painter, professor; Vladena Krykorkova, book illustrator; Thomas Kaberle, hockey player; Josef Drapell, artist; Slava Duris, Toronto Maple Leafs player; Antonin Kubalek, pianist; Eda Vokurka, Jazz Violin; Dr. Milos Krajny, secretary of Ontario Allergy Society, president of Toronto Philharmonia, founding member of Mozart Society in Toronto; Pavel Kantorek, caricaturist, professor nuclear physics; Ladi Horak, owner of Creative Post; Ing. Vladimir Kavan, founder of Canadian International.

Contributors: J.R.C. Cermak, Radmila Locher, Secretary General, Czech and Slovak Association of Canada.

Consulate, Trade Commission and Tourist Bureaus

♦ CONSULATE GENERAL OF THE CZECH REPUBLIC (Tel. 416-972-1476, 2 Bloor St. W.). Consul General: Richard Krpač.

The Danish Community

Most of the Danish immigrants, who are still living in Toronto, arrived in the 50s and 60s and are now of retirement age. Although they have integrated into the local communities, many still maintain Danish traditions and have shared their traditions, skills and Danish food specialties with their neighbours. In numerous ways, Danes have contributed to the cultural fabric of Toronto. One of the most famous contributors is probably the renowned Danseur Noble Erik Bruhn, who unquestionably made his mark as the **National Ballet of Canada**'s artistic director, and in whose name a prize was established to be awarded to outstanding senior male student dancers.

Many Danish establishments, such as restaurants, delicatessens, gift and furniture stores, were opened in the 1950s and 1960s by post-war settlers. Torontonians fondly recall **The Copenhagen Room**, **The Little Mermaid** and **The Viking** restaurants as well as **George Jensen Jewelers** and several furniture stores, among others. The **Danish-Canadian Chamber of Commerce** can attest to the continuing, but changing, successful Danish business community in Toronto.

The first Danes to come to Canada were early explorers, who braved the seas to reach the coast of North America. Jens Munk, searching for a Northwest Passage to China, landed his vessel at the mouth of Churchill River and named it Munk's Bay in 1619. Other Danish sailors and fur trappers soon followed. However, the first wave of immigration occurred in the late 19th century, when Danish farmers, servants, blacksmiths, and journeymen left the United States to settle in the Maritimes, the prairies, and Northern and Southwestern Ontario.

The first Danish settlement in Canada was established in New Brunswick in 1872, when New Denmark was founded and since then has developed into a very successful potato farming area. A second settlement was established at Pottersburg (London, Ontario) in 1893 by John Ginge, who built a large pork-packing plant, attracting many Danish butchers and sausage makers to the area.

In the 1920s, Danes arrived hoping to acquire homesteads. Many later moved to the cities, where they formed communities. In Toronto, the first worship service for Danish Lutherans was held at **St. Ansgar's Danish**

Evangelical Lutheran Church in 1925. The community organized other groups, including the **Ladies Aid Society**, a Sunday school, and the **Dana College Choir**. In 1931, St. Ansgar purchased the Methodist rectory on Sherbourne Street and organized a library of Danish books and newspapers. Between 1951 and 1960, thousands of Danish professionals and highly skilled workers such as carpenters, bricklayers, mechanics and electricians were attracted by the city's economic opportunities. Today, there are about 20,000 Danish-Canadians living in Toronto.

Places to Go

Sunset Villa Kro, (Tel. (519) 824-0539, R.R. #2, 7150 Concession #1, Puslinch), is located 100 km west of Toronto. The Danish inn and retirement home was established in 1950 by the Sunset Villa Association on a 52-acre park site with a pond, playground, and camping grounds. The home operates a library and a licensed inn (kro), which offers open-faced sandwiches and other Danish specialties.

Danish Pastry Shop, (Tel. 416-425-8877, 1017 Pape Ave), was established in 1961 by Hans and Anna Hansen. Practically everything for "Det Kolde Bord" (Danish smörgåsbord) is available here as well as authentic Danish pastries and rye bread, baked on the premises, and imported Danish delicacies. On the first Sunday of every month, many of the bakery's products are available for sale at Sunset Villa.

Danish Style Bake Shop and Delicatessen, (Tel. 416-694-5333, 1027 Kingston Rd). For more than two decades, Bjarne Hansen has baked Danish pastries such as almond sticks, buttercakes, and almond pastries with raisins. Also available are ingredients for the 'cold table' as well as Danish alcohol-free beverages. The shop also carries a variety of other Scandinavian products.

Church

The predominant religion among Danes is Lutheran.
◆ DANISH LUTHERAN CHURCH, (Tel. 416-222-2494, 72 Finch Ave. W). This white building was designed by a Danish architect and is typical of the simple and unassuming architecture of churches in Denmark. Built in 1966, the church has a Danish pipe organ and its inside supports have been compared to the longboats of early Danish sailors. The Danish church is home to many social functions as well as Sunday school, a folk-dance group, the Golden Age Club and various youth activities. Services are held every Sunday at 10:30 a.m. with two

services a month in Danish and two in English. Further information is available on the web site www.dlctoronto.on.ca. A vicarage, adjacent to the church, is provided for the Pastor, Dorte Pedersen.

Holidays and Celebrations

- FASTELAVN, held the week before Lent, is the Danish Mardi Gras. This event takes place at the Danish Lutheran Church and at Sunset Villa.

- QUEEN OF DENMARK'S BIRTHDAY (QUEEN MARGRETHE II) is celebrated on April 16 with a dinner and entertainment organized by the church congregation and the Danish Guards' Association.

- CONSTITUTION DAY, June 5, celebrates the day in 1849 when the first Danish liberal constitution became law. Every year, on the Sunday closest to this date, Sunset Villa is alive with hundreds of Danes, who meet here to commemorate this important event. The program includes an outdoor church service, speeches, a picnic, children's games and folk dancing.

- ST. HANS (JOHANNES) DAY on June 24 marks the longest day of the year and honours St. John the Baptist. The event is celebrated on the evening prior with singing and dancing and a large bonfire.

- MORTENSAFTEN (SAINT MARTIN'S EVE). The legend tells the story of Saint Martin of Tours, who did not wish to become bishop. He hid in a goose nest but was found when the geese's cackle gave him away. He became bishop and is celebrated on November 11. On the evening prior, Danes traditionally eat goose in memory of the geese that betrayed Saint Martin.

- SANTA LUCIA. Even though this is a Swedish tradition, Danes celebrate December 13, Lucia Day, in the Danish Church, nursing homes and hospitals as well as many schools and day-care institutions. A group of young girls in white dresses perform a traditional ritual, which includes their entrance, carrying candles and singing the Santa Lucia song. The girls are dressed in white, and the Lucia Bride, who leads the procession, wears a wreath with candles on her head. The custom was introduced in Denmark during the German Occupation in 1944.

- CHRISTMAS is celebrated on the evening of December 24. Following the afternoon church service (English or Danish), families gather for Christmas dinner, which usually includes pork roast with crackling, goose or duckling accompanied by pickled red cabbage, sugared potatoes, and vegetables. Rice porridge may precede the meal or riz a l'amande (rice with whipped cream and almonds, accompanied by cherry sauce) may follow the meal. Christmas carols and hymns are sung around a candle-lit tree and gifts are distributed by a younger member of the family.

♦ **GREAT PRAYER DAY (STORE BEDEDAG)**, is a special Danish festival falling on the fourth Friday after Easter Sunday. Both the previous evening and on Great Prayer Day itself, warm wheat buns (Hveder) are served. This day combines several lesser fast and prayer days. Under the law, all trade, work, etc. were forbidden on this day. The bakers therefore came up with the idea of baking some wheat buns, which could be heated up and eaten the following day.

See Holidays and Celebrations in Glossary.

Danish Constitutional Day, held June 5.

Organizations

♦ **DANISH CANADIAN CHAMBER OF COMMERCE**, (Tel. 416-923-1811, Fax 416-962-3668, 151 Bloor St. W., Suite 310). Chairman: Mr. Anders Fisker.

♦ **DANES WORLDWIDE**. (Tel. 416-493-1594) Representative for Toronto and southwestern Ontario: Eva Terp.

♦ **ROYAL DANISH GUARDS' ASSOCIATION**. (Tel. 416-260-2938) The members are former guards of the Danish Royal Palace. President: Jakob Noergaard.

♦ **SCANDINAVIAN-CANADIAN CLUB OF TORONTO**, (Tel. 416-782-4604, 91 Stormont Ave). The members represent the five Nordic countries, Denmark, Finland, Iceland, Norway and Sweden.

- SUNSET VILLA ASSOCIATION, (Tel. (519) 824-0539, R.R. #2, 7150 Concession #1, Puslinch), operates a group of retirement residences for elderly Danes on the Sunset Villa property. President: Linda Larsen.
- SUNSET MINDEPARK, (Tel. (519) 821-9296, R.R. #2, Puslinch). Founded in 1992 this beautiful memorial garden and urn cemetery is located on the Sunset Villa grounds. President: Lis Sondergaard.

Consulate/Trade Commission

- ROYAL DANISH CONSULATE GENERAL, (Tel. 416-962-5661, 151 Bloor St. W., Suite 310). Consul General / Trade Commissioner: Bjarne B. Jensen. Honourary Consul General: Mr. Arne Nordtorp.

Contributor: Eva Terp.

The Danube Swabian Community

Danube Swabian farmers are among the vegetable producers in the Holland Marsh and Leamington, Ontario, farm areas. Many of Ontario's small industrial plants that make everything from plastics to custom parts for the space industry were founded or are headed by Danube Swabians. Tradesmen and supervisors have been involved in major construction projects, including Toronto's **Rogers Centre**.

Danube Swabians are ethnic Germans from the Danubian Lowlands (now part of Hungary, Romania, and Yugoslavia). In the late 17th-century the Habsburg rulers in Vienna decided to colonize these lowlands and embarked on an energetic "impopulation" program. German colonists were considered to be very desirable by the authorities in Vienna because they possessed special skills to build the towns and cities, and they would introduce superior, Western methods of agriculture. Also, they were known to be steady, industrious, and above all politically neutral.

The first Danube Swabian to immigrate to Upper Canada was a Lutheran minister who settled in Markham Township. In the 1890s, some Danube Swabian farmers became homesteaders in the prairie Provinces as well as Ontario. Other Danube Swabians arrived in Canada in two waves, one in the 1920s and the other beginning in 1948 and lasting for approximately 10 years. Beginning in 1944, Danube Swabians were expelled from their homes and their lands were collectivized by the Communists, who assumed power at that time.

Presently, there are approximately 32,000 Danube Swabians living in Toronto.

Places to Go

Association of Danube Swabians, (Tel. 416-290-6186, Fax 416-290-6186, 1686 Ellesmere Rd., Scarborough). In 1994, after 40 years at its previous location of 214 Main St., the Association moved to a new location. The facility includes an attractive restaurant and banquet and meeting rooms able to accommodate everything from moderate receptions for 50 people to gala events for 450 people. The centre boosts a state-of-the-art kitchen that offers savory Canadian and traditional cuisine.

Donauschwaben Park Waldheim, Blackstock, (Tel. 905-985-9087), is a 135-acre private park, cottage and sport complex. Throughout the year, friends and families gather to participate in special occasions such as youth sports and Thanksgiving dinners. President: Tony Sax. At **St. Michaelswerk**, (Tel. 416-598-4835, 131 McCaul St) dinner, dances and entertainment are offered in October for **Erntedankfest** (Thanksgiving Dinner), in November for the **Kathrein Ball**, in January for the **Faschingsball** (Carnival Ball), and in May for Mother's Day Dinner. President: Anton Wekerle.

Religious Centres, Schools and Other Institutions

Members of the Danube Swabian community attend the city's Lutheran and Catholic German churches. The two most frequented churches are:

- ST. GEORGE'S LUTHERAN CHURCH, (Tel. 416-921-2687, 410 College St).
- ST. PATRICK GERMAN PARISH, (Tel. 416-598-4835, 131 McCaul St). This is the traditional church of Danube Swabian Catholics, who still form a large share of the membership.

Holidays and Celebrations

- NEW YEAR'S EVE. "Silvester" is celebrated with merrymaking at the **Danube Swabian Club** and at the **St. Patrick's German Parish**.
- KINDERMASKENBALL (CHILDREN'S MASQUERADE) is held on a Sunday afternoon in February. Children dress in outlandish costumes and partake in fun and games.
- THE SCHLACHTFEST is held twice a year, once in February and again in the fall. It is a nostalgic reminder of similar old-country feasts, and demonstrates home cooking of pork products, with particular emphasis on homemade sausages.
- TRACHTENFEST, in April, sees Danube Swabians wear their native trachten, the traditional costumes worn on Sundays in Danube Swabian villages. This spring festival attracts dance groups from across southern Ontario.
- THE ROSE BALL, in May, is a formal dance, where "Miss Blue Danube," the princess of the pavilion, is chosen. The pavilion has been hosted by the Danube Swabian Club for more than two decades.
- MOTHER'S DAY, in May, is observed with a banquet to honour mothers.
- PILGRIMAGE. On the second Sunday in June, an annual pilgrimage to Mary Lake, King City, Ontario attracts over 3,000 Danube Swabians,

who attend an open-air mass and memorial service to give thanks for
their regained freedom.

♦ **YOUTH FESTIVAL**. An annual gathering of Danube Swabian youth
groups from Canada and and the United States is held every July,
usually at Donauschwaben Park Waldheim. Jugend-Treffen features
sporting events and other activities.

♦ **SENIORS' PICNIC**. In August, a picnic for seniors is held at Donauschwaben Park Waldheim.

♦ **OKTOBERFEST**. In September, Danube Swabians join in Oktoberfest festivities with a polka competition. Although Oktoberfest is not a Danube
Swabian custom, they were the first to bring the festival to Toronto in
1970.

♦ **KIRCHWEIHFEST (CONSECRATION OF THE CHURCH FESTIVAL)** is held in
November. Traditionally, each community celebrated its own Kirchweihfest to commemorate the dedication of the earliest church. It has
become a secular festival, with dancing and merriment to the sounds
of a brass band. The girls wear "Trachten" and the boys don hats
decorated with flowers and coloured ribbons.

♦ **KINDER RESCHERUNG (CHILDREN'S CHRISTMAS PARTY)** is celebrated in
December. Children sing traditional songs and visit with Santa. A
family banquet is held the second week of December as well.

See Holidays and Celebrations in Glossary.

Media

♦ **DEUTSCHE PRESSE**, (Tel. 416-595-9714, 87 Judge Rd).

♦ **GERMAN HOUR**, CHIN Radio 100.7 FM, (Tel. 416-531-9991, 622
College St). Saturday, 6:00 a.m. Host: Rickle Marcus. Saturday,
6:30 a.m. Host: Jan Dziuma. Saturday, 7:00 a.m. to 9:00 a.m. Host:
Julli Jeschke, Ulrich Jeschke.

♦ **HEIMATBOTE**, (Tel. 905-881-6350, Fax 905-886-3794, 17 Doncrest Dr.,
Thornhill). The voice of the Danube Swabians in North America.
Editor-in-chief: Anton Wekerle.

♦ **NEUE WELT**, German language bi-weekly newspaper, (Tel. 416-237-
0591, Fax 416-237-9590, www.neueweltonline.com, 2 Billingham Rd.
Suite 203). Publisher & Editor-in-chief: Karsten Mertens

Organizations

♦ **ASSOCIATION OF DANUBE SWABIANS**, (Tel. 416-290-6186, 1686 Ellesmere
Rd). Fosters Danube Swabian culture, customs, the use of the German

language, as well as the physical well-being and good fellowship of its members. Supports six dance groups, two choirs, women's auxiliary, and a sports group. President: Mrs. Bridgette Wecker.

- ♦ ST. MICHAELSWERK, (Tel. 416-598-4835, 131 McCaul St). Attends to the needs of the Danube Swabians with respect to cultural, social, and charitable aspects of the community. Organizes annual pilgrimage to Mary Lake in King City, Ontario on the second Sunday in June. President: Anton Wekerle.

Member of youth group of St. Michaelswerk.

Since they form part of the German-speaking community of Toronto, Danube Swabians make use of German cultural institutions, libraries, and theatres. Some children attend the various German language schools that are found throughout Metro.

Prominent Torontonians

Andrew Brandt, former Chair and Chief Executive officer of LCBO, former leader of the Ontario Progressive Conservative Party; Ernst Roch, graphic artist, designer of the 1976 Olympic Games logo, a 1962–63 series of postage stamps, and the six-cornered emblem of the National Arts Centre in Ottawa; Dr. Gerda Wekerle, Professor, York University; Dr. Christine Wekerle, Professor of University of Toronto; Dr. Lorenz Eckert; Klaus Hartmann, B.A., LL.B.; Peter Reiss, B.A., LL.B.

Contributors: Tony Baumann, President, the Association of Danube Swabians; Anton Wekerle, President, St. Michaelswerke.

Sources: A. Baumann, A. Wekerle, B.A.

The Dutch Community

The country of Rembrandt and Van Gogh was also the birthplace of artist Albert Jacques Franck (1899–1973), who arrived in Canada in 1927. Franck worked out of a Gerrard St. store restoring paintings in what was then Toronto's artists' colony. His depictions of sleepy neighbourhoods, gabled homes, and wintry street scenes inspired many of the city's younger artists. In memory of the late artist, the **Albert Franck Artist Exchange Programme** was setup to provide an annual exchange of creative talents between Toronto and its twin city, Amsterdam.

Many of the first Dutch settlers were United Empire Loyalists who left the U.S. following the American Revolution. A prominent member of the early community was Egerton Ryerson (1803–1882), chief superintendent of education for Upper Canada, who pioneered the education system of Ontario. He founded **Ryerson Polytechnical Institute** and is commemorated with a statue on the campus.

Toronto's Dutch population began to burgeon in the 1920s and 1930s as southwestern Dutch farmers moved to the city seeking jobs in industry. Following the Second World War, Dutch war brides, skilled workers, and professionals settled in Toronto. Some were employed as agricultural and horticultural workers, and later became self-employed landscape gardeners or worked for Toronto's Parks Department.

Presently, an estimated 85,000 Dutch Canadians live in Toronto, the majority having arrived in the last 50 years. Dutch-owned companies in the city include **ABN-AMRO Bank**, **Voortman Cookies Ltd.**, **Philips Electronics**, **Rabobank Canada**, **ING Canada**, **Amsterdam Brewing Company**, **Hudson Movers Inc.**, **DeBoer's Furniture**.

Since the 1950s, a number of Dutch cultural, religious, and commercial groups have emerged. Several Christian Reformed Church parishes have been established. The **DUCA Community Credit Union** is among the ten largest of all credit unions in Ontario, with 40,000 members and assets valued at more than $400 million.

A special bond was created between Toronto and Amsterdam following the Second World War. Visiting dignitaries have included Queen Juliana in 1967, Queen Beatrix in 1988, and Princess Margriet in 1995. To celebrate the 25th anniversary of the liberation of Holland by Canadian soldiers,

Dutch Canadians from across Canada formed an organization: **1945–1970, Thank You Canada**. In appreciation of their new homeland, this Toronto-based group raised money for a concert organ as a gift to the National Arts Centre in Ottawa. In 1995, the 50th anniversary was commemorated coast to coast, with Canadian veterans as featured guest.

Places to Go

The flowered **Amsterdam Square Parkette**, St. Clair Avenue W. and Avenue Road, commemorates the twinning of Amsterdam and Toronto in 1974. The parkette has a 1928 replica of the **Van Karnabcek Fountain**, named after one of the founders of the Peace Palace at The Hague (the seat of the Dutch government).

In 1967, as part of their contribution to the Canadian Centennial festivities, the Dutch community donated an artistic maze (doolhof) of shrubs and bushes to Toronto's Centre Island. This permanent gift to the city reflects the Dutch skill for landscaping while providing a playground for children of all ages.

A popular Dutch meal is koffietafel, a light lunch of smoked sausage or meat and cheese sandwiches. Marinated herring dishes are Dutch specialties. Indonesian cuisine—which has influenced Dutch foods since Indonesia was a Dutch colony—includes the popular rijsttafel (rice table), and bahmi goreng (spiced fried noodles). The national drink of the Netherlands is jenever, gin made from a variety of spices, and another popular drink is advocaat—a potent egg spirit. **Heineken** beer is prized internationally.

Specialty stores carry imported products and Dutch-style smoked sausages, cocktail and tongue sausages, plus Holland's famed gouda, edam, and blue cheeses. Imported Dutch cookies, koffie waffles, fig rolls, salted licorice, chocolates, and baked goods, such as almond-filled shortbread and boterkoek (apple cake), are also available.

One of the first Dutch establishments in the city, **Simon De Groot Meat Products**, was located on Church and Maitland Street, surrounded by a large Dutch settlement. Today, the Dutch are mostly living in the suburbs and that is the reason you will find **Simon's Smokehouse** there, (Tel. 905-453-1822, 2 Fisherman Dr, Brampton).

Other stores that carry Dutch imported products and pastries include **Dutch Dreams Frozen Yoghurts & Ice Creams**, (Tel. 416-656-6959, 78 Vaughan Rd); **Niemeyer's Gift and Deli**, (Tel. 905-764-0302, 10 East Wilmot, Unit 9); and **Petit Paris Cake & Coffee Shop**, (Tel. 416-769-9881, 2382 Bloor St. W).

Little Dollhouse, (Tel. 416-489-7180, 612 Mount Pleasant Rd). sells handmade dolls. Dutch-owned furniture stores include **DeBoer's Furniture**, (Tel. 416-226-3730, 5051 Yonge St, and Tel. 416-596-1433, 444 Yonge St.); **Idomo Furniture International**, (Tel. 416-630-3622, www.idomo.com, 1100 Sheppard Ave. W); **Elizabeth DeBoer's Heritage Interiors**, (Tel. 416-398-5560, 1100 Sheppard Ave. W); and **Danish Style Bake Shop/Jennifer's Original Gluten Free Bread**, (Tel.416-694-5333, 1027 Kingston Rd).

Religious Centres, Schools and Other Institutions

Many Dutch follow the Roman Catholic or Protestant faiths. Churches frequented by the community include:

◆ CHRISTIAN REFORMED CHURCH, Central office, (Tel. 416-535-6262, 1088 Bathurst St).

◆ FIRST CHRISTIAN REFORMED CHURCH OF TORONTO, (Tel. 416-481-4912, 63–67 Taunton Rd).

◆ FREE CHRISTIAN REFORMED CHURCH, ELIJAH CHURCH, (Tel. 416-661-0216, 1130 Finch Ave. W).

◆ GRACE CHRISTIAN REFORMED CHURCH OF SCARBOROUGH, (Tel. 416-293-0373, 25 Channel Nine Crt).

◆ REHOBOTH FELLOWSHIP CHRISTIAN REFORMED CHURCH, (Tel. 416-622-9647, 800 Burnhamthorpe Rd).

◆ COVENANT REFORMED CHURCH OF TORONTO, (Tel. 416-747-1179, 265 Albion Rd).

◆ HOLLAND CHRISTIAN HOMES INC. (SENIOR CITIZENS' COMPLEX), (Tel. 905-459-3334, 7900 McLaughlin Rd. S., Brampton). Contact: Jon Masselink, Activation Co-ordinator.

◆ DUCA COMMUNITY CREDIT UNION, (Tel. 416-223-8502, www.duca.com, head office, 5290 Yonge St., North York). Branches: Etobicoke, 1451 Royal York Rd., Tel. 416-245-2413; Toronto, 245 Eglinton Ave. E., Tel. 416-485-0789; Rexdale, 2184 Kipling Ave., tel. 416-747-1791; Scarborough, 1265 Morningside Ave., Tel. 416-724-2957; Brampton, 7900 McLaughlin Rd. S., Tel. 905-453-1971; Newmarket, 17310 Yonge St., Tel. 905-898-4543.

Holidays and Celebrations

◆ QUEEN'S BIRTHDAY. Although her birthday is actually in January, Queen Beatrix of the Netherlands celebrates her birthday in April. Every year an Orange Ball is organized by the Dutch Canadian Association of Greater Toronto in her honour. The Consulate General of the Netherlands usually holds a reception.

◆ LIBERATION DAY, May 5, commemorates of the end of the Second World War.

◆ ST. NICHOLAAS OR SINTERKLAAS DAY, December 5, honours of the saint renowned for his kindness and charitable deeds to children. Legend has it that on the night of December 5, the saint appears on a white horse as a long-bearded bishop dressed in a robe, red cassock, and a mitre; he carries a golden crozier or staff. His helper, a Moorish boy named Black Peter, is dressed as a medieval page and carries the saint's sack with presents for good children and switches for the bad. In their wooden shoes, the children leave hay and carrots for the saint's horse. An annual St. Nicholaas children's party is organized by the Dutch Canadian Association in Toronto.

◆ NETHERLANDS BAZAAR is held every two years in October to raise money for needy Dutch Canadians in Ontario. In 2007, over $120,000 was collected.

See Holidays and Celebrations in Glossary.

Media

◆ DE NEDERLANDSE COURANT (THE DUTCH CANADIAN BI-WEEKLY), (Tel. 905-333-3615, 1945 Four Season Dr., Burlington). Published for almost 60 years; a bi-weekly with subscription sales of 5,800 and a readership of 25,000. Publisher: Theo Luykenaar.

◆ "DUTCH TOUCH" RADIO PROGRAM, CJMR 1320 AM, (Tel. 416-229-1753). Host: Martin Van Denzen.

Organizations

◆ CANADIAN-NETHERLANDS BUSINESS AND PROFESSIONAL ASSOCIATION, (Tel. 416-757-5523, 69 Hazelton Ave). Networking organization to promote trade between the Netherlands and Canada. President: Lisa Stam; Secretariat: Duco Itordijk.

◆ **DUTCH CANADIAN ASSOCIATION OF GREATER TORONTO**, (Tel. 416-229-1753, 207 Newton Dr., Willowdale). President: Martin Van Denzen. An umbrella organization for the community established in 1956.

◆ **ONTARIO CHRISTIAN MUSIC ASSEMBLY**, (Tel. 416-636-9779, 90 Topcliff Ave). Director: L. Kooy.

Various other clubs operate in the city, including: **DUCA Social Dance Club**; **Gezelligheid Kent Geen TIJD**, **Klaverjasclub "Zonder Naam"**; **Ladies Contact Club Welkom**; **Marines Canada**, veterans organization of the Dutch marines.

Consulates, Trade Commissions and Tourist Bureaus

◆ **CONSULATE GENERAL OF THE NETHERLANDS**, (Tel. 416-598-2520, Fax 416-598-8064, 1 Dundas St. W., Suite 2106). Consul General: Mr. Johan Kramer.

Prominent Torontonians

John de Visser, photographer; Dick Loek, photographer; Jake Mol, visual arts; Patricia Rozema, filmmaker; Huibert Sabelis, visual arts; Professor Robert Siebelhoff, teaches Art History at the University of Toronto; Martin Van Denzen, President: Dutch Canadian Association; Ernest Hillen, author; Michael Horn, Canadian Studies at York University; Case Ootes, Toronto City Councillor; Tim Hogenbirk, President of Netherlands Lunchen club; Maria Jacobs, President of CAAS Toronto; Mau Coopman, Credit Union; Henry Hoogstraten, The Netherlands Luncheon Club; Aleida Limbertie, The Netherlands Folklore Group; G. Spaans, The Netherlands Bazaar; Ada Wynston, Holocaust Education.

Contributors: Sophia Geenen, Leonard Vis, G. Spaans, Ada Wynston, Thea Schryer, Fritz Begemann, Cees Bijl, Elizabeth Verhaag.

The English Community

The English dominated Toronto's early history, establishing many industries and institutions, and shaping politics, law, and the arts in the city. The contributions of English-born Governors General and senior military officers such as Sir George Yonge, Lord Dufferin, and Earl Bathurst are remembered in the names of Toronto's main thoroughfares. **Osgoode Hall** is a reminder of London-born William Osgoode, who was the first Chief Justice of Upper Canada. **Massey (Music) Hall**, built in 1894, and **Hart House** at the **University of Toronto** are cultural monuments contributed by the family who founded the country's largest farm machinery manufacturer, **Massey Ferguson**.

In the 15th century, the English sponsored John Cabot's northern exploration that led to the discovery of Labrador and furthered British settlement of what is now Canada. Sixteenth-century English explorer Martin Frobisher, who sought a route to Asia through Greenland, and 17th-century explorers Henry Hudson, William Baffin, and Thomas James are memorialized in Canadian geographic features.

The first English colony in Canada was established in Newfoundland in 1611 by a small group of fishermen who came to Conception Bay from Devon, England. In 1670, the **Hudson's Bay Company** was granted an exclusive monopoly on trade through Hudson Strait and possession of Rupert's Land, which led to subsequent explorations by Englishmen based at the company's fort.

Large-scale English immigration began with the American Revolution, when thousands of settlers of British origin joined the United Empire Loyalists in leaving the United States between 1775 and 1783. As a British colony, Canada's early institutions adopted the British model of responsible government and English common law.

The Constitutional Act of 1791 divided Quebec into the provinces of Upper and Lower Canada, and Englishman John Graves Simcoe was appointed the first Lieutenant-Governor of Upper Canada. Simcoe founded York, a name which was used for the site until its incorporation as the City of Toronto in 1834.

British immigration to Canada increased significantly in 1816 after the Napoleonic Wars, when an economic depression forced many small farmers, artisans, factory workers, and ex-soldiers to emigrate. Between 1815 and 1855, almost one million British immigrants—a large percentage of whom were English—landed in British North America.

At the turn of the century, British children from poor families were sponsored to settle in towns across Canada. The Empire Settlement Act of 1922 provided training and financial assistance to new settlers, and resulted in 130,000 new immigrants settling in the country.

Following the Second World War, ex-servicemen, war brides, and many trained industrial workers, technicians, and professionals arrived in Canada. The Suez Crisis in 1956 sparked further English immigration, as did Canada's Centennial Year, 1967. Many Canadian institutions have English roots. The **Boy Scouts** were organized in 1908, and the **Girl Guides** were brought to Canada from England in 1910. The **Canadian Red Cross** began in 1896 as a branch of the **British National Society for Aid to the Sick and Wounded**. In the arts, the English have made important contributions in establishing the **CBC**, the **NFB**, the **Canada Council**, the **National Ballet**, and **Stratford festival**.

Toronto's Cabbagetown, which was settled in the 1850s by the Irish and English, contains reminders of early British history, including Parliament Street, once the site of the Town of York's parliament buildings. The neighbourhood's early Anglican churches include **St. Peter's** (1866), **All Saints** (1874), and **St. Simon's** (1888).

Rosedale was named after the wild roses found on the estate of Colonel William Botsford Jarvis, and High Park's Grenadier Pond took its name from the British soldiers who trained on its frozen surfaces. The park, once the estate of London-born architect John Howard, was bequeathed to the city in the 1870s.

Many of the prominent people of Toronto's early days were members of the **St. George's Society of Toronto**, which was founded in 1834. Today, the English community maintains ties with its heritage through the Society, which has an active social calendar and programme of charitable activities. English traditions are also carried on in the city's sports fields with soccer, rugby, and cricket matches. The **Toronto Cricket Club**, the oldest cricket club in North America, was founded by English soldiers in the 19th century and continues to be a popular sports club among those of British descent.

LONGWOOD
PUBLIC LIBRARY

800 Middle Country Rd
Middle Island, NY 11953
(631) 924-6400   longwoodlibrary.org
Library Hours:
Monday-Friday 9:30am-9pm
Saturday 9:30am-5pm
Sunday 1pm-5pm (Sept-June)

04/15/2019

Items checked out to:
p21713376

Title: **Toronto's many faces / Tony Ruprecht.**
Barcode: 30641004532417
Call #: 917.1354 RUP
Due: **05-13-19**

Total items checked out: 1

**You just saved an estimated $15 by
using the Library today.**

Thank you for visiting!

Places to Go

Memories of Old England linger in The Beaches with houses built in the style of mock-Tudor half-timbering, beach-type cottages, and a townhouse development that resembles a street in an English village. The Beaches is loosely defined as the area stretching from Woodbine Avenue to Victoria Park and from Lake Ontario to Gerrard Street. Street names like Hammersmith, Kenilworth, and Waverley Road reflect their previous English denizens, as do the neighbourhood's British pubs. The mock-Tudor **Beaches Library** was built in 1915 to commemorate the tercentenary of the death of William Shakespeare, and the **Glen Stewart Park** contains a pretty garden and a fountain typical of an English country home.

Institutions include the **Kew Beach Lawn Bowling Club**, (Tel. 416-694-4371, Lee Ave), one of the oldest recreational organizations in Canada, founded in the 1890s, and the century-old **Balmy Beach Canoe Club**, (Tel. 416-691-9962, Beech Ave), built on land donated by one-time Toronto mayor Sir Adam Wilson. Club teams won championships in lawn bowling, and hockey, and its football team won the Grey Cup in 1927 and 1930. The **Gardener's House**, (30 Lee Ave), was built in 1902 by Joseph and Jane Williams who turned their estate, **Kew Gardens** (named after the famous botanical gardens in London), into picnic grounds for summer visitors. **Ashbridges Bay Park** was named after the family who first settled the area in 1794. The Ashbridges' original farmhouse still stands at 1444 Queen St. E.

Toronto's British pubs are popular gathering places where dart playing is accompanied by the drinking of heavy beers such as **Newcastle Brown** and **Worthington E**. Popular pub dishes include steak and kidney pie, bangers and mash (sausages and mashed potatoes), fish and chips, and shepherd's pie. Pork and lamb dishes, eggs, Yorkshire pudding, and fish such as kippers (smoked herring) and haddock often appear on English menus. Tea is often served with buns, biscuits and cakes.

Feathers, (Tel. 416-694-0443, 962 Kingston Rd), takes its name from the classic pub in Ludlow. The mayor of Ludlow once made a speech over the phone to the patrons of Toronto's Feathers. The restaurant/pub serves fish and chips, bangers and mash, roast beef, steak and mushroom pie, steak and kidney pie, and Lancashire Hot Pot (lamb casserole). A midday snack is the ploughman's lunch (cheese plate with double Gloucester cheese, branston pickle, and pickled onion) and another popular dish is kedgeree (fish casserole with cream and curry). Scottish owner Ian Innes has added British atmosphere with dartboards and photographs of everyday life in Britain.

English burgers, fries, meatpies, pasties, beer, and pop can be found at: **Elephant and Castle Pub**, (Tel. 416-598-4003, 378 Yonge St).

In Cabbagetown, a few Victorian mansions still stand, along with elegant row houses that date from 1875. Original farmhouses and worker's cottages can be found in the area, as well as Queen Anne houses, and Victorian Gothic townhouses. The **Spruce Court Apartments**, built in Tudor style, was the city's first low-cost housing project, erected in 1913 by the **Toronto Housing Company. Allan Gardens**, (Tel. 416-944-2973, 120 Carlton St, Suite 417). The **Palm House** was designed after British examples. First built in 1879, then replaced in 1909 after a fire, the structure was used for concerts, balls, promenades, and floral displays.

Monuments found in the city's **Queen's Park** include statues of Queen Victoria, King Edward VII, Toronto's co-founder General John Graves Simcoe, and Robert Raikes, the founder of Sunday School in Gloucester, England, in 1780. Among the monuments along University Avenue is a memorial to the **Sons Of England** and those who died during the Great War (1914–1918) which was funded by the Toronto district **Sons of England Benefit Society**. On the lawns of Toronto's City Hall is a standing bronze figure of Sir Winston Churchill inscribed with many great quotations from speeches of the former British Prime Minister.

The oldest surviving structure in Toronto is **Gibraltar Light House**, or Centre Island. Built in 1808, the lighthouse was used by British soldiers to protect the island. **Fort York**, (Tel. 416-392-6907, Garrison Rd. off Fleet St), was a British garrison that defended the settlement of York during the War of 1812, notably during the Battle of York in 1813. Military displays and demonstrations are held at the fort.

Todmorden Mills, (Tel. 416-396-2819, 67 Pottery Rd), was built by early English settlers and contains remnants of a brewery, paper mill, and the old **Don Station. Casa Loma**, (Tel. 416-923-1171, 1 Austin Terrace), was built by architect E.J. Lennox using architectural styles of English castles. The original proprietor, Sir Henry Pellatt, employed stonemasons and imported stones from Scotland to build the 98-room house which features towers and secret panels. The paneled walls of Peacock Alley were fashioned after Windsor Castle.

Colborne Lodge, High Park, (Tel. 416-392-6916). The cottage was built by John Howard in 1836 and was made into a museum in 1927. Hours are Tuesday to Sunday, 12:00 p.m. to 5:00 p.m. Closed Mondays.

The Grange, (Tel. 416-977-0414, ext. 338, 317 Dundas St. W), was built in 1817 for the Boulton family, who named it after their ancestral home in England. The house became the **Art Museum of Toronto** between 1913 and 1918, until a new adjoining gallery was built. The Grange was restored and opened as a house museum in 1973.

The Henry Moore Sculpture Centre, Art Gallery of Ontario, (Tel. 416-977-0414, 317 Dundas St. W). World-renowned British sculptor Henry Moore donated the largest collection of his works—some 100 sculptures, drawings and prints—to the people of Toronto. Torontonians supported the completion of his controversial sculpture **The Archer**, which sits in the civic square of Nathan Phillips Square. His sculpture, **Large Two Forms**, is found on the corner of Dundas and McCaul streets, in front of the **Art Gallery of Ontario**.

The **Arthur Conan Doyle Room, Metro Toronto Library**, (Tel. 416-393-7000, 789 Yonge St), houses one of the world's largest collections of Sherlock Holmes memorabilia, including records, films, photos, books, manuscripts, and letters.

The English parlour tradition of tea-drinking is carried out in several establishments in the city. Tea is served with scones, whipped cream, and jams, and often accompanied by smoked salmon, cucumber, and watercress sandwiches served on silver trays. **Four Seasons Hotel**, (Tel. 416-964-0411, 21 Avenue Rd), serves afternoon tea in the lounge every day from 2:30 p.m. to 5:30 p.m. Ten different types of tea are served in **Royal Doulton** china along with scones with **Wilkin & Sons** jams and **Devon** cream. The **Meridian King Edward Hotel**, (Tel. 416-863-9700, 37 King Street E), built in 1903, also serves afternoon tea every day.

The institution of the British pub has been revived in the city with the **Duke of York**, (Tel. 416-964-2441, 39 Prince Arthur Ave). There are now a number of 'Dukes' offering fine pub fare including Scotch eggs, Cornish pastries, shepherd's pie, and British beer and ale on tap. These include the **Duke of Gloucester**, (Tel. 416-961-9704, 649 Yonge St); **Duke of Westminster**, (Tel. 416-368-2761, 100 King St W); **Duke of Kent**, (Tel. 416-485-9507, 2315 Yonge St).

The **Rose & Crown**, (Tel. 416-487-ROSE(7673), 2335 Yonge St), shares its name with some one thousand pubs in England. Other pubs include: **The Black Sheep**, (Tel. 416-224-0741, 4901 Yonge St); and **The Artful Dodger**, (Tel. 416-964-9511, 12 Isabella St); and **Red Lion Pub**, (Tel. 416-967-5551, 449 Jarvis St). **Ben Wicks Restaurant**, (Tel. 416-961-9425, 424 Parliament St), is an English-style pub named after the retired Toronto cartoonist.

The Bay, a descendant of the Hudson's Bay Company, has operated stores in Canada since the early 17th century. **William Ashley China Ltd.**, (Tel. 416-964-2900, 55 Bloor St. W, Manulife Centre), sells **Wedgwood**, **Crown Derby**, and **Royal Doulton** china.

Religious Centres, Schools and Other Institutions

About 50 percent of church-going Canadians of English descent belong to the Anglican church, while the rest belong to the United church and some smaller Protestant sects. A small minority are Roman Catholics.

There are almost 100 Anglican churches located throughout the city:

◆ THE ANGLICAN CHURCH OF CANADA, head offices and bookstore, are located at (Tel. 416-924-9192, 80 Hayden St). The Toronto Diocese office is at, (Tel. 416-363-6021, 135 Adelaide St. E).

◆ ST. JAMES CATHEDRAL, (Tel. 416-364-7865, 65 Church St), was designed in Gothic style by Frederick W. Cumberland and completed in 1874. The spire, which is the tallest in Canada, was once used to guide ships into harbour. Stained glass windows are dedicated to the Hon. William Jarvis, and a stone inside the church bears the name of the Jarvis family, for whom a city street is also named. Bishop Strachan, rector at St. James in 1812, is buried in the chancel.

◆ ALL SAINTS CHURCH, (Tel. 416-368-7768, 315 Dundas St. E), was built in 1874 in High Victorian style.

◆ BELLEFAIR UNITED CHURCH, (Tel. 416-691-3951, 2 Bellefair Ave).

◆ EMMANUEL HOWARD PARK UNITED CHURCH, (Tel. 416-536-1755, 214 Wright Ave). Built at the turn of the century, the church organ was once played by Glenn Gould and has been used by the **Orford String Quartet** to record songs.

◆ HOLY TRINITY CHURCH, (Tel. 416-598-4521, 19 Trinity Square). Built in 1847 by architect Henry Bowyer Lane.

◆ LITTLE TRINITY CHURCH, (Tel. 416-367-0272, 425 King St. E). Built between 1843 and 1845, this church has Tudor Gothic features.

◆ ST. JAMES-THE-LESS CHAPEL, (635 Parliament St). Built in 1858 in the style of a 13th century English parish church.

◆ ST. JOHN'S NORWAY ANGLICAN CHURCH, (Tel. 416-691-4560, 470 Woodbine Ave). The 142-year-old church has been designated a historic site. Sparkling stained glass windows are admired by art students, and a chime of eight bells can be heard over a cemetery of 68,000 graves of the city's early settlers.

◆ ST. PAUL'S ANGLICAN, (Tel. 416-961-8116, 227 Bloor St. E). The city's largest church, built in 1861 in the style of a medieval English village church.

◆ ST. PETER'S ANGLICAN CHURCH, (Tel. 416-924-1891, 188 Carlton St). Built in 1865.

◆ ST. SIMON THE APOSTLE CHURCH, (Tel. 416-923-8714, 525 Bloor St. E).

◆ **WAVERLEY ROAD BAPTIST CHURCH,** (Tel. 416-694-3054, 129 Waverley Rd).

There are two traditional English schools in Toronto:

◆ **ROYAL ST. GEORGE'S COLLEGE,** (Tel. 416-533-9481, 120 Howland Ave).

◆ **UPPER CANADA COLLEGE,** (Tel. 416-488-1125, 200 Lonsdale Rd), is a private school based on the English public school system.

Holidays and Celebrations

◆ **ST. GEORGE'S DAY** on April 23 honours the patron saint of England, once a Roman soldier who advanced to high military rank under the Emperor Diocletian. He was arrested and executed for protecting his new-found Christian faith. The flag of St. George (and of England, also forming part of the Union Jack) is a red cross on a white background. The St. George's Society of Toronto celebrates St. George's Day with its Red Rose Ball, held on or near April 23rd, and the Society's colours are processed at a service at St. James Cathedral the Sunday following.

See Holidays and Celebrations in Glossary.

Organizations

◆ **ST. GEORGE'S SOCIETY OF TORONTO,** (Tel. 416-597-0220, Fax 416-597-1438, www.stgeorges.to, 14 Elm St). Founded in 1834 to help English and Welsh immigrants who had fallen upon hard times, the Society still maintains an active charitable programme whilst at the same time furthering and preserving English heritage and culture.

◆ **BRITISH PENSIONERS ASSOCIATION CANADA,** (Tel. 416-253-6402, 605 Royal York Rd., #202). Open weekdays 10:00 a.m. to 2:00 p.m.

◆ **QUEEN'S OWN RIFLES OF CANADA,** (Tel. 416-635-2761, www.qor.com, 130 Queen St. E).

◆ **THE TORONTO CRICKET, SKATING AND CURLING CLUB,** (Tel. 416-487-4581, www.torontocricketclub.com, 141 Wilson Ave).

Consulates, Trade Commissions and Tourist Bureaus

◆ **BRITISH CONSULATE GENERAL,** (Tel. 416-593-1290, 777 Bay St., Suite 2800). Consul General: Mr. Jonathan Dart.

◆ **BRITISH CANADIAN CHAMBER OF TRADE AND COMMERCE,** (Tel. 905-274-7100, P.O. Box 1358, Station K). Executive Director: Caroline Ross.

Prominent Torontonians

Peter Appleyard, jazz vibraphonist; Dr. Robert Buchman, physician, author and TV personality; Betty Kennedy, media personality; Ted Medland, stockbroker; Bette Stephenson, former Ontario Cabinet Minister; Veronica Tennant, former ballerina; John Tory, radio personality, lawyer, former CEO of Rogers, former MPP and leader of the Progressive Conservative Party of Ontario; Rita Tushingham, stage and film actress; David Feldman, developer and philanthropist.

Contributors: Frances Sommerville, Gail Rayment, St. George's Society.

The Eritrean Community

The original home country for all Eritreans is located in the northeast corner of Africa. Eritrea gained its independence from Ethiopia after a bitter war that lasted 30 years. The war ended in 1991, and marked the birth of a new nation. Because of the war, thousands of Eritreans were forced to leave their country and live in Sudan, Europe, the Middle East and North America. The migration of Eritreans to Toronto gained momentum in the late 1970s and early 1980s. Today, over 10,000 Eritreans make the GTA their home.

Eritreans make up a diverse population, reflecting many languages, cultures and religions. There are nine Eritrean nationalities: Afar, Bilen, Hedareb, Kunama, Nara, Rashaida, Saho, Tigre and Tigrigna. While many Eritreans speak Arabic, the Rashaida speak Arabic exclusively. The most widely used languages in the community of the Greater Toronto Area, including Mississauga are Tigrigna, Tigre and Arabic.

Places to Go

There are several restaurants and cafés that serve fine Eritrean cuisine. These are mostly located in the West end of Toronto. Eritrean food is as diverse as the culture and languages of Eritreans. Usually it is hot and spicy.

Religious Centres, Schools and Other Institutions

Eritreans profess Christianity and Islam; the Christians include Coptics, Roman Catholics and Protestants.

Holidays and Celebrations

National Holidays

- INDEPENDENCE DAY is celebrated on May 24.
- INTERNATIONAL WOMEN'S DAY, March 8.
- MARTYRS DAY, June 20.
- START OF INDEPENDENCE ARMED STRUGGLE, September 1.

Religious Holidays

- CHRISTMAS, December 25 (Roman Catholic).
- COPTIC CHRISTMAS, January 7.

Media

♦ MEKALH is a newsletter published by the Eritrean Canadian Community Centre (see below).

♦ MERHABA is a newsletter published by the **Eritrean Canadian Society for Youth Advancement** (see below). Both newsletters feature news, views, articles, etc. that cater to the needs of the community.

Organizations

♦ THE ERITREAN CANADIAN COMMUNITY CENTRE (ECCC), (Tel. 416-658-8580, Fax 416-658-7442, 729 St. Clair Ave. W). Established in 1985, the ECCC provides services to the Eritrean community of Toronto, including children, youth and women. These services include adaptation and settlement, heritage language training, informal counselling, information and referral, translation and interpretation, advocacy, recreation, employment and career options, and stay-in-school program for youth.

♦ ERITREAN CULTURAL AND CIVIC CENTRE, (Tel. 416-516-1246, 120 Carlton St).

♦ ERITREAN CANADIAN ASSOCIATION OF ONTARIO, (Tel. 416-536-3229, www.ecao.ca, 296 Concord Ave). President: Astier Negash.

Source: Amanuel Melles.

Eritrean cultural display at the Eritrean Canadian Community Centre.

The Estonian Community

Tartu, in Estonia, is home to one of Europe's oldest and most venerated universities, founded in 1632. Some of the educational and architectural wisdom of the old-world city is captured at **Tartu College**, an 18-storey educational centre and student's residence located on Toronto's Bloor Street. Designed by Estonian architect Elmar Tampold, the college was established to promote the study of Estonian heritage and other cultures. Its founding contributors included former graduates of the ancient university, now members of Toronto's 12,000-member Estonian community.

This community is the largest concentrated group of Estonians living outside the homeland. Estonia, one of the Baltic countries, was an independent nation until it was annexed by the USSR in 1940. Some 80,000 Estonians escaped to take refuge in Sweden and Germany in 1944. Approximately 15,000 Estonians arrived in Canada from these countries in the late 1940s and '50s. Estonia regained its independence during the last stages of the dissolution of the Soviet Union. On August 20, 1991, Estonia declared its independence, thus continuing its statehood (which began on February 24, 1918). On September 6, 1991, Estonian independence was recognized by the Soviet Union. Recognition by other countries followed swiftly, with Canada among the early ones to do so.

Initially, most Estonians in Canada worked as contract labourers. As their knowledge of English improved, Estonians found jobs in the skilled trades and some started their own businesses.

In 1960, the growing Toronto community purchased the old **Chester School** building on Broadview Avenue. Today, this building is a cultural centre known as **Estonian House**.

With more than 100 cultural, social, professional and political organizations, Toronto's Estonians have firmly established their roots in the city. There are nine church congregations, 22 fraternities and sororities, as well as kindergarten and language schools. The Estonians have built a Lutheran and a Baptist church and, with the Latvians, they jointly own **St. Andrew's Estonian Evangelical Lutheran Church** on Jarvis Street.

Estonian academics, business people, and artists are among Toronto's prominent professionals. Through the efforts and talents of Estonian architects, the first co-op apartment complex in Canada was built in the 1950s on Queen Street East, and today, several corners of the city contain condo-minium complexes built by Estonians. In sports, Estonians were the first to introduce Canadians to the graceful movements of rhythmic gymnastics, and to the excitement of orienteering (the sport of wilderness running). In the wooded areas outside Toronto, three youth camps promote the Estonian language, folk dancing, and sporting traditions. **Jõekääru**, located near Uxbridge, features one of the first stadiums in Canada to use metric measurement. In the Muskoka wilderness, **Kotkajärve** is the site for open-air weddings, and in August, holds a "University in the Forest." **Seedrioru**, located near the town of Elora, maintains an open-air theatre and a field dedicated to those who died for freedom in Estonia. Annual Estonian festivals at Seedrioru attract from 3,000 to 5,000 people.

One of the city's most colourful events occurs when Toronto's Estonian community hosts the **Estonian World Festival**. Folk dancers, massed choirs, gymnasts, and theatrical performers set the stage in 1972 when more than 10,000 Estonians from around the globe gathered for the festival held in Toronto.

Places to Go

Estonian Arts Centre located at **Eesti Maja (Estonian House)**, (Tel. 416-461-7963, www.estohouse.com, 958 Broadview Ave), contains a collection of Estonian paintings and graphic arts, and a library of Estonian music which can be visited by appointment, (Tel. 416-259-9779). Eesti Maja also houses a lending library of Estonian literature, archives chronicling the nation's history, and two gift and bookstores that hold a wealth of Estonian culture in the city.

Open for lunch and dinner, **Esto Café**, (Tel. 416-465-3229, 958 Broadview Ave), serves typical Estonian fish, pork and sauerkraut dishes, which reflect the influence of Swedish and German cuisine.

Religious Centres, Schools and Other Institutions

Toronto's Estonians belong to Lutheran and Baptist churches. All of Toronto's Estonian churches have community halls. Churches include:

◆ ESTONIAN EVANGELICAL CHURCH, (Tel. 416-488-1754, 21 Swanwick Ave).

◆ ST. ANDREW'S ESTONIAN EVANGELICAL LUTHERAN CHURCH, (Tel. 416-923-5172, 383 Jarvis St).

◆ ST. PETER'S ESTONIAN EVANGELICAL LUTHERAN CHURCH, (Tel. 416-483-5847, 817 Mount Pleasant Rd).

Estonian Arts Centre located at Eesti Maja (Estonian House), 958 Broadview Ave.

- ◆ TORONTO ESTONIAN BAPTIST CHURCH, (Tel. 416-465-0639, 883 Broadview Ave).
- ◆ EESTI KODU INC., (Tel. 416-281-1792, 50 Old Kingston Rd), is a condominium complex built by Estonians in 1977. The complex has a library, and woodworking and craft workshops take place in recreational rooms. In 1982, **Ehatare**, 40 Old Kingston Rd., which is a senior's residence, was added. It is maintained by the **Estonian Relief Committee**.
- ◆ TARTU COLLEGE, (Tel. 416-925-9405, www.tartucollege.com, 310 Bloor St. W), was established in 1970. The institute arranges lectures and seminars, and supports Estonian language courses through the **University of Toronto**, where a chair of Estonian studies has been established. Tartu houses a 300-seat auditorium, archives and a library that has a collection of 4,000 books and 30,000 entries of publications on Estonian topics.
- ◆ THE ESTONIAN SCHOOLS IN TORONTO, (Tel. 905-669-5930), offers Estonian language, history, and culture classes. Contact: Elle Rosenberg.

The community's financial centre is:

◆ THE ESTONIAN (TORONTO) CREDIT UNION, (Tel. 416-465-4659,
www.estoniancu.com, 958 Broadview Ave).

Holidays and Celebrations

◆ INDEPENDENCE DAY. February 24 celebrates the day in 1918 that
Estonia became an independent democratic nation. Each year, on the
closest weekend, the Toronto Estonian community commemorates
Independence Day with a colourful cultural program and reception.

◆ COMMEMORATION DAY is observed on June 14 by Estonians, Latvians,
and Lithuanians in remembrance of the thousands of people deported
to Siberia by the Soviets.

◆ VICTORY DAY. June 23 marks Estonia's successful struggle for independence against Russian and German forces from 1918 to 1920.
Soldiers who died for the cause are honoured on Victory Day.

◆ ST. JOHN'S DAY is celebrated on June 24. This midsummer night celebration follows ancient traditions and festivities, including folk-
dancing, singing, and all-night folkloric rituals that welcome the
summer solstice.

◆ 1991 INDEPENDENCE DAY. On August 2, Estonians celebrate the day in
1991 Estonia declared its independence.

See Holidays and Celebrations in Glossary.

Media

◆ MEIE ELU (OUR LIFE), (Tel. 416-466-0951, 958 Broadview Ave). A
weekly newspaper published by the **Estonian Publishing Co. Toronto Ltd**.

◆ VOITLEJA (THE COMBATANT), (958 Broadview Ave). A periodical
published by the **Estonian War Veterans League**.

◆ ESTONIAN LIFE, (Tel. 416-733-4550, www.eesti.ca, 3 Madison Ave).
Editor: Mrs. Elle Puusaag.

Organizations

There are more than 100 Estonian organizations and clubs in Toronto.

◆ ESTONIA HOUSE, (Tel. 416-461-7963, 958 Broadview Ave), accommo-
dates the following organizations: Estonian Central Council in
Canada, (Tel. 416-465-2219); **Estonian Federation in Canada**;
Estonian Canadian Festival Foundation; **National Estonian**

Foundation of Canada; **Estonian Association of Toronto**; **Estonian Folkdance Group Kungla**; **Estonian Ethnographical Society**; **Estonian Chess Club**; **Toronto Estonian Choir of Mixed Voices**; **Pensioners' Club**; **Estonian Philatelists Club**; **Estonian War Veterans League**; and **Girl Guides** and **Boy Scouts** organizations. General Manager: Ulo Isberg.

◆ ESTONIAN RELIEF COMMITTEE, (Tel. 416-724-6144, 40 Old Kingston Rd).

◆ THE ESTONIAN ARTS CENTRE (EAC), (Tel. 416-466-8885, 958 Broadview Ave., Suite 204), is a non-profit charitable organization formed in 1974 to support, preserve, and promote the Canadian Estonian arts. Since the rebirth of the free Estonia in 1991, the EAC has been building cultural bridges between Canada and Estonia. It has arranged numerous musical and other cultural events with soloists and groups of performers from Estonia. It now represents the "**Eesti Kontsert**" and **Estonian Institute in Canada**. EAC organizes a **Seven Arts Camp** in Elora every summer and the **Estonian Concert** Management presents a yearly concert series. President: Stella Pahapill, (Tel. 416-259-9779).

◆ ESTONIA, (140 Erskine Ave). Mixed choir.

◆ ESTONIA CONCERT BAND, (34 Woolton Cres).

◆ ESTONIAN CANADIAN HISTORICAL COMMISSION, (4092 Dunmow Cr., Mississauga).

An Estonian confirmation.

◆ KALEV-ESTIENNE, (3 Pebble Beach Gate, Thornhill). Rhythmic gymnastics group. Contact: Evelyn Koop, Tel. 905-889-4167.

◆ RITMIKA, (Tel. 416-747-7868, www.ritmika.ca, 161 Deerhide Cres). Modern rhythmic gymnastics club.

◆ SOCIETY OF ESTONIAN ARTISTS IN TORONTO, (Tel. 416-250-1245, www.ekkt.org, 175 Hilda Ave., Suite 610). President: Mai Reet Jarve.

Consulates, Trade Commissions and Tourist Bureaus

◆ CONSULATE GENERAL OF ESTONIA, (Tel. 416-461-0764, 958 Broadview Ave). Honorary Consul General: Mr. Laas Leivat.

Prominent Torontonians

Urjo Kareda, theatrical director, journalist and broadcaster; Udo Kasemets, composer and choir conductor; Avo Kittask, formerly with the Canadian Opera Company and the Stratford Festival; Evelyn Koop, educator who popularized rhythmic gymnastics in Canada and founded the Kalev-Estienne gymnasts; Tom Kristenbrun, prominent restaurateur; Abel Lee, graphic artist; Norman Reintamm, first Director of the new Toronto Pops Orchestra; Elmar Tampold, architect; Osvald Timmas, artist; Ruth Tulving, artist; Arved Viirlaid, writer.

Contributors: Stella Pahapill, Former president, Estonian Arts Centre, and concert pianist; John Pahapill, Vice-Chairman, Advisory Board, Estonian Arts Centre; Marta Kivik, Estonia House; Tony Naelapea, Meie Elu, Elle Puusaag, Vaba Eestlane.

Source: Halve Massakas.

The Filipino Community

Throughout the city, a group of residents warmly call each other kababayan (countrymen). Although the members of Toronto's 100,000 member Filipino community are dispersed—living in Parkdale, St. Jamestown, North York, Scarborough, and Mississauga—they are a closely knit community bonded by a unique culture which is a mix of Indo-Malay, Spanish, Chinese, and American influences. At Toronto's multicultural festivals, popular Filipino dance troupes perform the tinikling, a dance which imitates the movements of the rice bird stepping through clashing bamboo poles. The community's rich traditions in music, dance, and drama have added to Toronto's cosmopolitan character.

Following the Second World War, Filipino nursing students began entering the United States. On expiry of their American visas, a small number came to Canada and settled in Toronto, Montreal, Winnipeg, and Vancouver. Nurses and laboratory technicians were employed by the six major teaching hospitals in Toronto. Many sponsored their spouses and families for immigration to Canada. In the late 1960s, young professionals unable to find work emigrated from the Philippines, and as a result of martial law introduced in their homeland in the 1970s, a large number of clerical and manufacturing workers also entered Canada.

Members of the Toronto community moved into the Maitland and Yonge streets area, and the St. Jamestown area, close to the hospitals and offices where they worked. Close by were Catholic churches frequented by the community: **St. Basil's Church** on Bay Street, **Our Lady of Lourdes Church** on Sherbourne Street, and the **Holy Family Church** on King Street. More recently, members of the community have settled in Crescent Town and Massey Square on Victoria Park, along the Danforth, in Thorncliffe Park near Don Mills, and in Mississauga, Brampton, and Markham.

Many members of the community are employed as nannies and domestics. Filipino entrepreneurs have added to the city's commercial sector with food stores, craft shops, travel agencies, and hair salons found along Queen Street West and in other parts of the city.

Places to Go

A sign posted on the outside wall of the **Kababayan Community Centre** on Queen Street West welcomes visitors to the oldest Filipino neighbourhood in the city.

Amidst the Greek restaurants along Danforth Avenue are a few Filipino establishments. The varied cuisine of the Philippines combines tropical fruits and vegetables with pork, chicken, and seafood. National dishes include lechon (barbecued suckling pig), adobo (varieties of garlic, chicken, and pork casserole), sinigang (stewed fish with vegetables), and lumpia (vegetable roll). Rice is the staple dish served with every meal. The merienda is a favourite pastime—a mid-afternoon snack consisting of sweet cakes, tarts and fritters.

Mayette's, (Tel. 416-463-0338, 2038 Danforth Ave), specializes in Filipino dishes including crispy pata, kare-kare (oxtail, tripe, and tropical vegetables with sauce), kaldereta (goat meat stew), pancit palabok, pancit guisado, nilaga, and paksiw. Other restaurants located throughout the city that offer Philippine cuisine include: **Aristokrat Restaurant**, (Tel. 416-635-6812, 355 Wilson Ave); and **Ellen's Place**, (Tel. 905-629-9559, 1090 Kamato Road, Mississauga), offers fine Filipino cuisine.

Philippine Oriental Food Market, (Tel. 416-466-6938, 1033 Gerrard St. E).

The Filipino Centre, (Tel. 416-928-9355, 597 Parliament St., Suite 116). Services include Filipiana collection, employment networking, individual tax preparation, free estate planning, workshops for new comers to Canada, and health services.

Religious Centres, Schools and Other Institutions

Many Filipinos are Roman Catholics, while others belong to different religious denominations. Community churches include:

- COMMONWEALTH AVENUE BAPTIST CHURCH, (Tel. 416-267-8073, 83 Commonwealth Ave).
- FILIPINO CANADIAN SEVENTH DAY ADVENTIST CHURCH, (Tel. 416-633-4631, 788 Sheppard Ave. W).
- FIRST FILIPINO BAPTIST CHURCH, (Tel. 416-534-4342, 382 Lippincott St).
- HOLY FAMILY CATHOLIC CHURCH, (Tel. 416-532-2879, 1372 King St. W).
- IGLESIA NI CRISTO, (Tel. 416-231-6006, 310 Burnhamthorpe Rd).
- JOHN XXIII COMMUNITY, (Tel. 416-429-4000, 150 Gateway Blvd).
- OUR LADY OF LOURDES CATHOLIC CHURCH, (Tel. 416-924-6257, 11 Earl St).
- SEVENTH-DAY ADVENTIST, (Tel. 416-636-2471, 535 Finch Ave. W).

- ST. BASIL CATHOLIC CHURCH, (Tel. 416-926-7110, 50 St. Joseph St).
- ST. PATRICK CATHOLIC CHURCH, (Tel. 416-598-3269, 141 McCaul St).

Holidays and Celebrations

- EASTER is an especially festive occasion for Toronto's Filipino community. The 2,000-year-old rite of Salubong is celebrated just prior to Easter Sunday with church services. The Lenten season is observed with solemnity and great devotion, with different activities scheduled each day of the Holy Week. On Good Friday, friends and relatives gather to re-enact the passion and death of Christ by quoting passages from the story of the resurrection and pasyon (singing).
- SANTACRUSAN. On the last day of May, a procession representing biblical characters winds through the streets of the city—the culmination of the Flores de Mayo. The Santacrusan is a religious celebration honouring St. Helena, the Greek Emperor Constantine's mother who travelled in search of the wooden cross on which Christ was crucified. The last figure in the parade is a girl dressed to resemble Queen Helena, carrying a small cross and escorted by the young Prince Constantine.
- INDEPENDENCE DAY. On July 4, 1946, the United States of America granted the Philippines independence, freeing the country from centuries of Spanish rule. Philippine Independence Day is on June 12 because on that date General Emilio Aguinaldo (President of the First Revolutionary Government of the Philippines) first announced the independence of the Philippines. Filipinos in Toronto hold a parade starting at City Hall and ending with a fiesta celebration in a park followed by a dinner dance. On the eve of the celebration, a gala ball is held.
- CHRISTMAS sees gatherings of family and friends and includes lantern contests where prizes are given for the most colourful and symbolic lanterns. Children dress up as pastores (shepherds) and perform plays depicting the nativity scene for which they are awarded gifts. Filipino groups like the Kagayanons, Culture Philippines, and the Carolinians sing Christmas carols as a fund-raising event for worthy projects. Filipinos traditionally kiss the hands of elders to earn blessings.
- DANCES. Throughout the year, cultural groups, such as the award-winning **Fiesta Filipina Dance Troupe**, perform dances like the maglalatik, featuring male dancers who play bamboo shells that are attached to their bodies; the pandango sa ilaw, a dance that creates a

festival of lights performed with oil lamps; and the itik itik, which imitates the movement and rhythm of ducks.

See Holidays and Celebrations in Glossary.

Media

◆ ATIN ITO (monthly newspaper), (Tel. 905-855-8380, 1544 Southdown Rd., Mississauga). Publisher: Eduardo Lee.

◆ THE FILIPINO BULLETIN BOARD, (Tel. 416-724-9077, 48 Millhouse Cr). Contact: Carlos Unas.

◆ FILIPIANA (monthly newspaper), (Tel. 416-534-7836, 1531 Queen St. W). Publisher: Bin Kon Loo.

◆ FILIPINO RADIO PROGRAM, CHIN 1540 AM, (Tel. 416-531-9991, 622 College St). Sunday, 6:00 p.m. to 7:00 p.m. Hosts: Joel Recla and Agatha Luna.

◆ MANILA MEDIA MONITOR, (Tel. 416-285-8583, 98 Comrie Terrace). Contact: Ace Alvarez.

◆ THE PHILIPPINE REPORTER (by-weekly newspaper), (Tel. 416-461-8694, Main Floor, 807 Queen St. E). Editor: Hermie Garcia.

Tony Ruprecht visiting the Kababayan community centre.

Organizations

There are more than 300 Philippine community cultural organizations in Toronto, organized by regional, provincial, municipal, and local dialect affiliations in the Philippines.

◆ KABABAYAN COMMUNITY CENTRE, (Tel. 416-532-3888, www.kababayan.org, 1313 Queen St. W., Suite 133). Co-ordinates educational, cultural, and social activities for Filipino immigrants. Contact: Flor Dandal.

◆ SILAYAN FILIPINO COMMUNITY CENTRE, (Tel. 416-926-9505, 476 Parliament St. Suite 301). A drop-in centre established in 1969 to provide new Canadians with information on welfare, legal aid, benefits, and services for seniors. President: Delfin Palileo.

◆ BARANGAY FILIPINO, (Tel. 905-276-2264, 2813 Kingsberry Cres., Mississauga). President: Cesar Arias.

◆ CULTURE PHILIPPINES, (3471 Martin's Pine Cres., Mississauga). President: Pepe Buenavides.

◆ FIESTA FILIPINA DANCE TROUPE, (Tel. 905-566-5734, 829 Queensbridge Dr., Mississauga). This group has performed at the Olympic and Commonwealth games opening ceremonies. President: Onofre Aguinaldo.

◆ FILIPINO PARENTS ASSOCIATION OF TORONTO (FIL-PAR), (101 1665 Victoria Park Ave). President: Alejo Parucha.

◆ FILIPINO PERFORMING ARTS & CULTURE, (Tel. 416-467-0612, 251 Westlake Ave). President: Hermie Rosario.

◆ FOLKLORICO FILIPINO CANADA, (Tel. 416-281-2408, 81 Parade Sq). Executive Administrator: Wendy Arenas.

◆ HIMIG FILIPINO CHORAL ENSEMBLE, (5762 Greensboro Dr., Mississauga). Music Director: Cristina Sanchez.

◆ INTERNATIONAL COALITION TO END DOMESTICS' EXPLOITATION (INTERCEDE), (Tel. 416-483-4554, 234 Eglinton Ave. E). Director: Agatha Mason.

◆ KAGAYANON FOUNDATION (Toronto), (Tel. 905-707-8433, 50 Mowatt Crt., Thornhill). President: Betsy W. Abarquez.

◆ PHILIPPINE HERITAGE BAND, (91 Thornhill Woods Dr). A brass band that plays at various cultural events. Contact: Carol Banez.

◆ SAMPAGUITA SENIOR CITIZENS CLUB, (208-2305 South Millway, Mississauga).

◆ SAN LORENZO RUIZ CATHOLIC COMMUNITY CENTRE, (% INTERCEDE, 234 Eglinton Ave).

- UNITED AKLANON ASSOCIATION OF TORONTO, (3050 Constitution Blvd., Mississauga). President: Vic Sunico.
- UNIVERSITY OF THE PHILIPPINES ALUMNI ASSOCIATION, (525-121 Scadding Ave). President: Francis Rementilla.
- CATHOLIC COMMUNITY SERVICES OF YORK REGION, (7170 Warden Ave., Unit 15, Markham). Contact: Ms. Agnes Manasan.
- MARKHAM FEDERATION OF FILIPINO CANADIAN CENTRE, (Tel. 905-305-1320, Fax 905-472-0322, 1151 Denison St., Units 10 & 11, Markham).
- KABABAIHANG RIZALISTA INC, (Tel. 416-536-8234, Fax 416-534-9244, 174 Symington Ave). President: Araceli (Rose) V. Cruz.

Consulates, Trade Commissions and Tourist Bureaus

- CONSULATE GENERAL OF THE PHILIPPINES, (Tel. 416-922-7181, 161 Eglinton. Ave. E., Suite 800). Consul General: Minerva Jean A. Faloon.
- PHILIPPINE DEPARTMENT OF TOURISM, (www.wowphilippines.ca).
- PHILIPPINES LABOUR OFFICE, (Tel. 416-975-8252, Fax 416-975-8277, www.polocanada.org, 161 Eglinton Ave E. Suite 801).

Prominent Torontonians

Jim Ariz, president, Living Waters Residence Inc.; Mila Eustaquio, Vice-Counsellor on Women's Rights; Carmencita Hernandez, community activist; Dr. Victoria Santiago-Liu, dentist; Mel Catre, community leader; Cornelia Soberano, lawyer; Rosalina Bustamante, teacher; Monina Serrano, president of the Federation of Filipino Canadians.

Contributor: Hermie Garcia (Reporter, *The Philippine*).

The Finnish Community

In 1959, Kendal Park at Brunswick and Bernard avenues was renamed Sibelius Square in honour of Finnish composer, Jean Sibelius (1865–1957), best known for his composition **Finlandia**. Today, a bronze bust of the music master by Finnish artist Waino Valdemar Aaltonen, erected in 1959, overlooks the park—a dignified reminder of the great composer and of the 10,000 Finns who live in the city.

In 1987, Finns celebrated a century of settlement in Toronto. The founder and pioneer of the Toronto Finnish community was Jaakko Lindala, a tailor who arrived in 1887 and encouraged other Finnish tailors to emigrate. A spokesperson for Finns and other immigrants, Lindala was a mayoral candidate in 1907. Established at the turn of the century on York Street, Lindala's **Iso-Paja** (Big Shop) became a centre for the community's gatherings. The shop, which contained a public sauna, was the largest employer of Finnish men in the city.

A Finnish neighbourhood developed around Widmer Street, where Finnish women operated rooming houses and Holm's restaurant became a gathering place for single men. Finnish-owned bakeries (**Lopponen** was the first and **Miettinen's** the second), restaurants, and grocery stores were also established in the area. On weekends, bands, theatre groups, and a choir livened up Finnish dances, picnics, and cultural events.

Prior to the Finnish settlement in Toronto, the first Finnish migrants to North America helped establish the colony of New Sweden along the Delaware River in 1638. In the 19th-century, several hundred Finns settled in Alaska, and along the coast of British Columbia. In Ontario, Finns were among the pioneers who constructed the Welland Canal. A tide of Finnish immigration in 1902 brought tailors, artisans, seamstresses, and laundresses to Toronto. The Finns contributed to early city construction, and iron workers laboured over the building of railroads, ships, and bridges. In the heart of the Finnish neighbourhood on Adelaide Street, the **Parisian Laundry** employed Finnish women for over two decades.

The Finnish in Toronto started cultural, social, and sport groups and one of the famous sportsmen was E. Lopponen who was the national heavyweight champion in wrestling (1908–1912) and a member of the Canadian Olympic team.

Another large group of Finns—mostly professionals—arrived in Canada between 1950 and 1960. Today, many Finns work in the professions or in business, some as independent contractors specializing in construction and the aluminum siding industry. The showpiece of Finnish architecture in Toronto is the dual-towered New City Hall, designed by Finnish architect Viljo Revell, whose novel oyster-shaped design won the 1958 international competition for the new home of city council.

Places to Go

In front of the **Finnish Agricola Church**, (25 Old York Mills Rd), stands a granite monument dedicated to the Finnish soldiers who perished during the two World Wars on the eastern defense line of Finland. The rock was brought to Canada from Finland, where it was utilized as a blockade to prevent Russian tanks from crossing the border during the early part of this century.

Finnish foods, such as setsuuri (sweet and sour bread with caraway seeds), pulla (raisin bread), and piirakka (puff pastry stuffed with beef, ham, cabbage, vegetables, or apples) can be found in Finnish bakeries and delicatessens around the city.

Viking Foods & Imports, (Tel. 416-696-7011, 19 Industrial St), imports Finnish and other Scandinavian dry and canned foods, nakkileipa, kaneli and sokeri korppu, candies, cookies, marinated herring, lingonberries, cloudberries, and rice and cheese pies. Owner: Mika Harela.

Milbree-Viking Bakery Inc., (Tel. 416-425-7200, 133 Laird Dr), traditional Finnish rye bread, coffee bread and pastries baked onsite. Smoked Christmas ham, turkey, salmon, and whitefish.

Hillside Café, (Tel. 416-544-1222, 594 Mount Pleasant Rd), offers Finnish-style layer cakes, limppu (sour rye bread), pastries, and imported Scandinavian delicacies.

The **Finnish Place**, (Tel. 416-222-7575, www.finnishplace.com, 5463 Yonge St). The Forss family sells Finnish giftware such as the popular Iittala designer crystal, Arabia China, Marimekko bags and clothing, jewelry, glass, cookware, napkins, stainless steel, and sauna accessories such as soap and sponges.

Religious Centres, Schools and Other Institutions

- ◆ FINNISH LUTHERAN AGRICOLA CHURCH, (Tel. 416-489-7600, 25 Old York Mills Rd), has the second largest Finnish congregation outside of Finland with a membership of just over 2,000. Only the Stockholm Finnish Church is larger. Dean: Rev. Markku Suokonautio, former President of the Finnish Conference of the Evangelical Lutheran Church of Canada.

- ◆ SAALEM FINNISH PENTECOSTAL CHURCH, (Tel. 416-222-2291, www.saalem.ca, 2570 Bayview Ave). One of the oldest and largest Finnish Pentecostal Churches outside of Finland, started in the 1930s by Finnish immigrants. Services held in Finnish and English, as well as weekly services for children, youth and seniors. Saalem church has two choirs, a brass band, and an orchestra. Senior Pastors: Mika & Rommy Yrjola, Associate Pastors: Mark and Sarah Rytkonen.

- ◆ FINNISH UNITED CHURCH, (Tel. 416-483-3514, 795 Eglinton Ave. E). Pastor Martti Hokkanen. Congregational services held on rotating Fridays.

- ◆ TORONTO FINNISH LANGUAGE SCHOOL, (Tel. 416-445-0747, 25 Old York Mills Rd), offers evening classes for children and adults. High school credits also available. Contact: Anneli Ylanko.

Toronto Finnish folkdancers at the Finnish-Canadian Festival

◆ SUOMI-KOTI (TORONTO FINNISH CANADIAN SENIORS' CENTRE), (Tel. 416-425-4134, 795 Eglinton Ave. E). A modern housing development for senior citizens containing 88 apartments, the building has social facilities, a library, an auditorium, and a medical centre with a pharmacy and two Finnish-speaking family practitioners. In 1992, a 34-bed nursing home facility was added to the Centre.

◆ FINNISH (TORONTO) CREDIT UNION, (Tel. 416-486-1533, www.finnishcu.com, 191 Eglinton Ave. E), has a membership of 3,300. General Manager: Antero Elo.

Holidays and Celebrations

◆ MAY 1ST VAPPU. The Toronto community celebrates the occasion with a dance and a Miss May Day contest. Sima, a special lemon-flavoured drink, is served with a sweet bread known as tippaleipa.

◆ MIDSUMMER DAY, celebrated on the Saturday nearest June 24, recognizes the longest day of the year. A picnic is held in Ontario cottage country. A huge bonfire, meant to ward off evil spirits, is an important part of the event. Midsummer Day is also a religious holiday and the Finnish name, Juhannus, refers to John the Baptist.

◆ THE ANNUAL FINNISH CANADIAN GRAND FESTIVAL, held on August 1 weekend, is organized by local clubs and coordinated by the **Finnish Canadian Cultural Federation**. In 1940, concerned Finns in Sudbury organized a Song and Music Festival to collect money for Finland, which had just survived the Winter War (1939–1940) against the Soviet Union. The need for assistance of the homeland has ceased, but the festival which brings together Canadians of Finnish descent still takes place in a different city each year. On the August 1 weekend, performing Finnish artists are featured in three nights of arts and crafts exhibitions that include dances, religious services, and sporting events. Finns enthusiastically compete in a round-robin tournament of Finnish baseball in which an intrepid pitcher throws the ball high up in the air, while standing next to the hitter.

◆ INDEPENDENCE DAY on December 6 marks the day in 1917 that Finland declared its independence from Russia. Commemorative services are held in churches, where war veterans bear flags and a wreath is placed at the **Agricola Church** monument.

◆ RELIGIOUS HOLIDAYS: Christmas Joulu, Easter Paasiainen, Helluntai and New Year Uusivuosi are highlights for family gatherings. Tradition is to go with all members of the family to church.

◆ CANADA DAY is celebrated by the Finnish Torontonians. On July 1, 1999, the community, for the first time in Canada's history, marched from Queen's Park to Nathan Phillips Square. Organizer: Tony Ruprecht, M.P.P. Finns coordinated by Meeri Apunen.

Media

◆ VAPAA SANA, (FINNISH WEEKLY NEWSPAPER), (Tel. 416-321-0808, 191 Eglinton Ave. E., Suite 308). A weekly tabloid with a circulation of 3,500. General Manager: Markus Raty. Editor-in-chief: Matti Temiseva.

◆ TODISTAJA, a monthly newspaper put out by the **Finnish Pentecostal Church**.

Organizations

◆ FINNISH CANADIAN CULTURAL FEDERATION, (www.finnishcanadian.com). Established 1971 as an umbrella organization for 60 clubs and associations throughout Canada. Represents the Finnish cultural group to all levels of government, and also supervises the annual Finnish Canadian Grand Festival.

◆ BOWLING CLUB ROLLERS, (Tel. (705) 765-6265). Chair: Kimmo Salonen; Secretary: Ulla Campbell, (Tel. 416-385-8090).

◆ CANADIAN FRIENDS OF FINLAND, (Tel. 416-730-8350, P.O. Box 51, 4700 Keele St). President: Seppo Kanerva. Founded by Dr. Varpu Lindstorm, Professor of History, Member Board of Governors, York University.

◆ FINNISH THEATRE, FINNISH SOCIAL CLUB ACTORS, (Tel. 416-724-9856). Chair: Maarit Koivunen; Leading Actor: Esko Laakso.

◆ FINNISH CANADIAN TEACHERS ASSOCIATION, (Tel. 416-445-0747, 20 Lynedock Cres). President: Anneli Ylanko.

◆ FINNISH SOCIAL CLUB, (Tel. 416-225-1534) Owns its own building and the **Cedar Club** in Udora (60 miles north of Toronto), which is used for the Finnish summer camp and Finnish language (summer) school. Holds an annual cross-country ski race at the grounds in late January. Chairman: Kalevi Aho.

◆ FINNISH SOCIAL COUNSELLING SERVICE OF TORONTO INC., Since 1981. (Tel. 416-997-3056, 191 Eglinton Ave E., Suite 206). A charitable agency that assists with Canada and global pensions and provides community outreach services. An information centre operating in liaison with the government and non-governmental agencies.

President: Seppo Leinoren; Executive Director: Meeri Apunen, A.C.I., M.C.I., B.A., M.A.

◆ FINNISH WAR VETERANS OF CANADA, (Tel. 905-887-7357, Toronto Chapter, P.O. Box 266, Gormley). Chairman: Veikko Kallio.

◆ PENSIONERS CLUB, (Tel. (705) 877-8310, 276A Main St). Arranges trips and meets at Suomi Talo. Chair: Kaija Raiskinmaki.

◆ SISU ATHLETIC CLUB, (Tel. 416-487-0687, 276A Main St). A major sports club, including a female modern rhythmic gymnastics group, folk-dancing group, hockey team, track and field group, soccer and Finnish baseball teams, and a cross-country ski group. Chairman: Matti Suopaa.

◆ SUOMI-TALO (HOUSE OF FINLAND) ASSOCIATION, (Tel. 416-421-9614). An organization to support the establishment of the Finnish Cultural Centre in Toronto; owns a hall at 276A Main St. Contact: Aimo Heikurinen.

◆ TORONTO FINNISH MALE CHOIR, (Tel. 416-225-9906). The 40-member choir participates in Finnish cultural events and festivals in Canada and the U.S.; has also organized concert tours in Finland. Chair: Bill Paavola; Secretary: Raimo Nutikka.

◆ TORONTO FINLANDIA LIONS CLUB, (Tel. 416-499-0167), Chair: Anja Kaski; Secretary: Seija Hyhko.

◆ TORONTO SUOMI LIONS CLUB, (Tel. 416-267-9206), Secretary: Risto T. Puhakka.

◆ CEDAR PARK RESIDENTS' ASSOCIATION, (Tel. 416-282-3548, 52 Grantown Ave., West Hill). Chair: Timo Makela.

Consulates, Trade Commissions and Tourist Bureaus

◆ CONSULATE GENERAL OF FINLAND, (Tel. 416-964-0066, 1200 Bay St., Suite 604). Honourary Consul: Mr. Patrick Brigham.

◆ CANADA-FINLAND CHAMBER OF COMMERCE, Toronto Chapter, (Tel. 416-964-7400, 1200 Bay St., Suite 604). Contact: Leila Appleford, C/o Finland Trade Centre; President: Tommi Korhonen.

◆ FINNISH TOURIST BOARD, (P.O. Box 246, Station Q).

Prominent Torontonians

Gayle Christie, former Mayor of the City of York; Dr. Bengt (Ben) Gestrin, Executive Vice-President of the Imperial Bank of Commerce, former Privy Council member and Canadian representative with the OECD; Tapani Nousiainen, President of Habridge and Gross Ltd., contractors; Dr. Veli J.

Peter Nygård
Nygård International, Ladies
Fashion and Textile Manufacturers.

Ylanko, former Assistant Professor, University of Toronto, and founder of Toronto Finnish Canadian Senior Centre; Peter Nygård, Nygård International, ladies fashion and textile manufacturers; Urho Pehkonen, first editor, Vapaa Sana and recipient of the Order of Canada; Kimmo A. Innanen, professor, Dept. of Physics and Astronomy, York University, former Dean of the Faculty of Pure and Applied Science; Paavo Kivisto, Former Deputy Minister of Labour, Government of Ontario; Dr. Pekka Sinervo, Dean of Faculty of Arts and Sciences, Professor of Physics, University of Toronto; Hannu Halminen, President of Halminen Homes Lauri Toiviainen, Editor, Vapaa Sana Press Ltd. and recipient of Knight Order of Lion of Finland; Andrea Hansen, former Second Violinist, Toronto Symphony Orchestra, Founder and Music Director of Strings Across the Sky, and recipient of Order of Canada; Hans Myrskog, Honorary President, Finn Fest Canada USA 2005 and owner of Myr Constuction Ltd.; Tommi Korhonen, President, The Canada Finland Chamber of Commerce, managing director, Northern Europe Inc., GSA, Finnair Canada.

Contributors: Mrs. Leila Appleford, Finpro, Finland Trade Centre; Lauri Toiviainen, journalist, former President of the Finnish Canadian Cultural Federation; Meeri Apunen, Founder and Executive Director of the Finnish Social Counselling Service of Toronto Inc., member, Toronto Seniors Assembly, and recipient of many awards; Markus Raty, General Manager and English Section Editor, Vapaa Sana Press Ltd.

Source: Students; Marian Raty and Lily Korhonen, Suomalainen Sosiaalineuvontapalvelu, active members of Saalem Church.

The French Community

Every June, French culture in the city is celebrated during **Francophone Week**, culminating with a bonfire celebration on St. Jean Baptiste Day. During this week, French culture is exhibited with displays of art, theatre and patriotic songs as Toronto's French-speaking community gathers together to celebrate its heritage during **Franco-Fête**.

There are more than 220,000 French-speaking people from various backgrounds living in Toronto. The community is a multicultural mix of Franco-Ontarians, Québecois, Acadians, francophones from the western provinces, Franco-Americans, and French-speaking peoples from such countries as France, Haiti, Belgium, Switzerland, Morocco, Senegal, Congo, and other African nations. French-owned businesses include restaurants, pharmaceutical companies, clothing boutiques, and translation services.

An early French settler in Ontario was Etienne Brûlé, interpreter to Samuel de Champlain and the first known European to stand on the site of Toronto in 1615. La Salle, another famous explorer, used the route in his explorations and was the first to record the name Toronto from the original native Indian word. In the 1700s, the French built fur-trading fortifications in the city. On the grounds of the **Canadian National Exhibition**, a huge boulder with an inscription marks the place where Fort Rouillé, commonly known as Fort Toronto, once stood in 1749.

Baby Point, an affluent Toronto neighbourhood, was once the estate of the Bâby family. In 1762, French fur-trader Jacques Bâby opened a trading store on the Humber River, and his son James Bâby became a member of both the executive and legislative councils of the new province of Upper Canada. Toronto's St. George Street is named after Laurent Quetton de St. George who operated a successful mercantile business at the turn of the 19th century. Other places and streets, such as Agincourt and Roncesvalles, take their names from famous French battles.

In the 1890s, most of the French population was located in the vicinity of Seaton and Sackville streets, between King and Queen streets, and in Parkdale. The community consisted of French-Canadians and half a dozen families from France. The majority were employed in factories, while some worked as printers, tailors, shoemakers, barbers, and bookkeepers.

One of the earliest organizations was the **St. Joseph Society**, a social service organization. The centre of the community was the **Sacré Coeur Church**, established on Sherbourne Street in 1887. Many French children attended separate schools, continuing their studies at a variety of schools, including **De La Salle Institute**.

A second parish, **St. Louis de France**, was established in Don Mills in 1965 to meet the needs of a growing French population. An important organization at this time was **Chasse-Galerie**, which housed an art gallery, workshops, and a bookstore, and organized events to promote French-Canadian culture.

Founded in 1981, **ACFO-Toronto** is a community-based non-profit organization, created for the purpose of furthering the development of French-speaking Ontarians or Ontarians of French culture living in Toronto and assists the more than 75 francophone organizations in Toronto to provide their services to the Community.

L'Alliance Française de Toronto, one of the oldest French groups in the city, continues to promote French culture through exhibitions, cultural events, a resource centre, a library and language classes. The **Comité Français de l'Hôtel de Ville de Toronto**, which organizes Francophone Week, was formed to establish a direct link between Toronto's elected officials and the francophone community.

There are a number of French dance troupes, singing clubs, and theatre groups, as well as francophone radio and television stations in the city, and it is possible for students to begin and complete their education in French by attending Toronto's day care centres, French elementary schools, secondary schools, and colleges.

Places to Go

Théâtre Français de Toronto, (Tel. 416-534-7303, www.theatrefrancais.com, 21 College St, Suite 610), performs plays for both adults and children during its season.

Exhibitions of French paintings, sculptures, and books are displayed at **Maison de la Culture**, Glendon College, York University, (Tel. 416-487-6710, 2275 Bayview Ave). Contact: Sylziane de Roquebruna. **Alliance française de Toronto**, (Tel. 416-922-2014, www.alliance-francaise.ca, 24 Spadina Rd) exhibits works by new French artists.

Toronto abounds with French restaurants serving carefully prepared soups, stews, meat and fish dishes enhanced by sauces such as béarnaise and béchamel. Hors d'oeuvres usually include escargot (snails in garlic, butter, and parsley), pâté de foie gras (goose liver paté), and soupe a l'oignon (onion soup). Regional specialties may include ratatouille (eggplant, red peppers, tomatoes, and zucchini stewed in olive oil), bouillabaisse (a stew of fish, mussels, and shellfish), and cuisses de grenouilles (frog legs). Popular desserts are mousse, soufflé, and torte. The French are renowned for their excellent wines, and café au lait is a popular beverage.

Arlequin, (134 Avenue Rd), serves specialties from the south of France, including ratatouille, scallops, roast lamb, and rabbit with thyme. A food shop on the premises sells French gourmet products. Le Trou Normand, (Tel. 416-967-5956, 90 Yorkville Ave), specializes in the cuisine of Normandy and northwestern France, serving dishes such as marinated rabbit, veal escalope with cream sauce, and calf's brains. Le Petit Gourmet, (Tel. 416-966-3811, 1064 Yonge St), serves Basque-style fish stews and meat dishes. Provence, (Tel. 416-924-9901, 12 Amelia St), serves duck in nine of its main dishes with a variety of sauces; and Jacques Bistro du Parc, (Tel. 416-961-1893, 126A Cumberland St), offers 17 different types of omelettes. Le Papillon, (Tel. 416-363-0838, 16 Church St), is Toronto's original crêperie, serving seafood, vegetarian, and fruit crêpes.

Le Saint Tropez, (Tel. 416-591-3600, 315 King St. W), offers light-style French cuisine, including a selection of 40 different sandwiches for lunch; Marcel's Bistro, (Tel. 416-591-8600, 315 King St. W., 2nd floor); La Bodega, (Tel. 416-977-1287, 30 Baldwin St), provides the experience of eating sophisticated French cuisine in the charming elegance of an old home.

Other restaurants serving French cuisine include Auberge du Pommier, (Tel. 416-222-2220, 4150 Yonge St); Bistro 990, (Tel. 416-921-9990, 990 Bay St); La Maquette, (Tel. 416-366-8191, 111 King St. E); Le Montmartre French Restaurant, (Tel. 416-630-3804, 911 Sheppard Ave. W); Le Paradis, (Tel. 416-921-0995, 166 Bedford Rd); Le Select Bistro, (Tel. 416-596-6405, 328 Queen St. W); Scaramouche, (Tel. 416-961-8011, 1 Benvenuto Place); Olliffe Butcher Shop, (Tel. 416-928-0296, 1097 Yonge St), and Cumbrae Butchers, (Tel. 416-923-5600, 481 Church St).

Pastry shops include France Patisserie, (Tel. 416-752-0027, 435 Midwest Rd); and Patachou Patisserie, (Tel. 416-927-1105, 1095 Yonge St), which sells brioches, croissants, brie sandwiches, quiche, and imported paté.

Stores that carry imported goods from France include The French Collection, (Tel. 416-483-3861, 253 Eglinton Ave. W), importers of women's clothes.

Librairie Champlain, (Tel. 416-364-4345, www.librairiechamplain.com, 468 Queen St. E) is considered the best French-language bookstore in the country with more than 100,000 French-language books in stock. Maison de la Presse Internationâle, (Tel. 416-928-2328, 102 Yorkville Ave), carries

French dailies, weeklies, Quebec newspapers, and magazines. It also sells French classics, reference books, dictionaries, greeting cards, and music by French recording artists.

Religious Centres, Schools and Other Institutions

Many French-speaking Torontonians belong to the Roman Catholic church. French services are held at the following churches:

◆ CHURCH OF THE REDEEMER, (Tel. 416-922-4948, 162 Bloor St. W).

◆ ÉGLISE DU SACRE-COEUR, (Tel. 416-922-2177, 381 Sherbourne St). The church is more than 100 years old.

◆ JARVIS STREET BAPTIST CHURCH, (Tel. 416-925-3261, 130 Gerrard St. E).

◆ ST. LOUIS DE FRANCE, (Tel. 416-445-6433, 1415 Don Mills Rd).

French schools in the city include:

◆ ÉCOLE JEANNE-LAJOIE, (Tel. 416-397-2080, 150 Carnforth Rd).

◆ ÉCOLE MONSEIGNEUR-DE-CHARBONNEL, (Tel. 416-393-5537, 110 Drewry Ave).

◆ GEORGE BROWN COLLEGE, Centre français, (Tel. 416-415-2000, P.O. Box 1015, Station B).

◆ GEORGE ÉTIENNE CARTIER, (Tel. 416-393-5314, 250 Gainsborough St).

◆ GLENDON COLLEGE, (Tel. 416-487-6710, York University, 2275 Bayview Ave).

◆ GABRIELLE ROY, (Tel. 416-393-1360, 14 Pembroke St).

◆ LE COLLEGE FRANCAIS, (Tel. 416-393-0175, 100 Carlton St).

◆ SACRE-COEUR, (Tel. 416-393-5219, 25 Linden St).

◆ ST. MADELEINE, (Tel. 416-393-5312, 1 Ness Dr).

◆ ST. NOËL CHABANEL, (Tel. 416-393-5321, 1300 Wilson Ave).

◆ ST. JEAN DE LALANDE, (Tel. 416-393-5369, 500 Sandhurst Circle).

◆ TORONTO FRENCH SCHOOL, (Tel. 416-484-6533, www.tfs.on.ca, 306 Lawrence Ave. E).

Financial institutions in the city include:

◆ BANQUE PARIBAS DU CANADA, Royal Trust Tower, TD Centre, (Tel. 416-365-9600, 77 King St. W., Suite 4100, P.O. Box 31).

Holidays and Celebrations

◆ NEW YEAR'S DAY. On January 1, New Year's Day celebrations include the eating of tourtières and roast turkey. Réveillons (get-togethers) are held on December 31 in private homes.

◆ MARDI GRAS is held during the week before Lent begins. Celebrations include a masquerade ball and other social activities.

◆ ST-JEAN-BAPTISTE DAY, June 24, takes place in honour of the patron saint of French Canadians. **Francophone Week** takes place around this time with cultural activities at Harbourfront and Ontario Place, and a large bonfire celebration at **Glendon College**.

◆ LE FESTIVAL ACADIEN, August 15, is held in honour of the patron saint of all Acadians, Our Lady of Assumption. An all-day open-air festival is held at **Harbourfront** with displays of crafts, demonstrations of spinning and weaving, and singing and dancing.

◆ LA TIRE STE. CATHERINE is held on November 25. A French Canadian custom was started on this date in the 17th-century when Marguerite Bourgeoys made toffee candy for her students. The tradition continues to this day and celebrates unmarried women over 25 years of age.

◆ CHRISTMAS. On December 25, Christmas is celebrated with Le Réveillon (midnight supper). After attending Midnight Mass, it is customary for French Canadians to gather together to share tourtières, pastries, and other delicacies, along with Petit St. George wine. The festivities include dancing and singing.

◆ FRANCO-FÊTE. This is the largest French festival in Toronto. More than 10,000 francophones attend this celebration of **La Francophonie** held yearly between **St-Jean-Baptiste Day** and **Canada Day**. This family-oriented festival has featured great names in French music worldwide, such as Céline Dion, Robert Charlesbois, and Michel Rivard. Chair: Gérard Parent.

◆ LA NUIT BLANCHE, Since 2002, Paris has invited its inhabitants to take an artistic and nocturne round for one night. The objective is to make art and culture accessible to everyone and to emphasize urban space. This event now also takes place in Toronto on the first Saturday of October and attracts close to a million visitors.

◆ LA FÊTE DE LA MUSIQUE, On the 21st of June, since 1982, the summer solstice is a day of music. People get together in various locations including streets, squares and centres to listen to live bands, all for free. All towns and villages in France hold this festival, and this concept has now spread to countries all around the world. Today we can enjoy *La Fete de la Musique* in New York, London, Rio, Madrid or Toronto.

◆ LA SEMAINE DE LA FRANCOPHONE, Every year in March, Toronto has a French atmosphere. For old and young alike, dozens of activities are organized by French speaking assiciations and intitutions from Toronto, they gather and celebrate French as a common language.

See Holidays and Celebrations in Glossary.

Media

- ◆ ANNUAIRE FRANCOPHONE, CFT Centre Francophone, (Tel. 416-203-1220, 20 Lower Spadina Ave). An annual directory of services available in French.
- ◆ CJBC 860, FRENCH RADIO AND TV, (Tel. 416-205-3311 and 205-2522, Box 500, Station A). Same address: CBLFT-French television.
- ◆ TFO, (Tel. 416-968-3536, 21 College St., 6th Floor, P.O. Box 3005, station F). Publicist: Claudette Paquin.
- ◆ L'EXPRESS, (Tel. 416-465-2107, 17 Carlaw Ave). A weekly newspaper in French. Editor: Magaline Boutros.
- ◆ CLUB CANADIEN DE TORONTO, (Tel. 416-243-0662, www.clubcanadien.ca, 1116 Wilson Ave).

Organizations

- ◆ FRENCH CHAMBER OF COMMERCE, (Tel. 416-205-9820, 20 Queen St. W., Suite 2006).
- ◆ ALLIANCE FRANÇAISE DE TORONTO, (Tel. 416-922-2014, www.alliance-francaise.ca, 24 Spadina Rd). President: Lee MacNeil.
- ◆ ASSOCIATION DES PROFESSEURS D'IMMERSION DE NORTH YORK (APINY), (Tel. 416-488-8044, 56 Braeside Rd). President: Laurie Moir.
- ◆ FRANÇAIS ACCUEIL, (Tel. 416-544-8106, 24 Lower Village Gate).
- ◆ ASSOCIATION DES SCOUTS DU DISTRICT DE TORONTO, (Tel. 416-490-6313, 265 Yorkland Blvd., 2nd floor). Executive Director: Peter Sundborg.

Franco-Ontarian students celebrate the official adoption of their community's flag.

- LE CERCLE CANADIEN DE TORONTO, (Tel. 416-243-0662, 1116 Wilson Ave Suite 66030).
- CENTRE DE RECHERCHE EN EDUCATION FRANCO-ONTARIENNE (CREFO), (Tel. 416-923-6641, 242 Bloor St. W., #6-210). Director: Monica Heller.
- CENTRE D'ACCUEIL HÉRITAGE, (Tel. 416-365-3350, 33 Hahn Pl).
- CERCLE DE L'AMITIE, (Tel. 905-456-0606, Fax 905-542-8896, 1780 Meadowvale Blvd., Mississauga).
- COMITÉ FRANÇAIS DE L'HÔTEL DE VILLE DE TORONTO, (100 Queen St. W., 2nd Floor). President: André Duclos.
- CONSEIL DES ÉCOLES CATHOLIQUES DU GRAND TORONTO, (Tel. 416-222-8282, 80 Sheppard Ave. E).
- EVEIL FÉMININ, (Tel. 416-922-2177). President: Anne Perry.
- FRANCOSCOPE, (Tel. 416-449-8738, 61 Ternhill Cres). A French cultural club. President: Paul Ceurstemont.
- GARDERIE LAJOIE, (Tel. 416-759-5095, 150 Carnforth Rd). President: Julie Ethier.
- L'ASSOCIATION DES FEMMES D'AFFAIRES FRANCOPHONES, (Tel. 905-827-6189, P.O. Box 7147 Oakville). Contact: Colette Mockfyd.
- LA FARANDOLE (GARDERIE), (Tel. 416-363-1841, 14 Pembroke St). Contact: Doina Iliescu.
- LA GARDERIE RAYON DE SOLEIL, (Tel. 416-444-3464, 1 Ness Dr). Contact: Celine Mousseau.
- LE CENTRE MEDICO SOCIAL COMMUNAUTAIRE, (Tel. 416-922-2672, 22 College St., Main floor). Executive Director: Jean-Gilles Pelletier.
- LE PETIT CHAPERON ROUGE (GARDERIE), (Tel. 416-463-3955, 250 Gainsborough Rd). President: Kip Daechel.
- LES BOUTS D'CHOUX (GARDERIE), (Tel. 416-960-9929, 25 Linden St). Director: Julie Meta.
- SOCIÉTÉ D'HISTOIRE DE TORONTO, (Tel. 416-497-5354, 552 Church St., P.O. Box 93). President: Rosland Smith.
- UNION DES ARTISTES, (Tel. 416-485-7670, 625 Church St., Suite 103).

Consulates, Trade Commissions and Tourist Bureaus

- THE FRENCH CONSULATE, (Tel. 416-847-1900, 2 Bloor St. E, Suite 2200). Consul General: Mr. Jérôme Cauchard.
- FRENCH TRADE COMMISSION, (Tel. 416-977-1257, 20 Queen St. W., Suite 2004). Trade Commissioner: Eric Morand.
- FRENCH CULTURAL SERVICE, (Tel. 416-847-1900, 2 Bloor St. E, Suite 2200). Contact: Mr. Joel Savari.

◆ **FRENCH CHAMBER OF COMMERCE**, (Tel. 416-205-9820, 20 Queen St. W., Suite 2006). Executive Director: Mrs.Laurence Jollivet.

Prominent Torontonians

Mira Godard, art gallery owner; Jacques Loic-Lorioz, entertainer; Jean Malavoy, formerly of the Ontario Arts Council; Micheline Montgomery, artist; Daniel Pokorn, sculptor; Marius Vitry, singer; Heidi Bouraoui, writer; Diana Leblanc, actress; Brigitte Bureau, journalist and writer; Gerard Lévesque, conseil de la vie française en Amérique–Ontario representative.

Contributors: Anne-Marie Couffin, former Executive Director, COFTM Centre Francophone; François Guérin, Chair ACFO.

Source: Anne Rich.

The German Community

From the building of the world's longest street by early settlers to the masterful designs of city landmarks by individual architects, Toronto's German-speaking residents have made their mark upon the city. Along Front Street, remnants of Old York mixed with modern developments chronicle Toronto's growth from a town to a metropolis. **Berczy Park** on the boulevard of Front and Wellington streets is named for architect and artist William Moll Berczy who co-founded Toronto (York) with John Graves Simcoe in 1794. Not far from this downtown respite is Yonge Street, which was cleared and constructed by Berczy and other German settlers. **German Mills Settlers Park** (Leslie and John Streets in Markham) commemorates the 64 German families that Berczy brought to settle in Upper Canada.

The sleek black façade of the **Toronto Dominion Centre** bears the famous markings of Ludwig Mies van der Rohe's international Bauhaus style, while architect Eberhart Zeidler's designs of top tourist attractions, such as the **Eaton Centre**, **Ontario Place**, and **Queen's Quay Terminal**, stand as silhouettes on Toronto's skyline.

The first recorded German settler in Canada was Hans Bernard, who purchased land in Quebec in 1664. In the mid-18th century, 2,000 German newcomers landed at HaliFax. Early German-speaking immigrants to Canada came not only from the various states of Germany, but also from the former Austro-Hungarian Empire and other European countries. After the American Revolution, German settlers from New York State, disbanded German auxiliary troops of the British crown, and Mennonites from Pennsylvania came in search of free land in Upper Canada.

By 1850, Toronto's community began to organize as a group; German Lutherans formed the congregation of the **First Lutheran Church of Toronto**. German builders, architects, manufacturers, and craftsmen started their own businesses, including Theodore August Heintzman, who turned his kitchen trade into **Heintzman and Company**, a world-renowned manufacturer of pianos. Sir Adam Beck was knighted for establishing the **Hydro Electric Power Commission of Ontario** in 1903. German musicians gave Toronto's early arts community a boost when Augustus

Stephen Vogt formed the **Mendelssohn Choir of Toronto** in 1894, and Luigi Maria von Kunits revived the **Toronto Symphony Orchestra** in 1912. Included in the 100,000 German-speaking immigrants who arrived in Canada following the First World War were farmers, artisans, shopkeepers, and labourers. In Toronto, a German neighbourhood formed around **St. Patrick's Church** on McCaul Street. A Catholic Settlement House was added to the church and functioned as a social and cultural centre with a library and a hall for holding classes, theatre evenings, concerts, and dances. The parishioners also formed a credit union and a funeral society.

Toronto's industries and economic opportunities attracted more German immigrants following the Second World War, when a number of professionals such as doctors, scientists, engineers, and academics settled in the city. This post-war community formed cultural organizations, including the **German-Canadian Club**, the **Danube-Swabian Club**, the **Hansa Club**, and the **Historical Society of Mecklenburg Upper Canada** (publisher of the *German-Canadian Yearbook*). The **Kolping Society of Ontario** served to help Catholic German tradesmen—stonemasons, welders, watchmakers, and toolmakers.

While a neighbourhood for Toronto's 220,000 member German community in 2005, has gradually dispersed throughout the city, examples of German artistry, craftsmanship, and business acumen are manifested throughout the city.

Places to Go

Across from the **St. Lawrence Centre** on Front St., in **Berczy Park**, an elegant bronze statue, sculpted by Almuth Lutkenhaus, honours the William Berczy family. Charles Albert Berczy, the youngest son, was the first president of the **Consumers' Gas Company** from 1847 to 1856, and postmaster of Toronto. William Bent Berczy was a member of the legislative assembly of Upper Canada and a gifted painter like his father.

Rising above a stately boulevard at University Avenue and Queen Street is a bronze figure of Sir Adam Beck, who was once called "Ontario's greatest public servant." The monument on top of a massive granite base was designed by Emanuel Hahn and unveiled in 1934.

At **Black Creek Pioneer Village** (Jane Street and Steeles Avenue), the buildings of this open-air museum have been arranged around the early 19th-century farm of the Pennsylvanian German immigrant, Daniel Stong.

A plaque marks the former residence of 19th century piano manufacturer Theodore Heintzman at 288 Annette St.

A German library is housed at the **Goethe Institute**, (Tel. 416-593-5257 (hotline 593-5258), 100 University Ave, North Tower). The library is open Tuesday, Wednesday, and Thursday, 12:30 p.m. to 6:30 p.m., Friday, 12:00 p.m. to 4:00 p.m., and Saturday, 10:00 a.m. to 4:00 p.m. Closed Tuesdays following a holiday Monday.

Among the European establishments in the High Park area and along Roncesvalles Avenue, there are a few stores and restaurants that carry the foods of Germany. The staple diet includes kassler rippchen (smoked loin of pork), wurst (sausage), sauerbraten (sweet and sour marinated pot roast), and sauerkraut (salted fermented cabbage). Famous German pastries are sacher torte (chocolate-iced chocolate cake filled with jam), nuss torte (nut cake), and obstkuchen (cake topped with fruit).

German restaurants found around the city include: **The Musket**, (Tel. 416-231-6488, 40 Advance Rd); **Blackhorn Dining Room**, (Tel. 416-449-2841, 251 Ellesmere Rd); and **Blue Danube Restaurant**, (Tel. 416-290-6186, 1686 Ellesmere Rd., Scarborough), which serves German-Viennese delicacies.

Another feature that has become an integral part of the culinary life of the city is German specialty and delicatessen stores. **Brandt Meats**, (Tel. 905-279-4460, 1878 Mattawa Ave., Mississauga), is well known. **Dimpflmeier Bakery**, (Tel. 416-239-3031, 26-34 Advance Rd), has homemade breads, wonderful tarts, pastries, and a specialty: their "stollen," considered to be better tasting than the original versions from Germany, are now a trademark. Another well-known bakery is **Rudolph's Specialty Bakeries**, (Tel. 416-763-4375, 390 Alliance Ave). Also, **Lein Delicatessen**, (Tel. 416-251-5858, 3262 Lakeshore Blvd. W).

Specializing in German pastries are: **Fabian Cafe**, (Tel. 416-438-1561, 876 Markham Rd); and **Cafe Bavaria and Bakery**, (Tel. 416-264-4535, 3244 Eglinton Ave. E).

German Canadian Club, (Tel. 905-564-0060, 6650 Hurontario St., Mississauga).

Religious Centres, Schools and Other Institutions

Most German-Canadians belong to the Protestant churches, but many are Roman Catholic and some are Mennonites or Hutterites.

♦ ST. PATRICK'S GERMAN PARISH CATHOLIC CHURCH, (Tel. 416-598-4835, 131 McCaul St). The second oldest church was erected in 1908 in Romanesque Revival style.

- **THE FIRST LUTHERAN CHURCH**, (Tel. 416-977-4786, 116 Bond St). Elongated windows and buttresses highlight the neo-Gothic style of the oldest German church in the city.
- **CHRISTUS-KIRCHE**, (Tel. 416-494-2201, 2210 Warden Ave).
- **EPIPHANY CHURCH**, (Tel. 416-284-5922, 20 Old Kingston Rd., West Hill).
- **GERMAN UNITED CHURCH**, (Tel. 416-484-6849, 20 Glebe Rd. E).
- **HUMBERVALE PARK BAPTIST CHURCH**, (Tel. 416-231-6483 and 232-9191, 763 Royal York Rd).
- **MARTIN LUTHER CHURCH**, (Tel. 416-251-8293, 2379 Lakeshore Blvd. W).
- **ST. GEORGES LUTHERAN CHURCH**, (Tel. 416-921-2687, 410 College St).
- **WILLOWDALE (LUTHERAN) EVANGELICAL CHURCH**, (Tel. 416-223-3182, 236 Finch Ave. E).
- **GERMAN LANGUAGE SCHOOL FRIEDRICH SCHILLER SCHULE**, (Tel. 905-857-1841, 7073 Castelderg Rd).
- **TORONTO GERMAN SCHOOL**, (Tel. 416-922-6413, 427 Bloor St. W).

Holidays and Celebrations

- **CANADIAN-GERMAN FESTIVAL (ANNUAL EVENT)**, (Festival hotline: 416-376-7928, www.germanfestival.ca).
- **FASCHING KARNEVAL**. Masquerade parties and carnivals mark Fasching Karneval (Mardi Gras) held in January and February. The main festivities end on Shrove Tuesday, the day before the beginning of Lent. As part of the festivities, a new prince and princess are chosen.
- **GERMANY'S LABOUR DAY** on May 1st is remembered by German-Canadians, with special celebrations held by some of the clubs.
- **CONSTITUTION DAY** on May 23 celebrates the day West Germany established its own constitution.

Canadian German Festival. These traditional costumes are from the Black Forest region.

- ◆ PILGRIMAGE on the second Sunday in June, the annual pilgrimage of German Catholics to Mary Lake, King City, pays homage to Germans expelled from Eastern Europe.
- ◆ KIRCHWEIHFEST, the largest feast of the German congregation at St. Patrick's Church, is held on September 24, the annual church dedication day.
- ◆ OKTOBERFEST, with its oompah bands, sausages, sauerkraut, and beer, carries on a Munich tradition. Large festivities in Kitchener-Waterloo and other Ontario communities attract people of all ethnocultural backgrounds.
- ◆ REMEMBRANCE DAY, November 18, honours Germans who died in two World Wars. Today, most German-Canadians recognize November 11 as Remembrance Day and many pay their respects at the **Woodland Cemetery** in Kitchener on the Sunday nearest the date.
- ◆ ST. NIKOLAUS DAY. On the eve of St. Nikolaus Day, December 6, German-Canadian children leave notes in their shoes in hopes that the Saint will bring them gifts.
- ◆ CHRISTMAS. Lighted evergreen trees at Christmas, a tradition that originated in Germany in the 16th century, was introduced to Canada in 1781 by the Baroness Friederike von Riedesel.

See Holidays and Celebrations in Glossary.

Media

- ◆ CIAO (AM 530), (Tel. 905-206-1234, 5312 Dundas St W). Flottewell, 8:00 am to 1:00 pm with host Helmut Gschoesser.
- ◆ DEUTSCHE PRESSE, (Tel. 416-595-9714, 87 Judge Rd). The largest German weekly in the country. Publisher: Rolf Meyer. Managing Editor: Rosemarie Meyer.
- ◆ ECHO GERMANICA, (Tel. 416-652-1332, 118 Tyrrel Ave). A bi-weekly newspaper. Publisher: Sybille Forster-Rentmeister.
- ◆ GERMAN HOUR, CHIN 1540 AM/91.9 FM, (Tel. 416-531-9991, www.chinradio.com, 622 College St). Saturday, 4:00 p.m. to 5:30 p.m. Host: Ulrich Jeschke.
- ◆ HEIMATBOTE, (Tel. 905-881-6350, 17 Doncrest Dr., Thornhill). Monthly newspaper of the **Alliance of Danube Swabians** in Canada and the United States. Editor: Anton Wekerle.

- NEUE WELT, German language bi-weekly newspaper, (Tel. 416-237-0591, Fax 416-237-9590, www.neueweltonline.com, 2 Billingham Rd., Suite 203). Publisher & Editor-in-chief: Karsten Mertens
- RADIO HERZ, (Tel. 905-842-3144, www.radioherz.com, 1177 Imvicta Dr. Suite 201, Oakville). Twenty-four hours German language radio program.

Organizations

- DEUTSCHKANADISCHER KONGRESS (GERMAN-CANADIAN CONGRESS), (Tel. (519) 746-9006 or 1-800-364-1309, Fax (519) 746-7006, www.dkk-ont.net, 455 Conestogo Rd., Waterloo). Represents German-Canadians and promotes German culture in Canada. President (Ontario Chapter): Ernst Friedel.
- HISTORICAL SOCIETY OF MECKLENBURG UPPER CANADA, (Tel. 416-439-1546, www.german-canadian.ca, P.O. Box 1251, Station K). The most influential German-Canadian cultural organization in the Toronto area; offers lectures and films, publishes the *German-Canadian Yearbook*, and is co-founder of the German Heritage Museum. President: Chris Klein.
- CANADIAN-GERMAN CHAMBER OF COMMERCE, INC., (Tel. 416-598-3355, 480 University Ave., Suite 1410). President: Thomas Beck.
- DEUTSCHER AUTOMOBILE CLUB, (Tel. 416-282-9865, 66 Celeste Dr). Promotes racing in Canada. Contact: Claus Bartels.
- DEUTSCH-KANADISCHES SENIORENHEIM VON GROSS-TORONTO (GERMAN-SPEAKING SENIOR'S RESIDENCE), (Tel. 416-497-3639, 1020 McNicoll Ave., 4th floor). Contact: Gabriele Goldschmitd.
- DEUTSCHE SPRACHSCHULEN (METRO TORONTO) INC., (Tel. 905-773-5601, 27 Bond Cr., Richmond Hill). Administration: E. Oberparleiter.
- G.K.G. HARMONIE, (Tel. 416-231-8496). Contact: Gaby Schick.
- GERMAN-CANADIAN HISTORICAL ASSOCIATION, (Tel. (705) 445-1240, 80-56 Goodview Rd). Contact: Mark Grzeskowiak.
- GERMAN-CANADIAN CLUB HANSA, (Tel. 905-564-0060, 6650 Hurontario St., Mississauga). Contact: Elbira Tordan.
- GERMAN SOCIETY OF EASTERN HERITAGE, (P.O. Box 80533, 2300 Lawrence Ave. E). President: Mr. Siegfried Fischer.
- SUDETEN KLUB VORWARTS TORONTO, (Tel. 416-483-8240). Publishes a periodical called *Vorwarts*. President: Mr. R. Lawrence.
- GOETHE INSTITUTE, (Tel. 416-593-5257, 100 University Ave, suite 201). Director: Dr. Arpad Solter.

Painting by Moll Berczy "Clearing of Yonge Street in Muddy York" Historical Society of Mecklenburg Upper Canada.

Consulates, Trade Commissions and Tourist Bureaus

◆ CONSULATE GENERAL OF THE FEDERAL REPUBLIC OF GERMANY, (Tel. 416-925-2813, 2 Bloor St. East, 25th Floor). Consul General: Sabine Sparwasser

◆ GERMAN NATIONAL TOURIST OFFICE, (Tel. 416-968-1685, 480 University Ave., Suite 1410).

◆ GERMAN-CANADIAN CHAMBER OF COMMERCE, (Tel. 416-598-3355, 480 University Ave., Suite 1500).

◆ GERMAN CANADIAN BUSINESS AND TRADE PUBLICATION, (Tel. 416-465-9957, www.germancanadian.com, Box 106–2255B, Queen St).

Prominent Torontonians

Harald Bohne, former Director of the University of Toronto Press; Alfons Dimpflmeier, well known baked goods entrepreneur; Dr. Harmut Froeschle, historian and Professor of German at the University of Toronto; Dieter Hastenteufel, sculptor; Almuth Luetkenhaus, sculptor; Gerry Meinzer, former President of the Canadian-German Congress; Leonhard Oesterle, sculptor; Dr. John Polanyi, Professor of Chemistry and Nobel Prize winner; Eva Pracht, 1988 Olympic bronze medalist in dressage riding; Josef Stritzl,

Alfons Dimpflmeier started his famous bakery in 1959 and is known today as a generous philanthropist

famous industrialist; Luigi Maria von Kunitz, founder of the Toronto Symphony Orchestra; Dr. Hermann Geiger-Torel, former General Director of the Canadian Opera Company; Helmut Hofmann, founder and Chairman of Exco Technologies Ltd.; Frank Klees, MPP; Johanna van Kempen, painter; Eb Zeidler, designed Ontario Place, the Eaton Centre, and many other famous landmarks in Toronto and around the world; Ida Brandt and Otto Rosenmeier, Co-owners of Brandt Meat Products; Manfred J Von Vulte, Author.

Contributors: Rolf A. Piro; Wolfgang Pazulla, President, Deutsche Sprachschulen (Metro Toronto); Anton Wekerle, President, St. Michaelswerk; C.J. Klein, President, Historical Society of Mecklenburg Upper Canada; Ulrich Jeschke, CHIN Radio, Rolf & Rosemary Meyer, publishers/editors of the German weekly newspaper *Deutsche Presse.*

The Greek Community

Athens" sprang up in the sixties, bringing the tastes and sounds of the Mediterranean through shish kebab houses, tavernas, kafenions, and bouzouki music. Although many Greeks moved out of Toronto to suburbs in Etobicoke, York, North York, Mississauga, and Scarborough, the Greek business district has flourished for the last three decades. Today, along the Danforth strip between Chester and Jones Avenues, restaurants serve traditional Greek food and mezes to a new clientele.

Toronto's Greek community numbers around 130,000, a striking contrast to the 20 Greek names that appeared in the 1907 *Might's Directory*. Many of the first Greek immigrants in Canada were young men, most of them refugees, who came in the 1890s to work in agriculture or in Northern Ontario's mines, forests, and railways. The exception to these working-class settlers was Dr. Petros Constantinides, an eminent scholar and surgeon who arrived in Toronto in 1864. Today, the community is proud of its more than 15,000 professionals.

In 1909, members of the community established the **St. George Greek Orthodox** congregation and a year later opened a church in a former warehouse on Jarvis Street. One of the earliest organizations was the **Ladies Philoptochos (Friends to the Poor) Benevolent Society** which set up a school in the church building and provided social services for newcomers.

During the next decade, the Greek presence became more evident as businessmen opened restaurants, fruit stores, ice-cream parlours, shoe-shine shops, and billiard halls along Yonge, College, and Queen Streets. The **Greek Community of Toronto** was founded in 1911. Greeks were often victims of discrimination during the early years of the 20th century. This discrimination peaked in August of 1918 when veterans of the First World War, frustrated with Greece's late entry into the conflict, led a riot which resulted in the destruction of many Greek businesses.

In the early 1930s, the first cultural organizations and regional clubs were established to preserve Greek language and traditions. One of the first was the **Helleno-Macedonian Brotherhood of Ion Dragoumis**, which was established in 1936. Youth groups and the Greek Orthodox parish schools became instrumental in teaching the language and heritage of the Hellenes to the children of early immigrants. Large communal efforts during the

Second World War and beyond included the **Greek War Relief Fund**, set up to assist the homeland.

Following the Second World War, another wave of Greek settlers, most from Northern Greece—Epirus, Macedonia, and Thrace—came to Canada, many to Toronto. In the 1950s, the Greek community moved into the Danforth area—originally a neighbourhood for the Anglo-Saxon proletariat and later an Italian enclave.

Today, numerous restaurants and businesses, Greek street signs, and the classical architecture of the **National Bank of Greece** and other buildings bearing the names of Hellenic associations such as the **Pan-Arcadian Federation**, the **Pan-Macedonian Association**, the **Pontion Brotherhood**, the political party offices of the **PASOK** and the **Democracy** signify the neighbourhood's most prevalent and flourishing culture.

Prominent Greek Torontonians have included the internationally-renowned soprano Teresa Stratas, who began her career singing for nickels at her father's Cabbagetown restaurant. Andreas Papandreou, the late Prime Minister of Greece, and many other Cabinet Ministers have been members of Toronto's Greek community.

Places to Go

The line-ups for Toronto's shish kebab houses never seem to fade, and the selling of souvlaki (tender chunks of pork or lamb laced with a garlic sauce) is a multi-million dollar business. One of the first restaurants to introduce Toronto to the shish kebab was the **Astoria Shish Kebob House**, (Tel. 416-463-2838, 390 Danforth Ave). Elias Bonos and George Sciouris have expanded the **Astoria House** into a 300-seat establishment occupying a corner of Chester and Danforth Avenues. On weekends, line-ups stretch past both the hustling waiters and the sizzling shish kebab in the storefront kitchen, where roast potatoes, Greek salad, and tzaziki sauce (yogurt, olive oil, garlic, and herbs) are added to the souvlaki platter. A glass of ouzo (anise-flavoured aperitif) completes the Greek culinary experience.

Restaurants specializing in shish kebab and gyro include: **Omonia Restaurant**, (Tel. 416-465-2129, 426 Danforth Ave); **Florida Shishkebob House**, (Tel. 416-422-2567, 940 Pape Ave); and **Zorba's Restaurant**, (Tel. 416-406-1212, 681 Danforth Ave). In the last 20 years, **Mr. Greek**, (Tel. 416-461-5470, 568 Danforth Ave), has become one of the largest food chains in Toronto with over 20 restaurants.

While souvlaki is a popular dish, staples in Greek cooking are roast lamb, fish, feta (goat's milk cheese), and olives. Appetizers include taramasalata (pink caviar), warm bean salad, and octopus, while main dishes are moussaka (baked eggplant casserole), gyro (minced lamb eaten with pita bread), and dolmades (vine leaves stuffed with ground meat and rice). Desserts and snacks are often made with filo pastry (strudel dough), and filled with cheese, spinach, or ground nuts and honey (baklava) or custard (galactomboureko). Popular drinks include Greek coffee, mountain sage tea, Metaxa (Greek brandy), ouzo, and retsina (aromatic wine flavoured with pine resin).

For more than 45 years, **Carman's Club**, (Tel. 416-924-8697, 26 Alexander St), owned by Arthur Carman, has been recommended by various magazines and newspapers to be one of the three best restaurants in Downtown Toronto. A typical Carman's feast includes greek olives and garlic bread, salads and steak too good to leave.

Just outside Pape subway station are two of the oldest Greek establishments. **Avra**, (Tel. 416-463-0334, 702 Pape Ave), is usually humming with the Greek language as patrons sip Greek coffee and sample taramasalata, marinated octopus, and galactomboureko. Avra was the first Greek restaurant in the Danforth area, established in 1967. Using Corinthian columns, bas relief friezes, and statues of the three seasons, Tom and Zabeta Dimakopoulos have renovated their restaurant into a neoclassical temple worshipped by food lovers.

New Greek restaurants combine traditional Greek cuisine with upscale city living. **Christina's on the Danforth**, (Tel. 416-463-4418, 492 Danforth Ave), is a chic restaurant where Bay Street conversations can be heard through windows opened onto a small summer patio.

Other restaurants along the Danforth include: **Acropolis Restaurant**, (Tel. 416-465-8175, 708 Danforth Ave); **Athens Restaurant & Tavern**, (Tel. 416-465-4441, 707 Danforth Ave); **Flamingo Restaurant**, (Tel. 416-422-3710, 2104 Danforth Ave); **Nikos Place**, (1419 Danforth Ave., Tel. 416-469-8155); and **Patris Restaurant**, (Tel. 416-466-1967, 888 Danforth Ave).

Other popular restaurants include: the **Elegant Penelope's**, (Tel. 416-947-1159, 6 Front St. E); **Kalyvia Restaurant**, (Tel. 416-463-3333, 420 Danforth Ave); **Avli Restaurant**, (Tel. 416-461-9577, 401 Danforth Ave); **Mezes Restaurant**, (Tel. 416-778-5150, 456 Danforth Ave); **Megas Restaurant**, (Tel. 416-466-7771, 402 Danforth Ave); **Ampeli**, (Tel. 416-465-4001, 526 Danforth Ave); **Caffe Demetre**, (Tel. 416-778-6654, 400 Danforth Ave).

The Friendly Greek Restaurant can be found at numerous locations, including: 551 Danforth Ave (Tel. 416-469-8422), 4695 Yonge St. (Tel. 416-250-7880), and 55 Eglinton Ave. E (Tel. 416-488-5105).

The ingredients to whip up an authentic Greek dinner can be bought at a number of specialty stores, including **Greek House Food Market**, (Tel. 416-469-1466, 565 Danforth Ave); **Mister Greek Meat Market**, (Tel. 416-469-0733, 801 Danforth Ave).

Greek bakeries include: **Athens Pastries**, (Tel. 416-463-5144, 509 Danforth Ave); **Donlands Bakery**, (Tel. 416-421-3010, 1055 Pape Ave); **Elite Bakery**, (Tel. 416-754-7857, 1961 Kennedy Rd); **Menalon Bakery**, (Tel. 416-654-2932, 811 St. Clair Ave. W); and **Stany Greek Bakery**, (Tel. 416-423-9781, 1015^1/$_2$ Pape Ave).

The Parthenon Jewelry and Gift Shop, (Tel. 416-469-2494, 371 Danforth Ave), was the first Greek jewelry store in Toronto. Hand-made wall plaques from Greece trimmed in 24 carat gold, alabaster and copper statues, worry beads, crystal, Grecian vases, urns, incense burners, and coffee grinders are among the items sold by the Papadopoulos family. The back room caters to the Greek Orthodox clientele, selling wedding articles, candles for baptisms, and traditional table-cloths; **The Platon Book Store**, (Tel. 416-469-2593, 781 Danforth Ave), sells Greek magazines and newspapers.

The sounds of Greece can be heard on the street from **Greek City Video**, (Tel. 416-461-6244, www.greekcity.com, 452 Danforth Ave), the only Canadian distributors for Greek records, tapes, compact discs, and videos. Owners Peter Koutroumpis, Vicki Scholas, Freda Koutroumpis, and Anna Ivans stock the gamut of Greek music from traditional to contemporary. They carry releases from George Dalaras (the number one Greek recording artist), and the mellow, romantic sounds of John Parios and Haris Alexiou. Traditional folk songs have been recorded by the Trio Bel Canto and Nana Mouskouri.

Religious Centres, Schools and Other Institutions

The large white buildings, gilded domed roofs, and rounded crosses seen over the neighbourhoods of east Toronto are the most visible signs of their Greek residents. Every so often, the black robes and headpieces of a Greek Orthodox priest can be spotted in the shopping malls around Thorncliffe Park or in one of the Greek cafes.

The Orthodox Church is one of the most important links among Greek Canadians, since recognition by the Church community is the first step towards social advancement. Common faith also makes Greeks of the diaspora realize and maintain their national identity and heritage.

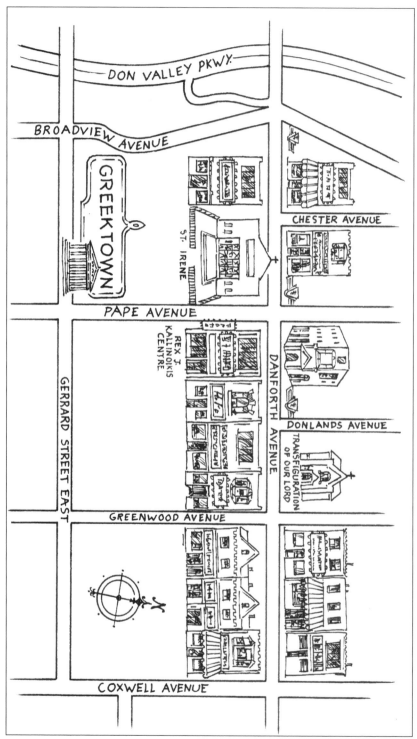

The role and contribution of the church to Greek immigrants has been very significant, becoming the link that connected them spiritually and mentally to the faith of their ancestors, traditions, and homeland. In 1996, the **Greek Orthodox Diocese of Canada** was elevated to Metropolis. His Emm. Archbishop-Metropolitan of Toronto Canada Sotirios Athanasoulias remains the head of the Church.

◆ THE GREEK ORTHODOX METROPOLIS OF CANADA, (1 Bartholomew Way), is the residence of the Archbishop.

◆ GREEK ORTHODOX ANNUNCIATION OF VIRGIN MARY, (Tel. 416-537-2665, 136 Sorauren Ave), the second oldest Greek church, is located in Parkdale, an early Greek settlement area.

◆ ST. GEORGE'S GREEK ORTHODOX, (Tel. 416-977-3342, 115 Bond St), the oldest church, was originally the Holy Blossom Temple. The church contains a mosaic of St. George and the dragon, and many of the icons on the walls were created by Greek monks.

In the Danforth area, there are several churches:

◆ ST. IRENE CHRISOVALANTOU GREEK ORTHODOX CHURCH, (Tel. 416-465-8213, 66 Gough Ave).

◆ ST. ANARGYROI GREEK ORTHODOX CHURCH, (Tel. 416-463-9664, 281 Jones Ave).

◆ ST. RAPHAEL GREEK ORTHODOX CHURCH, (Tel. 416-425-2232, 230 Glebemount Ave).

◆ THE TRANSFIGURATION OF OUR LORD GREEK ORTHODOX CHURCH, (Tel. 416-465-2345, 40 Donlands Ave).

◆ ALL SAINTS GREEK ORTHODOX CHURCH, (Tel. 416-221-4611, 3125 Bayview Ave).

◆ GREEK ORTHODOX CHURCH OF HOLY TRINITY, (Tel. 416-537-1351, 54 Clinton St).

◆ GREEK ORTHODOX CHURCH OF ST. CONSTANTINE & HELEN, (Tel. 416-241-2470, 1 Brookhaven Dr).

◆ GREEK ORTHODOX COMMUNITY OF MISSISSAUGA DISTRICT PROPHET ELIAS, (Tel. 905-238-5943, 1785 Matheson Blvd. E., Mississauga).

◆ HOLY NAME CHURCH, (Tel. 416-466-8281, 71 Gough Ave).

◆ ST. DEMETRIOS GREEK ORTHODOX CHURCH, (Tel. 416-425-2485, 30 Thorncliffe Park Dr).

◆ ST. JOHN'S GREEK ORTHODOX CHURCH, (Tel. 416-759-9259, 1385 Warden Ave).

◆ ST. NICHOLAS, (Tel. 416-291-4367, 3840 Finch Ave. E). The walls and ceilings of the church are covered in Byzantine-style icons. They were painted by Father Theodore Koufas, known as the "Michelangelo of Toronto" for his artistry and diligence in painting the entire church, a task that took more than four years to complete.

◆ THE GREEK ORTHODOX CHURCH OF ST. NEKTARIOS, (Tel. 416-537-7283, 1223 Dovercourt Rd), is not a Diocesan church and still follows the Julian calendar for all religious holidays.

◆ HELLENIC HOME FOR THE AGED, (Tel. 416-654-7700, www.hellenichome.org, 33 Winona Dr). The complex contains a seven-storey seniors' apartment, a recreational centre for arts and crafts, a cafeteria, and a lounge for watching Greek-language movies. In 2002, they opened a new long-term care facility.

The community's financial institutions include:

◆ BANK OF CYPRUS, REPRESENTATIVE OFFICE, (Tel. 416-461-5570, 658 Danforth Ave., Suite 302). Contact: Dimitri Maras.

◆ POPULAR BANK OF CYPRUS, REPRESENTATIVE OFFICE, (Tel. 416-466-8180, 484 Danforth Ave).

◆ THE NATIONAL BANK OF GREECE, (Tel. 416-461-7541, 661 Danforth Ave, and Tel. 416-751-6500, 2290 Lawrence Ave. E).

◆ GREEK ORTHODOX EDUCATION, (Tel. 416-463-7222, 30 Scarsdale Rd).

Members of Toronto's Greek community worship at the new St Pandelaimon Greek Orthodox church in Markham (Toronto)

Holidays and Celebrations

◆ NEW YEAR'S. The Greek Orthodox ring in the new year on January 1 with St. Basil's Day. At family celebrations, good luck is in store for the recipient of a gold coin found in the vasilopeta (New Year's bread).

◆ INDEPENDENCE PARADE. On the Sunday nearest March 25, children in national costumes, marching bands, and horsemen participate in a huge parade down Danforth Avenue. Store owners raise the Greek flag, and spectators wave blue and white banners. The parade commemorates Greece's independence from the Ottoman Empire in 1821 and coincides with the Feast of the Annunciation of the Virgin Mary. Both occasions are marked by church services, parades, speeches, and cultural programs.

◆ EASTER. Some of Toronto's residents may have witnessed an Easter candlelight procession at midnight around one of the many Greek Orthodox churches. Easter is the most important religious festival for the Greek Orthodox Church. After the midnight service, traditional Greek dishes and wine (retsina) are served with Easter eggs dyed red to symbolize love, the blood of Christ, and the renewal of life. Traditional food includes unleavened bread, mageritsa (a soup made of entrails of baby lamb seasoned with spring onions and egg lemon sauce), and baby lamb roasted on a spit. After dinner everyone samples the tsoureki (a sweet bread ring decorated with a red Easter egg).

◆ THE FEAST DAY OF THE HOLY CROSS. September 14, sees the Greek Orthodox community commemorate the finding of the Holy Cross by the Byzantine Empress St. Helena.

◆ OCHI DAY. Greeks wear national costumes in another parade down the Danforth on Ochi Day (Memorial Day), which honours those who lost their lives during the Second World War.

See Holidays and Celebrations in Glossary.

Media

◆ AVRAMIS GREEK TV SHOW, (Tel. 416-481-2941, 28 St. Clements Ave). Rogers Community Channel 10, Sunday 10:00 a.m. to 10:30 a.m.

◆ CHIR FM, (Tel. 416-467-4677, www.chir.com, 301 Donlands Ave., 2nd Floor). Broadcasting online 24 hours a day, 7 days a week. Director: Mike Agathos.

◆ CIRV RADIO INTERNATIONAL, 88.9 FM, (Tel. 416-537-1088, 1087 Dundas St. W). Monday to Friday, 9:00 p.m. to 10:00 p.m., Saturday, 8:00 p.m. to 10:00 p.m. Producer: Paul Marques.

◆ EDO KAI TORA, OMNI TV, (Tel. 416-260-0047, 545 Lakeshore Blvd. W). Sunday, 1:30 p.m. to 2:00 p.m. Producer: Stan Papulkas.

◆ EVODOMADA (THE GREEK-CANADIAN WEEKLY NEWSPAPER), (Tel. 416-461-3519, Fax 416-461-0774, 1009 Pape Ave). Publisher: Bill Sklavos.

- ◆ **GREEK CANADIAN RADIO**, CHCR 92.7 Cable FM, (Tel. 416-465-1112, 437 Danforth Ave., 3rd floor). Seven days a week, 24 hours, with eight newscasts. President and Producer: Peter Maniatakos.
- ◆ **GREEK PRESS** (bi-weekly), (Tel. 416-465-3243, Fax 416-462-3623, 6 Chester Ave). Publisher: Kostas Kranias.
- ◆ **GREEK PRESS PUBLISHERS AND TRANSLATORS**, (Tel. 416-778-7607, Fax 416-778-0811).
- ◆ **HELLENIC CANADIAN CHRONICLES (XPONIKA)**, (Tel. 416-465-4628, 437 Danforth Ave., 3rd floor). A weekly newspaper. Publisher: Peter Maniatakos.
- ◆ **LAMPSIS**, OMNI TV, (Tel. 416-260-0047, 545 Lakeshore Blvd. W). Sunday, 12:00 p.m. to 12:30 p.m.
- ◆ **MUSIKH PARE LASE**, CHEX TV, (Tel. 416-461-4244, 270 Donlands Ave). Saturday, 11:30 a.m. to 12:00 p.m. Contact: Kostas Mike Agathos.
- ◆ **ONTARIO'S GREEK TELEPHONE DIRECTORY & ALMANAC**, (Tel. 416-445-0111, 939 Lawrence Ave. E., P.O. Box 47529, Don Mills).
- ◆ **ODYSSEY TV**, (Tel. 416-462-1200, 437 Danforth Ave., Suite 300). Contact: Peter Maniatakos.
- ◆ **PATRIDES: A CANADIAN REVIEW IN GREEK-ENGLISH**, (Tel. 416-921-4229, P.O. Box 266, Station O). Publisher: Thomas Saras.
- ◆ **THE GREEK JOURNAL**, (Tel. 416-406-2949, 45 Overlea Blvd., P.O. Box 22064). Contact: Nikos Terzis.

Organizations

- ◆ **CANADIAN HELLENIC CONGRESS**, (Tel. (866) 355-4637, www.helleniccongress.com, 1550 Don Mills Rd, Suite 705). President: Crist Geronikolos.
- ◆ **HELLENIC CANADIAN CONGRESS**, (Tel. 416-463-9714, Toronto Office: 846 Pape Ave., 2nd floor), is a nation-wide organization representing Greek communities and Greek organizations across Canada. President: Jim Sidiropoulos.
- ◆ **HELLENIC HERITAGE FOUNDATION**, (Tel. 416-447-7107, www.hhf.ca, 18 Wynford Dr., Suite 503). President: John Dagonas.
- ◆ **PAN-MACEDONIAN ASSOCIATION OF ONTARIO**, (Tel. 416-466-1951; Fax 416-466-7335, 406 Danforth Ave). Founded in 1960, it represents some 60 associations from Macedonia, Greece. President: James G. Karas.
- ◆ **THE GREEK COMMUNITY OF TORONTO**, (Tel. 416-425-2485, 30 Thorncliffe Park Dr). Established in 1911, as an umbrella organization for three of the city's 12 Greek churches. **The Hellenic Cultural**

Centre houses the organization's central offices along with a Greek history and language school, dance, theatre, and music departments. The centre maintains a museum with books, copies of classic sculptures, and the remnants of an authentic Mycaenean-era mosaic. President: Kostas Menegakis.

◆ ALL SAINTS CULTURAL CENTRE, (Tel. 416-221-4611, 3125 Bayview Ave).

◆ ALEXANDER THE GREAT YOUTH CENTRE AND ATHLETIC COMPLEX, (Tel. 416-755-8867, 1385 Warden Ave). All three centres have choirs, dance groups, and soccer teams.

There are many Greek regional clubs which organize their own social and cultural events:

◆ PANARCADIAN FEDERATION OF CANADA, (Tel. 416-778-9471, 450 Danforth Ave).

◆ CRETANS ASSOCIATION OF TORONTO KNOSSOS, (Tel. 416-463-3965, 131 Coxwell Ave).

◆ CYPRIOT COMMUNITY OF TORONTO, (Tel. 416-696-7400, Fax 416-696-9465, 6 Thorncliffe Park Dr). President: Sotirios Nicolaou.

◆ FOLK DANCING GROUP OF THE GREEK COMMUNITY, (Tel. 416-696-4700, 6 Thorncliffe Park Dr).

◆ GREEK CANADIAN SENIOR CITIZEN CLUB, (Tel. 416-465-2020, 864 Pape Ave).

◆ GREEK COMMUNITY OF METROPOLITAN TORONTO INC. SOCIAL SERVICE CENTRE, (Tel. 416-469-1155, 760 Pape Ave). Provides family and individual counselling, information, and orientation, and holds weekly women's group meetings.

◆ GREEK COMMUNITY YOUTH CENTRE (ALEXANDER THE GREAT), (Tel. 416-755-8867, 1385 Warden Ave). President: Costas Varlkosta.

◆ GREEK MUSICIANS ASSOCIATION/ORPHEUS CHOIR OF TORONTO, (Tel. 416-530-4428, 651 Dufferin St). Performs programs of original Greek music. The choir of Orpheus participated in the opening of the 1976 Olympic Games in Montreal.

◆ GREEK ORTHODOX EDUCATION, (Tel. 416-463-7222, 40 Donlands Ave).

◆ GREEK ORTHODOX FAMILY SERVICES AND COUNSELLING, (Tel. 416-462-1740, 40 Donlands Ave). Counselling and referral agency specializing in legal, financial, housing, medical, employment, and education issues. Also offers interpreter services and arranges short-term accommodation.

◆ HELLENIC BENEFIT ASSOCIATION ANTARIKON, (Tel. 416-656-1794, 1774 St. Clair Ave. W).

◆ HELLENIC CANADIAN BOARD OF TRADE, (Tel. 416-410-4228, P.O. Box 801, 31 Adelaide St. E). President: Aristotle Christou.

◆ HELLENIC CANADIAN FEDERATION OF ONTARIO CHARITABLE & EDUCATIONAL FOUNDATION, (Tel. 416-463-9714, 846 Pape Ave., 2nd floor).

Consulates, Trade Commissions and Tourist Bureaus

◆ CONSULATE GENERAL OF GREECE, (Tel. 416-515-0133 and 416-515-0134, 365 Bloor St. E., Suite 1800). Consul General: Mr. Dimitris Azemopoulos.

◆ CONSULATE GENERAL OF CYPRUS, (Tel. 416-944-0998, Fax 416-944-9149, 365 Bloor St. E., Suite 1010). Consul General: Evagdras Vryonides.

◆ GREEK NATIONAL TOURIST ORGANIZATION, (Tel. 416-968-2220, 1300 Bay St). Director for Canada: George Tambakis.

◆ GREEK TRADE OFFICE, (Tel. 416-515-0135, Fax 416-515-0708, 365 Bloor St. E., Suite 1802).

Prominent Torontonians

Mirkopoulis Brothers, entrepreneurs, Cinespace Studios, Toronto contractors; Dr. Peter Fountas, physician, cardiologist; Jim Karygiannis, MP Scarborough—Agincourt; Peter Maniatakos, President and CEO, CHCR-FM Radio and Chronicles newspaper; John Sotos, lawyer; His Emm. Metropolitan Sotirios; George Stroumboulopoulos, TV personality; Mr. Lazarides, Co-Chair RIM; Justice Andromache Karakatsanis, judge of the Court of Appeal for Ontario; Bill Fatsis, Justice of the Peace; Dr. Dimitrios Oreopoulos, Professor of Medicine at the University of Toronto; John Cannis, MP; John Fanaras, Scientist; Thomas S Saras, President and CEO National Ethnic Press and Media Council of Canada; Lou Vavaroutsos, Entrepreneur.

Contributors: Dr. Anastasios Karantonis, physician and former President of the Greek Community; Eugenia Kourakas, educator; Angela Dimou-Kabouris; Maria Saras; Spiros Voutsinas, Nick; Thomas S Saras, President and CEO National Ethnic Press and Media Council of Canada.

The Gujarati Community

The Gujarati Community is independently described for the first time in this edition, having previously been included as part of the East Indian Community. "Gujarati" refers to both the people of the western Indian province of Gujarat and the language that they speak.The majority of Gujaratis follow Hinduism but many parctice Jainism, Zoroastrianism, or Islam. Zoroastrians who migrated from Persia to India are known as Parsi or Parsee. In Toronto, amongst the many who have maintained their cultural traditions, it is common to see a Parsi speaking Gujarati or an Ismaili or Muslim reading a Gujarati magazine.

During the 1940s many Gujaratis dispersed to the East, the Middle East, and Africa in search of a better livelihood. In short order they adapted to their new environments and became well-established, but with the political changes of the 1960s in East Africa many fled, often without their belongings, to England; a few returned to India. Of those who settled in Britain, large numbers later emigrated to Canada or America, and today there are about 60,000 Gujaratis living in the Toronto region.

Many young Gujaratis arrived in Toronto in the 1970s, then called upon their families to join them. In contrast to western individualism, Gujarati culture emphasizes "family" as the basic social unit; family members learn from each other, and values of warmth, sharing, caring for others, and staying together are emphasized. *Dadaji* (grandfather), *Dadima* (grandmother), *Ba* (mother), *Bapuji* (father), and children will live together for long periods. As long as the Dada-Dadi and Ba-Bapuji are alive their sons will live together, even with their own children; unmarried daughters also share the household.

The second generation of Gujaratis are experiencing a cultural shift as they become more assimilated to Canadian culture, moving away from arranged marriages and striking out on their own, away from the traditional family unit. But there remains a desire to maintain connections with long-standing tradition, and many return to India for short periods to work or provide aid.

Adventurous entrepreneurs, many Gujaratis keep an eye toward lucrative business opportunities. Initially, many took jobs as engineers, teachers, accountants, and medical doctors; later, others worked in import-export, wholesale and retail, local trade, IT, real estate, marketing, finance, and motels. Principles of non-violence and, by extension, vegetarianism have kept most Gujaratis out of the meat and wine industries, heavy duty manual labour, and the armed forces. Few work in government service or for the police, firefighting, or transport, and while they hold an appreciation for art, they tend to avoid careers in painting, dance, drama, music, and other cultural fields.

Gujaratis have not tended to live together near places of worship, as many other ethnic communities do, and as a result they are spread widely throughout the Greater Toronto Area.

Places to Go

Gujarati shops and restaurants are scattered throughout Toronto, but many can be found at the India Bazaars on Gerrard Street and in the Islington area. Clothing, jewelry, groceries, spice, paan (a palate cleanser and breath freshener), and other things can be purchased at Gujarati shops, which include: **Lodhia Jewellers**, 170 The Donway West, Tel. 416-441-2856; **Mayur Dave Gems**, 21 Dundas Square #909, Tel. 416-363-6831; and **Aprile Florist**, 2883 Keele St., Tel. 416-635-5759 or (800) 968-8695. DVDs, videos, and casettes can be found at **Mr Joshee Video**, 470 McNicoll Ave., tel 416-502-0022. **The State Bank of India**, 200 Bay St., Suite 1600, Tel. 416-865-0414 (with other branches at 3471 Sheppard Ave. E., Tel. 416-754-0039; 1450 Meyerside Dr., Suite 100, Mississauga, Tel. 905-565-8959; and 248 Queen St. E., Brampton, Tel. 905-874-7186), **ICICI Bank** (with multiple branches in the Greater Toronto Area), and the **Tourist Bureau of the Government of India**, 60 Bloor St. W., Suite 1003, Tel. 416-962-3787, serve Gujaratis and others.

Several Gujarati community groups have come together to form the **Sanatan Mandir Cultural Centre**, 9333 Woodbine Ave., Markham, Tel. 905-887-7777; and the **Hindu Mandir & Cultural Centre**, 6875 Professional Ct., Mississauga, Tel. 905-678-1166. Originally envisioned as full-service community cultural complexes, as constructed each centers on a religious temple.

Gujaratis' hospitality is well-known and food is one of their specialties. Any of their events can be successful with a good dinner and even the best of programmes is incomplete without good food. Favorite meals include *thali* for lunch or dinner with *rotli* or *puri*, *undhiyu*, *dal* (lentil soup), or *kadhi*, *patra* or *dhoka*, and sweet items like *srikhand*, *basundi*, or mango pulp; also rice, pickles, *chhas* (buttermilk) and *papad*. Gujarati fare can be found at **Gujarat Durbar**, 1368 Gerrard St. E., Tel. 416-798-4449; **Kala's Kitchen**, 5359 Timberlea Blvd., Mississauga, Tel. 905-602-9594; and **Bhakta Foods**, 3001 Islington Ave., Tel. 416-743-4682. Other restaurants, which also provide catering, include: **White Gold Sweets**, 3176 Ridgeway Dr., Mississauga, Tel. 905-607-6776; and **Amish Sweets & Catering**, 287 Glidden Rd., Unit 14, Brampton, Tel. 905-457-8333. Groceries can be purchased in the west at **Brampton Cash & Carry**, 158 Kennedy Rd. S., Brampton, Tel. 905-796-1104; and in the east at **Indian Groceries and Spices**, 1983 Lawrence Ave. E., Tel. 416-752-7157. Wholesale goods can be found at **Surti Sweet Mart**, 26 Carnforth Rd., Tel. 416-752-3366; and **Trupti Enterprises**, 2 Thorncliffe Park Dr., Unit 40, Tel. 416-421-0191.

Religious Centres, Schools and Other Institutions

The Gujarati community celebrates at temples and other places of worship:

◆ SANATAN MANDIR & CULTURAL CENTRE, 9333 Woodbine Ave., Markham, L6C 1T5, Tel. 905-887-7777, www.sanatanmandir.com. Hindu-Jain Temple with a large hall and dining facility.

◆ JAIN SOCIETY OF TORONTO, 48 Rosemeade Ave., M8Y 3A5, Tel. 416-251-8112, jsot.netfirms.com. Jain centre with temple, lecture hall, and dining facility.

◆ SHRI SWAMINARAYAN MANDIR (BAPS), 61 Claireville Dr., Toronto, M9W 5Z7, 416-798-2277. *Haveli* with many facilities including a large auditorium.

◆ VISHNU MANDIR, 8640 Yonge St., Richmond Hill, L4C 6Z4, Tel. 905-886-1724, www.vishnumandir.com. Temple with Hindu Museum of Civilization and a splendid statue of the great Gujarati, Mahatma Gandhi.

◆ HINDU MANDIR & CULTURAL CENTRE, 6875 Professional Ct., Mississauga, L4V 1Y3, Tel. 905-678-1166. Hindu temple.

◆ PUSTIMARGIYA VAISHNAV SAMAJ, SHREENATHJI HAVELI, 58 Clarke Ave., Thornhill, L3T 1S5, Tel. 905-771-3939.

The Gujarati language is taught by the Board of Education as a heritage language; classes are conducted at the Swaminarayan Haveli. *Pathshala* (religious classes) are taught at the temples, and private classes are held for dance and music. Gujarati books are available at the **Metro Toronto Reference Library**, which provides catalogues, inter-library transfers, and home delivery for seniors.

Holidays and Celebrations

Celebrations and festivals are integral to the Gujarati community. Religious festivals are characterized by excitement, joy, and solemn prayer. Since Hindus, Jains, and Ismailis follow the lunar calendar, their holy days do not fall on the same dates each year.

Gujaratis join other Canadians in celebrating this nation's holidays, such as Canada Day, and other Indians in celebrating occasions like India's Republic Day on January 26 and Independence Day on August 15. Gujarati-speaking Muslims of Pakistani origin celebrate that nation's holidays.

◆ NAVRATI, or "Nine Nights", is a Hindu festival special to Gujaratis. Although a religious celebration, Navarti has increasingly focused on modern music, dancing, and entertainment, especially amongst younger Gujaratis. The exuberant celebration features *garba* (rhythmic dancing in a circle) in traditional *chaniya choli* and *sari* costumes, and *raas*, a dance with sticks. Many "introductions" take place during these nine nights, sometimes resulting in marriage.

Many other Hindu, Muslim, and Ismaili festivals and holidays are described in other chapters or in the Glossary of Holidays and Celebrations; important Jain occasions are outlined below. Jain festivals and observances are characterized by renunciation, self-restraint, learning, meditation, forgiveness, repentance, and expressing devotion to the moral values brought to life by the *Tirthankars*.

◆ MAHAVIR JANMA KALYÄNAK, usually in April, commemorates the birthday of the 24th and final *Tirthankar Mahavir* of this era. "Tirthankar" means "spiritual victory", one who has attained omniscience. Vardhaman was the last of these, and took the honorific Mahavir, meaning "Great Hero". On this occasion Jains gather to read the life and mission of Mahavir and listen to his teachings.

◆ PARYUSHAN PARVA, falling during the months of August and/or September, is the most important eight-day festival of Jains. During these days Jains fast and carry out religious activities. It is a period of repentance for acts done during the year, and austerities to help shed the accumulated *karmas*. On the eighth day, known as *Samvatsari*, Jains ask for forgiveness from family, friends, and foes alike for any harmful act they might have committed during the previous year. They in turn forgive others, and the next day all who have observed fasts are honoured.

Other festival days observed include **Guru Purnima** (day of reverence for *Guru*, or teacher), **Gnan Panchami** (day of obtaining knowledge), **Dev Diwali** (day of prayer), and **Maun Agiyaras** (day of fasting with a vow of silence).

See Holidays and Celebrations in Glossary.

Media

◆ GUJARAT ABROAD, Tel. 905-265-0984, www.gujaratabroad.ca. Weekly newspaper. Editor and publisher: Vipul Jani.
◆ SWADESH, 713 Markham Rd., M1H 2A8, Tel. 416-996-7755 or 416-273-7075, www.swadeshmedia.com. Fortnightly newspaper.
◆ GUJARAT EXPRESS, Tel. 905-457-2498, www.gujaratexpress.ca. Weekly newspaper.
◆ VATAN NEWS, 695 Markham Rd., Suite 33, M1H 2A5, Tel. 416-486-0374.
◆ ATN, www.asiantelevision.com. While there are no local television broadcasts and very limited radio programming available in Gujarati, the Asian Television Network provides programming from India's Zee TV through Rogers digital cable, bringing news, entertainment, music, and religious programming.

Organizations

◆ FEDERATION OF GUJARATI ORGANIZATIONS. There are about fifty Gujarati associations and organizations in Toronto, from small to large, and many are linked with the Federation of Gjuarati Organizations (FOGA). Some groups are caste-based, like the Lohana Cultural Association, Vanik Samaj, Brahman Society, and Oswals; others center around locations, including the 24-Gam Patidar Samaj (Patidars of 24 Villages), 24-Gam Patel Association, or the Surti Samaj (People of the city of Surat). FOGA organizes annual *raas* and *garba* (folk dance) competions, and its many affiliated groups arrange annual picnics, sporting events, entertainment programs, conferences and conventions, and festive events. They also raise funds and provide aid in the event of natural calamities, and invite dance and drama troupes from India.
◆ GUJARATI SENIORS' SAMAJ OF MISSISSAUGA, is one of the few active Gujarati seniors' associations.
◆ YOUNG GUJARATI HORIZON, is a youth organization.

- ◆ **YOUNG GUJARATI NETWORK**, Tel. 905-457-3649, is another group for young Gujaratis. Founder: Danny Mistry.
- ◆ **VISHWA GUJARATI SAMAJ**, www.vishwagujaratisamaj.org, based in Ahmedaba, Gujarat, and with the backing of the government of Gujarat, is a worldwide organization that links Gujaratis across the globe. The Canadian chapter is based in Toronto.
- ◆ **SHABDA SETU**, Tel. 905-770-8298, meaning "a bridge of words," is a Canadian Gujarati literary group.

Prominent Torontonians

Jay Gajjar, businessman, writer, former professor, recipient of the Order of Canada; Keshave Chandaria, President of Comcraft Group, recipient of the Order of Ontario; Dr. Chandrakant Shah, educator, author of medical textbook, recipient of the Order of Ontario; Rohinton Mistry, internationally famous author and winner of Giller Prize; M. G. Vassanji, best-selling author, twice winner of the Giller Prize, Member of the Order of Canada; Navin Chandaria, President and CEO of Conross Group, recipient of Canada's Confederation Medal; Ramesh Chotal, businessman; Mac Champsee, real estate broker; Lata Champss, community leader.

Principal Contributor: Prakash Mody.

The Hungarian Community

The area known as "Little Budapest" can be found in two sections of Toronto: along Bloor Street West, between Spadina and Bathurst streets, where Hungarian restaurants serve goulash and shops carry traditional sausages and pastries; and on St. Clair Avenue West, centring around the **Hungarian Canadian Cultural Centre**, the largest Hungarian community centre outside of Hungary.

Many of Metro Toronto's 50,000 Hungarians have emigrated from Hungary or neighbouring countries such as Czechoslovakia, Romania, or Yugoslavia from areas that were part of Hungary for a thousand years, until the Trianon Treaty of Versailles, in 1920. The earliest Hungarians to arrive in Canada in the 1880s were drawn to the prairies by the promise of free land. By the early 1900s, there were Hungarian groups in Welland, Hamilton, Windsor, Brantford, and the Niagara region. Many who settled in the Delhi district of southern Ontario became successful tobacco farmers.

More Hungarians came to Canada as a result of the quota system imposed in the United States in the early decades of this century. New settlers included skilled tradesmen, butchers, carpenters, shoemakers, and blacksmiths. By the 1920s, the Hungarian community was large enough to organize itself into Roman Catholic and Presbyterian denominations. Toronto's Hungarian neighbourhood in the 1930s was bordered by Queen Street West, College Street, Spadina Avenue, and McCaul Street, and consisted of boarding houses, grocery stores, steamship and travel companies, and social clubs.

In the 1940s, a Hungarian neighbourhood developed in the area of Bedford Road and Bloor Street. The **Toronto Independent United Hungarian Society** bought a house at 245 College Street to serve as a cultural centre and welcome home. In 1974, a larger building was purchased at St. Clair Avenue West, which today houses the **Hungarian Canadian Cultural Centre**.

Hungarians arrived in Canada in large numbers following the Second World War. They consisted of emigrés who left Hungary for political reasons. Many were professionals—lawyers, doctors, engineers, military officers, embassy staff, journalists, and writers. These newcomers organized many of the first Hungarian cultural groups. Among the most popular were dramatic troupes who wore traditional costumes and used props typical of the Hungarian theatre. First started by settlers who arrived prior to the Second World War, the troupes were continued by the emigrés, who placed emphasis on passing on the culture and traditions of the homeland to their children.

The first troop of the **Hungarian Scouts Association** was founded in 1952 in Toronto. At present, there are six troops in the province, and three are located in Toronto. There are language schools in many churches as well as the **Arany Janos Hungarian School** in the **Hungarian Canadian Cultural Centre**, which promotes the education of Hungarian Canadian youth and adults. Following the 1956 revolution in Hungary, approximately 41,000 Hungarians immigrated to Canada; most were young, single, and had received their education from universities or technical schools. The newcomers founded new theatre companies, folkdance groups, and choirs.

Toronto is the centre of Hungarian publishing activity in Canada. The **Vörösváry-Weller Publishing Co.** (Stephen Vörösváry-Weller) published biographies, the Memoirs of Admiral Horthy, Regent of Hungary and The Memoirs of Cardinal Mindszenty, as well as countless fine literature works of Hungarian emigrè-authors like Sándor Márai and Ferenc Fáy. In 1978, a chair of Hungarian Studies was established at the **University of Toronto**. The former **Central Hospital** on Sherbourne Street was founded by two Hungarian doctors, Janos and Paul Rekai, who saw the need for a hospital serving those who speak little English. In the arts, Toronto sculptor Dora Pedery Hunt introduced medal sculpture to Canada and her design was used for the Canadian Olympic gold coin in 1976.

Places to Go

In 1966, to commemorate the tenth anniversary of the Hungarian Uprising and to express the gratitude of Hungarians to Canada, a steel sculptural fountain by Victor Tolgesy, inscribed with the words "Freedom for Hungary—Freedom for All," was erected in **Wells Hill Park** at the foot of Sunnyside. The site was renamed **Budapest Park** at the time of its dedication, and every year memorial services are held on the weekend nearest October 23rd.

The **Hungarian Canadian Cultural Centre**, (Tel. 416-654-4926, 840 St. Clair Ave. W), houses many activities. The **World Federation of Hungarian Veterans** maintains a museum of Hungarian military history containing hundreds of artifacts; along with a Hungarian Gendarmerie section, it features uniforms, weapons, documents, and insignia. The centre features weekly movies and also houses the Dr. Halasz Janos library collection of more than 24,000 books. A huge chandelier in the shape of the Hungarian Holy crown hangs over an enormous dance hall, and paintings hanging on the walls were completed by Toronto artist Lajos Kay. Reproductions of paintings by the Hungarian masters, including Szonyi Istvan (1894–1960) and Meszoly Geza (1844–1887), are also kept in the centre.

Hearty Hungarian cuisine includes soups and stews such as gulyas or goulash (traditionally cooked in a kettle and made with beef, veal, or pork, potatoes and onions) and tokany (pork and beef seasoned with paprika). Accompanying most meals are nokedli (noodle dumplings), goulash gravy, sour cream sauces, onions, and tomatoes. Popular dishes are lecsos kolbasz (stew with garlic sausages, onions, green peppers, tomato, and paprika), stuffed peppers, stuffed cabbage, and roast duck. The fatanyeros or wooden platter (mixed grill of breaded pork and sausages, served with pickled cabbage, cucumbers, and potato salad) dates from when the dish was prepared on a tree stump. Paprika flavours many dishes, such as chicken, veal, or chicken livers. Desserts are palacsinta (crepes filled with jam and sprinkled with ground walnuts), rigo Jancsi (chocolate-cream cake), poppyseed strudel, sacher torte (apricot jam between chocolate layers), and linzer (a tart filled with jam). Egribikaver (Bull's Blood of Eger) is the famous Hungarian red wine and Tokaji Aszu (Tokay) is a favourite sweet dessert wine.

The original "Little Budapest" in the Bloor-Spadina annex remains an area where you can hop from one restaurant or deli to another to enjoy authentic Hungarian foods. **Country Style Hungarian Restaurant**, (Tel. 416-536-5966, 450 Bloor St. W), owned by Judit Goda, is a homey restaurant popular with university students. The menu features daily specials that are typical of a dinner served in Budapest, including chicken soup with liver dumplings, ragout, fresh rye bread, beef with onions, lecso with sausages, hunter's stew, creamed lentils, chicken paprika, and Ujhazi chicken soup. The choices of schnitzels include wiener, parisien, natur, and Gypsy steak. Noodles Hungarian-style come with cottage cheese, and for dessert, poppyseed and ground walnuts, homemade strudel, and Hungarian-style crepes with cottage cheese or apricot are available.

Pannonia Hungarian Bookstore, (Tel. 416-966-5156, www.pannonia.ca, 300 St. Clair Ave. W), sells Hungarian novels, history books, dictionaries, encyclopedias, magazines, and records.

Other restaurants serving Hungarian foods include: **Gypsy Hungarian Restaurant**, (109 McCaul St); **European Sausage House**, (Tel. 416-663-8323, 145 Norfinch Dr); **Tuske Delicatessen**, (Tel. 416-588-8014, 586 Bloor St. W); **Paprika Restaurant**, (Tel. 416-789-3478, 3450 Bathurst St).

The **Coffee Mill**, (Tel. 416-920-2108, 99 Yorkville Ave), offers home-made soups, open-faced sandwiches, salads, hot entrees, and a variety of coffees, teas, and pastries. It also has a gourmet take-out counter. **Hungarian Honey Bear Delicatessen**, (Tel. 416-733-0022, 249 Sheppard Ave. E), carries Hungarian lekvar (jam), coffee, candies, herbal remedies, and beauty supplies.

Religious Centres, Schools and Other Institutions

The Hungarian community includes Roman Catholic, Greek Catholic, Presbyterian, United, Anglican, Lutheran, and Baptist congregations.

◆ ST. ELIZABETH OF HUNGARY ROMAN CATHOLIC CHURCH, (Tel. 416-225-3300, 432 Sheppard Ave. E). Established in 1928. It was originally located on Spadina Avenue; the church moved to its present location in 1985. It was the refugee reception centre for those fleeing Hungary during the 1956 Uprising. Many organizations are active at the church, including **The Hungarian Friends Circle**, a weekend language school, choir and scout troops, and the **St. Elizabeth Hungarian school**. In 1978, a Hungarian Jesuit noviciate—the only institution of its kind in the Hungarian diaspora—was established in Toronto.

◆ FIRST HUNGARIAN BAPTIST CHURCH, (Tel. 416-783-2941, 157 Falkirk St).

◆ FIRST HUNGARIAN PRESBYTERIAN CHURCH, (Tel. 416-656-1342, 439 Vaughan Rd).

◆ HUNGARIAN FULL GOSPEL CHURCH, (Tel. 416-760-9524, 51 Scarlett Rd).

◆ HUNGARIAN LUTHERAN CHURCH, (Tel. 416-977-4786, 116 Bond St).

◆ HUNGARIAN UNITED CHURCH, (Tel. 416-652-3809, 73 Mackay Ave).

Holidays and Celebrations

◆ REVOLUTION DAY. March 15 commemorates the anniversary of the 1848 revolution led by Louis (Lajos) Kossuth. Kossuth attempted to rid Hungary of the Austrian Hapsburg rule. For a short time, Hungary was virtually an independent state which abolished feudalism and established responsible government. Russia, upon request of Austria, invaded Hungary in 1849, ending its independence. The anniversary is commemorated on the nearest weekend to the date with speeches by prominent Hungarians and a cultural program.

◆ ARPAD DAY, usually held in April, honours the Hungarian national hero. The occasion is celebrated with a dinner and dance and recital.

◆ HEROES DAY. The last Sunday in May is known as Heroes Day in remembrance of those killed in the revolutions of 1845 and 1956 and

*Miss Budapest, elected
at the Hungarian
Community Centre.*

the two World Wars. A service is held in most Hungarian churches
and in the **Hungarian Canadian Cultural Centre** by the **World
Federation of Hungarian Veterans**.

◆ ST. STEPHEN'S DAY, August 20, is held in recognition of the King of
Hungary, who in 1001 A.D. embraced western Christianity and
received his crown from Pope Silvester II. St. Stephen is regarded as
the founder of the kingdom of Hungary. It has been celebrated in
Toronto since 1937, with church services, lectures, and cultural
programs.

◆ OCTOBER 6 honours the 13 Hungarian generals who took part in the
revolution of 1848 and were executed at Arad by the Austrians on
October 6, 1849. The day of mourning is commemorated with a
program in memory of the martyred heroes.

◆ THE ANNIVERSARY OF THE HUNGARIAN REVOLUTION, October 23. The
rebellion against Communist rule was quashed on November 4th by
the Soviet army. Thousands of people were killed and 200,000 refugees
left the country. On the weekend nearest to October 23, solemn services are held in memory of those who lost their lives.

See Holidays and Celebrations in Glossary.

Media

◆ INDEPENDANT HUNGARIAN RADIO TORONTO, CIAO 530 AM, (Tel. 416-693-8312, 695 Coxwell Ave., Apt. 601). Saturday, 5:00 to 7:00 p.m. Host: Bede Fazekas Zsolt.

◆ KANADAI/AMERIKAI MAGYARSAG (CANADIAN/AMERICAN HUNGARIANS), (Tel. 416-656-8361, 747 St. Clair Ave. W, Suite 103). Established in 1951, it is the largest Hungarian weekly newspaper outside Hungary. Publisher: Irene Vorosvary.

◆ MAGYAR ELET (HUNGARIAN LIFE), (Tel. 905-472-5704, 390 Concession 7, Pickering). A weekly newspaper published since 1957. Editor: Lazlo Bessenyei.

Organizations

◆ THE HUNGARIAN CANADIAN CULTURAL CENTRE, (Tel. 416-654-4926, www.icomm.ca/magyarhaz, 840 St. Clair Ave. W). Houses the Hungarian Canadian Federation, an umbrella organization for 42 cultural and church groups across Canada. Founded in 1951, its objectives are to represent Hungarian Canadians, assist refugees, and encourage and preserve Hungarian culture and tradition. President: Zoltan Forray; Secretary General: Steve Szabo.

Other clubs at the same address:

◆ HUNGARIAN HELICON SOCIETY AND THE HELICON YOUTH ASSOCIATION were established in 1951 to preserve, explain, and promote the cultural and historical heritage of the Hungarian nation. Lectures, performances, sports, and social events are organized. The highlight of the year's festivities is the Helicon Ball, where young women are introduced to society.

◆ RAKOCZI ASSOCIATION, composed of many former officers in the **Royal Hungarian Army**, operates a historical society, a memorial society, and a foundation to promote scholarships and funding for projects such as a **Heritage Handbook**.

◆ THE HUNGARIAN FREEDOM FIGHTERS ASSOCIATION is made up largely of refugees from the 1956 Hungarian Revolution and promotes the interest of political refugees.

◆ THE HARGITA CIRCLE, which preserves the folk arts of weaving, embroidery, wood burning, and ceramics paintings, was founded by Dr. Kover Janosne. The Kodaly Choir and Dance Group, founded in 1960 by Gyorgy Zaduban, performs traditional Hungarian dances and songs and has made several international tours.

- ◆ THE KODALY DANCE TROUPE, (www.kodaly.ca), founded in 1960.
- ◆ THE KOROSI CSOMA SANDOR HISTORICAL SOCIETY presents lectures from artists, musicians, poets, and writers.
- ◆ UNITED HUNGARIAN FUND, (509 St. Clair Ave. W., P.O. Box 73604). The fundraising arm of the Canadian Hungarian Federation; it promotes Hungarian cultural and educational activities, Hungarian language schools, and emergency fundraising for refugees. President: Gyula Keddy.

Other groups include: the **Bihari Dance Group**; the **Golden Age Club**; **Sports Club**; **Hungarian Veterans' Association**; **Hungarian House Women's Club**; **Hungarian Tradesmen's Circle**; **Hungarian Hunters and Anglers Association**; **Toronto Hungarian Landscapers**; **World Federation of Hungarian Engineers and Architects**; **Canadian Hungarian Authors Association**; The **Upper Hungarian Association**; and the **Royal Hungarian Gendermerie Veterans' Benevolent Association of Toronto**.

Prominent Torontonians

William (Bela) and Susan Aykler, Aykler Real Estate Inc. & Racoczi Foundation; Vera Barcza, Columbus Travel; Leslie Lewis Dan, Order of Canada and Order of Ontario, founded Novopharm; Rozalia Dancs-Telch, Author, Journalist; Frank Felkai Q.C., Solicitor, Rochon Genova LLP.; Dr. Peter Forbath, Cardiologist; Peter Ivanyi, Solicitor; Dr. Dezso Horvath, Order of Canada; George Jonas, Author; Peter Munk, Chairman and founder of Barrick Gold; Kati Rekai, Order of Canada; Fr. Szabolics Sajgo, Sj, Parish priest; Rev Zoltan Vass, Minister of First Hungarian Presbestrian church; Robert D. J. Wappel, LL.B. Solicitor, Wappel Toome Babits Laar & Bell (LLP.); Thomas (Tom) Wappel, Former MP.

Contributors: Mary Bodnar, Jim Torma.

The Icelandic Community

In March, when **Iceland** is still being heated by the island's dramatic hot springs, members of the **Icelandic Canadian Club of Toronto** try to appease the spirit of winter with an invitation to a communal feast called "**Thorrablot**." It takes place in the ancient Norse mid-winter month of Thorri, and is a festival of traditional food, music, and dance held in expectation that neither severe weather nor hardships will occur before spring approaches.

Toronto's Icelandic community, which is estimated at approximately 4,000 persons, consists mainly of second, third, and fourth-generation families whose professions include medicine, law, banking, business, and journalism. Many of the city's Icelanders arrived from Western Canada where their immigrant ancestors had settled more than a century ago.

Icelanders coming by way of Greenland were the first known European visitors to Canada, dating back to 896 A.D. when Eric the Red founded a settlement in Greenland. In the same year, Bjarni Herjolfsson sighted the northeastern coast of Canada. At the turn of the 11th century, Norsemen established a temporary settlement in Newfoundland, and it is believed that Snorri, son of community leader Thorfinnur Karlsefni, was the first European born in Canada.

Following his Norse ancestors, the first Icelander to land on mainland Canadian shores was Sigtryggur Jonasson, who arrived in Quebec in 1872. A year later, 150 Icelanders arrived in Quebec, and a second party of 351 followed in 1874, settling temporarily at Kinmount, Ontario. A monument to these pioneer settlers has been erected. Until the railway was built across the Canadian Shield, immigrants going to Western Canada, including groups of Icelanders, were routed through Toronto and stayed temporarily in the city's immigration sheds. The first permanent block settlement was established with the help of Jonasson along the shores of Lake Winnipeg.

In the 1870s, several families located in the Muskoka district near the village of Rosseau, Ontario. They named their community Hekkla, after a volcano in their island homeland. Descendants of these pioneers still live in the district, as well as throughout Southwestern Ontario.

The **Icelandic National League of North America** was founded in 1919 to promote community links and to assist in integration to Canadian society while recognizing and encouraging an awareness of their heritage. Chapters of this association are located throughout the country. A quarterly journal called *The Icelandic Canadian*, and a weekly newspaper, *Logberg-Heimskringla*, are published in English.

In 1959, the **Icelandic Canadian Club of Toronto** was started by a group of women. The association has a mailing list in excess of 800 households in Southwestern Ontario, and holds several events throughout the year, such as slide shows, lectures, socials, dances, and other cultural presentations relating to their heritage.

Among Toronto Icelanders are teachers, film makers, and novelists. A street is named after entrepreneur and real-estate broker Magnus Paulson, who founded Canada's first satellite city of Bramalea, Ontario. At the **Art Gallery of Ontario**, a room is named after Signy Stephenson Eaton, patron of the arts and wife of the late John David Eaton. Signy Eaton was a founding member of **York University** and a recipient of the **Order of the Falcon**, the highest honour awarded by the government of Iceland.

Places to Go

The **Archives of Ontario**, (Tel. 416-327-1600, www.archives.gov.on.ca, 77 Grenville St), has a research collection of government and private correspondence about early Icelandic immigration to Ontario, as well as publications on the topic.

Seafood specialties from Iceland and other Scandinavian countries can be found at **Viking Foods & Imports Ltd.**, with two locations (Tel. 416-425-7200, 133 Laird Dr, and Tel. 416-696-7011, 19 Industrial St).

Yarn Boutique, (Tel. 416-760-9129, 1719 Bloor St. W). Owner Margaret Haas carries Icelandic Lopi (soft twist) wool, patterns, and knitted items.

Religious Centres, Schools and Other Institutions

Historically, most Icelandic Canadians are associated with either the Lutheran or the Unitarian Church. Throughout the years a partial shift to other denominations has occurred and there are a good number affiliated with the United Church of Canada.

The **University of Toronto** offers courses in Old Norse, a classical language similar to modern Icelandic.

Holidays and Celebrations

◆ THORRABLOT, held in March, sees Icelanders eat a smorgasbord feast which includes traditional foods such as lax (salmon), flatbraud (flatbread), spice-rolled flank of mutton, smoked lamb, and desserts such as vinarterta, ponnukokur, and kleiner.

◆ ISLENDINGADAGURINN. The most important festival is one of the oldest annual ethnic gatherings in Canada. Islendingadagurinn (Icelandic Day) was first held in 1874 in North America by a group of immigrants in Wisconsin to celebrate Iceland's millennium. The biggest Islandingadagurinn is held in Gimli, Manitoba, at the beginning of August; in Ontario it is combined with a celebration of Iceland's Independence Day on June 17th and usually takes the form of a picnic at a farm outside Toronto.

See Holidays and Celebrations in Glossary.

Organizations

◆ THE ICELANDIC CANADIAN CLUB OF TORONTO (ICCT). Publishes a newsletter, organizes an annual dinner dance and picnic, and holds meetings at the **Unitarian Hall** on St. Clair Ave. It organizes six programs a year, featuring lectures, recitals, slide shows, and cultural presentations. In conjunction with the **Icelandic National League**, the ICCT sponsored a provincial historic site honoring immigration in 1874 from Iceland to Kinmount. The August 2000 unveiling of the monument was covered by **TV Ontario** and local newspapers. In addition, the club promotes the works of Canadian writers of Icelandic descent. It produced a millennial publication, *The Icelanders of Kinmount*, (Tel. 905-277-5298), which is available through the club. President: Leah Salt.

Memorial at Kinmount, Ont.
Sculptor: Gudrun S. Girgis
2000 Ontario Heritage
Foundation Historic Site

Icelandic settlement memorial at Kinmount, Ont., commemorating the 1874–1875 Icelandic settlement there.

Consulates, Trade Commissions and Tourist Bureaus

◆ CONSULATE GENERAL OF ICELAND, (Tel. 416-979-2211, 250 Yonge St., Suite 2400). Honorary Consul: Mr. Jon Ragnar Johnson.

Prominent Torontonians

Maja Ardal, actress, director, playwright, and former Artistic Director of the Young People's Theatre in Toronto; Dan Bjarnason, television journalist; Leslie Cochrane, artist; Tom Cochrane, Juno Award winner, rock singer-composer; Sturla Gunnarsson, award winning film producer-director (*Such a Long Journey* among others); Lorna Jackson, broadcaster; Linda Lundstrom, award-winning clothing designer and manufacturer; Helga Stephenson, Chair of Viacom Canada (former Executive Director of Toronto's Festival of Festivals); Betty Jane Wylie, author, journalist, playwright, and recipient of the Order of Canada; Don Johnson, Recipient of the Order of Canada; Oskar Sigvaldason, Chairman of the Energy Council of Canada and a Director, representing Acres International.

Contributors: Donald E. Gislason, researcher and author of articles about immigration from Iceland to Canada, former President of the Icelandic Canadian Club of Toronto; Magnus Paulson, commercial real-estate broker and founding member of Scandinavian Business Club; the late Rosa Hermansson Vernon, founding member of the Icelandic Canadian Club of Toronto and CBC radio concert soprano; Gail Einarson-McCleery, Past President, ICCT, Chair, Millennium Committee, and former Honorary Consul of Iceland in Toronto.

The Indo-Canadian Communities

In Shanti Uddyaan (Peace Park) on Yonge Street at Highway 7, a larger-than-life size statue of Mahatma Gandhi has been erected by Indo-Canadian communities as a gesture of thanks to Canada—the land of opportunities—for providing a peaceful new homeland. The monument is symbolic of the commitment of diverse cultural groups that make up Toronto's Indo-Canadian community, towards promoting peace and harmony. Gandhi, an enlightened soul wedded to truth and non-violence, liberated India from foreign rule through "Satyagraha" meaning peaceful civil disobedience. He identified himself with the people of India and more specifically with the poorest of the poor and the down trodden. India, before its independence on 15 August, 1947, was made up of 560 separate princely states. Today, there are a total of 25 states (provinces) in India, organised mainly on different cultural and linguistic considerations. The Toronto Indo-Canadian community includes Hindus, Muslims, Sikhs, Christians, Jains, Buddhists and Zoroastrians (Parsis), representing every nook and corner of India. Many of them came to Canada from Africa, the Carribeans or other parts of the world where their forefathers had migrated as bonded labour from India many generations ago. In fact, the first Indo-Canadians came to British Columbia from Punjab as early as 1897.

Of the 350,000 people of Indo-Canadian origin living in Ontario, approximately 100,000 are Hindus who reside mainly in Toronto. Immigration to Canada began as early as the mid-19th century, but it wasn't until the late 1960s that Indo-Canadian communities began to form in Ontario. Many of the early settlers came indirectly from either the United States or Britain, and were from India's professional class. Indo-Canadian entrepreneurs continue to operate in trade-oriented business, such as electronics, carpets, clothing, auto mechanics, travel, restaurants, and real estate.

From 1970 to 1975, a large influx of Sri Lankans came to Canada, settling in Toronto, Ottawa, and Montreal. The community is made up of many ethnic groups: Sinhalese, Tamils, Moors, Malays, Burghers (mixed European, Sinhalese and Tamil) and others. Members speak three languages: Sinhala, Tamil, and English, and follow one of four religions: Buddhism, Hinduism, Christianity, or Islam. The Buddhist Temple on

Kingston Road has served as the major religious centre and often acts as a community centre, also attracting non-Buddhist members to its events. A prominent Sri Lankan Torontonian is poet, novelist and film maker Michael Ondaatje, who has won Governor General awards for two books of poetry and his novel *The English Patient*.

Since the Second World War, the Ontario Zoroastrian community has grown to 350 families, making it the largest settlement in Canada. The Parsis (Parsees) or Zoroastrians migrated to India from Iran in the seventh century A.D. Members of the community are highly educated, devout, and volunteer many hours of their time to charities. In the 1960s, the Zoroastrian Society of Ontario purchased the former Bayview Avenue estate of writer Mazo de la Roche, and later established a prayer hall. Cultural and religious events include evenings of food and prayer called ghambar, and the navjot, a coming-of-age ceremony which is held before children reach their 11th year. Rohinton Mistry portrays this community, in Bombay and in Toronto, in his novels and stories, including *Such a Long Journey* which won the Governor General's Award for Fiction.

Jainism is one of the world's oldest surviving faiths. There are about five hundred Jain families living in Toronto. Another well-known community is Gujarati, one of India's prominent well-to-do and well-educated communities. Their community in Toronto is described in greater detail in a separate chapter.

Torontonians can observe classical Indian dance at various festivals that take place during the year. One of the most colourful Indian celebrations is Diwali, the Hindu festival of lights that takes place in autumn. Families and friends gather together to light lamps in honour of the goddess of strength, wealth, and prosperity.

Places to Go

A concentration of Indo-Canadian shops and restaurants are found in three commercial centers of Metro Toronto: Gerrard Street **Indian Bazaar**; Donlands Avenue **Indian Shopping Centre** in East York; and shopping areas in Malton and Brampton.

Along Gerrard Street, east of Greenwood Avenue, there are more than 40 stores and restaurants carrying spices, sarees, and East Indian cuisine. The neighbourhood formed around the Gerrard Street Theatre, which showed Asian films. Today, the **Indian Centre**, (1430 Gerrard St), has replaced the theatre; it features clothing shops, restaurants, and fast food outlets.

Toronto's Indian chefs use spices such as cardamom, turmeric, and hot chilies to create aromatic dishes. Rice is the staple, and Indian breads include nan (white flour bread) and puri (deep-fried puffy bread). Popular dishes are curried meat, chicken, vegetables, and fish. Specialties include bhelpuri (puffed rice, flour, potatoes, and onions in chutney); biriyanis (lamb, beef or chicken cooked with whole spices covered in rice and garnished with fruits and nuts); samosa (deep-fried turnover stuffed with spiced ground meat); pork vindaloo (hot curry made with vinegar base); and northern Indian tandoori meat dishes (baked in a clay oven and marinated in yogurt and spices). Popular sweets are carrot halwa (confection made from condensed milk and grated carrots), burfi, and Ras Malai (Bengal milk dessert).

Restaurants in other areas include **Brar Sweets Restaurant**, (Tel. 905-848-3933, 755 Dundas St. W, Mississauga). An excellent pure vegetarian Indian-Punjabi buffet. The owners, Pabla Brothers, specialize in high protein vegetarian cuisine, without a trace of animal products. Brar Sweets is always full of people. Other restaurants are **Mahar Restaurant**, (Tel. 416-466-6241, 1410 Gerrard St. E); and **Moti Mahal Restaurant Ltd.**, (Tel. 416-461-3111, 1422 Gerrard St. E).

The **Bombay Palace**, (Tel. 416-368-8048, 71 Jarvis St), is part of a worldwide chain with restaurants in New York, Montreal, and San Francisco. Bamboo sculptures decorate the restaurant and East Indian cuisine includes chicken tikka, tandoori prawns, seekh kabab (minced or ground lamb mixed with spices and cooked over charcoal), pasanda, lamb curry, pulao, nan, and chutney pickles. A daily luncheon buffet features 21 hot and cold dishes. **Swagat Restaurant**, (Tel. 905-475-5870, 415 Hood Rd), serves Tandoori and other traditional dishes from India. Both vegetarian and non vegetarian, including mixed vegetable curry and murg saag (chicken with spinach). **Annapurna**, (Tel. 416-537-8513, 1085 Bathurst St), serves vegetarian cuisine with East Indian spices in a room decorated with cards carrying words of wisdom in dedication to the philosophy of Sri Chimnoy. **Sangam Banquet Hall**, (Tel. 905-821-9688, 6991 Millcreek Dr., Mississauga);

Religious Centres, Schools and Other Institutions

The Indo-Canadian community represents practically all religions of India, including Hinduism, Islam, Christianity, Sikhism, Jainism, Buddhism, and Zoroastrianism. Of the city's numerous temples and churches, the main centres of worship are:

- HINDU PRARTHANA SAMAJ, (Tel. 416-536-9229, 62 Fern Ave).
- ISKCON/HARE KRISHNA TEMPLE, (Tel. 416-922-5415, 243 Avenue Rd)
- HINDU TEMPLE SOCIETY OF CANADA, (Tel. 905-568-1536, 4950 Albina Way, Unit 1404, Mississauga).
- JAI DURGA HINDU SOCIETY, (Tel. 416-297-1146, 37 Unita Grove).
- JAIN SOCIETY OF TORONTO, (Tel. 416-251-8112, 48 Rosemeade Ave). In July 1983, a formal temple was established at 247 Parklawn Road in the southwest section of Toronto. The **Jain Society**'s current location is used as a temple and hall for festivals and meetings. The **Sanatan Mandir**'s new facilities will make it easier for people from Northeast Toronto attend regular visitation (darshan) and prayers.
- HINDU SABHA, (Tel. 905-794-4638, 9225 The Gore Rd., Bramalea).
- VEDIC ARYAN MANDIR (TEMPLE) AND CULTURAL CENTRE, (Tel. 905-475-5778, 4345 14th Ave., Markham).
- ARYA SAMAJ, TORONTO, (Tel. 905-475-5778, 4345 14th Ave., Markham).
- TORONTO BUDDHIST CHURCH, (Tel. 416-534-4302, 918 Bathurst St).
- ZOROASTRIAN TEMPLE, (Tel. 416-733-4586, 3590 Bayview Ave).
- BUDDHIST TEMPLE, (3595 Kingston Rd).
- STATE BANK OF INDIA (CANADA), (Tel. 416-865-0414, Royal Bank Plaza, North Tower, 200 Bay St., Suite 1600), is the community's financial institution.

Holidays and Celebrations

Most East Indian holidays are according to the Hindu calendar and do not fall on the same day each year.

- PONGAL-SANKRANTI. In January Pongal-Sankranti is celebrated. Commemorating a three-day harvest festival celebrated in India. Traditionally, Pongal, the newly harvested rice, is fed to cows; in Ontario, the festival is celebrated as a general get-together and cultural evening.
- INDIA'S REPUBLIC DAY. January 26 is India's Republic Day, celebrating the day in 1950 that India became a republic. On the weekend closest to the holiday, The **Indo-Canadian Association** makes an address, followed by a cultural program and refreshments.
- HOLI. March is the month of Holi, a boisterous Hindu festival where friends throw coloured water on each other. It is celebrated with dancing, singing, and food.
- JAMSHEDI NAVROZ. March 21 is Jamshedi Navroz, a Zoroastrian festival which is associated with the spring solstice and held in honour

of an emperor of Iranian legend. The festival is celebrated by holding a jashan, a thanks-giving ceremony celebrated with get togethers.

◆ BIRTHDAY OF LORD RAMA. In April, the birthday of Lord Rama is celebrated by all Hindus with prayers and recitations from the Ramayana.

◆ BAISAKHI DAY. April 13 is generally Baisakhi Day, celebrated as New Year's Day for Hindus, Jains, and Buddhists.

◆ BUDDHA PURNIMA. In May, Buddha Purnima is celebrated in honour of the birth, enlightenment, and salvation of Buddha, the founder of Buddhism.

◆ INDEPENDENCE DAY, on August 15, marks India's Independence Day, which was first celebrated in 1947. On the weekend closest to the day, India's Consulate General in Toronto holds a reception.

◆ JANMASHTAM. A full-day festival with a dinner in honour of the birth of Lord Krishna is held in August. As a religious observance, it involves all-night prayer vigils, as well as devotional singing and dancing.

◆ PATETI, in August, is the beginning of the New Year on the Zoroastrian calendar. It is celebrated by holding a jashan.

BAPS Shri Swaminarayan Mandir, Toronto, Canada

The BAPS Shri Swaminarayan Mandir complex is located in Northwest Toronto.

- ◆ HARE KRISHNA TEMPLE. In mid-August, the **Hare Krishna Temple** celebrates Rathyatra with a procession down Avenue Road and University Avenue to Centre Island.
- ◆ HARVEST FESTIVAL OF KERALA. In honour of Onam, the harvest festival of Kerala, India, a social and cultural evening is held in September.
- ◆ DURGA PUJA AND DUSSEHRA. In September or October, Durga Puja and Dussehra are held to celebrate the triumph of good over evil. A three-day celebration with colourful religious ceremonies, it is comparable to Thanksgiving.

See Holidays and Celebrations in Glossary.

Media

- ◆ MIDWEEK, (Tel. 905-670-3687, 1310 Midway Blvd., Unit 31, Mississauga).
- ◆ THE WEEKENDER, (Tel. 416-855-9192, www.theweekender.ca).
- ◆ COMMUNITY DIGEST, (Tel. 416-283-3373, 7305 Woodbine Ave., Suite 616).
- ◆ INDIA ABROAD, (Tel. 416-622-2600, 42 Deanewood Cres). A weekly newspaper published in English in Toronto and New York. Associate Editor: Ajit Jain.
- ◆ INDIA CALLING, (Tel. 416-823-2541 or 416-233-9577, 41 Mabell Ave., Suite 1908). Publisher and Editor: Sanyogta (Sonia) Singh.
- ◆ CANADIAN TIMES OF INDIA NEWSMAGAZINE, (Tel. 416-490-0091, 7 Axsmith Cres). Editor Umesh Vijaya. At the same address: *Sangam*, a bi-monthly Hindu newspaper. Publisher: Umesh Vijaya.
- ◆ EAST INDIAN PROGRAM, 530 CIAO AM, (Tel. 416-453-7111, 50 Kennedy Rd. S., Unit 20, Brampton). Saturdays 7:00 p.m. to 9:00 p.m.
- ◆ SOUTH ASIAN NEWSWEEK, CFMT Channel 47, (Tel. 416-260-0047, 545 Lakeshore Blvd. W). Tues. to Sat., 6:00 a.m. to 7:00 a.m. Mon. to Fri., 8:00 p.m. to 9:00 p.m. Producer: Stan Papulkas.
- ◆ GEETMALA (Hindi), CHIN 100.7 FM, (Tel. 416-531-9991, 622 College St). Sunday, 9:00 p.m. to 12:00 a.m. Host: Darshan Sahota.
- ◆ EYE ON ASIA (Hindi), CITY-TV, Channel 57, ℅ CHIN Radio/TV International, (Tel. 416-531-9991, 622 College St). Saturday, 10:00 a.m. to 11:00 a.m. Sunday, 10:00 a.m. to 11:00 a.m. Contact: Darshan Sahota.

Organizations

The Indo-Canadian community is one of the youngest and most diversified communities in Ontario. Many Indo-Canadian organizations are small, with meetings taking place in the home of the organizer.

◆ **BRAHMA KUMARIS**, (Tel. 416-537-3034, 3000 Islington Ave.) National Coordinator: Denise Lawrence

◆ **SOUTH ASIAN SOCIAL SERVICES ORGANIZATION**, (Tel. 416-431-4847, 1200 Markham Rd). Formerly the **Indian Immigrant Aid Services**. Established in 1972. One of the first East Indian organizations in Toronto. Provides settlement for new immigrants, orientation, resume preparation, and job search assistance.

◆ **INDO CANADA ASSOCIATION**, (Tel. 416-592-4215, 163 Lyndhurst Dr., Thornhill). Founded in 1961, it is one of Toronto's oldest East Indian organizations. Its mandate is to promote friendship between Canada and India and preserve Indo-Canadian culture.

◆ **EIPROC**, (235 Yorkland Blvd). A club of professionals from India.

◆ **ARYA SAMAJ VEDIC CULTURAL CENTRE**, (Tel. 905-475-5778, Fax 905-475-2883, 4345 14th Ave). Provides various cultural, social and religious activities to the East Indian Community.

◆ **ASSOCIATION OF WOMEN OF INDIA (AWIC)**, (Tel. 416-499-4144, 3030 Don Mills Rd., Lower Level Mall).

◆ **BHARATHI KALA MANRAM**, Canada, (Tel. 905-568-1536, Box 22097, 45 Overlea Blvd). Contact: R. Venkataraman.

◆ **CANADIAN COUNCIL OF HINDUS**, (Tel. 905-471-1211, P.O. Box 295, Station O). Contact: Amar Erry.

◆ **HINDU CULTURAL SOCIETY**, (Tel. 416-284-6282, 1 Morningview Trail, Scarborough), Contact: Hari Chopra.

◆ **HINDU FEDERATION OF CANADA**, (Tel. 416-756-0583, 64 Hobart Dr). Contact: President Shori Lal Katyal.

◆ **JAIN SOCIETY**, (Tel. 416-251-8112, 48 Rosemeade Ave). Established in 1974, in 1977 it was registered as a religious non-profit and charitable organization.

◆ **ONTARIO FEDERATION OF INDIAN FRIENDSHIP CENTRES**, (Tel. 416-956-7575, 219 Front St. E).

◆ **MARATHI BHASHIK MANDAL**, (Tel. 905-479-0313, 10 Glamorgan Crt). Contact: K.M. Ghanekar.

◆ **NARGIS DUTT FOUNDATION**, (Tel. 905-471-1211, 40 Coppard Ave). Co-ordinator: Amar Erry.

The Indo-Canadian community occasionally receives visits from divine leaders. Pictured above is Her Holiness Amma Sri Karunamayi and below His Holiness Swami Hari Prasad with avid believers.

- ◆ SOUTH ASIAN FAMILY SUPPORT SERVICES, (Tel. 416-286-3878, 1154 Morningside Ave., #205; Tel. 416-431-4847,Tel. 416-431-4847, 4352 Kingston Rd., 2nd Floor).
- ◆ SOUTH ASIAN MEDIA ALLIANCE OF CANADA, (Tel. 905-455-9839, Fax 905-452-8133, 45 Radford Dr., Brampton).

- SOUTH ASIAN WOMEN'S CENTRE, (Tel. 416-537-2276, 1332 Bloor St. W).
- VEDANTA SOCIETY OF TORONTO, (Tel. 416-240-7262, 120 Emmett Ave).
- YOGI DIVINE SOCIETY, (Tel. 905-678-1166, 6875 Professional Ct, Mississauga).
- ZOROASTRIAN SOCIETY OF ONTARIO, (Tel. 416-733-4586, 3590 Bayview Ave) Chair: Moti Kaka PaTel.

Consulates, Trade Commissions and Tourist Bureaus

- CONSULATE GENERAL OF INDIA, (Tel. 416-960-0751, 1835 Yonge St., #400). Consul General: Mrs. Preeti Saran.
- INDIAN GOVERNMENT TOURIST OFFICE, 60 Bloor St. W., M4W 3B8, Tel. 416-962-3787.
- INDO CANADA CHAMBER OF COMMERCE, 45 Sheppard Ave. E., Suite 900, M2N 5W9, Tel. 416-224-0090, Fax 416-224-0089, www.iccc.org.

Prominent Torontonians

Kanta Arora, community leader; Shan Chandrasekar, TV executive producer; Dr. Budhendra Doobay, doctor and religious leader, recipient of the Order of Ontario; Dr. Lorna D'Silva, physician; Harish Jain, human rights expert; Gian Rajan, religious commentator; Shil Sanwalka, barrister and solicitor, Q.C.; Dr V. Kumar, President of the Toronto Amma centre.

Contributors: Avinashi Agnighodri, community organizer; Amar Erry, social and religious leader, President, Vedic Cultural Centre; Shori Lal Katyal; Prakash Mody, Jain Rep; Hari Krishna Chopra.

Sources: Ashok Parihar, Krishan Sehgal, Rosey Weston, Shori Lal Katyal, Ajit Jain.

The Indonesian Community

Indonesians have broadened Toronto's cultural horizons by introducing the city to a cuisine of savoury spices, the lovely art of batik, and the music of bamboo instruments such as the angklung and the gamelan.

The community, with just over 5,000 members, consists mainly of people who arrived from the Southeast Asian islands in the late 1960s and early 1970s. The early settlers included students who applied for citizenship, and seniors who wanted to spend their retirement in a different country. Some Indonesians immigrated to Canada from the Netherlands, Hong Kong, and China. The majority of the Toronto community is of Chinese origin.

Although there is not an Indonesian neighbourhood in the city, many live in Etobicoke and Mississauga. Well-educated members of the community include civil servants and scientists, and among Indonesian-owned businesses in the city are real estate agencies and pharmacies.

Every year, culture sharing between Canada and Indonesia is extended through an exchange program, when the youth from the two countries switch residences for three months.

Places to Go

Indonesian cooking uses a number of spices in both meat and vegetable dishes. Rijsttafel features a bowl of steamed rice accompanied by spiced meats, vegetables, and sauces. Sate is barbecued beef, lamb, pork, or chicken with a spicy sauce.

Restaurants serving Indonesian cuisine include: **Simon's Smokehouse**, (Tel. 905-453-1822, 220 Clarence St., Brampton).

Indonesian dry foods and snacks can be obtained at **Oey Trading** (Mrs. Elke Oey), (Tel. 416-609-1201, 3520 McNichol Unit #2); and **La Rissa Food** (Mrs. Clara Ong), which specializes in tempe (soya beans), (Tel. 416-297-6936, 2250 Midland Ave., Unit #25).

Religious Centres, Schools and Other Institutions

The Indonesian community is made up of Muslims, Buddhists, and Christians who worship at the city's churches and temples.

◆ INDONESIAN CHRISTIAN CHURCH CANADA (ICCC), (Tel. 416-665-4777, Fax 416-665-8298, www.icc-toronto.org, 1000 Petrolia Rd).

◆ UMAT KATOLIK INDONESIA (UKI—INDONESIAN CATHOLIC COMMUNITY OF THE GREATER TORONTO AREA), ℅ Priest of the Sacred Heart, (Tel. 416-535-3145, 58 High Park Boulevard). Contact: Father Blasius Sukoto SCJ.

◆ MASYARAKAT ISLAM INDONESIA TORONTO (MIIT—INDONESIAN MOSLEM COMMUNITY IN TORONTO). Contact: Teddy Natanegara, e-mail: tnatanegara@yahoo.com.

◆ INDONESIAN FULL GOSPEL FELLOWSHIP (IFGF), ℅ Cawthra Park United Church, (Tel. 905-278-7376, 1465 Leda Ave., Mississauga). Contact: Pastor Henry Suhady, e-mail: henrysuhadys@yahoo.com.

◆ INDONESIAN ALLIANCE CHURCH, (Tel. 905-403-1345), contact: Pastor Polin Siringo Ringo.

Holidays and Celebrations

◆ INDEPENDENCE DAY, August 17, recognizes the day in 1945 that Indonesia proclaimed its independence from the Netherlands. The day is celebrated by Indonesian Torontonians with a flag ceremony at the Consulate. Sports competitions are held, including tournaments in soccer, table tennis, badminton, volleyball, tennis and other sports.

See Holidays and Celebrations in Glossary.

Media

◆ RADIO SUARA PENGHARAPAN (THE VOICE OF HOPE), (www.harapan.ca), Saturday, 8 p.m. to 9 p.m. on 1430 AM. E-mail for programs and advertising: (program@harapan.ca).

Organizations

◆ INDONESIAN CANADIAN SENIOR CITIZEN CENTRE (INCASEC), (Tel. 905-821-3090, Fax 905-821-0048, 1205 Vanrose St., Mississauga). Contact: Mrs. Annie Liem.

- MUDA-MUDI KATOLIK INDONESIA (MUDIKA-INDONESIAN CATHOLIC YOUTH), (Tel. 905-567-3296, 2842 Castlebridge Dr). Contact: Christopher Leo.
- INDONESIAN CHRISTIAN FELLOWSHIP, (Tel. 416-665-4777, Fax 416-665-8298, 1000 Petrolia Rd). Contact: Pascal Aswinata.
- INDONESIAN CANADIAN COMMUNITY ASSOCIATION (ICCA), (4294 Fieldgate Dr., Mississauga). Vice President: S. Sugiharto.

Consulates, Trade Commissions and Tourist Bureaus

- THE CONSULATE GENERAL OF THE REPUBLIC OF INDONESIA, (Tel. 416-360-4020, Fax 416-360-4295, www.indonesiatoronto.org, 129 Jarvis St). Consul General: Mr. Bambang Cahyo Gunawan.

Prominent Torontonians

Willy Kurnia, famous designer in GTA; Handy S. Atmaja, artist (painter) and film actor; Dr. herna Halim, Dentist; Dr. Roy Kwee, Family Doctor; Dr. Sie Kian Gwan, Family Doctor; Dr. Wie Giap Liaw, Dentist; Dr. Linda The, Gynecologist; Dr. Ivone Surya, Dentist; Dr. Anne Sutikno, Dentist.

Contributors: Ms. Sylvia Shirley Malinton, Head of Information—Social & Culture, Consulate General of the Republic of Indonesia in Toronto.

The Iranian Community

An annual "yellow page" directory known as *Zarvaragh* (www.zarvaragh.com) published by **Shahram Saremi** lists the large number of Canadian Iranian professional services and business activities in the city. Toronto's Iranians are involved in almost all areas of business, including the insurance and real-estate businesses, import/export and international trading, construction, banking, and financial services, education, politics, and medicine. Most of Toronto's 120,000 Iranians are highly educated— physicians, engineers, bankers, teachers, lawyers, architects, and business people—from the Islamic Republic of Iran, formerly known as Iran. The majority of immigrants have arrived since the late 1970s.

The first recorded Iranian immigrants to Canada were predominantly students who came between 1946 and 1965. Non-student immigrants began to arrive after 1966, and the third wave, from 1979 to 1981, brought Iranians seeking refuge from political upheaval in their homeland. Other Iranians have come to Canada indirectly from the United States, England, France, Germany, and other countries.

Iranians are spread throughout Toronto but there is a concentration in North York, and Richmond Hill, where the first language and cultural heritage school was established. In 1982, an Iranian soccer league was formed with four teams. In 1983, a special ceremony was held to honour the year's champions and to encourage participation in the Iranian Soccer League.

Hints of ancient Persian culture can be unearthed around Toronto. Persian musicians playing various musical instruments and theatrical troupes are regular performers at Toronto's theatres. The **Persian Traditional Art and Cultural Foundation of Ontario** has organized a number of events, including an international folk songs concert; a Persian Traditional Concert to commemorate Ontario's bicentennial; arts exhibitions and cultural seminars; and an International Congress on Persian Heritage to celebrate the 800th anniversary of the birth of Sa'di, Iran's greatest poet. The foundation plans to start a library and open a community centre.

Places to Go

Traditional popular Persian entertainment and foods, including Chelow Kabab, cornish hen marinated in saffron served with yogurt drink (with herbs and flavoured mint), and grilled tomatoes, Persian tea, coffee, desserts, and pasteries, are served in dozens of restaurants and pastry shops, including: **Karoon Restaurant**, (Tel. 905-886-4443, 5 Glen Cameron Rd., Thornhill); **Zaffron**, (Tel. 416-223-7070, 6200 Yonge St); **Shirini Sara Pastry House**, (Tel. 416-510-1050, 1875 Leslie St., #6); **Red Rose**, (Tel. 416-223-5551, 6184/5467 Yonge St); and **Via Egnatia Restaurant**, (Tel. 416-766-2332, 395 Keele St).

Popular Iranian foods, such as dried lime, saffron, and basmati rice are available at over a dozen stores, including: **Super Khorak**, (Tel. 416-221-7558, 6125 Yonge St). Books, videos, and cassettes in the Farsi (Persian) language are available at **Pars Video**, (Tel. 416-512-2414, 6113 Yonge St).

Iranian owned businesses prominently display their colourful signs in Toronto.

Religious Centres, Schools and Other Institutions

The majority of Iranians are Muslims but the eastern Christian and Bahai faiths are also represented in the community.

Farsi language courses are offered at:

◆ GLENVIEW PUBLIC SCHOOL, (Tel. 416-393-9390, 401 Rosewell Ave).

◆ THE SCHOOL OF CONTINUING STUDIES, (Tel. 416-978-2400, www.learn.utoronto.ca, at the University of Toronto, 158 St. George St) offers classes in Farsi.

Holidays and Celebrations

◆ NOW-RUZ (IRANIAN NEW YEAR), March 20–22, is held at the beginning of spring. Traditions include baking cookies, buying new clothes, planting vegetables, and setting the table with haft-sin: seven things that begin with the letter "S" in the Persian language—for example: vinegar (serkeh), coins (sekkeh), and apples (sib). Mirrors are symbolic of light and universe, candles honour fire, and apples represent productivity. The **Iranian Association of Ontario** holds a reception party on this day.

◆ LONGEST NIGHT OF THE YEAR. December 20–22 is a joyous celebration that marks the end of the longest night of the year. The holiday provides a break in the long winter season.

See Holidays and Celebrations in Glossary.

Media

◆ IRAN STAR (WEEKLY NEWSPAPER), (Tel. 905-763-9770, Fax 905-763-9770, www.iranstar.com, 72 Steeles Ave. W., Suite 205, Thornhill). Editor-in-Chief: Bijan Binesh.

◆ SHAHRVAND NEWSPAPER, (Tel. 416-739-1086, Fax 416-739-6418, www.shahrvand.com, 4610 Dufferin St., Unit 208). Editor: Hassan Zerehi.

Organizations

◆ MOTHER'S VOICE, (Tel. 416-789-7092, 377 Ridelle Ave., Unit 1822).

◆ IRANIAN COMMUNITY ASSOCIATION OF ONTARIO, (Tel. 416-441-2656, 5330 Yonge St. Suite 205). Provides support services for newcomers and arranges various cultural events, picnics, and parties.

◆ IRANIAN WOMEN'S ORGANIZATION, (Tel. 416-296-9566, Fax 416-496-0881, 2975 Don Mills Rd., 2nd floor).

◆ IRANIAN CANADIAN CONGRESS, (Tel. 416-840-3222, Fax 416-222-7422, 5330 Yonge St., Unit 202, www.iccongress.ca).

The **University of Toronto** has an Iranian Students' Group, **Ryerson University** and **York University** have Iranian Students' Associations set up to help Iranian students familiarize themselves with Canada.

Consulates, Trade Commissions and Tourist Bureaus

◆ IRANIAN EMBASSY, (Tel. (613) 233-4726, Fax (613) 236-4726, www.salamiran.org, 245 Metcalfe St., Ottawa). Consul General: Mr. Hadi Karimitabr.

Prominent Torontonians

Nasser Akmal, owner of Persian Alborz Rugs; Shane Baghai, developer; Sheida Gharachedaghi, composer; Mr. Hakim, owner of Hakim Optical; Edik Hovespian, conductor; Mihan Kazemi, computer graphic designer and miniaturist, portraitist, publisher; M. Sadegh Kazemi, author and founder of Persian art and cultural foundation; Dr. Lotfi Mansouri, former Director General of the Canadian Opera Company; Dr. Arsalan Mohajer, recipient of the Roy Thomas Award; Dr. Reza Moridi, MPP; Dr. Fahimeh Mortazavi, member of Immigration and Refugee Board, and community leader; Reza Navabi, artist and architect; Dr. Siavash Taheri, lawyer; Mr. Admad Tabrizi, entrepreneur; Fariba Motamed, architect; Jafar Amini, Ph.D., a designated consulting engineer in Ontario; Norman Ahmet, former director of the city of York Board of Education; Jian Gomeshi, musician and radio personality.

Contributor: Massood Mashadi, Shahrvand Newspaper.

Sources: Shahin Assayesh; Anoush Binesh; B. Binesh; Dr. F. Mortazavi; K. Rezvanfar; Dr. M.H. Yazdanfar; and Ali Tahbazian.

The Irish Community

In the lower rotunda of the **Royal Ontario Museum**, a bronze statue honours one of Toronto's best-known Irish Canadians. Timothy Eaton (1834–1907) was an Irish-born merchant who turned his Toronto dry-goods store into Canada's largest privately owned department store. In 1907, the **T. Eaton Company** employed more than 9,000 people. Today, the **Timothy Eaton Memorial Church** on St. Clair Avenue West stands as a reminder of the contributions of the great Irish Torontonian.

Irish settlers have lived in Canada since the early 17th century. The Irish may have constituted as much as five percent of the population of New France, and during the 18th century, the Irish began to settle in the new British colonies. More Irish settlers were among the Loyalists who arrived in Canada following the American Revolution.

The potato crop failure and famines in Ireland in the 1840s resulted in a large number of settlers arriving in Toronto. Early Irish working class neighbourhoods along Toronto's waterfront and the Don Basin were called Slab Town, Paddy Town, and Cork Town. Irish Claretown developed around Bathurst and Queen streets, and by the 1890s, the junction area of west Toronto became home to many Irish. Cabbagetown is reputed to have been named for the Irish working class who planted cabbages in their front yards.

The first Irish Catholic churches in the city were **St. Paul's** in Cabbagetown, **St. Michael's Cathedral** (1848), **St. Basil's Church** (1856), and the original **St. Patrick's Church**, established in the 1860s. The churches were centres for education and social activities. The pioneer charitable organization was **St. Vincent de Paul Society**, whose members also founded the **Toronto Savings Bank** and the **Catholic Children's Aid Society of St. Vincent de Paul**.

In the 1850s, **St. Michael's College**, now part of the **University of Toronto**, became a seminary school under the **Basilian Fathers** to provide higher education for Irish Catholics. The **Christian Brothers** established **De La Salle** as a secondary and commercial school, complementing the schools of the **Sisters of Loretto** and of **St. Joseph**. St. Michael's Hospital was opened in the late 19th century by the **Sisters of St. Joseph** (who were assisted by the Irish Catholic laity), followed by the establishment of **St. Joseph's** and **Our Lady of Mercy** hospitals.

In the second half of the 19th century, there were a large number of Ulster Protestants living in the city. Lodges of the **Orange Order**, a predominantly Protestant society founded in 1795 and named in honour of King William III, Prince of Orange, were established in the 19th century. The main meeting-halls were the **Eastern Orange Hall** on Queen Street East, as well as the **Western District Orange Hall** on Euclid Avenue. The lodges provided social services, health care, and illness and death benefits. The needy received additional aid from the ancillary organizations of the **Ladies Loyal True Blues** and the **Irish Protestant Benevolent Association**.

Irish Torontonians have contributed greatly to the city's development in the political, business, and sports sectors. The first Orange Mayor, W.H. Boulton, took office in 1845 and, during the rest of the century, 20 of Toronto's 23 mayors were Orangemen. Irish-born lawyer Edward Blake became the second premier of Ontario; Irish nationalist John Lynch was the first Roman Catholic Archbishop of Toronto. Sir John Craig Eaton, son of Timothy Eaton, was knighted in 1915 for his philanthropic activities. Irish-born bankers include William McMaster (1811–1887), founder of the **Bank of Commerce**, who bequeathed his estate to the establishment of **McMaster University**. Among Toronto's most popular sports figures were the late King Clancy and former Canadian boxing champion and Olympic silver medalist Shawn O'Sullivan.

In Toronto today, some 485,000 people have some Irish ancestry. The community has numerous cultural, charitable, social, and sporting organizations, many with Gaelic (Irish language) names.

Places to Go

Many of Toronto's notable buildings were designed by Irish architects. Belfast-born John Lyle designed the **Royal Alexandra Theatre** (1906) and was chiefly responsible for the design of **Union Station**. He designed hundreds of bank buildings across Canada; the best known in Toronto is the **Bank of Nova Scotia** at King and Bay streets. Architect Edmund Burke (b. 1850) was among the architects responsible for **Simpson's Department Store** (now **The Bay**), **CTV Queen Street** (formerly **Chum/City Building** and the **Wesley Building**) on Queen Street, and the **Royal Conservatory of Music** on Bloor Street West. Architect Joseph Connelly (b. 1840) designed over 30 Roman Catholic Churches in Ontario. Architect Kivas Tully (b. 1820 in County Laois) became senior architect of the **Ontario Public Works Department** in 1868, and designed the **Custom House** at Yonge and Front streets. David Roberts and his son designed the **Gooderham and Worts Distillery**, the **York Club** at St. George and Bloor, and the **Gooderham** (Flat-Iron) Building at Wellington and Front St. East.

Montgomery's Inn, (Tel. 416-394-8113, www.montgomerysinn.com, 4709 Dundas St. W), was built and operated by Irishman Thomas Montgomery in the 1840s. Today, it houses a museum of early British settlement in Canada. Open Tuesday to Friday, 9:30 a.m. to 4:30 p.m., and weekends, 1:00 p.m. to 5:00 p.m.

In 1848, Irish brewer Enoch Turner established Toronto's first free school. **Enoch Turner School House**, (Tel. 416-863-0010, www.enochturner schoolhouse.ca, 106 Trinity St), restored in the 1970s, is Toronto's oldest standing school building. It can be visited by appointment.

Spadina Museum, (Tel. 416-392-6910, 285 Spadina Rd), was the 1866 home of businessman and financier James Austin. Visiting hours vary, depending on season.

The **Royal Ontario Museum**, (Tel. 416-586-5549, www.rom.on.ca, 100 Queen's Park), contains over 100 canvases by Irish-born artist and explorer Paul Kane, who arrived in York around 1822. He travelled the Great Lakes, painting portraits and scenes of Canadian Natives. A commemorative plaque to the artist is also located at 56 Wellesley St. E., the site of **Paul Kane House** and **Paul Kane Park**.

Irish cuisine has several traditional staples, including oatmeal, milk products, leeks, and, of course, potatoes. Popular dishes include champ (a mound of hot mashed potatoes in a pool of melted butter); Cumberland pie (a baked dish of two layers of potato pastry with slices of bacon and eggs); trotters (pigs feet); bath chaps (cured cheeks and tongues breaded and fried); mince pies; and oatmeal for breakfast. Tea is a popular beverage, and the Irish toast each other's health—"Slainte" (pronounced slawn'che in Gaelic)—with beer and Irish whiskey.

An Irish brewing dynasty was founded by John Labatt (1803–1866), a native of Laois, and in the 1890s, Eugene O'Keefe founded **O'Keefe Breweries**, Canada's largest brewery at that time.

Irish pubs include **Galway Arms**, (Tel. 416-251-0096, 838 The Queensway), hosts: Tom & Della Keane; and **Mick E. Fynn's Restaurant**, (Tel. 416-598-0537, 45 Carlton St), which has Irish entertainment two nights a week. Both **The New Windsor House**, (Tel. 416-364-9698, 124 Church St) and **The Unicorn Pub an Irish Rovers Free House**, (Tel. 416-482-0115, 175 Eglinton Ave. E), feature nightly entertainment; **Dora Keogh Restaurant**, traditional music and dance, (Tel. 416-778-1804, 141 Danforth Ave), with host Dora Geogh. **Allens Restaurant**, traditional music and dance, (Tel. 416-463-3086, 143 Danforth Ave), your host: John Maxwell; **P.J. O'brien Restaurant**, (Tel. 416-815-7562, 39 Colborne St), host: Patt Quinn; **Failte**, (Tel. 905-276-2212, 201 City Centre Dr., Mississauga), hosts: Damian & Charlotte Kerr; **Scruffy Murphy's**, (Tel. 416-484-6637, 150 Eglinton Ave. E), host: Tony Byrne; **McMurphy's**, (Tel. 416-489-1111, 381 Eglinton Ave. E), host: Jack Murphy; **Irish Rose**, (Tel. 416-763-2478, 1095 Weston Rd), hosts: Michael & Mary McConnell; **The Belfast Lounge**, (Tel. 905-212-9048, 5165 Dixie Rd., Mississauga); **The Brogue Inn**, (Tel. 905-278-8444, 136 Lakeshore Rd. E., Port Credit), host: Tommy Donnelly; **Starfish Oyster Bed & Grill**, (Tel. 416-366-7827, 100 Adelaide St. E), imports fresh Galway mussels, year round; **Gold & Shamrock**, (Tel. 416-366-1247, 211 Yonge St, Suite 201).

Religious Centres, Schools and Other Institutions

Irish Torontonians attend Protestant and Roman Catholic churches.

♦ ST. BASIL'S CHURCH, (Tel. 416-926-7110, 50 St. Joseph St).

♦ ST. CECILIA'S CHURCH, (Tel. 416-769-8163, 161 Annette St).

♦ ST. MICHAEL'S CATHEDRAL, (Tel. 416-364-0234, 200 Church St).

♦ TIMOTHY EATON MEMORIAL CHURCH, (Tel. 416-925-5977, 230 St. Clair Ave. W).

♦ WHITE FEILD CHRISTIAN SCHOOL, (Tel. 416-297-6569, 1600 Neilson Rd).

Holidays and Celebrations

♦ ST. PATRICK'S DAY, March 17, commemorates the patron saint of Ireland, a preacher and a teacher who helped to establish churches and schools. One of the legends of St. Patrick tells how he drove the snakes out of Ireland. He is credited with using the shamrock to explain symbolically the Christian Trinity of Father, Son, and Holy Spirit. Shamrock and leprechaun souvenirs are signs of St. Patrick's Day celebrations in the city. After a lapse of 110 years, Toronto held its first Saint Patrick's Day parade in 1988, and it is now an annual event on the Sunday prior to March 17th. The parade winds its way down Yonge Street with marching bands and colourful floats supplied by members of the community.

◆ THE ORANGEMEN'S CELEBRATION OF THE BATTLE OF THE BOYNE IN 1690 occurs on July 12. The first "Twelfth" parade was held in Toronto in 1822. Today, Orange parades continue the tradition with a colourful display of flags, banners, bands, and regalia.

◆ BLOOMSDAY. Every year the Irish community holds a Bloomsday celebration on June 16, with readings celebrating the character from James Joyce's novel, *Ulysses.*

See Holidays and Celebrations in Glossary.

Media

◆ COOL DAYS CRAIG IRISH, radio show, CHKT 1430 AM, Saturdays, 11 a.m. to 12 p.m. Music, news, sports from Ireland. Host: Eamonn O'Loghlin.

◆ HUGO STRANEY SHOW, CHIN 1540 AM, Sundays, 10 a.m. to 11 a.m., (Tel. 416-491-6195, Fax 416-531-5274, 77 Cairnside Cres). Host: Hugo Straney.

◆ SONGS FROM HOME, CHIN 1540 AM, (Tel. 416-531-9991, 622 College St). Sunday, 10:00 a.m. to 11:00 a.m. Regular features include the Sunday sports results from Ireland. Host: Hugo Straney.

◆ THE SENTINEL, (Tel. 416-223-1690, 94 Sheppard Ave. W). Founded in 1875; published four times a year by the **British America Publishing Company** and the official organ of the **Loyal Orange Association**. Managing Editor: Jeremy Dowdell.

◆ IRISH CONNECTIONS CANADA, (Tel. 416-621-7373, www.irishcanadamag.com, 121 Decarie Circle). A quarterly magazine published by The Irish Canadian Aid and Cultural Society. Editor: Eamonn O'Loghlin.

Organizations

◆ THE TORONTO IRISH PLAYERS, (Tel. 416-440-2888, www.torontoirishplayers.org), a theatre group, has been performing plays for 20 years from the Irish dramatic repertoire.

◆ CANADIAN ORANGE HEADQUARTERS, (Tel. 416-223-1690, Fax 416-223-1324, 94 Sheppard Ave. W). Sponsors several events throughout the year, including the annual Orange Parade. It publishes a magazine called *The Sentinel.* Secretary: Jeremy Dowdell.

◆ THE IRELAND FUND OF CANADA, (Tel. 416-367-8311, Fax 416-367-5931, www.irlfunds.org/canada, 67 Yonge St., Suite 401), is dedicated to raising funds to support programs of peace and reconciliation, arts and culture, education and community development in Ireland, North and South. The Fund is also dedicated to promoting Irish importance and preserving Irish identity here in Canada. Executive Director: Eleanor McGrath.

◆ IRISH DANCE TEACHERS ASSOCIATION, (www.irishdancecanada.com). A network for over a dozen Irish dance schools in Toronto. Contact: Yvonne Kelly, Regional Director.

◆ MACKENZIERO, (Tel. 416-769-2529, www.mackenziero.com, 156 High Park Ave). Professional theatre company dedicated to producing works that reflect their Irish heritage.

◆ ST. PATRICK'S DAY PARADE SOCIETY, (Tel. 416-487-1566, www.topatrick.com, 165 University Ave., Suite A200). Runs the annual parade and other events throughout the year.

◆ THE IRELAND SUPPORTER'S CLUB, (Tel. 905-607-8912, 4120 Ridgeway Dr., Unit 39, Mississauga).

◆ IRELAND PARK FOUNDARION, (Tel. 416-601-6906, 67 Yonge St, Suite 1101).

◆ EMERALD ISLE SENIORS SOCIETY, (Tel. 416-469-5394, 1190 Danforth Ave), Mon–Fri: 12 pm–5 pm.

◆ O'CONNOR IRISH HERITAGE HOUSE, (60 Rowena Dr).

◆ TORONTO IRISH ASSOCIATION, (Tel. 647-722-0841, www.torontoirish association.com).

Most Irish counties are represented by county associations including Antrim, Carlow, Cavan, Clare, Cork, Derry, Down, Donegal, Dublin, Fermanagh, Galway, Kerry, Kildare, Kilkenny, Laois/Offaly, Leitrim, Longford, Limerick, Mayo, Meath, Monaghan, Roscommon, Sligo, Tipperary, Tyrone, Waterford, Westmeath, Wicklow.

Consulates, Trade Commissions and Tourist Bureaus

◆ CONSULATE GENERAL OF IRELAND, (Tel. 416-366-9300, Fax 416-947-0584, 20 Toronto St., Suite 1210). Honorary Consul General: Edward J. McConnell.

◆ IRISH TRAVEL BUREAU, (Tel. 416-482-0449, 90 Eglinton Ave. W).

◆ IRELAND-CANADA CHAMBER OF COMMERCE, Toronto Chapter, (Tel. 416-621-7373, Fax 416-621-3433, 121 Decarie Cir). Executive Director: Eamonn O'Loghlin.

◆ TOURISM IRELAND, (Tel. 416-925-6368, www.tourismireland.com, 2 Bloor St. W., Suite 3403). Marketing Manager: Mrs. Jayme Shacklesord.

Prominent Torontonians

Matthew Barrett, former President, Bank of Montreal; John Dunne, former Chairman and CEO, A&P/Dominion; Cardinal Emmett Carter; Edward J. McConnell, investment counsellor and Irish Hon. Consul; Tony O'Donohue, former politician; Shawn O'Sullivan, former Canadian Boxing Champion and Olympic silver medallist; Hilary M. Weston, former Lieutenant Governor of Ontario; Bob White, former labour leader

Contributors: Paul Farrelly, former Executive Director, the Ireland Fund of Canada; Jonathan Kearns, architect; Eamonn O'Loghlin, Editor, Toronto Irish News; Sandra McEoghain.

The Ismaili Muslim Community

The Shia Imami Ismaili Muslims, generally known as the Ismailis, live in over 25 different countries and span many different cultural and linguistic groups. A Muslim sect, they venerate the religious leader Ismail (d. 760) as the seventh Imam. His Highness Prince Karim Aga Khan, a direct descendent of the Prophet Muhammad, is the 49th Imam.

The first Ismailis arrived in Canada in the mid-1960s from the United Kingdom and other Western European countries. Many were professionals who found work in the areas of education, health, and business. This steady growth continued until the early 1970s when political changes in East Africa and Asia led to a second large wave of Ismailis moving to Canada.

Today, Ismailis are settled throughout Canada, and number some 70,000 to 75,000. An estimated 20,000 Ismailis live in Toronto. Ismaili Torontonians play a significant role in community affairs. Over the years, the community has launched several fundraising events. They have several fundraising activities for charities, including a ten-kilometre annual run to raise funds for the **Canadian Cancer Society** and the **Arthritis Society**, **Child Find**, **North York General Hospital Foundation**, **The Hospital for Sick Children Foundation**, and the **United Way of Greater Toronto**. The community has also held blood donor clinics in conjunction with the **Red Cross Society** and more recently **Canadian Blood Services**. Toronto Ismailis have also participated in the annual **Ontario Multicultural Theatre Festivals** and **Easter Seal Telethons**. Members of the community occupy senior positions in the professions, government, and business.

The Ismaili community in Canada is governed by volunteers under the aegis of **His Highness Prince Aga Khan Shia Imami Ismaili Council of Canada**, headquartered in Toronto. Local Ismaili Councils are based in British Columbia, Alberta, Ontario, and Quebec.

Religious Centres, Schools and Other Institutions

The Ismaili community is centred around various jamatkhanas (religious centres):

- HEADQUARTERS, (Tel. 416-751-7821, 149-151 Bartley Dr).
- BRAMPTON, (Tel. 905-450-8504, 525 North Park Dr).

◆ DON MILLS, (Tel. 416-696-7882, 80 Overlea Blvd).
◆ ETOBICOKE, (Tel. 416-674-2388, 100 Skyway Ave).
◆ HALTON, (Tel. 905-335-0033, 5341 John Lucas Dr., Burlington).
◆ OSHAWA, (Tel. 905-725-1626, 83 Byng Ave).
◆ RICHMOND HILL, (Tel. 905-770-9600, 102 Yorkland Blvd).
◆ UNIONVILLE, (Tel. 905-513-9862, 350 Apple Creek Blvd., Markham).

Holidays and Celebrations

Ismailis celebrate all the major Muslim festivals. They also celebrate Eid-e-Ghadir (commemorating the Prophet Mohammad's designating his cousin and son-in-law Ali as the Imam); the birthday of Hazrat Ali; and Navroz (the beginning of the new year). The dates for each event are calculated according to the Muslim calendar.

See Holidays and Celebrations in Glossary.

Media

◆ THE ISMAILI, (Tel. 416-467-0199, 789 Don Mills Rd., Suite 786). Managing Director: Alam Pirani.

Organizations

◆ ISMAILI COUNCIL FOR CANADA, (Tel. 416-467-7261, Fax 416-467-0961, 789 Don Mills Rd., Suite 786). The objectives of the Councils in relation to their active areas of jurisdiction are the social, governance, administration, guidance, supervision, and coordination of the activities of the community and its institutions and organizations. President: Firoz Rasul.
◆ ISMAILI COUNCIL FOR ONTARIO, (Tel. 416-751-4001, Fax 416-751-6401, 149-151 Bartley Dr). President: Shiraz Lakhani.
◆ ISMAILI TARIQAH & RELIGIOUS EDUCATION BOARD, (Tel. 416-751-0440, Fax 416-751-6126, 149-151 Bartley Dr). Provides religious education for members of the community and training for teachers. Chair: Bashir Rahemtulla.
◆ IPS INDUSTRIAL PROMOTION SERVICES, (Tel. 905-475-9400, Fax 905-475-5003, 60 Columbia Way, Suite 720, Markham). President: Nizar Alibhai.

The Aga Khan Museum is visible from the Don Valley Parkway and is the biggest Islamic museum in the Western World.

◆ FOCUS HUMANITARIAN ASSISTANCE CANADA, (Tel. 416-423-7988, Fax 416-423-4216, 789 Don Mills Rd., Suite 786). An agency established to provide emergency humanitarian assistance. It also facilitates the reparation of displaced persons and resettlement of refugees.

Prominent Torontonians

Barkat Ali, President, Chestwood Stationery; Aziz Bhaloo, engineer, and President, Shorim Investments; Shams Hirji, philanthropist and businessman; Mahumd Jamani, chartered accountant, Ernst & Young; Amin Jivraj, President, Angelo Retail Corporation, and Director, Retail Council of Canada; Nizar Kanji, Vice-President, Alexis Nihon Developments; lqbal Kassam, President: Equitable Trust Company; Yasmin Rattansi, Principal, Bottom Line Consulting; Murad Velshi, former MPP.

Contributors: Allaudin Bhanji, Alam N. Pirani, Zahir K. Janmohamed, and Kamrudin Rashid.

The Italian Community

Oggi tutti si sentono italiani—it was a day that all Toronto felt Italian. In 1982, when Italy won the **World Cup of Soccer**, more than 100,000 members of Toronto's Italian community danced in the streets surrounding St. Clair Avenue West and Dufferin Street, waving tri-colour flags and shouting "Viva Italia." Other Torontonians joined in and the **CN Tower** marquee flashed the word "Italy" in response to the city's largest spontaneous celebration. Today, the event is remembered fondly through photographs displayed in the restaurants and cafes, elegant boutiques, and professional offices of Corso Italia.

Italians are the largest cultural group in Toronto next to the British. More than 500,000 live in the area, residing in York, North York, Mississauga, Woodbridge, and Richmond Hill.

Italians have played an important role in Canadian history ever since Giovanni Caboto (John Cabot) explored and claimed Newfoundland for England in 1497. Italian soldiers served in the military in New France, and among Toronto's early pioneers was the family of Filippo de Grassi, a retired British army officer who arrived in 1831. Today, a street and a school bear the family's name.

The first wave of immigration to Canada was between 1885 and 1924, when Italian men left the villages of southern Italy to work as seasonal labourers for Ontario's railways, mines, and industries. Toronto's first Italian neighbourhood was formed in the area around College Street and University Avenue known as "The Ward"—where **Toronto General Hospital** now stands. Early settlers worked in road construction and needle trades, and small businesses such as shoeshine parlours, restaurants, meat markets, and fruit groceterias. Entrepreneurs began manufacturing pasta in factories on York Street and Centre Avenue. By 1912, half of the city's fruit dealers were Italian. The first Italian parish in the city was **Our Lady of Mt. Carmel** on St. Patrick Street, established in 1908. In the 1930s, Italian stonemasons and contractors provided the backbreaking labour that transformed Toronto into a metropolis with roads, sewer systems, sidewalks, streetcar lines, hospitals, and later, subway lines.

A second wave of settlers followed the Second World War, and in the 1950s, an Italian neighbourhood developed along College Street between

Euclid Avenue and Shaw Street, as well as around **St. Mary's of the Angels Church** at Dufferin Street and Davenport Road. Italian merchants formed a business association, and other organizations were established, including the **Italian Immigrant Aid Society**, which provided assistance to newcomers. Later **COSTI** was established to assist those immigrants experienced in a variety of trades to acquire Canadian credentials.

By the 1960s, the community began moving north and west to the St. Clair Avenue West district and the Downsview area. In Mississauga, Richmond Hill, and Woodbridge, the splendid homes and spacious properties developed by the Italian community during the 1970s and '80s reflect the achievement of its members, who came to Canada seeking a better life for their families, as expressed in the Italian song *La Casetta in Canada*. The City of Vaughan, north of Toronto, has become a destination for the second and third generations.

Italian entrepreneurs and restaurateurs have left their mark on the city. Today, 70 per cent of the construction industry in the province is directed by Italian Canadians, including the Fidani family of **Orlando Corporation**, the Del Zotto family of **Tridel Corporation**, Fred DeGasperis of **Con-Drain Company**, and Marco Muzzo of **Marel Contracting**. Many second-generation Italian Canadians are contributing to the city's professions as lawyers, doctors, and bank managers.

In 1966, Johnny Lombardi established Toronto's first multicultural radio station; and in 1979, Dan Iannuzzi, publisher since the mid-'50s of the Italian newspaper, *Corriere Canadese*, founded **MTV**, a multilingual television network.

As early as 1885, Italian composers and musicians widened the city's appreciation of opera and classical music. More than a century later the tradition is still carried on in events such as the **Italian Culture Institute's** presentation **Italy on Stage**, a month-long showcase of Italian culture featuring music, theatre, dance, visual arts, and collections of Renaissance ceramics and rare Franciscan manuscripts.

Architectural monuments that stand at the corner of Lawrence Avenue West and Dufferin Street reflect a united effort by two generations of Italian settlers. The impressive **Villa Colombo**, with its blend of cobblestone and fountains, is a home for the aged. Next door the **Columbus Centre**, a multifaceted community centre containing an art gallery, restaurant, and fitness facilities, provides the venue for cultural and social expression by the community. **Caboto Terrace** and **Casa Del Zotto** apartments for seniors complete the campus.

Places to Go

Toronto is home to a number of Italian neighbourhoods and commercial strips that are lined with cafes, espresso bars, Italian boutiques, and bakeries. **Corso Italia**, located along St. Clair Avenue West between Dufferin Street and Lansdowne Avenue, is an old-world neighbourhood and emporium for fine Italian food, fashion, and culture. The commerce of Corso Italia is conducted in Italian and the business association has tried to create a European flavour with potted plants and Italian-made cast-iron lamp posts and street signs, which read "Corso Italia." Elmwood Avenue was officially renamed Via Italia, and the corner is now occupied by the **Banca Commerciale Italiana of Canada**.

Outdoor cafes decorated with colourful umbrellas and canopies are an integral part of Corso Italia's night life, where panzerotti, pizza, veal sandwiches, cappuccino, and latte di mandorla (almond milk) are served.

Festoons of fruits and vegetables including hot peppers, zucchini, endive, escarole, and rapini (similar to spinach) are displayed outside Italian grocery stores. Suspended prosciutto hams and salami hang in delis and some 100 varieties of cheeses are available, including bocconcini, parmesan, romano, provolone, mozzarella, and gorgonzola. Store shelves are stocked with olives, olive oil, romano beans, imported mineral water, bread sticks, iced taralli biscuits, aniseed sponges, and shortbread cookies.

Toronto's Italian restaurants reflect regional influences from Venice, Rome, Sicily, and Calabria. Characteristic of northern cuisine is the use of butter and pasta enriched with eggs. Southern Italian cooking uses seasonings such as garlic and olive oil. Since Italy is close to the sea, specialties often include shellfish, octopus, and calamari (squid), along with anchovies, sardines, and salted herring. Pastas are the staple of an Italian meal, and include cannelloni (large tubes baked and stuffed), fettuccine (small ribbon pasta), and manicotti (rectangular shaped, stuffed and cooked). Popular cream pastries and gelati are often enjoyed with cappuccino and espresso.

Fieramosca, (Tel. 416-323-0636, 36A Prince Arthur Ave). One of the most well known italian restaurants has been owned by Mario Micucci for 25 years. Mario personally prepares simply wonderful italian dishes.

La Bruschetta, (Tel. 416-656-8622, 1317 St. Clair Ave W), owned by the Piantoni family, features specialties such as fettucine giuliana (pasta with chicken, cream, mushrooms, onions, and brandy), and mixed seafood platters with clams, mussels, shrimps, and veal with portobello and wild mushroom sauce.

At **Centro Trattoria & Formaggio**, (Tel. 416-656-8111, 1224 St. Clair Ave. W), the capicollo, prosciutto, and mortadella have been immortalized after making their debut in Norman Jewison's film Moonstruck. A picture of owner Tony Celebre and Cher hangs behind the counter of the deli, which also serves homecooked meals in its cafe. The shop carries mascarpone cheese, **Lavazza** coffee, and chocolates.

The three seas surrounding Calabria are incorporated in the name **Tre Mari Bakery**, (Tel. 416-654-8960, 1311 St. Clair Ave. W), owned by the Deleo family for more than 35 years. La dolce vita begins with fresh hot bread without additives, baked every half hour. Italian foods include rigatoni, frozen gnocchi and ravioli, almond and amaretto cookies, and desserts laced with liquor. Freshly made pizza, pasta, and meat dishes are served in an adjoining cafe. Also **Pane Vittoria Bakery Ltd.**, (Tel. 905-265-1438, 8633 Weston Rd);

Sophisticated men's wear is available at **La Scala**, (Tel. 416-652-1606, 1190 St. Clair Ave. W). At the 35-year-old **Genesis**, (Tel. 416-652-1386, 1188 St. Clair Ave. W), customers are offered a cup of cappuccino or espresso as they browse through Italian silk shirts, ties, finely tailored suits, and leather goods. Owner Gene Di Matteo offers labels by Pal Zileri and Brioni.

Wedding gowns, designer sportswear, and elegant dresses are available at Corso Italia's boutiques. The establishments include **Sposabella**, (Tel. 416-652-7777, 1176 St. Clair Ave. W), owner John Gianopolous; and **Gente Fashions**, (Tel. 416-657-1461, 1232 St. Clair Ave. W). Gente's co-owner Joe Luizza travels to Milan's trade shows to find new imports and selections of different European designers.

There are more than 20 stores carrying imported shoes, belts, leather bags, Italian gold jewelry, and accessories from Italy. Five children's clothing stores are located in three blocks along St. Clair Avenue W.

At **Ital Records**, (Tel. 416-654-8272, 1339 St. Clair Ave. W), films by Fellini and operas by Puccini are among the Italian records, tapes, and videos sold by Lina and Pat Colangelo. The 45-year-old store sells a range of music, including classical recordings by Luciano Pavarotti, Italian folksongs, and new music. More than 20 Italian weekly magazines including Sportivi (Sport News) are also available.

The original **Little Italy**, located in the College Street area, has become a largely Portuguese neighbourhood. However, remnants of the Italian community still remain, including red and green "Little Italy" signs donated by the City of Toronto in 1980. It is home to the landmark **Sicilian**

Ice Cream Company, (Tel. 416-531-7716, 712 College St), and the headquarters of **CHIN International Radio**, (Tel. 416-531-9991, 622 College St). Italian establishments in the area include **Trattoria Giancarlo**, (Tel. 416-533-9619, 41 Clinton St), which serves Italian cuisine. Others include **Diplomatico Cafe and Restaurant**, (Tel. 416-534-4637, 594 College St). **Bitondo Snack Bar and Pizzeria**, (Tel. 416-533-4101, 11 Clinton St); and the 60-year-old **San Francesco Foods**, (Tel. 416-534-7867, 10 Clinton St), which serves pizza, veal sandwiches, and Italian coffees; **Riviera Bakery**, (Tel. 416-537-9352, 576 College St), is a neighbourhood landmark.

A grassed section of **Nathan Phillips Square** holds a fourth-century granite Roman column, presented in 1957 to Mayor Nathan Phillips by the Hon. Umberto Tupini, Mayor of the City of Rome, as a token of friendship between the citizens of the two cities. A sculpture found on the plaza outside **Union Station** was donated to the City of Toronto by the Italian community.

Columbus Centre, (Tel. 416-789-7011, 901 Lawrence Ave. W), houses the **Joseph D. Carrier Art Gallery**, (Tel. 416-789-7011). It has displayed acclaimed exhibits, including a drawing by Leonardo Da Vinci combined with facsimiles of the artist's major works. Italian cuisine is available at **Ristorante Boccaccio**, (Tel. 416-789-5555), and cultural arts courses are taught at the centre. Guests to the centre have included the President of Italy and tenor Luciano Pavarotti, who held a lifetime membership.

Italian restaurateurs have also given Toronto a fine cuisine served in sleek, elegantly decorated interiors that reflect the grandeur and beauty of Italian design. Peter Costa is credited with introducing northern Italian cuisine to Toronto. **Centro Restaurant & Lounge**, (Tel. 416-483-2211, 2472 Yonge St), is decorated with Italian marble and columns.

New upscale restaurants have their own following, including **La Fenice**, (Tel. 416-585-2377, 319 King St. W); **Grano**, (Tel. 416-440-1986, 2035 Yonge St) and **Mastro's Place**, (Tel. 416-636-8194, 890 Wilson Ave).

In Yorkville, **Il Posto Nuovo**, (Tel. 416-968-0469, 148 Yorkville Ave), along with the many outdoor cafes in the area, contributes to the European and Italian atmosphere of the neighbourhood. At **Lenny's Ristorante-Pizzeria**, (Tel. 416-239-2222, 4748 Dundas St. W), owners Leonardo and Rosalba Fuda's house specialities are linguine primavera, and cozze marinara, with a finale of a tiramisu.

Popular pizza haunts are **Filippo's Gourmet Pizzeria**, (Tel. 416-658-0568, 744 St. Clair Ave. W); **Regina Pizzeria**, (Tel. 416-535-2273, 782 College St); **Camarra's Pizzeria & Restaurant**, (Tel. 416-789-3221, 2899 Dufferin St); and **La Sem Ltd.**, (Tel. 905-624-8888, 1275 Eglinton Ave. E., Mississauga).

A strip of restaurants along Avenue Road have made the North York neighbourhood a popular dining area. They include **Rossini Dining Lounge**, (Tel. 416-481-1188, 1988 Avenue Rd); Other Italian Restaurants in Toronto include **Biagio**, (Tel. 416-366-4040, 155 King St. E); **Terroni on Adelaide**, (Tel. 416-203-3093, 57 Adelaide St E); **Romanga Mia**, (Tel. 416-363-8370, 106 Front St E); **Sotto Sotto**, (Tel. 416-962-0011, 116A Avenue Rd); **Sotto in the Village**, (Tel. 416-322-8818, 425 Spadina Rd); **Mistura**, (Tel. 416-515-0009, 265 Davenport Rd), and **Fieramosca Trattoria**, (Tel. 416-323-0636, 36A Prince Arthur Ave) Owned by Mario Micucci.

There are many shops that carry Italian cheeses, including local super-markets and several cheese manufacturers such as **International Cheese Ltd.**, (Tel. 416-769-3597, 67 Mulock Ave); **Pasquale Bros. Downtown Ltd.**, (16 Goodrich Rd.); **Siena Foods Ltd.**, (Tel. 416-239-3967, 16 Newbridge Ave); **Grande Cheese Co. Ltd.**, (22 Orfus Rd., 175 Milvan Dr., and 6 Scott Dr., Richmond Hill); and **Il Centro del Formaggio**, (Tel. 416-531-4453, 578 College St. W).

Contemporary Italian design furniture and home furnishings are avail-able at **Abitare Design**, (Tel. 416-363-1667, 130 Melford Dr); **Italinteriors**, (Tel. 416-366-9540, 69 Front St. E.); and **Martin Daniel Interiors Inc.**, (Tel. 416-667-0080, 2663 Steeles Ave. W). Contact: Marcello Tarantino.

The **Joseph J. Piccininni Community Centre**, (Lansdowne Ave. and St. Clair Ave. W), features two indoor bocce courts, and recreational rooms for playing Italian card games such as stoppa, tressette, and briscola. The centre was named after the city's first Italian Canadian alderman.

For fine Italian clothing, **Marcello Tarantino's**, (Tel. 416-925-2464, 17 Hazelton Ave).

Religious Centres, Schools and Other Institutions

The vast majority of Toronto's Italians are Roman Catholic.

- ◆ ST. FRANCIS OF ASSISI CHURCH, (Tel. 416-536-8195, 72 Mansfield Ave), was built in 1904 and continues to be a spiritual centre for the commu-nity, with 20,000 attending on Good Friday and St. Anthony's Day.
- ◆ HOLY ANGELS CHURCH, (Tel. 416-255-1691, 61 Jutland Rd).
- ◆ IMMACULATE CONCEPTION, (Tel. 416-651-7875, 4 Richardson Ave).
- ◆ OUR LADY OF VICTORY, (Tel. 416-769-1171, 117 Guestville Ave).
- ◆ ST. ALFONSO, (Tel. 416-653-4486 540 St. Clair Ave. W).
- ◆ ST. AMBROSE, (Tel. 416-251-8282, 782 Brown's Line).
- ◆ ST. ANTHONY'S CHURCH, (Tel. 416-536-3333, 1041 Bloor St., W).

- ST. AUGUSTINE OF CANTERBURY CHURCH, (Tel. 416-661-8221, 80 Shoreham Dr).
- ST. BERNARDO, (Tel. 416-241-6738, 1789 Lawrence Ave. W).
- ST. BRIGID, (Tel. 416-696-8660, 300 Wolverleigh Blvd).
- ST. CATHERINE OF SIENA, (Tel. 416-466-9433, 1099 Danforth Ave).
- ST. CHARLES, (Tel. 416-787-0369, 811 Lawrence Ave. W).
- ST. CLARE, (Tel. 416-654-7087, 133 Westmount Ave).
- ST. CLARE OF ASSISI, (Tel. 905-653-8000, 150 St. Francis Ave., Woodbridge).
- ST. JOHN BOSCO, (Tel. 416-651-1491, 402 Westmount Ave).
- ST. LEO, (Tel. 416-251-1109, 277 Royal York Rd).
- ST. MATTHEW, (Tel. 416-653-7191, 706 Old Weston Rd).
- ST. NORBERT, (Tel. 416-636-0213, Ancaster and Regent).
- ST. PHILIP NERI, (Tel. 416-241-3101, 2100 Jane St).
- ST. ROCH, (Tel. 416-749-0328, 2889 Islington Ave).
- ST. SEBASTIANO, (Tel. 416-536-2302, 20 Pauline Ave).
- ST. THOMAS AQUINAS, Tel. 416-782-8943, 640 Glenholme Ave).
- ST. WILFRID'S, (Tel. 416-638-0313, 1675 Finch Ave. W).
- VILLA COLOMBO HOME FOR THE AGED, (Tel. 416-789-2113, 40 Playfair Ave), built in 1976, is a 268-bed centre for seniors, which offers a daycare centre, a chapel, and a bus fleet named after Christopher Columbus's three ships. Caboto Terrace, and Casa Del Zotto next door, provide 460 geared-to-income apartments for seniors, and l Vita Community Living Services operates group homes and offers programs for the developmentally handicapped.
- CENTRO SCUOLA E CULTURA ITALIANA AND DANTE SOCIETY OF TORONTO, (Tel. 416-789-4970, 901 Lawrence Ave. W), organizes heritage language classes and cultural programs and exchanges. Director: Alberto Di Giovanni.

The University of Toronto has the largest Italian department with the highest number of students taking Italian studies in North America. The Murray Elia Chair at York University encourages research in Italian Canadian studies.

- BANCA COMMERCIALE ITALIANA, (Tel. 416-654-1920, 1241 St. Clair Ave. W., and Tel. 416-245-5145, 1617 Wilson Ave.)

Holidays and Celebrations

◆ NATIONAL DAY, June 2, celebrates the day Italians voted in favour of a republic following the Second World War. The Italian consulate usually hosts a reception, and a parade takes place in Corso Italia.

◆ CHIN PICNIC. Listed by the *Guinness Book of World Records* as the "largest outdoor free picnic in the world," the CHIN International Picnic was first held in 1966 at Toronto's **Centre Island**. The picnic, usually held on the July 1st Canada Day weekend at the **Canadian National Exhibition** Grounds, has outgrown its Italian roots to include multicultural folklore performances, beauty pageants, marching bands, and international entertainment.

◆ ITALIAN DAY, held the 3rd Sunday in August, was first staged in 1973 and takes place every summer at Ontario Place. The event features live entertainment, contests and games.

◆ ITALIAN FILM FESTIVAL, (1287 St. Clair Ave. W., Suite 7).

See Holidays and Celebrations in Glossary.

Media

◆ CORRIERE CANADESE AND TANDEM MAGAZINE, (Tel. 416-785-4300, www.corriere.com and www.tandemnews.com, 101 Wingold Ave). Editor: Paola Bernardi.

◆ JOHNNY LOMBARDI'S ITALIAN VARIETY SHOW, CITY-TV, Channel 57, % CHIN Radio/TV International, (Tel. 416-531-9991, 622 College St). Sunday, 12:00 p.m. to 2:00 p.m.

◆ LO SPECCHIO, (Tel. 905-856-2823, www.lospecchio.com, 160 Woodbridge Ave., Unit 101, Woodbridge). A weekly tabloid. Also publishes the monthly magazine Donna. Editor: Sergio Tagliavini.

◆ STUDIO APERTO, Television Program on OMNI Television, CFMT-TV, (Tel. 416-260-0047, 545 Lakeshore Blvd. W). Tuesday to Saturday, 6:30 a.m. to 7:00 a.m.

◆ TELELATINO NETWORK INC., (Tel. 416-744-8200, 5125 Steeles Ave. W). Daily, 1:00 p.m. to 3:00 p.m. and 7:30 p.m. to 1:00 a.m.

◆ CHIN RADIO/TV INTERNATIONAL, (622 College St., M6G 1B6, Tel. 416-531-9991.) The broadcasting system provides information and entertainment for more than 30 linguistic and cultural communities—only Vatican Radio broadcasts in more languages. The centre provides 24 hours a day of radio programming and 13 hours a week of television programming. Contact: Ali Bidabadi.

The Venitian Ball is held annually in Toronto. Participants enjoy the masked revelry for which Venice is famous.

Italian programs on CHIN 100.7 FM include:

◆ ITALIA BY NIGHT, Monday, 1:00 a.m. to 3:00 a.m. Host: Giorgio. Tuesday to Friday, 12:00 a.m to 3:00 a.m. Host: Giorgio. Saturday, 12:00 a.m. to 2:00 a.m. Host: Franco Valli. Sunday, 12:00 a.m. to 3:00 a.m. Host: Franco Valli.

◆ SPORT PROGRAM, Sunday, 10:00 a.m. to 12:00 p.m. Host: Alfonso Ciasca.

◆ SU DI GIRI, Monday to Friday, 3:00 p.m. to 7:00 p.m. Contact: Fiorella and Franco Valli.

Italian programs on CHIN 1540 AM include:

◆ ATTENTI A QUEI DUE, Saturday, 10:00 a.m to 3:00 p.m. Host: Ornella.

◆ CANTA NAPOLI, Saturday, 9:00 a.m. to 10:00 a.m. Host: Alfonso Ciasca.

◆ IL SABATO DEL VILLAGIO, Saturday, 7:00 a.m. to 9:00 a.m. Host: Ontario Sarracini.

◆ ITALIAN FOLKLORE, Saturday, 3:00 p.m. to 5:45 p.m. Host: Italo Kuci and Salvatore. (Folklore from various regions of Italy.)

◆ MUSIC OF YOUR LIFE (ITALIAN STYLE), Monday to Friday, 1:00 p.m. to 3:00 p.m. Host: Nico Navarra.

◆ PER VOI TUTTI, Monday to Friday, 9:00 a.m. to 10:00 a.m.
Host: Vittorio Coco.

◆ RAI (from Italy), Monday, Thursday, 3:00 a.m. to 6:00 a.m.; Friday,
midnight to 1:00 a.m.

◆ TUTTO TUO, Monday to Friday, 11:00 a.m. to 1:00 p.m. Host: Ornella.

◆ WAKE UP ITALIAN STYLE, Monday to Friday, 6:00 a.m. to 9:00 a.m.
Host: Vittorio Coco.

◆ WEEKEND ITALIAN, Sunday, 1:00 p.m. to 6:00 p.m.

Organizations

◆ VENETO FEDERATION, (Tel. 905-851-5551, 7465 Kipling Ave., Woodbridge).

◆ CANADIAN ITALIAN BUSINESS AND PROFESSIONAL ASSOCIATION OF
TORONTO, (Tel. 416-782-4445, 901 Lawrence Ave. W).

◆ COSTI-IIAS, (Tel. 416-658-1600, 1710 Dufferin St). A non-profit
community organization initially organized to assist Italian workers in
the construction industry. Today, it provides a number of educational
and social welfare services for Italians and other immigrants.
President: Mr. B. Suppa.

◆ COLUMBUS CENTRE, (Tel. 416-789-7011, 901 Lawrence Ave. W). Home
to the **Canadian Italian Advocates Association; Canadian Italian
Business and Professional Association of Toronto**, (Tel. 416-782-
4445). President: Mario Cinelli.

◆ ITALIAN CULTURAL INSTITUTE, (Tel. 416-921-3802, www.iicto-ca.org,
496 Huron St). Under the jurisdiction of the Italian Foreign Office,
this Institution promotes Italian culture through lectures, exhibitions,
and conferences. Housed in an 1879 Queen Anne style building with
Palladian elements. Director: Carlo Coen.

◆ THE NATIONAL CONGRESS OF ITALIAN CANADIANS (TORONTO DISTRICT),
(Tel. 416-531-9964, www.canadese.org, 756 Ossington Ave), is the
voice and unifying force for more than one million Italian Canadians.
Originally called **FACI (Federation of Italian Canadian Clubs and
Associations)**, it is an umbrella for more than 55 associations, sports
clubs, village clubs, and churches. It holds seminars on Italian history
and has played an important role in the development of Villa Colombo
and other community activities. President: Anthony Carella.

◆ VILLA CHARITIES INC., (901 Lawrence Ave. W., M6A 1C3, Tel. 416-
789-7011, www.villacharities.com), was established in 1971 as a charitable community organization that has developed, raised money, and
built and operated the Columbus Centre, Villa Colombo, and others.
President: John Gennaro. Director: Palmacchio Di Iulio.

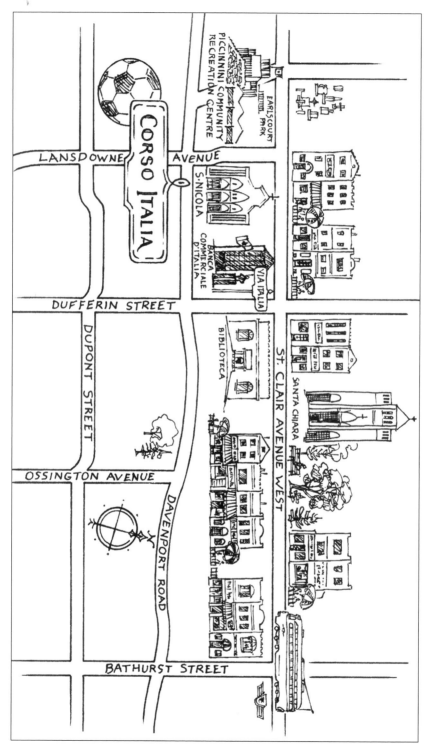

There are more than 300 incorporated and unincorporated social and regional Italian clubs in the city:

◆ FAMEE FURLANE—TORONTO, (Tel. 905-851-1166, 7065 Islington Ave., Woodbridge). The largest and most organized regional Italian club has meeting rooms, club rooms, a restaurant, and senior residences.

◆ SOCIETA FEMMINILE FRIULANA, (7065 Islington Ave., Woodbridge). A women's group with over 800 members. Activities include theatre groups, library exchanges, picnics, and bowling. President: Susan Giust.

Consulates, Trade Commissions and Tourist Bureaus

◆ ITALIAN CONSULATE, (Tel. 416-977-1566, 136 Beverley St). The Italian consulate is housed in the former George Breadmore mansion built in 1872. Consul General: Mr. Gianni Bardini.

◆ ITALIAN CHAMBER OF COMMERCE, (Tel. 416-789-7169, www.iccbc.com, 80 Richmond St W, Suite 1502).

◆ ITALIAN GOVERNMENT TOURISM BOARD, (Tel. 416-925-4882, 175 Bloor St. E., Suite 907).

◆ ITALIAN TRADE COMMISSION, (Tel. 416-598-1555, 180 Dundas St. W, Suite 2002, Box 2).

Prominent Torontonians

Ron Barbaro, President, Ontario Casino Corporation, and former Chairman of the Metro Zoo; Maurizio Bevilacqua, MP; Rudy Bratty, developer; Mike Colle, MPP; Fred DeGasperis, developer; Elvio Delzotto, lawyer and developer; Joe Pantalone, former Deputy Mayor; Mario Sergio, MPP; Joseph Volpe, MP; Greg Sorbara, MPP and former Minister of Finance; Lenny Lombardi, President of CHIN Radio and Television; Lorenzo Berardinetti, MPP; Laura Albanese, MPP; Rosario Marchese, MPP; Alberto Di Giovanni, director, centro scuola-e-cultura; Corrado Paina, poet, Executive Director: Italian Chamber of Commerce of Ontario; Sergio Marchi, former MP and Cabinet Minister; Gianni Bragagnolo, President of Albatours; Nick Di Donato, Liberty Entertainment Group; Sam Di Michele, Executive Vice-President and General Manager of Cineplex Odeon; Consiglio De Nino, Senator of Canada; Gabriella Martinelli, founder of Capri Films; Franco Prevedello, entrepreneur of Italian cuisine in Toronto; Donald J.P. Ziraldo, Managing Director and Co-Founder of Inniskillin Wines.

Contributors: Palmacchio Di Iulio, Gino Cucchi, Armand Scaini, Antonio Nicaso.

The Japanese Community

The Japanese Canadian Cultural Centre stands as a monument to the Issei—the pioneers of the community who ventured across the Pacific at the turn of the century to establish roots in Canada. The cultural centre provides a venue for Toronto's 20,000 Japanese Canadians to express pride in their heritage, and for other Torontonians to experience Japanese cultural traditions, such as ikebana (the art of flower arranging) and martial arts (kendo, judo, karate, and iaido).

Japanese migration to Canada occurred during the first two decades of the 20th century. Early settlers were from Japan's farming and fishing villages. By 1914, there were 10,000 Japanese in Canada, mostly young men who had settled primarily in Vancouver and Victoria.

A photo of J. Kono, dated 1885, is the earliest evidence of Japanese settlement in Ontario. The first Japanese names to appear in the City of Toronto Directory were Kenji Ishikawa and Shigesaburo Ubukata in 1897. The two partners were silk jobbers who expanded their business into an enterprise with offices across Canada. Today, the **Ubukata Bursary**, established in 1926, is still available to Japanese-born students at the **University of Toronto**. Another prominent member of the early Toronto community was Takatsuna Kurata, who became an assistant curator at the **Royal Ontario Museum**.

Until 1941, the Toronto community consisted of approximately six families. Merchants sold imported Japanese wares, and others worked in hotels and restaurants, or were employed by the **Canadian Pacific Railway**. Following the bombing of Pearl Harbor by Japan, the Canadian government ordered the removal of Japanese Canadians from an area within 160 km of the Pacific coast. As the Second World War drew to a close, Japanese Canadians began to move east to other parts of Canada.

By 1947, there were 5,000 Japanese Canadians living in Toronto. The arrival of a Japanese minister under the sponsorship of the **United Church** marked the beginning of the Japanese Church in Toronto. Early organizations included the **Nisei Men & Women's Committee**, established to help with housing and jobs; the **Japanese Canadian Committee for Democracy**; and the **National Japanese Canadian Citizens' Association**, located on Gerrard Street.

In the 1950s and '60s, more Japanese Canadians arrived from the West, settling in the city and later moving to suburbs such as Scarborough and Etobicoke. As a result of changes to Canada's immigration laws, new settlers from Japan's urban middle class arrived in Canada. Called the Shin Issei, they were the first new migrants to arrive from Japan in almost 50 years. The third generation of Japanese Canadians (Sansei) were born during the 1950s and raised in the Canadian community; many speak little or no Japanese, 92% live in either Ontario, British Colombia or Alberta.

Prominent Japanese Canadians that have contributed to the city include the late George Tanaka, a renowned landscape artist and civil rights activist, and the late Ken Adachi, columnist and author of *The Enemy That Never Was: A History of the Japanese Canadians.*

Places to Go

The **Japanese Canadian Cultural Centre** (JCCC), (Tel. 416-441-2345, www.jccc.on.ca, 6 Garamond Ct). In 1999 it moved into a building remodeled by **Bruce Kuwabara and Associates**. The JCCC houses a library of books by Japanese and Japanese Canadian writers. A gift shop carries origami supplies, flower pots, gifts, and books. In 1988, Noboru Takeshita, the former Prime Minister of Japan, paid a visit and left behind as a gift a ceremonial wooden cask of sake. Classes are held in ikebana, sumi-e (brush painting), shodo (calligraphy), sogetsu, bunka shishu (embroidery), conversational Japanese, Japanese cooking, bonsai, norizome, and other crafts. Instructions are given in karaoke (singing) and taiko (drums), and in the martial arts, including judo, kendo, karate, and iaido (the way of harmonizing spirit). The centre holds art shows, lectures, and demonstrations of creative arts, music, and dance. Annual events include the Spring Festival, Issei Day, the Artisan Show, ikebana and bonsai exhibitions, sumi-e painting displays, and a bazaar. Director: James Heron.

Japanese cherry trees are planted in **High Park**, which also contains two commemorative plaques from the Canadian Pavilion at **Expo '70**, held in Osaka, Japan.

The **Japanese Temple Bell** on the west island of Ontario Place was erected on the occasion of the centennial anniversary of the Japanese in Canada. The bell is rung on New Year's Eve and in July for Obon, the Buddhist remembrance day for deceased relatives.

Japanese cuisine is well known for sushi (little vinegared rolls of rice topped or filled—usually with raw fish). The staples of Japanese cuisine are rice, seafood, soybean products, noodles, vegetables, and dried seaweed.

Meals include appetizers such as miso soup (fermented bean paste) and sashimi (sliced varieties of raw fish) dipped in sauces, and several entrees, including chawan mushi (sliced chicken, shrimp, and mushrooms covered with egg custard), fish or vegetable tempura (deep fried and served with dips), and teriyaki dishes (marinated in soy sauce and sweet rice wine). Popular desserts include green tea ice cream and orange mandarin cream pie. Favoured Japanese beverages are Kirin (beer), hot green tea, and warm sake (rice wine).

In Japanese restaurants, many dishes are cooked on grills or barbecues in front of diners. Meals are eaten with chopsticks, and diners can experience Japanese-style seating by removing their shoes and sitting at tatami tables (low tables in private rooms).

Many Japanese restaurants contain sushi bars where patrons sit at a counter and select sushi from a display case of seafood. At **Shogun Japanese Restaurant**, (Tel. 416-964-8665, 154 Cumberland Ave), sushi is served in lacquered boxes from the bar which features a display of yellowtail, sea urchin, flounder, sea bream, squid, and octopus sushi.

At **Nami**, (Tel. 416-362-7373, 55 Adelaide St. E), private rooms with sliding doors are popular among visiting celebrities, including the Japanese diplomats who visited Toronto during the Economic Summit in 1988. The restaurant was designed by Raymond Moriyama, and its decor includes brush paintings, a sushi bar, and a robata counter where meals are cooked by Chiz Uyeyama, Canada's only female robata chef. (Robata is a charcoal grill used for teppanyaki-style cooking.) The menu includes suimono, teriyaki, and tempura dishes, eel steamed with egg, and grilled yellowtail with daikon.

Other examples of Japanese-style cooking are found at **Benihana of Tokyo, Royal York Hotel**, (Tel. 416-860-5002, 100 Front St. W), where steaks, chicken, shrimp, lobster, and vegetable dishes are prepared at tables by chefs performing the ancient art of hibachi cooking. **Yamato Japanese Steak House**, (Tel. 416-927-0077, 18 Bellair St), has ten teppanyaki tables at which Japanese chefs prepare dishes such as steak flambe with brandy and vegetable teppanyaki.

Mariko, (Tel. 416-463-8231, 348 Danforth Ave), features health-conscious foods such as tofu dishes and vegetable sushi.

Around Toronto

AKANE Japanese & Korean Restaurant, (1344 Kennedy Rd); **Asakusa**, (Tel. 416-598-9030, 389 King St. W); **Ginko**, (Tel. 416-248-8445, 655

Dixon Rd); **Ichiricki**, (Tel. 416-923-2997, 120 Bloor St. E); **Katsura Japanese Restaurant**, (Tel. 416-444-2511, The Prince Hotel, 900 York Mills Rd); **Mikado**, (Tel. 416-421-6016, 114 Laird Dr); **Okonomi House**, (Tel. 416-925-6176, 23 Charles St. W); **Rikishi**, (Tel. 416-538-0760, 833 Bloor St. W); **Sasaya Japanese Restaurant**, (Tel. 416-487-3508, 257 Eglinton Ave. W); **Sushiman**, (Tel. 416-362-8793, 20 Richmond St. E); **Sushi Bistro**, (Tel. 416-971-5315, 204 Queen St. W); **Takesushi**, (Tel. 416-862-1891, 22 Front St. W); **Tokyo Grill**, (Tel. 416-968-7054, 582 Yonge St); **Zen Japanese Restaurant**, (Tel. 416-265-7111, 2803 Eglinton Ave. E).

At the **Japan Food Centre**, (Tel. 905-967-1033, 145 Main St. S, Newmarket), owner Relko Mitsuishi, carries a full line of food products including rice, rice crackers, soup mixes, Japanese vegetables, and frozen fish such as squid, mackerel, octopus, and tuna, as well as dried fish and sushi products. Other stores carrying Japanese foods are **Kealson**, (Tel. 416-261-2297, 2501 Eglinton Ave E); **Sandown Market**, (Tel. 416-496-9083, 4385 Sheppard Ave. E., and Tel. 416-259-8260, 826 Browns Line).

Ozawa Canada Inc., (Tel 905-731-5088, 135 East Beaver Creek Rd., Richmond Hill).

Japanese Shopping Centre, (3160 Steeles Ave. E., Markham), includes grocery shopping, fish store, sushi restaurant, bookstore (JAP), gift shop, bakery, and more.

Religious Centres, Schools and Other Institutions

Members of the Japanese community follow Buddhism, Christianity (many are Protestant), and Shintoism.

- ◆ JAPANESE (LANGUAGE) UNITED CHURCH, (Tel. 416-536-7004, 49 Bogert Ave).
- ◆ KONKO CHURCH OF TORONTO, (Tel. 416-261-9619, 398 Kennedy Rd).
- ◆ NICHIREN BUDDHIST CHURCH, (Tel. 416-463-9783, 20 Caithness Ave).
- ◆ ST. ANDREW JAPANESE CONGREGATION, ℅ St. David's Church, (Tel. 416-461-8399, 49 Donlands Ave).
- ◆ TENRIKYO, (Tel. 416-247-9791, 160 Gracefield Ave).
- ◆ TORONTO BUDDHIST CHURCH, (Tel. 416-534-4302, 1011 Sheppard Ave. W).
- ◆ ZEN BUDDHIST TEMPLE, (Tel. 416-658-0137, 297 College St).

Japanese language classes are held at:
- ◆ DON MILLS COLLEGIATE INSTITUTE, (Tel. 416-395-3190, 15 The Donway East).

- **TORONTO JAPANESE LANGUAGE SCHOOL**, Orde Street Jr. PS, (Tel. 416-393-1900, 18 Orde St).

Several banks and trust companies from Japan have offices in the city, including:

- **THE BANK OF TOKYO-MITSUBISHI CANADA**, (Tel. 416-865-0220, Royal Bank Plaza, South Tower, Suite 1700).
- **NOMURA SECURITIES CO. LTD.**, (Tel. 416-868-1683, 2 Bloor St. W., Suite 700).
- **DAI-ICHI KANGYO BANK (CANADA)**, (Tel. 416-365-9666, Commerce Court West, Suite 5025).
- **SANWA BANK CANADA**, (Tel. 416-366-2583, BCE Place, Canada Trust Tower, 161 Bay St., Suite 4400).

Holidays and Celebrations

- **NEW YEAR'S DAY** on January 1 is celebrated with house parties. On New Year's Eve many Japanese eat soba (buckwheat noodles) to bring the old year to a happy ending and to welcome the new. The first meal of the new year consists of ozoni—symbolic of realizing dreams—mochi (rice cakes) which are boiled with vegetables such as satoimo (a kind of potato believed to drive away evil spirits), and daikon (a large white radish with strong roots that represents a firm family foundation). Kobu (seaweed) is considered to be a lucky food as its name forms part of the word yorokobu (to be glad).
- **HINA-MATSURI (DOLLS' FESTIVAL)**, is celebrated in March. Traditionally, ceremonial dolls and miniature household articles are arranged on the Hina-Dan (tiered shelves covered with a red cloth). The dolls are bought for the first daughter in a family and become family heirlooms.
- **HARU MATSURI**. In Toronto, the **Japanese Canadian Cultural Centre** holds Haru Matsuri (spring festival) on the first weekend of March. Japanese cuisine is served; Hina-Matsuri dolls are displayed; and Japanese dancing, drumming, crafts such as sumi-e, ikebana, shodo, bunka shishu, and martial arts are performed.
- **TANGO-NU-SEKKU**, the traditional Boys' Festival of Japan, is celebrated on May 5. Also known as Children's Day, paper streamers in the shape of a carp are hung on a pole in the garden. The carp, with its great power and determination, is an example for young boys.
- **BIZAAR**. On the first Saturday in May, the **Japanese Canadian Cultural Centre** holds a bazaar offering Japanese gifts, leather goods, plants,

boutique items, dry goods, hardware, and paper flowers for sale. Dining facilities are available for sampling sushi, udon, and tempura dishes.

◆ OBON FESTIVAL, Held sometime between mid-July and mid-August, is a Buddhist festival of lighted lanterns meant to guide the spirits of departed ancestors on their annual visit to the family home. Celebrations are held in honour of the returning spirits. The festival ends with a circular folk dance. On the second Saturday of the month, Buddhist dancers perform at City Hall, and a bell-ringing ceremony takes place on the second Sunday of the month at the site of the Japanese Temple Bell at **Ontario Place**.

◆ ARIGATO DAY. The Centre holds a Karaoke Concert and Arigato Day to say thank you to its volunteers with a dinner and celebration.

◆ PICNIC. An annual community picnic is held in Caledon, at the **JCCC**'s recreational area, along with the annual picnics of the Japanese Anglican and Buddhist churches. The grounds have facilities for fishing, swimming, skating, and cross country skiing, and a farm area for growing Japanese vegetables such as daikon and gobo. Small wedding parties, conference, and business groups rent the facilities.

◆ THE YUSUZUMI (SUMMER) DANCE is held in August at the Japanese Canadian Cultural Centre.

◆ ISSEI DAY, in October, honours the first generation of Japanese in Canada with an anniversary dinner and dance for the Nisei-Sansei and friends.

◆ ARTISAN, a show and sale of crafts, is held every November, along with **Aki No Uta Matsurl** (a song fest).

◆ KOHAKU UTA GASSEN, a song contest, is held for men and women in December. **Haru** and **Aki No Uta Matsuri** (Spring and Fall Song Festivals) are musical variety shows of Japanese songs, odori (traditional dances), skits, and kayo drama (comedy plays). The festivals are highlighted by colourful Japanese seasonal backdrops and life-like props.

◆ NEW YEAR'S EVE is celebrated with a dance held at the **Japanese Canadian Cultural Centre**.

Every year, the **Toronto Japanese Garden Club** exhibits the art of flower arranging and landscaping with displays of ikebana, bonsai, asagao, and Japanese gardens. These shows are held each year:

◆ ASAGAO at the **Prince Hotel** in August.

◆ CHRYSANTHEMUM AND FLOWERS at the **JCCC** in October.

See Holidays and Celebrations in Glossary.

Media

◆ OMNI-TV, CHANNEL 47, (Tel. 416-260-0047, 545 Lakeshore Blvd. W). News from ANN (Tokyo), local community events and announcements. Host: Susan Tsuji.

◆ NIKKEI VOICE, (Tel. 416-516-1779, 382 Harbord St). A monthly publication and national forum for Japanese Canadian community. Publisher: Frank Moritsugu. Editor: Jesse Nishihata.

◆ THE NIKKA TIMES, (Tel. 416-923-2819, 720 Spadina Ave., Suite 420). A weekly newspaper established in 1969; published in Japanese. Publisher-Editor: Nobuo Iromoto.

◆ THE NEW CANADIAN, (Tel. 416-593-1583, 524 Front St, W, 2nd Floor).

◆ BITS MAGAZINE, (Tel. 416-964-2599, 360 Bloor St. W, Suite 207)

Organizations

◆ JAPANESE CANADIAN CULTURAL CENTRE, (Tel. 416-441-2345, 6 Garamond Ct). President: Marty Kobayashi.
At the same address:

◆ THE NEW JAPANESE CANADIAN ASSOCIATION, (Tel. 905-475-7173, Fax 905-261-9384). Assists new immigrants with citizenship and provides social, recreational, and educational information. President: Mr. Keiko Ono, Vice President: Yoshi Nagaishi.

◆ JAPANESE SOCIAL SERVICES, (www.jss.ca) social support service for Japanese speakers.

◆ ASSOCIATION FOR JAPANESE CULTURE. Established in 1978, members of the association teach school children and other interested persons about Japanese culture through demonstrations, videos, and stories. Every year, some 6,000 students from Ontario's elementary schools attend the centre for an introductory lesson on Japan. The instructors make their presentations wearing kimonos, and lessons include the ritual of the Tea Ceremony, paper-folding, and topics such as trade between Canada and Japan. The program is sponsored by the Japanese Government through the Japanese Consulate General in Toronto.

Arts groups include:

◆ THE AYAME KAI DANCE GROUP, begun in 1964 as the **Sansei Choir-Dancers**, which performs odori dances.

◆ THE IKENOBO STYLE AND SOGETSU STYLE IKEBANA SOCIETY OF TORONTO, offers classes in flower arrangement.

◆ TORONTO JAPANESE GARDEN CLUB, organized in 1953, practises the art of horticulture and holds several shows each year.

◆ THE KARAOKE CLUB is a singing club made up of enka (popular song) enthusiasts who perform at various functions.

◆ THE SAKURA KAI DANCE GROUP, organized in 1960, which performs the buyo or odori, traditional Japanese dances.

◆ YAKUDO DRUM GROUP has the largest collection of taiko (drums) outside of Japan.

Groups for seniors include:

◆ THE ANNEX SENIORS, a social group whose activities include the making of crafts for sale at bazaars.

◆ HI FUMI STEPPERS (SENIOR) GROUP, which performs line dancing and Japanese folk dancing wearing ukata kimonos and happi coats.

◆ HI-FU-MI (JAPANESE FOR 1-2-3), which signifies all three generations of Japanese Canadians participating in dance groups.

◆ WYNFORD SENIORS' CLUB MOMIJI KAI, organized in 1969 to assist elderly Issei in enjoying activities together.

◆ MOMIJI SENIORS CENTRE, (Tel. 416-261-6683, www.momiji.com, 3555 Kingston Rd),Executive Director: Brigitte Robertson.

Other groups include: The **Women's Auxiliary**, organized in 1960, which has lent support to the community through volunteer work at JCCC's events and fundraising causes; **3 Pitch League**; **Kendo Club** (The Way of Sword-manship); **Student Association**; **Baseball League**; **Japanese Canadian Citizens Association**; **Friday Night Duplicate Bridge Club**; **Judo Club**; **Aikido Club**; **Karate Club**; **Sunday Niters**, a social club that participates in ballroom dancing; **Friday Niters**, a social club; and **Ken Jin Kais**, organized in the pre-war days, which are groups made up of people from the same prefecture in Japan.

◆ BUKYO KAI DANCE GROUP, (918 Bathurst St), based at the Toronto Buddhist Church.

◆ CANADIAN ASSOCIATION OF JAPANESE AUTOMOBILE DEALERS, (Tel. 416-620-9717, 1 Eva Rd., Suite 101).

◆ JAPAN AUTOMOBILE MANUFACTURERS ASSOCIATION OF CANADA, (Tel. 416-968-0150, www.jama.ca, 151 Bloor St. W., Suite 460).

◆ THE GREATER TORONTO CHAPTER OF THE NATIONAL ASSOCIATION OF JAPANESE CANADIANS (NAJC), (Tel. 416-516-1375, 382 Harbord St). Established in 1986, one of 14 chapters under the **National Association of Japanese Canadians,** the Toronto NAJC was incorporated in 1993, as a not-for-profit community-based organization to strive for equal rights and liberties. President: Tracy Matsuo.

◆ TORONTO JAPANESE ASSOCIATION OF COMMERCE AND INDUSTRY, (Tel. 416-360-0235, www.torontoshokokai.org, 3244 Yonge St).

Consulates, Trade Commissions and Tourist Bureaus

◆ CONSULATE GENERAL OF JAPAN, (Tel. 416-363-7038, Suite 3300, Royal Trust Tower, Toronto Dominion Centre, 77 King St. W). Consul General: Mr. Tetsuo Yamashita.

◆ JAPAN INFORMATION CENTRE, (Tel. 416-363-5488, 6 Garamond Ct).

◆ JAPAN NATIONAL TOURIST ORGANIZATION, (Tel. 416-366-7140, 481 University Ave Suite 306).

◆ JAPAN EXTERNAL TRADE CENTRE (JETRO), (Tel. 416-861-0000, 181 University Ave., Suite 1600).

Prominent Torontonians

Dennis Akiyama, actor; Kaz Hamazaki, sumi-e (landscape) artist; Gene Kinoshita, architect and President, Royal Academy of Arts; Joy Kogawa, poet and author; Bruce Kuwabara, architect; Roy Matsui, architect; Dr. David Suzuki, scientist, columnist, and host of CBC-TV "The Nature of Things"; David H. Tsubouchi, former Chair, Management Board of Cabinet, Government of Ontario; Sam Yamada, photographer and sculptor.

Contributors: Harry Taba, Publisher, Canada Times; Martin Koyabashi, JCCC; Elaine Taguchi, National Association of Japanese Canadians; Rui Umezawa, Japan Information Centre.

The Jewish Community

was Judah Joseph who arrived in 1838 and opened a jewelry shop on King Street. Since then, the entrepreneurial spirit of Jewish Torontonians has promoted commerce and industry in the city, while Toronto's art's scene has flourished with the help of its Jewish benefactors, participants, and artists.

The late 1830s brought European Jewish families to Toronto from England and Germany, the United States, and Quebec. In 1856, the **Toronto Hebrew Congregation** was established at Yonge and Richmond streets, providing services for some 20 families. The congregation still exists as **Holy Blossom Temple**, the largest Reform synagogue in Canada.

Following the assassination of Czar Alexander II in 1881, Jewish refugees fleeing the Russian Empire arrived in Toronto. They first settled along York and Richmond streets and gradually moved to the area known as The Ward, bounded by University Avenue and Queen Street, and College and Yonge streets.

Jewish businessmen in the salvage trades could be seen pushing their carts through the streets of The Ward. The neighbourhood was close to the factories where labourers worked and contained the shops of Jewish barbers, shoemakers, grocers, bakers, and pawnbrokers. Ice-cream parlours became centres for socializing and holding meetings.

Of the dozen synagogues that were established, **Goel Tzedec** was founded in 1883 on Richmond Street, followed by **Beth Hamidrash Hagodol Chevra Tehillim** in 1887. Both merged in 1952 to form **Beth Tzedec**, Canada's largest synagogue. **Shomrai Shaboth**, established in 1889, is the only early Toronto institution to remain traditionally Orthodox.

The first lodge of **B'nai Brith Canada** was founded in 1875, and today it is the oldest Canadian Jewish service organization in the world. At the turn of the century, the **Mozirer Sick Benefit Society** was formed as well as the **Pride of Israel Sick Benefit Society**, which is now the largest organization of its kind in the city. The **Toronto Hebrew Religion School** was established in 1907 on Simcoe Street and is the ancestor of today's **Associated Hebrew Schools**.

The Jewish neighbourhood eventually moved west to Spadina Avenue and Dundas Street where Jewish clothing stores, garment factories, and delicatessens thrived and **Kensington Market** developed into a Jewish marketplace. In the 1920s and '30s, approximately 60,000 Jews lived around Spadina Avenue, building synagogues and operating small shops as tailors, furriers, and bakers. Spadina was nicknamed "Little Jerusalem" for its Jewish establishments.

Following the Second World War, 60,000 survivors of the Holocaust arrived in Canada, and Toronto's expanding Jewish community moved to the suburbs, as far north as Thornhill. Today, North York and Thornhill form the heart of Toronto's Jewish neighbourhood, where synagogues, bookstores, kosher markets, and delis stretch along Bathurst Street, reflecting the presence of the 180,000-member community.

In the 1960s, Jews arrived from Israel and the United States, and non-Yiddish-speaking Sephardic Jews immigrated from North Africa. The community now includes additions from Iran, Iraq, India, and Russia.

Jewish Torontonians have been entrepreneurs in almost every kind of enterprise, from mining to paper mills, real estate to manufacturing. There are more than 2,000 Jewish doctors and lawyers practising in the city. In politics, Phil Givens was one of the city's most respected mayors, and **Nathan Phillips Square** at City Hall is named after Toronto's first Jewish mayor. In North York, **Mel Lastman Square** recognizes the mayor who dominated North York politics for close to two decades before being elected first mayor of the Toronto "megacity." A library at the **University of Toronto** and a museum of Canadiana arts are named after steel merchant and collector Sigmund Samuel. The **Bluma Appel Theatre** at the **St. Lawrence Centre** was named after its benefactor.

Late businessman and patron of the arts Ed Mirvish has his name in lights on two city blocks. Located in the Annex is **Honest Ed's**, the world-famous bargain shopping centre, and on a lively stretch of King Street West are Mirvish's **Royal Alexandra** and **Princess of Wales** Theatres. Other prominent Jewish Torontonians include the Reichmanns, real estate developers of such enterprises as **First Canadian Place** and **Harbourfront's Queen's Quay Terminal**.

Among Jewish landmarks in the city are **Mount Sinai Hospital**, which evolved from a 1909 dispensary on Elizabeth Street; and the **Baycrest Centre for Geriatric Care**, which began in 1917 as the **Jewish Home for the Aged**.

Places to Go

On Saturday mornings, commerce on Bathurst Street in North York slows, although the sidewalks are filled with people out on their Sabbath walk to the synagogue. Some Jewish men wear traditional satin coats and fur-trimmed hats or yarmulkes and carry talith (prayer shawls) on their way to the synagogues. The **Lipa Green Building**, (Tel. 416-635-2883, 4600 Bathurst St), named after a prominent Jewish builder, houses some of the community's social service organizations, and a museum, library, and archives.

The **Ontario Jewish Archives** hold manuscripts and printed documents, personal papers, notebooks, diaries, financial and cemetery records, passports, newspapers, films, paintings, tape recordings of interviews, and artifacts. The archives can be viewed by appointment from Monday to Thursday, 9:00 a.m. to 4:45 p.m., and Friday, 9:00 a.m. to 2:00 p.m. Contact: Dr. Ellen Scheinberg.

The **Koffler Centre of The Arts**, (Tel. 416-636-1990 ext. 270, with a second location at 750 Spadina Ave), offers social, athletic, and cultural activities and operates theatre, dance, and music schools. The **Koffler Gallery**, (Tel. 416-636-2145), exhibits fine art and crafts. The annual Jewish Book Fair sells works by Jewish authors and features guest speakers and youth programs. Director: Jane Mahut.

Next door to the **Lipa Green Building** is the **Bathurst Jewish Centre**, North Branch, (Tel. 416-636-1880, 4588 Bathurst St,. The Bloor Branch is at Tel. 416-924-6211, 750 Spadina Ave). The building's recreational centre includes a swimming pool, cafeteria, meeting halls, dance studio, and gymnasium. Plays and concerts are performed at **Leah Posluns Theatre**, (Tel. 416-636-1880, ext. 354). Contact: Reva Stern.

Further south on Bathurst Street, the **Beth Tzedec Reuben and Helene Dennis Museum**, (Tel. 416-781-3511, 1700 Bathurst St), is located in Canada's largest synagogue and maintains a collection of pottery, coins, Hanukkah menorahs (candelabrum), and spice boxes. Curator: Dorion Liebgott.

Earl Bales Park at Sheppard Avenue and Bathurst Street has become a recreational locale for the community's elderly, who often stroll along Raoul Wallenberg Road, the park's main thoroughfare, named after the Swedish war hero who saved thousands of Jews from concentration camps. **Earl Bales Senior's Centre** offers fitness classes, swimming, tennis, dance, and art exhibits. The **Skylight Theatre** is constructed in the style of a classical amphitheatre.

Many of the bakeries, restaurants, and shops along Bathurst Street follow Jewish dietary laws. The mixing of dairy products and meat is forbidden, as is the eating of pork and shellfish. Meat is slaughtered by trained kosher slaughterers only. **Kashruth Directory**, (Tel. 416-635-9550, www.cor.ca), published by the **Kashrut Council**, lists supervised retail and commercial products and services that meet the requirements of Jewish dietary laws. They also have a kosher information service. Some of the bakeries listed include: **Isaac's**, (Tel. 416-789-7587, 3390 Bathurst St., and Tel. 416-630-1678, 221 Wilmington Ave); **Richman's**, (Tel. 416-636-9710, 4119 Bathurst St). Restaurants and delicatessens listed in the directory include: **Hartman's Kosher Meats**, (Tel. 416-663-7779, 5988 Bathurst St); and **Marky's Glatt Kosher Delicatessen and Restaurant**, (Tel. 416-638-1081, 280 Wilson Ave).

Jewish cuisine, influenced by European cooking, features delicatessen meats, smoked fish, borscht (beet soup), kasha (cracked buckwheat cooked until tender), and pirogen (stuffed dough pockets). Popular Jewish dishes include blintzes (crepes rolled around cheese or fruit fillings), gefilte fish (fish balls made from ground, cooked freshwater fish); knishes (baked pastry shell filled with potato, cheese, meat, fruit); knaidel (matzo meal dumpling); kugel (pudding or pudding soufflé). Popular breads are bagels (ring-shaped rolls), matzo (thin flat unleavened bread), and challah (braided egg bread served on the Friday night Sabbath meal).

Sunday mornings produce throngs of weekend shoppers who form lineups at the dozen or more bakeries along Bathurst Street between Lawrence and Wilson avenues. The **Open Window Bakery**, (Tel. 416-787-4246, 3507 Bathurst St), carries bagels and challahs, while a block away is **Gryfe's Bagel Bakery**, (Tel. 416-783-1552, 3421 Bathurst St), where Art and son Moishe Gryfe carry on a tradition started by Art's father in 1915. The Gryfes opened the **Crown Bakery** in Kensington Market in the 1930s, and today the bakery makes close to 4,000 whole wheat, poppy seed, sesame seed, and salt-free bagels a day. **Hermes Bakery**, (Tel. 416-787-1234, 2885 Bathurst St), is another spot for those searching for the perfect bagel.

At **Toronto Kosher**, (3459 Bathurst St., Tel. 416-633-9642), opened in 1956, co-owner Rabbi Shmuel Stroli often serves customers personally. The market sells strictly kosher TV dinners, smoked meats, and kosher poultry. **Daiter's Creamery and Appetizers**, (Tel. 416-781-6101, 3535 Bathurst St), is known for its creamed cheese, smoked fish and herring, and party trays. Kosher products from New York include **Manischewitz** jarred gefilte fish, crackers, matzo meal, and matzos. Everything chocolate is strictly kosher at **Chocolate Charm**, (Tel. 416-787-4256, 3541 Bathurst St). Chocolate Torahs and centrepieces are popular, along with gift baskets filled with chocolates and candies. For a quick meal and snack, **Grodzinski**, (Tel. 416-789-0785, 3437 Bathurst St), offers kosher fast foods. **Milk'n Honey**, (Tel. 416-789-7651, 3457 Bathurst St), serves vegetarian and dairy dishes. Traditional foods include Israeli salad, potato latkes, blintzes with a choice of sauces, and lox and cream cheese. And **Sonny Langer's Dairy and Vegetarian Restaurant & Bakery**, (Tel. 905-881-4356, 180 Steeles Ave. E), also serves vegetarian cuisine. **Aleph Bet Judaica**, (Tel. 416-781-2133, 3453 Bathurst St), carries religious articles and giftware for holy days, including menorahs and shamos imported from Israel or New York. Hundreds of books line the shelves of the shop along with Jewish tapes, videos, silver jewelry and precious stones from Israel, napkins embossed with the word "shalom," and Jewish newspapers. **Negev Book Store and Gift Shop**, (Tel. 416-781-9356, 3509 Bathurst St). Offers English and Hebrew texts, cassetes, religious articles, gifts, and more.

Historic buildings housing synagogues, delicatessens, bagel bakeries, and dry-goods wholesalers can still be found among the myriad of Chinese, Vietnamese, and West Indian shops and restaurants along Spadina Avenue. Lower Spadina to Dundas Street, known as the fashion district, contains a number of Jewish garment manufacturers, wholesalers, and retailers. **Mills Nadal Jewish Community Centre**, (Tel. 416-924-6211, South Branch, 750 Spadina Ave), has a recreational centre, gymnasium, lounge, chapel, nursery, and theatre.

Just like New York's Jewish Lower East Side, Toronto has a **Katz's Deli**, (Tel. 416-782-1111, 3300 Dufferin St). The deli seats up to 275 with party rooms and an outdoor patio. Katz's makes its own corned beef, pastrami, Montreal-style smoked meats, hot dogs, salads, and cakes. **Yitz's Delicatessen**, (Tel. 416-487-4506, 346 Eglinton Ave. W), is a family-owned restaurant first opened by Yitz Penciner in 1972. The eatery specializes in pastrami and corned beef sandwiches and also features chicken soup with matzo balls, salads, specialty breads, and potato latkes. In the theatre district, **Shopsy's** (restaurant and catering), (Tel. 416-365-3333, 33 Yonge St), serves its famous hot dogs, corned beef sandwiches, knishes, cabbage rolls, and deli platters.

Thousands of Torontonians anticipate the annual **Hadassah-WIZO Bazaar**, (Tel. 416-630-8373, 638A Sheppard Ave. W., Unit 209), held on the last Wednesday in October, where new and used clothes, furniture, arts and crafts, and household wares are sold.

Religious Centres, Schools and Other Institutions

The city has more than 90 synagogues representing all branches of Judaism from Reform (or liberal) to the very orthodox Hasidic community. Jews follow three different religious streams: Orthodox, Conservative, and Reform. Orthodox Jews adhere to strict dietary laws and eat only kosher food. The men wear a head covering called a yarmulka, and most married women wear hats or wigs in the synagogue. The Sabbath begins 18 minutes before sundown on Friday and ends 42 to 72 minutes after sundown Saturday for Orthodox Jews. During this time no work is done and Orthodox Jews do not drive.

Synagogues are community centres as well as locations for religious studies, senior clubs, self-help groups, and choirs. Many of the city's synagogues are historic sites that feature interesting art and architecture.

Conservative synagogues include:

- ◆ ADATH ISRAEL SYNAGOGUE, (Tel. 416-635-5340, 37 Southbourne Ave).
- ◆ BETH DAVID B'NAI ISRAEL BETH AM, (Tel. 416-633-5500, 55 Yeomans Rd).
- ◆ BETH EMETH-BAIS YEHUDA, (Tel. 416-633-3838, 100 Elder St). With a membership of 2,000 families, it is one of the largest Conservative synagogues in the country.
- ◆ BETH SHOLOM SYNAGOGUE, (Tel. 416-783-6103, 1445 Eglinton Ave. W). It was built in 1947 and features 18 stained glass windows depicting biblical and modern Israeli scenes.
- ◆ BETH TZEDEC SYNAGOGUE, (Tel. 416-781-3511, 1700 Bathurst St). The country's largest synagogue. England's **Canterbury Cathedral** was the inspiration for the foyer's spiral staircase. Designed by architect Peter Dickinson, the synagogue features marble and has reliefs and a 60-foot-high mosaic wall. A second mosaic is patterned after the 1,500-year-old Beth Alpha synagogue in northern Israel.
- ◆ BETH TIKVAH, (Tel. 416-221-3433, 3080 Bayview Ave). **Beth Tikvah Hebrew School**, (Tel. 416-221-3433, ext. 301.

Orthodox synagogues include:

- ◆ ANSHEI MINSK, (Tel. 416-595-5723, 10 St. Andrews St). One of the few remaining synagogues in the Kensington Market area and the only Orthodox synagogue in the downtown area to hold daily services.
- ◆ BETH JACOB V'ANSHEI DRILDZ CONGREGATION, (Tel. 416-638-5955, 147 Overbrook Pl).

- **B'NAI TORAH**, (Tel. 416-226-3700, 465 Patricia Ave).
- **CHABAD LUBAVITCH COMMUNITY CENTRE**, (Tel. 905-731-7000, 770 Chabad Gate, Thornhill).
- **CLANTON PARK**, (Tel. 416-633-4193, 11 Lowesmoor Ave).
- **MAGEN DAVID (SEPHARDIC) CONGREGATION**, (Tel. 416-636-0865, 10 McAllister Rd).
- **PETAH TIKVAH ANSHE CASTILLA (SEPHARDIC)**, (Tel. 416-636-4719, 20 Danby Ave).
- **SHAAREI SHOMAYIM**, (Tel. 416-789-3213, 470 Glencairn Ave). Has the largest Orthodox congregation in Canada, with more than 1,000 families. The synagogue is also known for its 50-member all-male choir.
- **SHOMRAI SHABOTH**, (Tel. 416-782-8849, 585 Glengrove Ave. W).
- **SHAAREI TEFILLAH**, (Tel. 416-787-1631, 3600 Bathurst St).

Reform synagogues include:
- **HOLY BLOSSOM TEMPLE**, (Tel. 416-789-3291, 1950 Bathurst St). Founded in 1856, Holy Blossom (with a membership of more than 2,000 families) is one of the largest reform temples in North America. The temple is modelled after the **Temple Emanu-El** in New York City and features a cathedral-like sanctuary, stained glass, and an organ.
- **SOLEL CONGREGATION**, (Tel. 416-820-5915, 2399 Folkway Dr., Missisauga).
- **TEMPLE HAR ZION**, (Tel. 905-889-2252, 7360 Bayview Ave., Thornhill).
- **TEMPLE SINAI**, (Tel. 416-487-4161, 210 Wilson Ave).

Other synagogues and religious institutions include:
- **FIRST NARAYEVER**, (Tel. 416-927-0546, 187 Brunswick Ave). A traditional / Egalitarian synagogue founded in 1915 by immigrants from Galicia. The synagogue allows the full participation by women.
- **BENJAMIN'S PARK MEMORIAL CHAPEL**, (Tel. 416-663-9060, 2401 Steeles Ave. W).
- **DARCHEI NOAM (RECONSTRUCTIONIST)**, (Tel. 416-638-4783, 864 Sheppard Ave. W).
- **LODZER CENTRE HOLOCAUST CONGREGATION**, (Tel. 416-636-6665, 12 Heaton St).
- **PRIDE OF ISRAEL SYNAGOGUE**, (Tel. 416-226-0111, 59 Lissom Cres).
- **STEELES-COLLEGE MEMORIAL CHAPEL**, (Tel. 905-881-6003, 350 Steeles Ave. W., Thornhill).

Synagogues and other institutions conduct afternoon schools. In addition, Jewish Day Schools include:

♦ ASSOCIATED HEBREW SCHOOLS OF TORONTO, (Tel. 416-494-7666, Central Administraion, 252 Finch Ave. W).

♦ BIALIK HEBREW DAY SCHOOL, (Tel. 416-783-3346, 2760 Bathurst St).

♦ EITZ CHAIM DAY SCHOOLS, (Tel. 416-789-4366, 1 Viewmount Ave).

♦ NER ISRAEL YESHIVA, (Tel. 905-731-1224, 8950 Bathurst St., Thornhill).

♦ OR HAEMET SEFARDIC SCHOOL, (Tel. 905-669-7653, 7026 Bathurst St., Thornhill).

♦ UNITED SYNAGOGUE DAY SCHOOL, (Tel. 416-225-1143, 3072 Bayview Ave).

♦ YESHIVA BNAI AKIVA OR CHAIM, (Tel. 416-630-6772, 159 Almore Ave).

Seniors' institutions include:

♦ BAYCREST CENTRE FOR GERIATRIC CARE, (Tel. 416-785-2500, 3560 Bathurst St), is a multi-service facility which includes the **Jewish Home for the Aged**, **Baycrest Terrace** (minimal care institution), **Baycrest Hospital** (including day hospital, psychiatric day hospital, and Alzheimer's unit), **Baycrest Day Care Service**, and the **Joseph E. and Minnie Wagman Multi-Purpose Activity Centre.**

♦ BERNARD BETEL CENTRE FOR CREATIVE LIVING, (Tel. 416-225-2112, 1003 Steeles Ave. W), is a multipurpose activity centre for seniors aged 55 and up that provides educational, social, and recreational activities.

Holidays and Celebrations

♦ PURIM (THE FEAST OF LOTS) falls in February or March. It is based on the story of the Book of Esther and acts as a reminder that evil can be defeated. During the celebration, a three-cornered pastry is eaten that represents the hat of Haman, whose plan to kill all Jews was thwarted by Esther and Mordecai.

♦ PASSOVER OR PESACH, in March or April, celebrates the exodus of the Hebrews from the land of Egypt, where they were enslaved by the pharaohs. During the eight-day festival, matza (unleavened bread) is eaten as a reminder of the bread the Jews ate when they departed from Egypt. On the eve of Pesach, the family gathers for Seder, a meal and worship service performed according to an ancient book called the Haggadah. As the meal is eaten, the symbolism of each of the traditional foods is explained.

- ◆ **WARSAW GHETTO UPRISING** is commemorated in April. It honours the heroism of the Jews in the Warsaw ghetto and the memory of Jews who perished during the Second World War. The day of celebration is Yom HaShoah—Holocaust Memorial Day.
- ◆ **ISRAELI INDEPENDENCE DAY**, April or May, celebrates the anniversary of the 1948 declaration of Israeli independence.
- ◆ **SHAVUOTH, OR PENTECOST**, falls seven weeks after Passover. It is a commemoration of the giving of the Ten Commandments to Moses at Mount Sinai.
- ◆ **HIGH HOLY DAYS** take place in September or October. Rosh Hashanah (New Year) and Yom Kippur (Day of Atonement) are the most important festivals of the Jewish religious year, during which Jews reflect on their lives and ask God to forgive their sins. The days between the holidays are known as the Days of Awe.
- ◆ **ROSH HASHANAH (NEW YEAR)**, sees people pray in synagogues for a year of peace and happiness. The blowing of the shofar (ram's horn) reminds the congregation of the need for doing good and for living a God-fearing life. Families celebrate with a festive dinner that includes the eating of an apple or other fruits dipped in honey in hopes of a year filled with sweetness.
- ◆ **YOM KIPPUR (DAY OF ATONEMENT)** is for the confession of sins and prayers for forgiveness. An evening service, called Kol Nidre, is followed by prayer which continue until sunset the next day. The holy day of prayer and fasting ends with the long blast of the shofar, and the congregation says, "Hear, O Israel, the Lord Our God, the Lord is One," followed by "Next Year in Jerusalem."
- ◆ **SUKKOTH.** In September or October, Jews celebrate Sukkoth (Feast of Tabernacles), a eight-day harvest festival commemorating the time the ancient Israelites gathered in the harvest and offered thanks to God. During the synagogue service, a palm branch, myrtle twigs and willow branches are held in the right hand and an ethrog (citron) in the left. These are waved in all directions to symbolize the universality of God's presence.
- ◆ **HOSHANA RABBA** is observed as the final judgement day of man. With lulav (palm branch and a few sprigs of myrtle and willow) in one hand and ethrog in the other, members of the congregation parade around the synagogue seven times singing hosannas, the prayers for salvation.
- ◆ **SHEMINI ATZERETH**, the seventh day of Sukkoth, sees the congregation offers special prayers for rain.

80th annual Toronto Hadassah-WIZO bazaar.

- ◆ **SIMHATH TORAH** is the eighth and final day of Sukkoth. And celebrates the end of the year's reading of the Torah and the reminder that the study of God's word is an unending process. The last chapter of Deuteronomy and the first chapter of Genesis are read on this day.
- ◆ **HANUKKAH OR CHANUKA**, in December, is the Feast of Dedication. The festival honours the first victory for religious freedom, when the Jewish people refused to convert to the ways of Antiochus IV, a Syrian-Greek Emperor who reigned in 165 B.C. The eight-day festival is celebrated with gift-giving and a candle-lighting ceremony at home and in the synagogue. The candles are arranged in a special candelabrum (called a menorah) and are lit with a shamos (helper candle), one every night until all eight candles are lit. During the holiday it is traditional to serve latkes (potato pancakes).

Media

- ◆ **B'NAI BRITH JEWISH TRIBUNE**, (Tel. 416-633-6224, 15 Hove St). Publisher: Frank Dimant.
- ◆ **SHALOM, CHIN 100.7 FM**, (Tel. 416-531-9991, 622 College St). Monday to Friday, 10:00 a.m. to 11:00 a.m. Host: Zelda Young.
- ◆ **SHALOM**, CHIN 1540 AM, Sunday, 8:30 a.m. to 10:00 a.m.
- ◆ **CANADIAN JEWISH NEWS**, (Tel. 416-391-1836, www.cjnews.com, 1500 Don Mills Rd., Suite 205). A weekly newspaper founded in 1960. Editor: Mordechai Ben-Dat.
- ◆ **SHALOM TORONTO ISRAELI NEWSPAPER INC.**, (Tel. 416-744-1385, 61 Alness St. Suite 201).

Organizations

◆ CANADIAN JEWISH CONGRESS, ONTARIO REGION, (Tel. 416-635-2883, 4600 Bathurst St), represents the Jewish community to fellow Ontarians and to government. It acts as a vehicle for advocacy on a broad range of public policy and social justice issues. Congress promotes intergroup relations and combats antisemitism and racism. It is committed to preserving and strengthening Jewish life throughout the province, stresses the centrality of Israel for Jews and Judaism, and fosters concern for the status of Jewish communities abroad.

◆ UNITIED JEWISH APPEAL FEDERATION OF GREATER TORONTO, **Lipa Green Building**, (Tel. 416-635-2883, www.jewishtoronto.com, 4600 Bathurst St). Established in 1937 as the **United Jewish Welfare Fund** to support local institutions, and later for overseas relief. Houses Jewish service organizations, including the **UJA Federation of Greater Toronto**, President: Moshe Ronen, **The Canadian Jewish Congress** is the parliament and official voice of Canadian Jewry set up to reflect the concerns of the Jewish community. The CJC represents the Jewish community before government on matters affecting the community's interest.

At the same address:

◆ CENTRE FOR THE EDUCATION ENHANCEMENT OF JEWISH EDUCATION, (Tel. 416-633-7770).

◆ JEWISH FAMILY AND CHILD, (Tel. 416-638-7800).

◆ JEWISH INFORMATION SERVICES OF GREATER TORONTO, (Tel. 416-635-5600).

◆ UNITED ISRAEL APPEAL OF CANADA INC., (Tel. 416-636-7655).

◆ TORONTO JEWISH LOAN CASSA, (Tel. 416-635-1217), gives low-interest business, educational and personal loans to recent immigrants to Canada.

◆ B'NAI BRITH CANADA, (15 Hove St., 2nd floor, M3H 4Y8, Tel. 416-633-6224). The members sponsor programs in aid of Israel as well as adult education programs, youth activities, and senior citizen programs. At the same address: **B'nai Brith Canada's League for Human Rights**, an agency which fights racism and anti-Semitism and promotes inter-community relations; and **The Institute for International Affairs**, a think-tank that addresses international human rights abuses.

◆ CANADIAN COUNCIL OF CHRISTIANS AND JEWS, (Tel. 416-597-9693, www.cccj.ca, 4211 Yonge St., Suite 515).

◆ CANADIAN YOUNG JUDAEA, (Tel. 416-781-5156, 788 Marlee Ave).

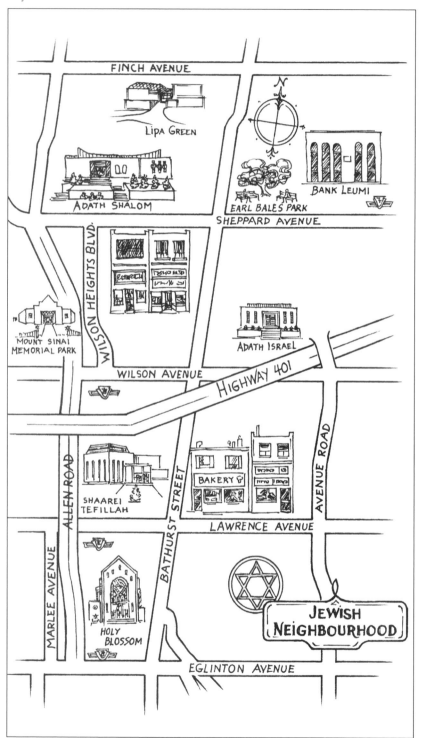

Bar Mitzva, Beth Sholom Synagogue.

- ◆ **JIAS (JEWISH IMMIGRANT AID SERVICES) TORONTO**, (Tel. 416-630-6481). Helps settle and intergrate jewish immigrants.
- ◆ **CIRCLE OF CARE**, (Tel. 416-635-2860, www.circleofcare.com, 530 Wilson Ave., 4th Floor). Provides an extensive range of services to the non-institutionalized elderly and their families.
- ◆ **HADASSAH-WIZO**, (Tel. 416-630-8373, 638A Sheppard Ave. W., Unit 209). An organization with 4,000 members in 72 chapters dedicated to furthering health and welfare in Israel.
- ◆ **JEWISH NATIONAL FUND**, (Tel. 416-638-7200, 1000 Finch Ave. W., Suite 700).
- ◆ **JEWISH RUSSIAN COMMUNITY CENTRE**, (Tel. 416-222-7105, 18 Rockford Rd).
- ◆ **JVS TORONTO**, (Tel. 416-787-1151, 74 Tycos Dr), provides vocational guidance and job placement.
- ◆ **NATIONAL COUNCIL OF JEWISH WOMEN OF CANADA**, Toronto Section, (Tel. 416-633-5100, 4700 Bathurst St).
- ◆ **REENA FOUNDATION**, (Tel. 905-889-6484, www.reena.org, 927 Clarke Ave., W). Serves adults and children with developmental disabilities and their families.

Consulates, Trade Commissions and Tourist Bureaus

◆ CONSULATE GENERAL OF ISRAEL, (Tel. 416-640-8500, 180 Bloor St. W., Suite 700). Consul General: Mr. Amir K Gissin.

Prominent Torontonians

A. Alan Borovoy, civil liberties advocate; David Caplan, MPP and former cabiner minister; George A. Cohon, Chair, McDonald's Restaurants of Canada Ltd.; Leslie Dan, President, Novapharm; Mendel M. Green, Q.C., Founding Chairman of the Immigration Section of the Canadian Bar Association, lawyer; Paul Godfrey, former Metro Chairman, CEO Financial Post; Mel Lastman, former Mayor of Toronto; Stephen Lewis, former leader of the Ontario New Democratic Party, former Canadian ambassador to the UN; Joseph Rotman, philanthropist; Barry Sherman, President, Apotex; Joseph Tanenbaum, patron of the arts; Monte Kwinter, MPP and former cabinet minister; Lawrence Tanenbaum, Chairman and CEO, Kilmer Van Nostrand Co., and philanthropist; Peter Shurman, MPP; Joe and Wolf Lebovic, Developers and philanthropists; Frank Dimant, CEO, B'nai Brith Canada; Murrey and Marvelle Koffler, Founders of Shoppers Drug Mart; Rosalie Abella, Supreme Court Justice; Les Scheininger, former president of Canadian Jewish Congress; Jerry Gratstein, former Senator.

Sources: Barbara Barak, Albert Latner, Isadore Sharp, Aubrey Zidenberg.

Lawrence Tanenbaum, Chairman and CEO Kilmer Van Nostrand Co. Limited, and noted philanthropist.

The Korean Community

Lined with restaurants, herb stores, acupuncture centres, and shops selling imported giftware from Seoul, Toronto's Koreatown bustles with the activity of an Asian sidewalk market. The neighbourhood, located along Bloor Street West, between Bathurst and Christie streets, was one of the community's first areas of settlement. Today, few Koreans live in the area but it still contains the highest concentration of Korean restaurants and shops in the city. One of the city's two Korean banks and a credit union are open for business, while offices along the strip bear the names of Korean lawyers, doctors, and other professionals who have made Toronto their home.

Canada and Korea officially opened their diplomatic relations in 1963, but the first association between the two countries began as early as 1888 through the Christian missionary system. By the 1940s, church-sponsored students who had come to Canada to study began changing their status from student to landed immigrant. In the late 1960s and the early '70s, the first large wave of Koreans arrived in Canada.

A collective effort by the community resulted in the establishment of a church, and in 1967, the first Korean Sunday service was held at **St. Luke's United Church** on Sherbourne Street. The parish was named the **Toronto Korean United Church** and became the centre for community activity, sponsoring lectures, a Korean language school, and the **Toronto Korean-Canadian Choir**.

Today, the 100,000-member Toronto Korean community boasts highly skilled workers, professionals, and small business entrepreneurs who operate drycleaning depots, fast food outlets, delicatessens, print shops, and real estate and insurance agencies. More than 76 percent of the grocery and variety stores in Toronto are owned and operated by Koreans.

Koreans have widened Toronto's cultural range with dance, music, arts, sports, and martial arts such as Tae Kwon Do (the art of self defence). Korean companies such as **Korean Airlines**, **Hyundai Corporation** and **Gia Masters** (automobile manufacturers), **KIA Motors**, **LG electronics**, and **Samsung Electronics**, have established regional offices in the city.

South Koreans remember with gratitude the 20,000 Canadian soldiers who were sent to help rescue South Korea from invading North Korean forces during the Korean War. Koreans across Canada donated more than $50,000 to the **Federation of Korean Canadians** to help erect the **Korea Veterans' National Wall of Remembrance** in Brampton on July 27, 1997. A bond between the two cultures is also reflected by replicas of granite pagodas located on the grounds of **Victoria College** at the **University of Toronto**. The pagodas were dedicated by the graduates of **Victoria Medical College** in memory of Dr. O.R. Avison, a graduate of the college who founded the first occidental-style hospital and medical college in Seoul in 1893.

Places to Go

Storefronts of restaurants in Koreatown display dishes of sophisticated Korean cuisine, which gained greater appreciation among Torontonians following the **24th Summer Olympic Games** held in Seoul in 1988. A simple Korean meal consists of soup, rice, a bowl of fish or meat, and kimchee (pickled cabbage). Rice dishes and rice mixed with barley, beans, and potatoes are staple Korean foods. The popular after-dinner beverage is Korean tea.

The oldest Korean restaurant in Toronto is **Korea House**, (Tel. 416-536-8666, 666 Bloor St. W). Specialties include kimchee, kalbi ribs (spare-ribs marinated and barbecued in a special sauce), and bibimbab (rice topped with marinated beef, fried egg, mixed vegetables, and hot sauce). **Moolraebang-A**, (Tel. 416-534-6833, 3 Christie St), is well known for its bul-go-gee dinner (a mound of thinly sliced sirloin marinated in soy sauce and grilled). It comes with kimchee, spiced chunks of Asian radish, and black beans.

Korean Village, (Tel. 416-536-0290, 628 Bloor St. W), serves starters such as mandoo gook (Korean won ton soup), guhun mandoo (meat-stuffed won tons fried with seasoned soy sauce for dipping), bindae dock (dried-green-bean flour egg pancakes with bits of ham), and kimchee that comes with bowls filled with pickled juliennes of radish, bean sprouts in sesame oil, pepper-stewed daikon, and sun-dried fish. House specialties include ohjung un begum (squid in a hot chili sauce with rice), cow shank soup, and the bul-go-gee dinner that patrons barbecue at their table.

Other popular Toronto dining spots include **Seoul House**, (Tel. 416-782-4405, 3220 Dufferin St), where kalbi and bul-go-gee (spicy barbeque) are specialties. A chimney above each table draws smoke away from tabletop barbecues. **Missihana**, (Tel. 905-803-9870, 90 Dundas St. W., Mississauga), is a large restaurant serving both traditional Korean and

Traditional Korean costume

Japanese dishes. **Shin-Ra**, (Tel. 416-247-2007, 1161 Weston Rd), and **Masamune**, (Tel. 905-625-1852, 5200 Dixie Rd., Mississauga), feature karaoke. Other Korean restaurants in the city and vicinity include: **Ho-Shim**, (Tel. 416-368-0125, 100 King St. W); and **Spring Garden**, (Tel. 416-250-6094, 39 Spring Garden Ave).

P.A.T. Korean Market, (675 Bloor st. W). The oldest Korean supermarket with branches in North York, Thornhill, Mississauga and Scarborough. **H Mart**, (Tel. 905-883-6200, 9737 Yonge St).

Religious Centres, Schools and Other Institutions

There are approximately 200 Christian churches frequented by members of Toronto's Korean community. They include:

- ◆ YOUNG NAK KOREAN PREBESTRIAN CHURCH, (Tel. 416-494-0191, 650 McNicoll Ave).
- ◆ TORONTO KOREAN PRESBYTERIAN CHURCH, (Tel. 416-447-5963, 67 Scarsdale Rd., North York).
- ◆ TORONTO KOREAN UNITED CHURCH, (Tel. 416-968-1800, 300 Bloor St. W).

Buddhist Koreans worship at three Korean temples in the city:

- ◆ DAE GAK SA, (Tel. 416-588-3251, 1000 Queen St. W).
- ◆ HANMAUM SEON CENTRE, (Tel. 416-750-7943, 20 Mobile Dr). The oldest Korean community Church founded in 1967.
- ◆ KOREAN CREDIT UNION, (Tel. 416-863-0415, 489 Don Mills Rd).

◆ KOREA EXCHANGE BANK OF CANADA, **Head Office, Madison Centre**, (Tel. 416-222-5200, 4950 Yonge St., Suite 1101; and Tel. 416-533-8593, 627 Bloor St. W).

Holidays and Celebrations

◆ NEW YEAR'S. Although Koreans observe New Year's Day by the solar and lunar calendars, most Korean Canadians follow the solar calendar and celebrate it on January 1st. It is customary to wear new clothing at this time and to prepare a traditional dish called ttogguk (a soup with rice cake). To wish their elders health, happiness, and a long life, the younger Koreans kneel and touch their foreheads to the floor. This special act of respect is called sebae. The elders respond with gifts of money and food.

◆ NATIONAL INDEPENDENCE DAY, March 1, commemorates the day in 1919 that Koreans attempted to gain independence from Japan. The uprising lasted approximately two months before being suppressed.

◆ BUDDHA'S BIRTHDAY usually falls in April or May. Korean Buddhists celebrate the day similarly to Christmas with colourful festivities at their three Toronto temples.

◆ LIBERATION DAY, August 15, celebrates the day in 1945 that Korea was liberated from Japan after 36 years of colonial rule.

◆ CHOOSUK (MOON FESTIVAL DAY), a celebration similar to Thanksgiving Day, is celebrated on the same day as Liberation Day by the lunar calendar. It is considered the second most important holiday for Koreans.

◆ MAY FESTIVAL (DAN-O) is the largest festival of the Korean community. About 5,000 Koreans attend this festival every year, where Korean foods, gifts, clothing, etc., are sold. Traditional Korean games are played. Held annually on the first Saturday of June at **Christie Park**.

◆ FESTIVITIES ON OCTOBER 3 celebrate Korean Heritage Day and Korean Foundation Day in Ontario. The community also commemorates the day Korea was founded 4,000 years ago.

Media

◆ KOREA CENTRAL DAILY, (Tel. 416-533-5533, Fax 416-533-5500, 655 Bloor St. W). Publisher: Hyo Kim.

◆ AII TV, (Tel. 416-538-2211, Fax 416-588-6550, 1133 Leslie St., Suite 213).

Korean youth at Nathan Phillips Square.

- ◆ **ARIRANG KOREA**, OMNI-TV, (Tel. 416-260-0060, 545 Lakeshore Blvd. W). Entertainment and music from Korea, Saturday, 7:00 p.m. to 7:30 p.m. and Sunday, 8:00 a.m. to 8:30 a.m.

Organizations

The **Foundation for Korean Studies** at the **University of Toronto** has established a chair. Toronto's Koreans belong to a number of alumni organizations.

- ◆ **KOREAN-CANADIAN ASSOCIATIONS**, (Tel. 416-383-0777, Fax 416-383-1113, 1133 Leslie St). An umbrella organization that provides cultural and social activities for the Korean community. President: Samghoon Lee.
- ◆ **KOREAN CANADIAN WOMEN'S ASSOCIATION**, (Tel. 416-340-1234, 27 Madison Ave), which provides language classes and other classes to help the new immigrants settle in Canada. President: Linda Yoo.
- ◆ **ONTARIO KOREAN BUSINESSMEN'S ASSOCIATION**, (Tel. 416-789-7891, 130 Orfus Rd). This organization also operates its own co-op in three loca-

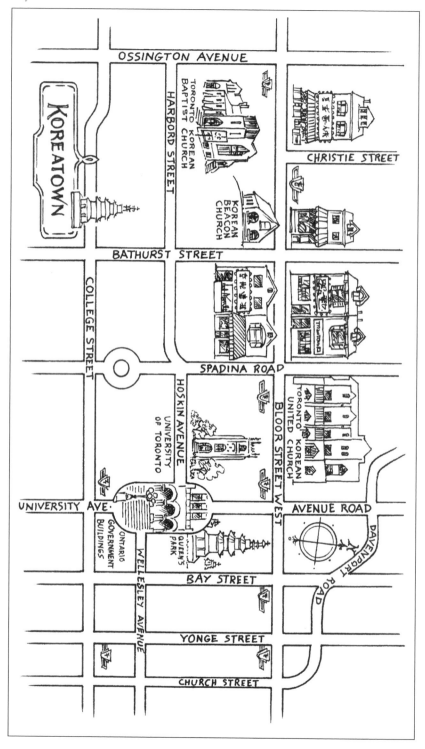

tions in Toronto to serve its members. Its annual revenue tops $60 million. A business and professional organization with 2,000 members. Eighty percent of the members are convenience store owners. President: Jong Sil Yoon.

- ◆ ASSOCIATION OF KOREAN CANADIAN SCIENTISTS AND ENGINEERS, (Tel. 416-449-5204, Fax 416-449-2875, 1133 Leslie St., #206).
- ◆ KOREAN SENIOR CITIZENS ASSOCIATION, (Tel. 416-532-8077, 476 Grace St). Executive Director: Hangim Kim.
- ◆ KOREAN VETERANS ASSOCIATION EASTERN CHAPTER OF CANADA, (Tel. 416-769-8739, Fax 416-763-3257, 285 St. John's Rd).
- ◆ KOREAN COMMUNITY CENTRE, (Tel. 416-538-9412, 721 Bloor St. W).
- ◆ ONTARIO KOREAN LIBERAL PARTY ASSOCIATION, (224 Brownridge Dr., Thornhill). President: Robert Pak.
- ◆ PHYSICALLY CHALLENGED KOREAN ADULT COMMUNITY CENTRE, (Tel. 416-604-7845, 139 Bond Ave).

Consulates, Trade Commissions and Tourist Bureaus

- ◆ KOREAN CONSULATE GENERAL, (Tel. 416-920-3809, 555 Avenue Rd). Consul General: Mr. Ji-in Hong
- ◆ KOREA TRADE CENTRE (KOTRA), (Tel. 416-368-3399, www.kotra.ca, 65 Queen St. W., Suite 600, Box 9).

Prominent Torontonians

Rev Sang-Chul Lee, former Moderator of the United Church of Canada; Dr. Sang-hwe Koo, senior researcher at the Hospital for Sick Children; Dr. Taek-Soon Yoon, Professor at the University of Toronto; Choon-Soo Lee, former President, Korean Canadian (Cultural) Association of Metro Toronto; Dr. Raymond Cho, Toronto Councillor; Sam T. Hahn, former President of the Korean-Canadian Cultural Association; Jong Park, master of Tae-kwon-do; Joo-yeon Lee, soprano; Dr. Hwe-Ja Yoo, organist and music conductor; Andrew Chang-Hun Chung, President of Pickering Toyota; Ben Chin, former broadcaster, former advisor to the Premier of Ontario, currently Vice-president of Communications at the Ontario Power Authority; Mi Young Kim, president of Korean Dance Co.

Contributors: Lawrence Kim, Mike (Hwi) Lee, Sam T. Hahn.

The Laotian Community

The Laotian community in Toronto consists of 5,000 people who honour their heritage through cultural and religious festivals, bands and dance groups, and organized sports teams. Laos is bordered by China, Vietnam, Kampuchea, Thailand, and Burma. The native language is Lao, but many people speak French as a result of the country's membership in the **French Union** up until 1954.

The Lao came to Canada in three waves of immigration. The first group arrived in the late 1960s as students who later applied for citizenship. A large group of political refugees came to Canada following the Laotian king's abdication and a Communist government takeover in 1975. In 1980, more Laotian refugees arrived—both professionals and blue-collar workers.

The community's most important festival is Lao New Year, usually celebrated in the spring with processions and prayers. Toronto's Lao practice the custom of chasing away evil spirits for the New Year by cleaning their homes and sprinkling their friends with water to wash away their sins. At the **Lao Buddhist Temple**, images of Buddha are washed during ritual ceremonies. The **Lao Association of Ontario** arranges an evening of entertainment with a band, choir, and dance group, and a feast of Lao foods is served with tea.

Places to Go

Businesses of interest include:

- NAM-MY, (Tel. 416-979-7384, 72 Huron St), carries medicinal herbs.
- WIN KUANG ASIAN FOODS, (Tel. 905-953-8445, 16925 Yonge St., Unit 18, Newmarket).
- VIENTIANE CO., (Tel. 416-743-2911, 2 Bradstock Rd).
- THUAN THANH SUPERMARKET, (Tel. 416-741-1930, 1989 Finch Ave., W).
- TUPTIM RESTAURANT, (Tel. 905-898-3599, 450 Mulock Dr., Newmarket).
- SALA THAI RESTAURANT, (Tel. 416-785-1727, 1100 Eglinton Ave. W).
- VIENG RATRI KARAOKE BAR, (Tel. 416-744-5067, 295 Eddystone Ave).

◆ SALA THAI RESTAURANT, (Tel. 416-785-1727, 1100 Eglinton Ave. W).
◆ VIENG RATRI KARAOKE BAR, (Tel. 416-744-5067, 295 Eddystone Ave).

Religious Centres, Schools and Other Institutions

The Lao are primarily Buddhists and frequent their own Buddhist temple:

◆ LAO BUDDHIST TEMPLE OF TORONTO, (Tel. 416-739-1784, 39 Hullmar Dr).
◆ WAT LAO VELUWANH, (Tel. 905-584-6886, www.watlao-veluwanh.com, 17969 Airport Rd., Caledon East).

Holidays and Celebrations

Dates for buddhist holidays are calculated according to the lunisolar calendar. The full moon days in each month are celebrated with ceremonies.

◆ MAKHA BOUXA, usually held in February, is a festival that calls together Buddha's disciples before his entrance into a state of nirvana. Prayers, processions, and offerings mark the ceremony.

Ho khao padap dinh (the feast of the dead), celebrated in August, honors the dead with gifts, prayers, and thoughts.

Laotian women display traditional dresses from various regions of their country.

- ◆ VIXAKHA BOUXA (ROCKET FESTIVAL), usually held in May, commemorates the birth, death, and enlightenment of Buddha.
- ◆ THE BOUN PHA VET, celebrated in February or March, is a day of reading by the bonzes (Buddhist priests) of the Life of the Buddha.
- ◆ KHAO VASSA (THE BEGINNING OF BUDDHIST LENT), held in July, sees the bonzes retire to their temples and recite the Patimokkha.
- ◆ HO KHAO PADAP DINH (THE FEAST OF THE DEAD), celebrated in August, honours the dead with gifts, prayers, and thoughts.
- ◆ HO KHAO SLAK in September is a traditional time for indulging children with toys and sweets.

- **OK VASSA (THE END OF BUDDHIST LENT)** in October is a general rejoicing and confession of evil and careless thoughts.
- **THE FESTIVAL OF THE WATERS** is a ceremony to drive out evil spirits. Houses are decorated with candles.
- **THAT LUANG FESTIVAL** in November celebrates the That Luang, supposedly containing a relic of the Lord Buddha. The occasion is celebrated with processions and prayers.

See Holidays and Celebrations in Glossary.

Organizations

- **LAO ASSOCIATION OF ONTARIO,** (Tel. 416-398-3057; Fax 416-398-3058, 956 Wilson Ave. W). A non-profit charitable organization thatassists newcomers to integrate into the Canadian community and also promotes Lao culture and identity in Canada. The organization arranges cultural, educational, and social activities. Sports teams and a dance group belong to the association. President: Mr. Thongsouk Vongphakdy.

Contributor: Somchith Saysourinho, Executive Director, Lao Association of Ontario.

The Latvian Community

Toronto becomes the scene of a melodious cultural celebration that originated in Latvia in the 19th century. For one week in July, thousands of voices and hands join together to perform Dainas, beautiful rhythmic folksongs central to the Latvian tradition. Symphony concerts, recitals, displays of fine arts and handicrafts, theatre performances, and folk dancing are part of the festivities. The festival was transplanted to Toronto in 1952, when the first Latvian Song Festival was held at Massey Hall.

Latvian Canadians have not only introduced Torontonians to their own culture but have enriched the city's artistic scene with accomplished composers, artists, and musicians. With 10,000 members—the largest concentration of Latvians in Canada—the Toronto community has become the centre for almost all Latvian cultural, social, and political life in the country.

Latvia was an independent Baltic state from 1918 to 1940, when it was annexed by the USSR, and is once again independent after the fall of the Soviet Union. The first Latvian settlers in Canada were farmers who arrived in the 1890s and settled in Western Canada, gradually moving east to find jobs in the cities.

During the Second World War, more than 110,000 Latvians fled their occupied homeland. Of this group, some 15,000 emigrated to Canada. In Toronto, the early community was scattered throughout the city, with higher concentrations in the High Park area, along Broadview Avenue, and in the suburbs of Willowdale and Weston. One of the earliest community groups was the **First Evangelical Lutheran Congregation**, established in 1949. Its temporary premises were replaced in 1951 when the group joined with the Estonian congregation and purchased the old **St. Andrew's Church** at Jarvis and Carlton Streets. The church was later named **St. Andrew Evangelical Lutheran Congregation**. In the 1950s, the large building housed a Sunday school, choirs, drama groups, and youth and senior citizen groups.

Today, other visible signs of the Latvian community include a memorial to the late president of Latvia, Dr. Karlis Ulmanis, located in Willowdale's **York Cemetery**. Latvian culture is fostered in the city at **Latvian House** on

College Street, and at the impressive modern complex of the **Latvian Canadian Cultural Centre** in Toronto.

Places to Go

The striking classical columns of **Latvian House**, (Tel. 416-922-2931, 491 College St), recall the old-world culture preserved inside. Formerly a Masonic temple, the building has been a cultural home to the Latvian community for more than 30 years. Paintings depicting scenes from the homeland hang in the entranceway and in the large hall. The House is the head office of the **Latvian Credit Union**, (Tel. 416-922-2551). Contact: Alvis Lubnevskis.

Concerts, dances, lectures, films, shows, poetry readings, and Sunday brunches are held at the **Latvian Canadian Cultural Centre**, (Tel. 416-759-4900, 4 Credit Union Dr). A historic display of Latvian costumes and exhibitions of art and artifacts are housed in the Centre's art gallery. An impressive collection of Latvian novels and reference and history books are found in the library resource centre, and books can be purchased at the **Latvian Bookstore**, (Tel. 416-757-1482, 4 Credit Union Dr). Souvenirs such as jewelry in amber—the gem of the Baltic—and handicrafts are found in the gift shop. **Umurkumurs** is the Centre's lounge, which is open evenings to members and their guests.

Daugavas Vanagi House, also at 4 Credit Union Dr, is a community centre which borrows its name from the largest river in Latvia. The centre maintains a library.

Religious Centres, Schools and Other Institutions

Most Latvians are members of the Lutheran Church, although some belong to Roman Catholic and Baptist churches.

◆ BARNABAS CHURCH, (Tel. 416-463-1344, 361 Danforth Ave). Toronto Eastern Evangelical Lutheran Latvian congregation shares this church with Lutheran Estonians. The parish has its own choir and owns **Talava**, a summer retreat with retirement homes located on the banks of the Nottawasaga River.

◆ ST. ANDREW'S EVANGELICAL LUTHERAN LATVIAN CHURCH, (Tel. 416-924-1563, 383 Jarvis St). The historic church with its green spire is home to the **Latvian Choir of St. Andrew's**, established in 1952 under the direction of the prominent composer Talivaldis Kenins. The congregation owns **Sidrabene**—a sixty-six acre property near

Burlington—with a Community Hall, cottages, an outdoor stage, an open-air stone altar, a sports field, a swimming area, and a children's summer camp.

- **ST. JOHN'S EVANGELICAL LUTHERAN LATVIAN CHURCH**, (Tel. 416-921-3327, 200 Balmoral Ave). The first church built by the Latvians in Canada. The parish has a choir and Sunday school, and owns Saulaine, a vacation camp on Nottawasaga River in Essa township.

Latvian is the second oldest existing language within the Indo-European group of languages. The Latvian community supports Latvian language schools in Canada, three of which are located in Toronto:

- **VALODINA LATVIAN CENTRE**, (Tel. 416-759-4900, 4 Credit Union Dr), from kindergarten to Grade 8.
- **TORONTO LATVIAN SCHOOL**, (Tel. 416-755-2353, 4 Credit Union Dr).
- THE **LATVIAN HIGH SCHOOL**, (Tel. 416-922-2551, 491 College St).
- **KRISTUS DARZS (CHRIST'S GARDEN) HOME FOR THE AGED**, (Tel. 905-832-3300, 11290 Pine Valley Dr., Woodbridge), is the first Latvian retirement home in North America. The three-story building has more than 90 rooms. Administrator: Mr. Maris Inveiss. Founding Chair and Medical Director: Dr. S. Lusis.
- **LATVIAN CREDIT UNION**, (Tel. 416-922-2551, 491 College St), is the community's financial institution. Branch Office: 4 Credit Union Dr., Tel. 416-751-8982.

Holidays and Celebrations

- **CULTURAL APPEAL DAY** on January 28 recognizes the day in 1935 that Dr. Karlis Ulmanis, the last President of Latvia, appealed to the nation to support local schools, churches, and other cultural institutions.
- **MARCH 6** sees Latvians honour Colonel Oskars Kalpaks, Commander-in-Chief of the Latvian forces, who was killed in action during the War of Liberation in 1919. A special church service on the Sunday nearest the date honours those who gave their lives in the fight for Latvia.
- **COMMEMORATION DAY** is held on June 14 in memory of the thousands of Latvians who were deported to Siberia in 1941 by the occupying Soviet forces. The anniversary is organized by the Baltic Federation of Canada. Speeches and a cultural program are held.
- **JOHN'S DAY.** Traditional folk songs and dances are part of the festivities on John's Day, June 24. The custom predates Christianity in Latvia as a pagan celebration of the longest day of the year and the

beginning of harvest festivals. With the arrival of Christianity, this mid-summer festival has become a cultural celebration.

◆ INDEPENDENCE DAY. The independence of the Republic of Latvia was proclaimed on November 18, 1918. The nation lost its status in 1940, when occupied by the USSR, and regained it in 1991. A cultural program is held on this day each year.

◆ LATVIAN CULTURE DAYS are observed annually at proclaimed dates, but are generally held in early spring. A program on these days features presentations of Latvian cultural achievements on a particular theme, represented by music, literature, art exhibits, and lectures.

See Holidays and Celebrations in Glossary.

Media

◆ LATVIJA AMERIKA (LATVIA IN AMERICA), (4 Credit Union Dr). A weekly newspaper with a circulation of 3,000. It is published by the Daugavas Vanagi organization.

◆ LAIKS (TIMES). A semi-weekly newspaper published in New York with a large Canadian content.

Organizations

◆ DAUGAVAS VANAGI (DV) LATVIAN RELIEF SOCIETY OF CANADA, TORONTO BRANCH, (Tel. 416-757-1482, 4 Credit Union Dr). A large international organization founded at the end of the Second World War to provide relief for Latvians. It now has branches in many countries and has broadened its activities to include political work aimed at the preservation of Latvian culture. The organization publishes Latvija Amerika. Contact: Varis Pludonss.

◆ THE LATVIAN NATIONAL FEDERATION IN CANADA (LNAK), (Tel. 416-755-2353, 4 Credit Union Dr). Founded in 1949, LNAK acts as a unified voice for the community on issues such as politics, culture, education, and welfare. Chairman of General Assembly: Alexander Budrevics. President: Mr. Egils Tannis. Vice-President: Dr. G. Subins.

Other organizations at the same address:

◆ THE LATVIAN NATIONAL YOUTH FEDERATION IN CANADA organizes social and cultural activities, as well as political seminars, rallies, and demonstrations.

◆ DAUGAVINA DANCE GROUP. Manager: S. Gulena.

Latvians celebrate John's day with traditional songs and dances.

- ◆ DIZDANCIS LATVIAN DANCE GROUP. Manager: Mr. Z. Miezitis.
- ◆ LATVIAN ARTS AND CRAFTS ASSOCIATION OF CANADA. President: Ms. Vagness.
- ◆ LATVIAN GUIDES AND SCOUTS.
- ◆ LATVIAN SONG FESTIVAL ASSOCIATION IN CANADA. President: A. Purvs.
- ◆ LATVIAN BUSINESS AND PROFESSIONAL MEN'S ASSOCIATION, (Tel. 416-444-5201, 895 Don Mills Rd). President: Alexander Budrevics.
- ◆ LATVIAN CANADIAN HANDICRAFT ASSOCIATION, (4 Credit Union Dr).
- ◆ LATVIAN DANCE GROUP, VECAIS DIZDANCIS, (3032 St. Malo Circle, Mississauga).
- ◆ LATVIAN SENIOR CITIZENS' ASSOCIATION OF TORONTO, (4 Credit Union Dr).
- ◆ LATVIAN SOCIETY OF ARTISTS IN CANADA, (184 Westminster Ave).
- ◆ TORONTO LATVIAN SOCIETY, (Tel. 416-922-2931, 491 College St).

Consulates, Trade Commissions and Tourist Bureaus

- ◆ CONSULATE GENERAL OF LATVIA, (Tel. 416-932-8725, Fax 416-932-0920, 4 Credit Union Dr). Honorary Consul: Mr. Imats Purvs.

Prominent Torontonians

Alexsis Dreimanis, Professor of Geology; Arturs Ozolins, classical concert pianist; Ernests Reinbergs, wheat geneticist and developer of Tritical; Banuta Rubess, playwright, dramatist, and the second woman in Ontario to become a Rhodes Scholar; Tom Skudra, freelance photojournalist; Sarmite Bulte, M.P.

Source: Mr. Alexander Budrevies, Latvian National Federation in Canada.

The Lithuanian Community

Park Lithuanian at Keele Street and Glenlake Avenue signifies the presence and accomplishments of Toronto's 10,000 Lithuanians. Close by is a seniors' residence and the impressive Lithuanian community centre with a credit union and five halls. The **Lithuanian Church of the Resurrection** contains one of best collections of Lithuanian art in Canada, and in Mississauga, the **Lithuanian Martyrs' Parish** and the adjoining "**Anapilis**" **Cultural Centre** contain one of the largest halls in all Mississauga, as well as the **Lithuanian Museum Archives of Canada**. All the Lithuanian centres in the Greater Toronto area were built through the fundraising efforts of the community.

The first recorded Lithuanians in Canada were soldiers serving in the British Army in the early 19th century. The first wave of immigration occurred between 1900 and 1930. It was made up initially of people fleeing the mandatory 25-year service in the czar's army, and later of those looking to earn money to buy land back in Lithuania. Most of the early settlers found work on farms, the railways, in coal mines, and in the factories of Toronto and Montreal. Lithuanians—many of whom had come via England, Scotland, and the United States—began settling in the city around 1900.

The first Toronto Lithuanian organization was **St. Joseph's Society**, formed in 1907. It served as a mutual benefit relief organization providing insurance for its members. Another early organization was the **St. John the Baptist Relief Society**, from which grew the first Toronto Lithuanian parish. In 1928, the parish purchased a small Presbyterian church at Dundas Street and Gorevale Avenue. The basement hall was converted into a language school, and the church hall became a centre for social events and a meeting place for the choir, folk dance group, **Boy Scouts**, and **Girl Guides**. A small library was established at the parish and, in 1948, the sports club (**VYTIS**) was formed, attracting many young Lithuanian Canadians. In the interwar period there were also secular Lithuanian organizations, such as the **Sons and Daughters of Lithuanians** and the **S.L.A. (Susivienijimas Lietuviu Amerikoje)**, mutual benefit societies which also organized many cultural events.

The largest group of Lithuanians arrived in Canada after the Second World War, and consisted of political refugees who refused to return to

Lithuania after Soviet occupation ended the brief freedom of the Lithuanian Republic (1918–1940). Canada accepted Lithuanian workers under labour contracts in mining, lumber, agriculture, and domestic services. Of the 20,000 Lithuanians who came to Canada at this time, approximately 5,000 settled in Toronto.

In 1952 the **Lithuanian Canadian Community** was founded. It is still the main umbrella organization of all Lithuanians in Canada, with branches in all major cities including Toronto. In 1949 the weekly Lithuanian newspaper, **Teviskes Ziburiai**, was established in Toronto and is still going strong (although its offices are now in Mississauga), with subscribers all over the world.

In 1953, the **Resurrection Parish** officially opened and held services in a Parkdale theatre. The parish bought 25 acres of land on Georgian Bay at New Wasaga for a youth camp and formed the **Ausra Sports Club**. Other organizations located at the Resurrection Parish included the **Lithuanian Catholic Women's Association**, a library and bookshop, youth organizations, the pensioners' club, the **Toronto Lithuanian Philatelistic Club**, and the parish co-operative credit union.

Every year, Lithuanian culture is displayed at colourful cultural celebrations such as the **World Fall Dance Festival** which takes place in various cities and brings together 2,000 Lithuanian dancers from across Canada and the United States.

Places to Go

Lithuanian Community House, (Tel. 416-532-3311, 1573 Bloor St. W), is a community centre with five halls for accommodating social and cultural events. The centre is decorated with chandeliers, the regional flags of Lithuania, and plaques.

The **Lithuanian Museum Archives of Canada**, (Tel. 905-566-8755, 2185 Stavebank Rd., Mississauga). Founded by the Lithuanian Canadian community, documents the history of Lithuanian Canadians and displays Lithuanian textiles, rare books, coins, stamps, medals, and curios.

Religious Centres, Schools and Other Institutions

◆ ANAPILIS HALL, (Tel. 905-277-1270, 2185 Stavebank Rd., Mississauga). "Anapilis" (St. John's Hall) Community Centre with three halls.

- ◆ **ST. JOHN'S LITHUANIAN CEMETERY**, (2185 Stavebank Rd., Mississauga). The cemetery contains a large number of headstones of artistic merit in a pleasant park-like setting.
- ◆ **LITHUANIAN CHURCH OF RESURRECTION**, (Tel. 416-533-0621, 1 Resurrection Rd). The church contains one of the best collections of Lithuanian art in Canada. The parish hall is also located at 1 Resurrection Rd. In 1987, Lithuanians celebrated 600 years of Christianity.
- ◆ **LITHUANIAN LUTHERAN CHURCH OF THE REDEEMER**, (Tel. 416-766-1424, 1691 Bloor St. W).
- ◆ **LITHUANIAN MARTYRS CHURCH**, (Tel. 905-277-1270, 494 Isabella Ave., Mississauga).
- ◆ **VILNIUS MANOR**, (Tel. 416-762-1777, is at 1700 Bloor St. W). For Lithuanian Senior Citizens.

The community's financial institutions are:

- ◆ **LITHUANIAN RESURRECTION CREDIT UNION**, (Tel. 416-532-3400, 3 Resurrection Rd), which has accumulated a balance of $62 million since being founded in 1963.
- ◆ **PARAMA LITHUANIAN CREDIT UNION**, (Tel. 416-532-1149, 1573 Bloor St. W., and Tel. 416-207-9239, 2975 Bloor St. W), which has accumulated $107 million since 1952 to become the largest Lithuanian credit union in Canada.

Holidays and Celebrations

- ◆ **INDEPENDENCE DAY** is held on February 16 in celebration of the day in 1918 that Lithuania became an independent democratic nation. The nation lost its independence in 1940 when it was occupied by the USSR. After a struggle by dissidents which lasted many decades and captured the world's headlines in 1989–1990, Lithuania again became an independent country in 1991. An official ceremony including a cultural program is held on the weekend nearest to the date.
- ◆ **ST. CASIMIR'S FEAST** on March 4 honours Lithuania's patron saint. A special church service is held on the nearest Sunday. A fundraising bazaar organized by the Lithuanian **Boy Scouts** and **Girl Guides** is usually held on this day.
- ◆ **DAY OF REMEMBRANCE**. On June 14, the thousands of Lithuanians, Latvians, and Estonians who were deported to Siberia by occupying Soviet forces in 1941 through 1953 are remembered by the community.

A commemorative program is organized by the Baltic Federation of Canada.

- **LITHUANIANS IN CANADA DAY** is celebrated in September or October. Initiated in 1956, the day is commemorated with a convention, held in a different city each year, and a program featuring social functions, a religious service, and cultural performances.
- **ARMED FORCES DAY**, November 23, commemorates the day in 1918 that the armed forces were organized in Vilnius to protect the reborn nation of Lithuania. On this day, the community remembers those who died in the struggle for freedom.

See Holidays and Celebrations in Glossary.

Media

- **TEVISKES ZIBURIAI (THE LIGHTS OF THE HOMELAND)**, (Tel. 905-275-4672, www.tzib.com, 2185 Stavebank Rd., Mississauga). A weekly newspaper published since 1949. Editor-in-Chief: Dr. Pranas Gaida.

Organizations

- **LITHUANIAN CANADIAN COMMUNITY NATIONAL EXECUTIVE**, (Tel. 416-533-3292, www.klb.org, 1 Resurrection Rd). A national umbrella organization with nearly 20 local branches located throughout Canada. All Lithuanian Canadians are considered members of the **Lithuanian Canadian Community**, founded in 1952. The National Executive also maintains links with the **World Lithuanian Community**. President: Ruta Zilinskas.
- **LITHUANIAN COMMUNITY HOUSE**, (Tel. 416-532-3311, 1573 Bloor St. W). Home to the head offices of many Lithuanian Canadian organizations.

At the same address:
- **ATZALYNAS CULTURAL ARTS & FOLK DANCE GROUP INC.** President: Walter Dauginis.
- **VOLUNTEERS OF LITHUANIAN INDEPENDENCE ASSOCIATION.**
- **LITHUANIAN CANADIAN FOUNDATION.**
- **LITHUANIAN NATIONAL FUND IN CANADA.**

Other popular groups within the community are the Gintaras Folk Dance Ensemble; ARAS men's choir; and Volunge (mixed) choir.

Consulates, Trade Commissions and Tourist Bureaus

◆ CONSULATE GENERAL OF LITHUANIA, (Tel. 416-538-2992, 1573 Bloor St. W.) Honorary Consul General: Mr. Paul Kuras.

Prominent Torontonians

Juozas Bakis, sculptor; John Govidas, musician; Algis Pacevicius, Prominent Lawyer: Al Pace Law Firm; V. Rudinskos, Lawyer; Erin Link, Senior member of OPS; Leo Rautins, first Canadian to play in the National Basketball Association; Snaige Sileika, artist; Violeta Nesukaitis, former table tennis champion of Canada; Antanas Sileika, writer; Shaige Sileika, artist; Arthauas Sileika, novelist; Paul Kravecas, artist.

Al Pacevicius (Pace), prominent lawyer, former president of the Canadian Lithuanian community.

The Macedonian Community

On the first weekend in August, Toronto's Macedonians participate in a memorial service at **St. Clement of Ohrid Church** in Toronto to honour the heroes of Macedonia's past. The 1903 Ilinden Uprising of the Macedonians against the Ottoman Empire is commemorated with a picnic and a ceremony that includes the placing of a wreath at a stone monument dedicated to the Unknown Soldier, at the **National War Memorial**, Ottawa.

Toronto is a centre for one of the largest Macedonian communities in the world. Macedonia is now a nation state that broke away from the former Yugoslavia. Macedonians also live in the region that stretches through Bulgaria, Greece, and Albania.

Relatively few Macedonians immigrated to Canada before the turn of the century. With the failure of the Ilinden Uprising, many people emigrated to escape the aftermath; others arrived following the Balkan Wars of 1912–1913.

Early Macedonians found work in tannery and fur-processing plants located in Cabbagetown. Machine operators and labourers were employed by the garment industry on Spadina Avenue or in the iron and sheet metal industries, silk mills, and knitting factories. Macedonians worked as railroad navvies and in the meat-packing industry. As slaughterhouses and abattoirs moved westward in the city, the Macedonian community settled near the Municipal Abattoir in the Niagara Street district or near the west-end railway junctions. Many factory workers became supervisors and union stewards, while entrepreneurs started their own small businesses such as meat markets, barber shops, shoeshine parlours, grocery stores, and haberdasheries. Having gained experience as waiters and busboys, many ventured into the restaurant business. The **Dufferin Grill** was one of the first Toronto Macedonian-owned restaurants.

Macedonian organizations in the city included **Slave Petroff and Company**, a steamship and banking agency which offered the services of a labour bureau. The Baptist church in Toronto also established a labour exchange and information bureau at the **Macedonian and Bulgarian Mission Hall.**

The third wave of immigration resulted from the expulsion between the two World Wars. By the end of the Second World War, there were an estimated 50,000 Macedonians in Canada. Today, Macedonians are found in all jobs and professions, from doctors, lawyers, engineers, and teachers to factory workers and business owners.

Places to Go

Macedonian national foods like stuffed peppers, cabbage rolls, musaka, guvech, tavche gravche, and skara, are served in restaurants including **Madera**, (Tel. 416-465-2653, 836 Danforth Ave); **Red Violin**, (Tel. 416-465-0969, 95 Danforth Ave) and **Burgundy's**, (Tel. 416-924-1186 780 Yonge St).

Canadian Macedonian Historical Society, (Tel. 416-755-3117, www.macedonianhistory.ca, 850 O'Connor Dr). A historic display of Macedonian costumes and exhibitions of art and artifacts are housed in the Society's museum. An impressive collection of over 2,000 Macedonian history books are found in the library resource centre. Books in english on Macedonian history can be purchased through the society.

Religious Centres, Schools and Other Institutions

In addition to the following churches, Macedonians also attend several other Eastern Orthodox and Greek Orthodox churches.

- ◆ ST. CLEMENT OF OHRID MACEDONIAN ORTHODOX CHURCH, (Tel. 416-421-7451, 76 Overlea Blvd). The first Macedonian Orthodox Church in Canada, built in 1964. The congregation features the twenty-voice **Canadian Macedonian Choir**, and Macedonian Language heritage classes are held at the church.
- ◆ ST. ILIJA MACEDONIAN ORTHODOX CATHEDRAL, (Tel. 905-821-8050, 1775 Bristol Rd. W, Mississauga). Groups at the church include the **Ladies Auxiliary** and **Ilinden Folklore Group**.
- ◆ ST. DIMITRIJA OF SOLUN MACEDONIAN ORTHODOX CHURCH, (Tel. 905-471-5555, 188-201 Main St. N., Markham).
- ◆ ST. NEDELA MACEDONIAN ORTHODOX CHURCH, (Tel. 905-426-5355, 485 Bayly St. W., Ajax).

Holidays and Celebrations

Easter and Christmas are celebrated according to the Gregorian and Julian calendars.

- **ST. JOHN THE BAPTIST DAY** is January 18. It is celebrated with a baptismal ceremony, usually held in front of the church.
- **THE BIRTHDAY OF MACEDONIAN FREEDOM-FIGHTER GOTSE DELCHEV,** who led the 1903 Ilinden Uprising, is celebrated on February 4.
- **SAINTS CYRIL AND METHODY DAY** is May 24. Macedonians worldwide pay tribute to the two brothers from Salonika. Apostles to the Slavs, they are best known for creating the first Slavonic alphabet, which later became known as Cyrillic script.
- **ILINDEN UPRISING.** August 2 commemorates the anniversary of the Ilinden Uprising of 1903. Festivities include dances, a beauty contest, and a picnic held the first Sunday in August.
- **SEPTEMBER 8** is the celebration of the independence of the Republic of Macedonia.
- **THE FORMATION OF THE REPUBLIC OF MACEDONIA** in 1944 is celebrated by some members of the community on October 11.
- **ST. CLEMENT'S DAY,** December 8, is in honour of St. Clement of Ohrid, a disciple of Saints Cyril and Methody. St. Clement's Church in Toronto holds a dinner and dance and other celebrations on the nearest weekend to the day.

See Holidays and Celebrations in Glossary.

Media

- **MACEDONIAN EDITION,** Informative & Entertaining TV program, (Tel. 416-503-2285, www.macedonianadition.tv), Rogers TV, Channels 10, 63, 84, 18–25th St., #4. Alternate Saturdays, 3:30 p.m. to 4:00 p.m. Alternate Fridays, 6:00 p.m. Also broadcast on Macedonian Satellite. Producer and host: Pobeda Piskaceva.
- **MACEDONIAN HERITAGE,** OMNI-TV, (Tel. 416-260-0047, 545 Lakeshore Blvd). Saturday, 3:00 p.m. to 4:00 p.m. and Wednesday, 8:00 a.m. to 9:00 a.m. Producer: Bill Yancoff.
- **VOICE OF MACEDONIA,** CHIN 100.7 FM, (Tel. 416-531-9991, 622 College St). Sunday, 7:30 p.m. to 8:00 p.m. Also on CHIN 1540 AM, Monday to Friday 7:30 p.m. to 8:00 p.m. Host: Dragica Belchevska.
- **UNITED MACEDONIA,** Fairchild Radio, CHKT 1430 AM, (Tel. 905-763-3350, 135 East Beaver Creek Rd., Units 7–8, Richmond Hill). Saturday, 9:00 a.m. to 10:00 a.m.

- CANADIAN-MACEDONIAN NEWS, (1032 Pape Ave., Box 60002). A monthly newspaper distributed across North America. Editor and publisher: Lijana Ristova.
- ZDRAVETZ, (TEL. 416-755-9231, 850 O'Connor Dr), a periodical newsletter published by Canadian Macedonian Place,. Editor: Zlatka Cokov.

Organizations

- CANADIAN MACEDONIAN PLACE, (Tel. 416-755-9231, 850 O'Connor Dr). Home to the Daughters of Macedonia.
- MACEDONIAN COMMUNITY CENTRE, (Tel. 416-421-7451, 76 Overlea Blvd). With three halls and a library, the Centre houses several organizations, including: the award-winning **Makedonka**, **Macedonian Folk Ensemble** with 200 dancers; **Macedonia Drama Group**; the **Ladies' Auxiliary**; the **Miladonov Brothers**, a Macedonian literary association; **Macedonian Language School**; **Macedonian War Veterans Association**; **Macedonian Canadian Choir**; **Trsye Folklore Group**; **Macedonian Information**; the **Macedonian Youth Association**.

Youth in Macedonian costume.

- UNITED MACEDONIANS OF CANADA ORGANIZATION, (Tel. 416-490-0181,www.unitedmacedonians.org, 686 McCowan Rd., P.O. Box 66517). Established in 1959 to promote unity and friendship among Macedonians in North America and overseas. Sponsors cultural days, dances, picnics, and beauty pageants, and awards scholarships. The organization is home to the Macedonian folk dance group, **Gotse Delchev**; **United Macedonians Hockey Team**; and the **Solun Soccer Club**. President: Boris Mangov.

Other Organizations include:

- CANADIAN MACEDONIAN HISTORICAL SOCIETY, (Tel. 416-755-3117, 850 O'Connor Dr).

◆ CANADIAN MACEDONIAN HOCKEY LEAGUE, (Tel. 416-759-5309, 71 Gooderham Dr).

◆ MACEDONIAN CANADIAN RESTAURANT CO-OPERATIVE INC., (Tel. 905-831-3551, 774 Liverpool Rd., Pickering).

◆ SELYANI MACEDONIAN FOLKLORE GROUP, (Tel. 416-698-1747, 4 Osborne Ave). Director: James Nicoloff.

◆ CANADIAN MACEDONIAN HEALTH PROFESSIONALS ASSOCIATION, (Tel. 416-231-4417, 270 The Kingsway).

◆ MACEDONIAN STUDENTS ASSOCIATION AT YORK UNIVERSITY, (331 Student Centre, 4700 Keele St).

◆ CANADIAN MACEDONIAN BUSINESS NETWORK, (Tel. 905-764-7816, 3-100 West Beaver Creek Rd). President: Nick Kuburovski.

Consulates, Trade Commissions and Tourist Bureaus

◆ CONSULATE GENERAL OF THE REPUBLIC OF MACEDONIA IN TORONTO, (Tel. 416-322-2196, 90 Eglinton Ave. E., Suite 210). Consul General: Mr. Martin Trenevski.

Prominent Torontonians

Thea Andrews, TV personality; John Bitove Sr., Order of Canada founder of Canadian Macedonian Place; John Bitove Jr., President & CEO for 2008 Olympic Bid corp; Michael Close, artist; Georgi Danevski, iconographer; John Evans, Dora award winner actor; Peter Kondoff, engineering member of the Order & President Emeritus of Canadian Macedonian historical Society; Susan Niczowski, Canadian Woman Entrepreneur 2006; Dr. Andrew Rossos, historian; Dr. Boris Stoicheff, physicist; Lui Temelkovski, First Macedonian MP; Chris Paliare LSM, lawyer.

Source: V.A. Evans

The Malaysian Community

One of Toronto's greatest culinary discoveries is satay, the popular Malay dish consisting of meat barbecued on bamboo skewers and dipped in sweet chili and peanut sauce. Satay, along with the experience of eating a communal meal around a fire, is offered at the Malaysian restaurants that have sprung up in the city in the last two decades.

Malaysia, located in Southeast Asia, is a member country of the Commonwealth. Formed in 1963, Malaysia comprises the Federation of Malaya, Sarawak, and Sabah. Its population includes the Malays, Chinese, Indians, and other ethnic groups.

Between 1973 and 1980, Malaysian clerical workers arrived in Canada, followed by industrial labourers and professionals in the areas of science, engineering, math, and medicine. Students also form part of the Malaysian population. The Malaysian government is the only foreign administration to have established a separate students' department in Toronto to look after the welfare of its students.

The **Malaysian Association of Canada** serves as a meeting place for Malaysian and Singapore nationals, and assists newcomers in adjusting to Canadian society. Community organizations and student associations also encourage an awareness of Malaysian cultural traditions. Holidays are celebrated with festivals that include exhibitions of art, food, fashion and other aspects of life in Malaysia.

Places to Go

Among the most popular dishes found in Toronto Malaysian restaurants are rojak (boiled vegetables mixed with peanut gravy), rendang (beef braised with ginger), and panggang gold (spicy roast duck). Chinese dishes include bird's nest soup and shark's fin soup. Beer, coconut water, and fruit juices often complement a meal.

Gourmet Garden, (Tel. 416-332-8765, 4465 Sheppard Ave. E., Unit 46), specialties include Assam curry fish and Nyonya chicken curry. **Mata Hari Grill**, (39 Baldwin St.), is also a popular dining destination.

Malaysian food is also served in Asian restaurants in Toronto's downtown Chinatown.

Religious Centres, Schools and Other Institutions

Among Malaysians, there are Muslim, Hindu, Buddhist, and Christian followers who worship at the city's churches, mosques, and temples.

◆ MALAYSIAN SINGAPOREAN BIBLE CHURCH, (Tel. 416-322-8060, 288 Cummer Ave).

Holidays and Celebrations

◆ THE BIRTHDAY OF HIS MAJESTY, YANG DI-PERTUAN AGONG is celebrated on June 7. The country is an independent constitutional monarchy and the date is set aside by the government to honour the supreme head of state.

◆ MALAYSIA DAY is August 31. In 1948, Great Britain established the nine Malay states as the Federation of Malaya. Full independence was achieved in 1957. In 1963, Malaysia became a sovereign state within the Commonwealth of Nations.

See Holidays and Celebrations in Glossary.

Organizations

◆ MALAYSIAN ASSOCIATION OF CANADA, (Tel. 416-618 0966, Fax 905-629-0421, 89 Donalda Cres). A non-profit organization bringing together

Traditional and local costumes of Malaysian people.

Malaysians and non-Malaysians through educational, social, cultural, and economic activities. President: Gopal Simon.

Consulates, Trade Commissions and Tourist Bureaus

◆ CONSULATE OF MALAYSIA, (Tel. 416-364-6800, Fax 416-969-9225, 55 St. Clair Ave. W., Suite 225). Consul and Trade Commissioner: Mrs. Zalela Binti Jaafar.

Prominent Torontonians

Chin Lee, Toronto City Councillor.

Contributors: Mohamad B. Ahmad Thani Sani, former Consul and Director, Malaysian Students Department, Consulate of Malaysia; and H.J. Sahban Muksan, Consul and Director, Malaysian Students Department, Consulate of Malaysia.

The Maltese Community

Every year, a carnival dance kicks off the summer for Toronto's 6,000-member Maltese community—the largest in Canada. In the recent past, thousands of people have lined the streets for a parade which included resounding marching bands and festive floats. The parade passed **Malta Park**, a small parkette in the West Toronto Junction named in recognition of the contributions of Maltese-Canadians to Canada. Located at St. John's Road and Dundas Street West, the parkette is encircled by a Maltese neighbourhood with shops, clubs, and the community's landmark, **St. Paul the Apostle Roman Catholic Church**.

The Ontario community dates back to 1840 when early settlers arrived from Malta, a Mediterranean country comprised of three islands—Malta, Gozo, and Comino. Pre-Confederation pioneers included Louis Shickluna, a shipbuilder who arrived in 1836 and established a prominent shipyard on the Welland Canal in St. Catharines, Ontario.

By the turn of the century, Toronto had two Maltese neighbourhoods, one in the Dundas and McCaul streets area, and the other in the West Toronto Junction. Maltese living in the downtown neighbourhood worshipped at **St. Patrick's Shrine Church** and the **Church of Our Lady of Mount Carmel**, while early settlers in the West Toronto Junction attended **St. Cecilia's Church** until **St. Paul the Apostle** was built in 1930. Immigration continued from 1907 and through the 1920s. Maltese labourers found jobs in meat-packing factories, on the railway, and in various trades.

In 1922, meetings were held in a house on Simcoe Street by the **Maltese-Canadian Society of Toronto (MCST)**, the first North American Maltese organization. Its main purpose was to build the first Maltese national church. By 1930, **St. Paul the Apostle Church** in the West Toronto Junction was completed. For its efforts, the MCST became affectionately known as "il-kazin tal-Knisja" (the club of the church). Today, the names of the MCST members and church benefactors can be read on a large stone slab at the church's entrance.

During the Second World War, the **Malta Relief Fund**, headed by the **Maltese-Canadian Society of Toronto**, united the community in sending supplies and funds to their homeland. By the mid-1940s, the main community was concentrated in the Junction area surrounding the church, where some Maltese started their own businesses in 1955. **St. Paul the Apostle Maltese Church** was expanded after the Second World War when large numbers of Maltese settled in the area.

Community get-togethers for Malta's favourite sport have become a familiar sight on West Toronto soccer fields. Maltese have contributed to the economy with real-estate firms, travel agency, restaurants, and various businesses.

The 80-year-old statue of St. Paul is decorated during St. Paul the Apostle Church and the community's celebration of the Feast of Malta's patron, St. Paul.

Places to Go

Much of the Maltese cultural and commercial life in the city can be found on a stretch of Dundas Street West between Keele Street and Runnymede Road. Bakeries and delicatessens fill the air with the redolence of Maltese meat, pasta delicacies, and popular dishes, including fenkata (rabbit stew), bragioli (beef roulades), tumpani (a mixture of puff pastry, macaroni, meat, and eggs), octopus stew, Imquarrun-fil-forn (baked macaroni), and smoked herring, a favourite Maltese fish dish.

Photographs of Malta's churches and fishing villages embellish the stucco walls of the **Malta Bake Shop**, (Tel. 416-769-2174, 3256 Dundas St. W), serving hot pastizzi (pastry filled with cheese or peas), which can be a meal or a snack, depending on the appetite. Other foods available include tumpani and ftira (a pizza-like crust covered with potatoes, anchovies, peppers, and capers). Fenkata is made on special occasions and dessert temptations include gaghaq ghassel (pastry rings with molasses) and strizzi (pastry filled with chocolate, fruit, and almonds).

Buskett Bakery, (Tel. 416-763-2562, 3029 Dundas St. W), bears the name of Malta's only forest. Famous for homemade Maltese pastizzi, **Joe's Pastizzi Plus**, (Tel. 416-233-9063, 5070 Dundas St. W), and **Malta's Finest Pastries**, (Tel. 416-236-1253, 4138 Dundas St. W), offer a variety of Maltese foods, served in a Maltese ambience.

The city's largest collection of Maltese books is located at the library of the **Melita Soccer Club**, (Tel. 416-763-5317, 3336 Dundas St. W). The social club, which has a recreation room, serves as a gathering place for the Maltese community. The library is open on Tuesday and Thursday from 5:00 p.m. to 7:00 p.m. **Annette Street Public Library**, (Tel. 416-393-7692, 145 Annette

Members of the Malta Band Club performing a typical Maltese march in High Park.

St), has a large collection of books in Maltese, as well as books on the Maltese Islands.

Our Lady's Chapel in **St. Michael's Cathedral**, (200 Church St), was designed by Maltese-Canadian architect John Farrugia. A large Maltese cross is embedded at the main entrance of the cathedral. **St. Paul's Catholic Church**, (83 Power St), has a large painting of Malta on its ceiling.

Religious Centres, Schools and Other Institutions

◆ ST. PAUL THE APOSTLE CHURCH, (Tel. 416-767-7054, 3224 Dundas St. W). Dedicated to one of Malta's two patron saints, the church is run by the Missionary Society of St. Paul. It has a choir and an auditorium. The church museum houses a trophy won by The Maltese-Canadian Society of Toronto's **Knights of Malta Committee** for the best float in Toronto's centennial parade in 1934.

◆ MALTESE HERITAGE CLASS PARENTS AND TEACHERS ASSOCIATION. Maltese is a Semitic language of Punic-Arabic origin, containing some elements of other Mediterranean languages. The **Maltese Heritage Class Parents and Teachers Association** promotes Maltese culture, traditions, and language. Classes are taught at **St. Paul the Apostle Church**.

Holidays and Celebrations

◆ THE FEAST OF ST. PAUL THE APOSTLE, who converted the Maltese to Christianity in 60 A.D., is marked on February 10.

◆ DAY OF FREEDOM is celebrated on March 31 to commemorate the day in 1979 when the last foreign forces peacefully left the island.

◆ THE FEAST OF OUR LADY OF SORROWS sees statues of Our Lady of Sorrows and St. John carried outside **St. Paul the Apostle Roman Catholic Church** in a solemn procession held every April. Special masses are held in Maltese and English at the church during the Pashal season.

◆ THE FEAST OF SAINTS PETER AND PAUL (L'IMNARJA), held on June 29, sees a festival of folklore and music.

◆ THE FEAST OF OUR LADY OF VICTORY on September 8 commemorates Malta's victories during its two Great Sieges in 1565 and 1942.

◆ INDEPENDENCE DAY, September 21, commemorates the day Malta was recognized as an independent country within the Commonwealth.

- ◆ REPUBLIC DAY, December 13, recognizes the day in 1974 that Malta officially became a republic within the Commonwealth.
- ◆ CHRISTMAS. On December 25, Toronto's Maltese attend Christmas midnight mass at **St. Paul the Apostle Church**. Many homes display a nativity scene. Gifts are exchanged after Mass with a visit from Father Christmas. Dinner the next day consists of leg of pork, lamb, or a turkey. After the meal, family and friends toast each other with "Il-Milied it-tajjeb" (Merry Christmas).
- ◆ SENIORS' DINNER. Every year, the **Maltese-Canadian Federation** organizes the Senior Citizens Christmas Dinner Social which treats seniors of all ethnocultural backgrounds to a complimentary Christmas dinner and show.
- ◆ THE MISS MALTA OF CANADA PAGEANT is an annual event organized by the **Maltese-Canadian Society of Toronto, Inc**.

See Holidays and Celebrations in Glossary.

Media

- ◆ LEHEN MALTI, OMNI-TV, (Tel. 416-260-0047, 545 Lakeshore Blvd. W). Sunday, 6:00 a.m. to 6:30 a.m. and Saturday, 8:30 a.m. to 9:00 a.m.
- ◆ RICHARD CUMBO—FREELANCE MALTESE JOURNALIST, (Tel. 416-762-6613, 480 Windermere Ave).

Organizations

- ◆ MALTESE-CANADIAN FEDERATION, at **St. Paul the Apostle Church**, (Tel. 416-767-8185, 3224 Dundas St. W). Founded in 1974, this Federation is comprised of Maltese organizations in Ontario and other parts of Canada. Its goals are to foster co-operation and interaction amongst groups, act as a unified voice for the community, and organize community events. President: Henry Formosa.

The following organizations can also be reached through **St. Paul the Apostle Church**:

- ◆ 172ND SCOUT GROUP, BROWNIES, AND GUIDES OF ST. PAUL THE APOSTLE CHURCH, (Tel. 416-767-7054).
- ◆ THE MALTESE ACTORS GROUP, which promotes and performs traditional Maltese plays.

Other organizations include:

◆ MALTESE VETERANS ASSOCIATION OF CANADA, (Tel. 416-767-8185, 3 Baby Point Cres).

◆ THE MALTESE CANADIAN SOCIETY OF TORONTO, (Tel. 416-767-3645, 3132 Dundas St. W). Founded in 1922, MCST sponsors sports and social activities and provides services to the needy. The society cele-brated its 50th anniversary in 1972 with a spectacular parade, and in its 60th year produced a publication outlining its history. In 2002 the society marked it's 80th anniversary. President: Charlie Grixti.

◆ MELITA SOCCER CLUB INC., (Tel. 416-763-5317, 3336 Dundas St. W). Founded in 1963, the club borrows Malta's biblical name, Melita, and sponsors its own **Metropolitan Toronto Soccer Association** team, the Melita Soccer Club, which won first prize for its float in Toronto's sesquicentennial parade in 1984. It also stages popular social events.

Consulates, Trade Commissions and Tourist Bureaus

◆ CONSULATE GENERAL OF THE REPUBLIC OF MALTA, (Tel. 416-207-0922, Fax 416-207-0986, 3300 Bloor St. W., Suite 730, the Cierical Centre mezzaine West Tower). Consul General: Mrs. Fiona-Jayne Formosa.

Prominent Torontonians

Larry and Tito Attard, thoroughbred trainers and famous jockeys; Joe Sid, thoroughbred trainer; Mario Phillip Azzopardi, actor and director; Richard S. Cumbo, journalist and historian; Margaret Darmanin, archaeologist; Peter Muscat, artist and sculptor; Tony Tanti, former NHL hockey player; Charlie Theuma, soccer player and coach; Paul Zammit, prominent litiga-tion lawyer; Emily Zarb, fashion designer; George Zarb, Professor of Dentistry and lecturer; Roger Scannura, musician; Valerie Buhagiar, actress; John Portelli, professor at the University of Toronto; Millo Vasallo, former dean of the consular corps.

Contributor: Richard S. Cumbo, journalist, historian, and researcher.

Sources: Richard S. Cumbo; Milo Vassallo, former Consul General.

The Norwegian Community

Little Norway Park, opened in 1987 by Norway's King Olaf V, is located along Little Norway Crescent at the foot of Bathurst Street and the lakefront. In the administration building at **Toronto Island Airport**, Norway's military and air force flags are mounted on each side of a historical plaque dedicated to the 3,200 men of the Norwegian air force who trained in Canada in the 1940s.

During the Second World War, a landing strip and buildings near the airport were used as a recruit school and physical training facility until camp **Little Norway** was built on the mainland opposite Toronto Island. It was the first foreign air force training camp granted by the Canadian government. Today, a Norwegian flag and a granite boulder with memorial inscriptions mark the place where Little Norway's post office, hospital, schools, barracks, mess halls, and military stores once stood.

Long before, Norwegians had made their mark in Canada. Some 500 years before Columbus, Norsemen discovered and attempted to settle on Canada's shores. The earliest known instance of European settlement in North America is a Norse site on the shores of Newfoundland. L'Anse Aux Meadows is the only authenticated Norse site found in North America. Helge and Anne Stine Ingstad began excavating the site in 1961. The Northwest Passage was traversed from 1903 to 1906 by sailor Ronald Amundsen. Henry A. Larsen, of Norwegian birth, was the first Canadian to travel the Passage from east to west, in 1940–1942.

Major Norwegian settlements developed in the Canadian West between 1886 and 1929, largely made up of settlers who had migrated from the United States. Toronto's Norwegian community is a combination of descendants of early western pioneers who left the Prairies to seek careers in the cities, and others who came from Norway seeking jobs in Ontario's industries. These post–Second World War settlers were mainly from professional and clerical backgrounds.

Some Norwegian Air Force personnel immigrated to Canada, settling either in Toronto or Muskoka, where the "Little Norway" training camp was moved in 1942. A memorial stone at the site of the camp was erected 40 years after the camp's closing.

Many of Toronto's early Norwegian settlers were members of the **Scandinavian-Canadian Club**, founded in 1935, and the now defunct **Nordic Society**. Members preserved their culture through the celebration of holidays, cultural events, arts and crafts, and sporting activities such as cross-country skiing, orienteering, handball, and tennis.

Of the approximately 2,000 Torontonians of Norwegian descent, many are involved in business in the fields of contracting, manufacturing, plumbing, education, IT, business, and real estate.

Places to Go

The **Scandinavian-Canadian Club of Metropolitan Toronto**, (Tel. 416-782-4604, 91 Stormont Ave), sponsors Scandinavian dinners and houses a library with hundreds of books, newspapers, and magazines from Scandinavian countries. President: Irene Ingersol.

A favourite Norwegian snack is Knekkebrod (crisp round bread) eaten with aged cheeses. Flatbrod (a paper-thin unleavened crisp bread) is eaten with meals. Cured, pickled, and salted fish dishes including smoked salmon, lutefisk (salted codfish), and herring are popular. Meat dishes include fenalar (salted and smoked leg of mutton), skinke (cured ham eaten with scrambled eggs with chives), fankal (lamb and cabbage), and kjottkaker (meatballs). Rommegrot (flour-thickened sour cream) served with melted butter, cinnamon and brown sugar, is often served at the end of a meal.

Holidays and Celebrations

- ◆ CONSTITUTION DAY on May 17 honours the day Norway adopted its constitution. In Ontario, the holiday is celebrated on the nearest weekend with a cultural program consisting of a dinner, speeches, and a dance.
- ◆ DAY OF LIBERATION on May 8 marks the day in 1945 when the Second World War ended in Norway. On this day, Norwegian War Veterans, members of the **Norwegian Club** and **Scandinavian–Canadian Club** lay wreaths at the memorial stone in **Little Norway Park**, at Bathurst Street, finishing with a reception at the **Scandinavian–Canadian Club**.
- ◆ SUMMER SOLSTICE. On the weekend nearest June 24, Norwegian Canadians join together with other Scandinavian groups to celebrate the summer solstice. Midsummer Day events include dancing and singing.

- **WINTER SOLSTICE.** Since prehistoric times, Scandinavians have celebrated the winter solstice. According to the Julian calendar, this date
  was December 13. The celebration of the return of light to a northern
  country now coincides with the commemoration of Saint Lucia, who
  suffered a martyr's death in 300 A.D. for her Christian beliefs. Before
  being pierced by a soldier's sword, she miraculously withstood the
  flames of the pyre where she was sentenced to be burned to death. She
  is believed to appear every December 13 in the early morning, dressed
  in virginal white, with a blood-red sash from her martyr's death and
  wearing a crown of candles, symbolizing the flames that did not touch
  her. In Toronto a young woman wearing a crown of candles appears
  on the steps of Queen's Park followed by an entourage of white-clad
  attendants. Toronto's Lucia is chosen by Swedish organizations and
  the Scandinavian-Canadian Club, who jointly arrange the annual
  entourage.
- **CHRISTMAS EVE,** December 24, is the most important day of the festive
  season for Norwegians. They may leave a bowl of rice pudding out for
  Julenissen, a gnome-like creature who is said to live in the barn and
  take care of the animals' well-being, if the farmer is good to him. In
  towns, Julenissen, like Santa Claus, is believed to leave presents for
  children under the tree. Some Norwegians carry on the custom of
  feeding birds and animals, as they are revered for having witnessed
  Christ's birth.

See Holidays and Celebrations in Glossary.

Media

- **THE SCANDINAVIAN-CANADIAN CLUB OF METROPOLITAN TORONTO,**
  (Tel. 416-782-4604, 91 Stormont Ave), publishes a newsletter 10 times
  a year.

Organizations

- **NORWEGIAN CLUB,** (www.thenorwegianclub.org). This social and business club established in 1984 aims to maintain elements of Norwegian
  culture in the city, organizes festivities for Norway's national holidays,
  including Constitution Day and St. Hans (Midsummer's Eve). Dinners
  held during the year feature typical Norwegian food. President: Knut
  Larsen.

- ◆ THE DOWNSVIEW-NORWAY, ROYAL CANADIAN AIR FORCE (RCAF) ASSOCI-ATION, (Wing 451, 91 Stormont Ave). Founded in 1981 by a group of Norwegian veterans.

- ◆ THE SCANDINAVIAN-CANADIAN CLUB OF METROPOLITAN TORONTO, (Tel. 416-782-4604, 91 Stormont Ave). Holds Sunday afternoon family get-togethers once a month, and organizes hiking and canoeing expeditions, ski weekends, and theatre outings. Norwegian language classes are held at the centre. The club celebrates all of the Scandinavian countries' national days with a dinner dance and features speakers from the various countries. It helps organize the **Saint Lucia Pageant** every year, and holds a bazaar at Christmas and Easter each year with handmade goods and imports from Scandinavian countries. Arts and crafts classes are held monthly.

- ◆ NEEDLES AND KNITS, (Tel. 905-713-2066, 15040 Yonge St., Aurora). Owner: Tove Gilie, specializes in Norwegian knitting techniques and finishing, wool, novi needles, pewter buttons, and clasps. Knitting classes every week.

Consulates, Trade Commissions and Tourist Bureaus

- ◆ ROYAL NORWEGIAN CONSULATE GENERAL, (Tel. 905-671-3637, Fax (905) 671-3648, www.emb-norway.ca, 6150 Kennedy Rd., Unit #7, Mississauga). Honorary Consul General: Mr. Eivind Hoff.

- ◆ INNOVATION NORWAY (TRADE OFFICE FOR NORWAY), (Tel. 416-920-0434, Fax 416-920-5982, www.ntc-no/toronto, 2 Bloor St. W., Suite 504). Trade Commissioner and Consul: Arnfinn Hatterm.

Prominent Torontonians

Solveig Barber, singer, actress; Brit Missirlian, one of the founders of the Scandinavian Club and the Norwegian Club and active in the Advent Church in Toronto; Astrid Simola, first woman President of the Scandinavian Club, active in Boy Scouts; Eivind Hoff, successful businessman, current Counsel General for Norway in Toronto; Johann Olav Koss, famous speed skater President of "Right-To-Play."

Sources: Eivind Hoff, Greta Papageorgiu and Knut Larsen.

The Pakistani Community

Every August since 1978, members of Toronto's Pakistani community have marched in a parade from **Nathan Phillips Square** to **Queen's Park** to celebrate Pakistan's Day of Independence. This colourful ceremony, followed by speeches and a cultural program of patriotic songs and folk dances, symbolizes the close co-operation of the community's major organizations and media in celebrating Pakistani culture in the city.

Although the history of the Pakistanis dates back 5,000 years to the Mohan-Jo-Daro civilization, Pakistan is a relatively new nation that achieved its independence in 1947. The Islamic Republic of Pakistan is located on the Arabian Sea between Afghanistan and India. Following Pakistan's independence, there was a large exodus of Pakistanis, and in the late 1950s and early '60s, the first people began to immigrate to Canada indirectly from the United States, Britain, Germany, and France.

In the 1960s, the Muslim community established Islamic centres in a rented building on Dundas Street West and at **St. Mary's Church** on Bathurst Street. A building on Rhodes Avenue was purchased and became the **Islamic Community Centre**. Today, the focal point of religious life for Toronto's Pakistani community is the **Jami Mosque** on Boustead Avenue, established in the early 1970s. The Mosque is open 24 hours a day and has a major research library. It operates a weekly radio program and hosts lectures and programs featuring Muslim scholars from around the world.

In the early 1970s, a second wave of immigrants arrived from Pakistan. These new settlers eventually sponsored their families to come to Canada. Today, Toronto's Pakistani community numbers close to 50,000 people.

The **Pakistan Canada Association**, established in 1968, was the community's first organization in the city. In 1982, the **National Federation of Pakistani Canadians**, with headquarters in Ottawa, was formed as an umbrella organization to help promote the group's separate identity from the South Asian and East Indian communities in Canada. The federation sponsors seminars and publications on issues related to the Pakistani community in Canada and organizes a women's conference and youth conference on Labour Day weekend.

Shops carrying imported clothing and carpets from Pakistan can be found throughout Toronto. The community's rich cultural traditions are manifested through the music of the tabla and sitar, and art exhibits by internationally acclaimed Pakistani artists. In 1988, the community entered Metro's International Caravan for the first time with the Lahore Pavilion, which featured the exciting sword dances of the Pathan tribesmen, carpet weaving demonstrations, and a bazaar of brassware, fabrics, saris, jewelry, and artifacts.

Places to Go

Pakistani restaurants, spice shops, and sari boutiques are found around the city, particularly in East Toronto in the Pape, Gerrard, Coxwell, and Donlands area. Butcher shops sell Halal meat (slaughtered in a ritual manner), video stores carry Pakistani movies, and splendid Pakistani carpets are sold in rug stores.

Popular Pakistani cuisine includes tandoori chicken (cooked in a clay oven using charcoal), samosas (deep fried turnovers stuffed with spiced ground meat or potatoes and peas), chat (a sauce made with potatoes, onions, tomatoes, radishes, and mint), and chicken, lamb, and beef curries. Desserts include halwah (sweet wheat or carrot puddings), and accompanying most meals is naan (unleavened bread from a clay oven) and puris (puffy breads deep-fried in oil).

Shala-Mar, (391 Roncesvalles Ave), serves appetizers such as cumin-scented vegetable samosas and pakora with fresh vegetables in light batters; main courses include karahi chicken and lamb biryani and an assortment of curry dinners, including chicken, beef, shrimp, and vegetable.

Pakistani fare can be sampled at **Pita Delight**, (Tel. 416-299-3833, 2360 Midland Ave).

Pakistani videos can be rented from **Videohome**, (Tel. 416-748-1702, 130 Westmore Dr).

Halal meats such as lamb, goat, beef, and chicken, as well as other groceries are available at **Madina Halal Meat & Grocery**, (Tel. 416-461-0404, 1063 Danforth Ave); and **Indo Canada Bakery**, (Tel. 416-469-3753, 1002 Danforth Ave).

Rugs from Pakistan are sold at **Karakashian Rug Gallery**, (Tel. 416-964-1995, 1257 Bay St); and **Tapis d'Orient**, (Tel. 416-658-7518, 1440 Bathurst St).

Islamic literature can be found at **Islamic Centre of Toronto (Jami Mosque)**, (Tel. 416-769-1192, 56 Boustead Ave); and **ICNA Book Service**, (Tel. 416-609-2452, 100 McLevin).

Religious Centres, Schools and Other Institutions

- ◆ JAFFARI MOSQUE, (Tel. 905-881-1763, 7340 Bayview Ave., Thornhill).
- ◆ ISLAMIC CENTRE OF TORONTO (JAMI MOSQUE), (Tel. 416-769-1192, www.jamimosque.com, 56 Boustead Ave). The mosque is open 24 hours a day and holds services every Friday.
- ◆ ISLAMIC FOUNDATION OF TORONTO INC., (Tel. 416-321-0909, www.islamicfoundation.ca, 441 Nugget Ave). The foundation completed a project in 1995 on Markham Road, between Sheppard and Finch avenues, which includes a large prayer hall, research library/reading room, gymnasium, cafeteria, and other facilities that cater to the needs of Muslim Torontonians.
- ◆ MADINAH MASJID, (Tel. 416-465-7833, www.madinahmasjid.org, 1015 Danforth Ave).
- ◆ MAKKI MASJID, (Tel. 905-458-8778, 8450 Torbram Rd., Brampton).
- ◆ MALTON ISLAMIC ASSOCIATION, (Tel. 905-671-2991, 6836 Professional Ct., Mississauga).
- ◆ MASJIDE ALNOOR, (Tel. 416-658-6667, 277 Scott Rd).
- ◆ REXDALE MUSSALAH, (Tel. 416-744-3474, 1770 Albion Rd).
- ◆ ISLAMIC COMMUNITY SCHOOL, (Tel. 905-272-4303, 1525 Sherway Dr). A full-time elementary public school run by the Islamic community.

Holidays and Celebrations

- ◆ PAKISTAN NATIONAL DAY is celebrated on March 23 in commemoration of the Pakistan Resolution passed in 1940 in Lahore. Pakistan was declared a republic in 1956.

The Independence Day of Pakistan is celebrated by raising the Pakistani flag at Toronto City Hall every August 14.

◆ **INDEPENDENCE DAY**, on August 14, is a celebration of Pakistan's coming into existence as an independent Muslim state as a result of the efforts of the founder of the nation, Quaide Azem Mohammad Ali Jinnah. The day is celebrated with a parade and a cultural program.

See Holidays and Celebrations in Glossary.

Media

◆ **CRESCENT INTERNATIONAL**, (Tel. 905-474-9292, 300 Steelcase Rd. W., Unit 8, Markham). A bi-weekly published in English. Editor: Mr. Z. Bangash.

◆ **DHARTI SONHI PAKISTAN (URDU)**, **CITY-TV**, **CHANNEL 57**, (Tel. 416-531-9991, ℅ CHIN Radio/TV International, 622 College St). Saturday, 9:30 a.m. to 10:00 a.m.

◆ **EASTERN NEWS**, (Tel. 905-826-NEWS or (905) 858-7525, 5790 Riverside Pl., Mississauga). An alternative weekly Urdu language newspaper since 1979. Editor: Masood Khan.

◆ **PAKEEZA INTERNATIONAL URDU MAGAZINE**, (Tel. 905-337-3030). First weekly newsmagazine. Contact: Sabih Mansoor.

◆ **SOUTH ASIAN VOICE (WEEKLY NEWSPAPER)**, (Tel. 905-337-3030). Editor: Sabih Mansoor.

◆ **VOICE OF PAKISTAN**, ℅ CHIN 100.7 FM Radio, (Tel. 416-531-9991, 622 College St). Sunday, 8:00 p.m. to 9:00 p.m. Monday to Friday.

◆ **VISIONS OF PAKISTAN**, **VISION-TV**, (Tel. 416-368-3194, 80 Bond St). Saturday, 2:00 p.m. to 3:00 p.m. Producer: Bashir Khan.

◆ **DIL DIL PAKISTAN**, **VISION-TV**, (Tel. 416-368-3194, 80 Bond St). Saturday, 1:00 p.m. to 2:00 p.m. Producer: Dil Muhammad.

◆ **MEELAN (MUSIC OF PAKISTAN) RADIO PROGRAM**. Every Sunday, 12:30 p.m. to 2:00 p.m. on CJMR AM 1320. Broadcasting for last 25 years.

Organizations

◆ **CANADIAN LEAGUE OF PAKISTANIS**, (Tel. 416-609-2267, 145 Purcell Sq). Contact: Asif Khan.

◆ **ISLAMIC SOCIETY OF NORTH AMERICA, CANADA**, (Tel. 905-403-8406, Fax (905) 403-8409, 2200 South Sheridan Way, Mississauga).

◆ **PAKISTAN CANADA CULTURAL ASSOCIATION**, (Tel. 416-532-7556, Fax 416-532-6717, 54 Bartlett Ave). Formed in 1972, this Association

The Pakistani flag prominently displayed on Independence Day at Toronto City Hall.

provides cultural and social services and helps new immigrants settle in the city. President: Asaf Shujah.

◆ PAKISTANI WOMEN'S ASSOCIATION, (128 Brahms Ave., Willowdale). President: Nighat Sukhera.

Consulates, Trade Commissions and Tourist Bureaus

◆ CONSULATE GENERAL OF PAKISTAN, (Tel. 416-250-1255, 240 Duncan Mill Rd., Suite 402). Consul General: Mr. Sahebzada A. Khan.

Prominent Torontonians

Shamim Khan, singer and orchestra leader; Sabih-Ud-Din Mansoor, publisher; Dil Muhammad, pharmacist, philanthropist, and TV producer; Asaf Sujah, President, Pakistan Canada Cultural Association; Khalid Usman, Former Councillor, Markham; Gul Nawaz, accountant and prominent community leader; Adil D. Mama, recipient of the Queen Elizabeth Jubilee Medal, entrepreneur and senior government advisor; Dr. Shafiq Quaadri, MPP; Ashfaq Hussain, Author, famous poet and TV anchor; Naeem Chaudhry, Senior TV Producer; Dr Matanat & Shaheen Khan, Host and producer, Radio Sunshine, publisher, weekly ambassador; Latafat Siddiqui, Publisher and editor, Asian News; Maulana Asif Qasmi,

Prominent authority on Islamic Heritage; Athar Rizvi, Founder, Ghalib Academy, historian, author; Nuzhat Siddiqui, Recipient of Peace Award and famous poet; Salim Khan, Artist with a passion for Pakistani culture and heritage.

Sources: S. Abid Jafri, Malik Saaed, Asaf Shujah.

Dil Muhammad, pharmacist, philanthropist, and TV producer

The Polish Community

Just off Lakeshore Boulevard stands a memorial honouring one of Toronto's most distinguished citizens, Polish patriot Sir Casimir Gzowski. Gzowski helped start the **Grand Trunk Railway**, and in 1890 he was knighted at Windsor Castle by Queen Victoria. As a civil engineer, he pioneered the construction of the **International Bridge** at Niagara Falls, the **Erie Canal**, and the grading and surfacing of Yonge Street. Sir Casimir is an ancestor of former Toronto media personality and author Peter Gzowski.

Not far from Gzowski's monument is "**Little Poland**," a neighbourhood located along the strip of shops and delis on Roncesvalles Avenue between the Lakeshore and Dundas Street West. A statue of the first Polish Pope, John Paul II, was erected on the corner of Fern and Roncesvalles avenues, and, close by, **St. Stanislaus-Casimir Credit Union** displays a commemorative plaque in honour of his 1976 visit to the city. The statue of the Pope was funded by Toronto's 165,000-member Polish community.

As early as the 1860s, the city directory listed Polish names, but the first wave of immigration began in the 1890s with agricultural workers and artisans. They settled in The Ward in boarding houses on Chestnut, Elm, and Elizabeth streets. The Polish community eventually moved further south to Queen Street West, where the steel and iron industry provided work for some and others found employment as carpenters, piano tuners, and shoemakers.

The church became the focus of the community—the first religious gatherings were held at **St. Patrick's Catholic Church** on McCaul Street and **St. Mary's** on Bathurst Street. In 1911, the church building on Denison Avenue was donated to the Polish Community by Mr. Eugene O'Keefe. **Stanislaus Parish** was established there, within a large Polish neighbourhood. The parish became a centre for social groups, such as a brass band and a gymnastics association. One of the first religious teaching organizations was the **Felician Sisters**, first formed in Poland. It started a school on Augusta Street for Polish children and set up a university scholarship fund.

During the Second World War, Polish engineers and technicians who came to work in Canada's armament industry formed the **Association of Polish Engineers in Toronto**. Following the war, a large influx of Polish refugees and ex-military personnel streamed into Canada, consisting of professionals, academics, and artisans. The community established a parish credit union—which today is one of the largest in the world, and the **Canadian Polish Congress** emerged as an umbrella organization for most groups and associations.

Most of the post-war settlers were highly educated, reflected by the great number of Polish professors and professional engineers practising in the city. Polish engineers have contributed to projects such as **Roy Thomson Hall**, the **CN Tower**, and **TD Bank**.

In the 1980s, thousands of refugees fleeing martial law in Poland arrived in the city. Community members often join together to help new immigrants settle or to send food and supplies to Poland. Roncesvalles Avenue, with its churches, financial institutions, delicatessens, and cafes, remains a central meeting and marketplace for the community.

Places to Go

The **Sir Casimir Gzowski Memorial**, found in **Gzowski Park**, was donated by the **Institute of Engineers** (Gzowski was a founding member), the Toronto Polish community, and the City of Toronto. The tripodal concrete structure by Polish-born artist and architect Richard R. Dzwonnik contains an 1896 bust of Gzowski by sculptor Frederick A. Turner Dunbar. The three supports of the structure symbolize the facets of Sir Casimir's career—engineer, statesman, and military man—while the cabinets around the structure hold other Gzowski memorabilia.

The **Katyn Monument** at the foot of Queen Street and Roncesvalles Avenue is a 10-foot-high granite monument with a monolithic crack, surrounded by 15 blocks of cement. The monument was created by artist Tadeusz Janowski and sponsored by the **Canadian Polish Congress**. It was erected in remembrance of the 15,000 Polish prisoners of war who vanished in 1940 from camps in the USSR, and the 4,000 officers, professors, and other professional people who were later discovered in mass graves at Katyn.

Stately Victorian homes with manicured lawns and gardens adorn the tree-lined avenues of Little Poland. A stroll along Roncesvalles Avenue discloses shops named after Warsaw, Poland's capital city, and posters advertising Polish films, theatre, and events in the city.

An old Polish saying, "bread unites the strongest," reveals the importance of bread in the Polish diet, especially during religious feasts. Poles are connoisseurs of kashas (cereals), and meals are often accompanied by beets,

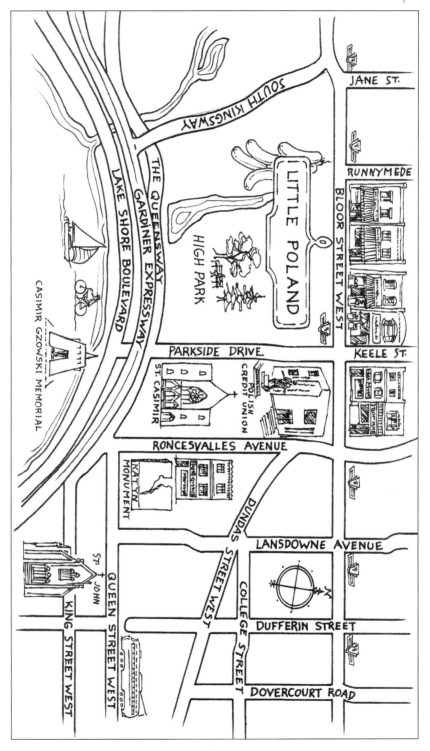

potatoes, cabbage, smoked and cured meats, and kielbasa (Polish sausage). Specialties are kasza (buckwheat groats or barley served with potatoes), pierogi (dumplings filled with meat, potato, or cheese), bigos (hunter's stew), kupusniak (sour soup), pieczony schab (roast pork loin), and flaczki (tripe). Popular desserts are nalesniki (savoury and sweet pancakes), and paczki (filled doughnuts). Popular drinks include vodka, beers, and excellent meads.

Krak Restaurant, (Tel. 416-536-6119, 153 Roncesvalles Ave), offers traditional Polish cuisine. Menu selections may include cheese and apple crêpes, breaded pork chops, goulash, and cabbage rolls. Polish drinks that are available are Krakus beer and vodkas such as **Wyborowa, Baltic, Zubrowka**, and **Winiak. Cafe Polonez**, (Tel. 416-532-8432, 195 Roncesvalles Ave), serves potato pancakes, pierogies, and beet soup with dumplings. Sketches of Warsaw decorate the walls of Irene and Zygmunt Zychla's restaurant. The daily specials might include beef tripe soup and veal schnitzel Polonez with fried mushrooms.

A view of the Polish quarter can be found at **Granowska's**, (Tel. 416-533-7755, 175 Roncesvalles Ave), which offers baked goods filled with plum jam and other preserves. Inside, mirrors reflect double rows of bread and puff pastries, and an outdoor cafe is a popular spot to try a Polish royal coffee (vanilla ice cream, espresso, grand marnier, whipped cream, and chocolate topping). Other bakeries carrying Polish pastries include: **Roncesvalles Bakery**, (Tel. 416-535-7143, 173 Roncesvalles Ave); **Pascal's Baguette & Bagels**, (Tel. 416-532-8762, 2904 Dundas St. W); **Ontario Bread Co. Ltd.**, (Tel. 416-532-4929, 178A Ossington Ave); **Piegus European Bakery**, (Tel. 416-431-6081, 3478 Lawrence Ave. E).

Other delicatessens carrying Polish products include: **Karl's Butcher**, (Tel. 416-531-1622, 105 Roncesvalles Ave); **Family Meat & Deli**, (Tel. 416-259-1380, 675 The Queensway); **Polka European Deli Inc.**, (Tel. 416-289-0379, 3482 Lawrence Ave. E., Unit 105); **Polonez Meat Products and Delicatessen**, (Tel. 416-251-0942, 2436 Lakeshore Blvd. W).

Named after the fossil resin found along the Baltic and North seas, **Amber European Restaurant**, (Tel. 416-763-6164, 2372 Bloor St. W), specializes in Polish and Eastern European cuisine. Owners Irena Gerlicz and Jadwiga Hoch greet patrons with "smacznego" (bon appétit). Traditional dishes include nalesniki (pancakes) and kotlety (meat balls).

Izba (Wooden Cottage), (Tel. 416-251-7177, 648 The Queensway), has a chalet-style decor furnished with dolls in regional costumes and Polish wall ornaments. Owners and chefs Monica and Mark Sarsh wear Polish costumes to serve dishes such as pork roast served with fried cabbage, dumplings, pierogi, and schnitzel. Monica provides the entertainment with violin and piano selections.

Other places in the city serving Polish cuisine include: **Chris's Diner**, (Tel. 416-251-1466, 709 The Queensway); and **Zagtoba**, (Tel. 416-530-0303, 317 Roncevalles Ave).

Polish imported foods, meats, and baked goods are available at: **Anna's Bakery and Deli**, (Tel. 416-769-8065, 2394 Bloor St. W); **Astra Meat Products**, (Tel. 416-763-1093, 2238 Bloor St. W); **Kingsway Meat Products**, (Tel. 416-762-5365, 2342 Bloor St. W); **Krakow Delicatessen**, (Tel. 905-897-0695, 2560 Sheppard Ave., Mississauga); and **Starsky Finest European Foods**, (Tel. 905-279-8889, 2040 Dundas St. E, Mississauga).

Religious Centres, Schools and Other Institutions

The Roman Catholic Church unites the Polish community and assists newcomers.

- POLISH BAPTIST CHURCH, (Tel. 416-239-3305, 2611 Dundas St. W).
- ST. JOHN'S CATHEDRAL POLISH CATHOLIC CHURCH, (Tel. 416-532-8249, 186 Cowan Ave).
- ST. CASIMIR'S, (Tel. 416-532-2822, 156 Roncesvalles Ave). Completed in 1954, it is one of the largest Polish churches in Canada with over 5,000 parishioners from across Toronto. Of the eight services held, seven are in Polish.
- ST. STANISLAUS ROMAN CATHOLIC CHURCH, (Tel. 416-504-4643, 12 Denison Ave). The oldest Polish church, along with St. Casimir's, it accommodates 350 children for Polish language and cultural classes held twice a week. The parishes also teach traditional Polish dance.
- ST. MAXIMILIAN KOLBE, (Tel. 905-848-2420, 4260 Cawthra Rd., Mississauga). The newest Polish church stands on eight acres in Mississauga, close to where many Poles live. It is the largest church to present with over 11,000 registered families.
- ST. MARY'S ROMAN CATHOLIC CHURCH, (Tel. 416-656-3130, 1996 Davenport Rd).
- ST. THERESA'S ROMAN CATHOLIC CHURCH, (Tel. 416-259-2933, 123 Eleventh St).
- COPERNICUS LODGE, (Tel. 416-536-7122, 66 Roncesvalles Ave), is a senior citizens' residence erected by the Polish community.
- ST. STANISLAUS' & ST. CASIMIR'S POLISH PARISH CREDIT UNION, (Tel. 416-537-2181, 220 Roncesvalles Ave), is one of the community's chief financial institutions. It is also one of the largest credit unions in the

world with 19 branches, 42,000 members, and assets of more than $340 million. The organization also provides educational and recreational facilities for young people.

Holidays and Celebrations

◆ KATYN DAY, in April, commemorates the discovery of mass graves of over 15,000 Polish officers murdered by the Soviet secret police in the Katyn forest in 1940.

◆ POLISH NATIONAL CONSTITUTION DAY, May 3, commemorates the day the constitution of 1791 was proclaimed. Usually a solemn mass is held, followed by a parade to the Katyn Memorial to pay tribute to the 15,000 Polish soldiers killed in 1940 in the Katyn forest.

◆ VISTULA REMEMBRANCE. August 15 commemorates the 1920 Polish victory in the battle called "Miracle on the Vistula River." An out-of-town picnic is held in Brampton's Paderewski Park (Highway 27 and 7), named after the world-renowned Polish pianist and politician.

◆ INDEPENDENCE DAY, November 11, was first recognized in 1918 when occupying forces were expelled from Poland. In 1939, Poland was invaded and occupied by both German and Soviet forces; and following the Second World War, a Polish people's republic was created. On this day the Polish flag is raised at Toronto's City Hall and an evening performance is held.

◆ ANNIVERSARY OF THE DECLARATION OF MARTIAL LAW, December 13. Laying wreaths at the Katyn Monument. On that day in 1981 the Solidarity Movement was crushed by the communist government by declaring martial law.

◆ CHRISTMAS EVE begins with the traditional meatless dinner, a 12-course meal beginning at dusk with the appearance of the first star in the sky. Grace is followed by the sharing of oplatek (thin unleavened wafers stamped with the figures of Jesus, the Blessed Mary, and the Holy Angels). Wafers, tied with a ribbon and a sprig of evergreen, are set on an embroidered cloth on a plate after being blessed in the church. The meal often includes barszcz (beet soup), uszka (dumplings with mushrooms), galabkl (cabbage rolls with rice or buckwheat), fish, sauerkraut with mushrooms, pasta with poppy seed, and a compôte made with dried fruits.

See Holidays and Celebrations in Glossary.

Media

- ◆ GAZETA, (Tel. 416-531-3230, www.gazetagazeta.com, 215 Roncesvalles Ave). The only Polish daily in Canada. Editor: Zbigniew Belz.
- ◆ GLOS POLSKI (POLISH VOICE), (Tel. 416-201-9601, 71 Judson St). A weekly tabloid. Contact: Michal Donda.
- ◆ ZWIAZKOWIEC (THE ALLIANCER), weekly. (Tel. 416-531-2491, 22 Roncesvalles Ave). Editor: Stanislaw Stolarczyk.
- ◆ PRZEGLAD TYGODNIOWY (POLISH WEEKLY), (Tel. 905-502-1984, 5346 Cosentino Gardens, Mississauga). Contact: Lidia Ambroziak.
- ◆ RADIO POLONIA, CHIN FM 100.7, (Tel. 416-531-9991, 622 College St). Monday-Friday, 12:00 p.m. to 3:00 p.m. Producers: Krystyna & Ryszard Piotrowski.
- ◆ POLISH STUDIO, Channel 57, Saturday 11:00 a.m. to 12:00 p.m. (Tel. 416-503-9465, C⁄o CHIN Radio/ TV International, 622 College St). Contact: Ted Lis.
- ◆ NA LUZIE, OMNI TV. Saturday, 7:30 p.m. to 8:00 p.m. Producer: Wojciech Sniegowski.
- ◆ Z UKOSA, OMNI TV. Saturday, 7:00 p.m. to 8:00 p.m. Friday 9:00 p.m. to 10:00 p.m. Producer: Wojciech Sniegowski.
- ◆ POLONEZ NEWS, (Tel. 416-516-0144, mgoldyn@poloneznews.com) Editor: Marek Goldyn.

Organizations

- ◆ CANADIAN POLISH CONGRESS, NATIONAL HEADQUARTERS, (Tel. 416-532-2876, 288 Roncesvalles Ave). The umbrella organization representing the Polish community in Canada, with over 200 member organizations. President: Wladyslaw Lizon.
- ◆ THE TORONTO DISTRICT OFFICE, (Tel. 416-971-9848, located at 206 Beverley St). President: Jan Cytowski.
- ◆ THE MILLENIUM FOUNDATION, (Tel. 416-532-2876, 288 Roncesvalles Avenue). Established in 1966 in recognition of 1,000 years of Christianity in Poland.
- ◆ THE POLISH CANADIAN RESEARCH INSTITUTE, (Tel. 416-532-2876, 288 Roncesvalles Ave). It compiles histories of Poles throughout Canada and their contributions to Canadian culture and science.
- ◆ THE COORDINATING COUNCIL OF WORLD POLONIA, (Tel. 416-532-2876, 288 Roncesvelles Ave).

- THE POLISH COMBATANTS' ASSOCIATION, (Tel. 416-979-2017, 206 Beverley St). President: Mr.Marcello Ostrowski.
- THE POLISH ENGINEERS ASSOCIATION, (Tel. 416-977-7723, 206 Beverley St).
- POLISH IMMIGRANT COMMUNITY SERVICES, (Tel. 416-233-0055, 3363 Bloor St). Director: Jadwiga Gaszynski.
- ASSOCIATION OF POLISH SCOUTS, (Tel. 416-499-8545. Contact: Teresa Berezowski.
- POLISH ALLIANCE CENTRE (POLISH CULTURAL CENTRE), (Tel. 416-252-9519, 2282 Lakeshore Blvd. W).
- POLONIA FOR THE FUTURE, (Tel. 416-531-3230 ext. 30, 215 Roncesvalles Ave). Established in 1997, it has four regional groups and works in the areas of culture, education, sports, etc. President: Zbigniew Belz. Media contact: Margaret Bonikowska.
- POLISH CANADIAN SOCIETY OF MUSIC, (Tel. 416-760-9745). Established in 1986, this society organizes music concerts and represents an orchestra and a choir. Manager: C. Maria. President: S. Chorzempa.
- POLISH CANADIAN WOMEN'S FEDERATION, (Tel. 416-255-8608, 2 Bradbrook Rd). President: Yvonne Bogorya-Buczkowski.
- THE POLISH INSTITUTE OF ARTS & SCIENCES IN AMERICA, Canadian Branch, Toronto Chapter, (Tel. 416-535-6233, 288 Roncesvalles Ave). Chair: Ywona Kirejcrk.
- POLISH NATIONAL HALL AND POLISH NATIONAL UNION OF CANADA, (Tel. 416-201-9607, % Polish Voice, 71 Judson St). President: Bogdan Adamczak.
- CANADIAN POLISH TEACHERS ASSOCIATION, (Tel. 416-532-2876, 288 Roncesvalles Ave).
- POLISH ALLIANCE CANADA, (Tel. 416-531-2491, 1586A Bloor St, W). President: Robert Zawierucha.
- WAWEL VILLA INC., (Tel. 905-823-3650, www.wawel.org, 880 Clarkson Rd. South., Mississauga), seniors retirement residence.
- MARIE CURIE SKLODOWSKA ASSOCIATION, (Tel. 416-621-8688, 16 Neilor Cres). A ladies charity organization founded in 1957 in memory of Marie Curie Sklodowska, the Polish scientist who was the first and only woman to be twice awarded the Nobel Prize. Her discovery of radium and radioactivity ultimately led to her death of radiation. President: Danute Warszawska.

Consulates, Trade Commissions and Tourist Bureaus

◆ CONSULATE GENERAL OF THE REPUBLIC OF POLAND, (Tel. 416-252-5471, Fax 416-252-0509, 2603 Lakeshore Blvd. W). Consul General: Mr. Marek Ciesielczuk .

◆ POLISH TRADE COMMISSION, (Tel. 416-233-6571, 3300 Bloor St. W., Suite 2250).

Prominent Torontonians

Dr. Yvonne Bogorya-Buczkowski, senior program consultant, Ministry of Education; Dr. Stanislaw Dubicki, Professor of Immunology; Lusien Conrad, former President, Canadian Polish Congress; Dr. George Korey-Krzeczowski, President and Professor of the Canadian School of Management; Dr. Zdzislaw Krynski, laryngologist; Jesse Flis, former Member of Parliament; Mark Starowicz, writer, CBC journalist, author of History of Canada (OMNI TV); Tamara Jaworska, artist (sculpture); Prof. Ted Jaworski, department of film York University; Prof. Tamara Trojanowska, University of Toronto dept of Slavic studies; Dr. Richard Russ; President and founder of Polish Orphans Charity, Maria Nowotarska, founder of the Polish theatre in Toronto; Jerzy Kolacz, director and actress, painter, Prof of Fine Arts at the Ontario College of Arts; Mathew Jaskiewicz, founder of the Polish Canadian Society of Music and Toronto Simfonietta; Andrew Rozbicki, founder Toronto Celebrity Orchestra; R. Grzymski, curator of The Royal Ontario Museum; Casimir Glaz, painter; Mr. Stan Orlowski, Prof Architect, former President of the Canadian Polish Congress; Mark Malicki, LL.B, former President of the World Polonia, currently president of the Millenium Foundation; Helena Jaczek, MPP; Chris Korwin-Kuczynski, Former Toronto City Concillor.

The Portuguese Community

Since the 1960s, scarlet-coloured houses and front yard shrines to Our Lady of Fatima have decorated the **Kensington Market** area—a neighbourhood and commercial district for the city's 170,000-member Portuguese-speaking community. On the first Saturday closest to the 10th of June, a two-hour-long parade featuring floats, bands, and cultural exhibits marks the Week of Portugal. Festivities and concerts organized by Toronto's largest cultural community are later held at either **Ontario Place** or at **Trinity Bellwoods Park**.

Among the first Europeans to sight Canada were 15th-century Portuguese explorers. Early sailors fished for cod on the Grand Banks and there were Portuguese families among the settlers in New France. In 1705, Pedro Silva, the first letter carrier, delivered letters from Montreal to Quebec City.

There was little immigration to Canada until 1953, when 85 Portuguese men arrived in Halifax aboard the *Saturnia*. They were recruited to work as farm labourers, but gradually moved into cities where they found jobs in construction or in factories. The first Portuguese welcome house in Toronto was a restaurant and inn on Nassau Street owned by Antonio Sousa. Sousa arrived aboard the *Saturnia* and began work as a dishwasher before earning his fortune with investment properties and in the food importing business. In the 1960s, **Alexandra Park** and the **Kensington Market** area became the nucleus of settlement when Portuguese-speaking people began arriving from the Azores Islands, Madeira, the former Portuguese territory of Goa in India, Macao, and from the Cape Verde Islands off the African coast.

The **First Portuguese Canadian Club** was incorporated in 1956 and began organizing early festivals and soccer teams. Portuguese-language services were first held at **St. Michael's Cathedral** in 1955, while a group from the island of Madeira frequented **St. Elizabeth's Church** at Spadina Avenue and Dundas Street West. The first Portuguese parish was formed in the 1960s at **St. Mary's Church**, followed by **Saint Agnes** (1970), **Santa Cruz** (1974), and others.

The neighbourhood has pushed westward as the Portuguese opened stores, restaurants, importing companies, and auto repair shops along Dundas Street, Ossington Avenue, and College Street. Today, street signs in the area read "**Portugal Village**," and two telephone directories list numerous Portuguese businesses in the city. Newcomers include skilled technicians and business people, and among second-generation Portuguese Canadians there are many professionals.

More than 70 percent of Portuguese Torontonians are from the Azores, a group of nine volcanic islands 300 miles southwest of mainland Portugal. The Azoreans held their first religious festival at the **CNE** grounds in 1966. Every year, the procession of **Senhor Santo Cristo dos Milagres** (Christ of the Miracles) draws thousands of people from across North America as the statue of Santo Cristo is led through downtown streets by men wearing opas (red capes) and children dressed up as biblical figures.

Many of the city's Portuguese hold dual citizenship and are allowed to vote in Portugal's elections, which has prompted politicians to come abroad and court votes. A visit by the Mayor of Lisbon on April 8, 1987, resulted in a friendship agreement between the two cities and the inspiration to plan projects that would reflect the contribution of the Portuguese people to Canada.

For the 1988 Olympics, the community, with the help of the **First Portuguese Canadian Cultural Centre**, supported their former homeland by sending a Portuguese bobsled team to the Calgary winter games and by providing the Portuguese Olympic sailing team with the *Comtor*, a sailboat named in honour of the Portuguese community of Toronto.

Places to Go

In High Park, a seven-foot-high monument commemorates the 25th anniversary of the arrival of Portuguese in Canada (1953–1978). The white granite column topped with a stone cross was the type used by Portuguese explorers to mark their arrival in a new land; the monument symbolizes Portuguese exploration, discovery, and imagination.

A bust of Luis de Camões, the famous Portuguese poet and author of **Os Lusiadas**, sits in **Jardim de Camões** at the **First Portuguese Canadian Cultural Centre**, (Tel. 416-531-9971, 722 College St). The centre has a seniors' department, and holds ESL and heritage language classes.

The Portuguese neighbourhood spans several city blocks, bordered by **Trinity Bellwoods Park**, Bloor Street, and Spadina and Lansdowne avenues. Canadian and Portuguese flags hang side by side in store windows, and on almost every block there are Portuguese restaurants, bakeries, cheese stores, and fish markets.

Portuguese-Canadian restaurants specialize in Portuguese fish dishes and in pork dishes cooked with oil instead of fat. Seafood dishes include santola recheada (stuffed spider crab), bacalhau no forno (oven-baked cod), lagosta grelhada (grilled lobster), and lagosta suada (poached lobster). The national soup of Portugal is caldo verde (fine shredded collards and potato broth with slices of smoked peppery sausage and garlic). Other entrées are meat or fish croquettes, frango no espeto (grilled chicken), stuffed pancakes or fritters, and rice garnished with shellfish, chicken, rabbit, onions, tomatoes, and turnips. Desserts usually contain fruit, and a favourite snack is macapao (marzipan). Portuguese wines include famous Madeira wines and the popular port, which is both an aperitif and an after-dinner drink.

Spring is the best time to visit Portugal according to **New Casa Abril**, (Tel. 416-654-9696, 475 Oakwood Ave). Lobsters can be personally selected from a huge aquarium, while Portuguese songs are performed by a trio of musicians. Owner Amadeu Goncalves offers authentic dishes, such as carne alentejana (a pork dish) and a seafood specialty called bacalau a braz (codfish mixed with eggs, onions, and shredded potatoes). In keeping with the Portuguese custom of concluding a meal with fruit, desserts include pineapple covered with Madeira wine and Orange La Casa served with Grand Marnier. Amendoa amarga (almond liqueur) is the favourite after-dinner drink.

Lisboa A Noite (Lisbon by Night), (Tel. 416-603-6522, 802A Dundas St. W), features nightly entertainment and seafood dishes prepared by mainland chefs. The second-storey restaurant is decorated with red tablecloths and surrounded by vast windows. Owner Americo Amaral offers his customers specialties such as The Seafood Revolution (a platter for two with steamed shrimp, lobster, clams, squid, and crabs). Tosta (dry toasted, tasty bread) accompanies most meals and can be enjoyed with Sagres beer or a choice from the private stock of Portuguese wines such as Dào Primavera 1972 and Bairrada Vintage 1976.

Ramboia means "goofing off," but quite the opposite is true of the kitchen of **Casa da Ramboia Restaurant-Gallery**, (Tel. 416-534-0407, 1282 Dundas St. W). A popular spot for lunch, the restaurant is decorated with brick and mirrors, which offer a view of meals being prepared in the kitchen. Specialties include bolhao pato (steamed clams or mussels in white wine and fresh coriander sauce) and gambas e alho (steamed large shrimps in white wine and garlic). Dishes broiled on an open flame include frango no churrasco (barbecued chicken). Many meals are concluded with Portuguese cheese and port wine.

The seafaring traditions of the Portuguese are evident in the names they choose for their restaurants. **The Boat**, (Tel. 416-593-9218, 158 Augusta Ave), provides Portuguese seafood specialties along with entertainment. The

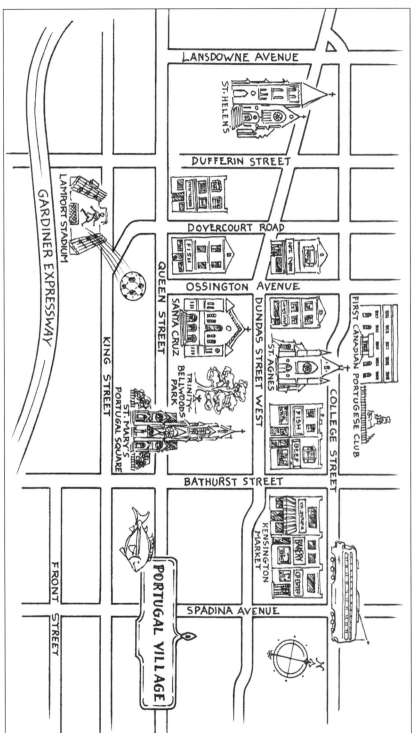

kitchen serves a seafood platter (lobster, crab, prawns, shrimp, clams, and squid) and other seafood selections, such as cod with pimentos, peppers, and grilled scups. Coffee is made with Portuguese brandy or Madeira wine, and soft Portuguese music is performed by musicians.

Other restaurants serving Portuguese foods include: **Amadeus Dining Lounge**, (Tel. 416-591-1245, 184 Augusta Ave., Toronto); **Bairrada Churrasqueira**, (Tel. 416-539-8239, 1000 College St); **Chiado Fine Dining**, (Tel. 416-538-1910, 864 College St); **Cataplana Restaurant**, (Tel. 416-538-1562, 936-938 College St).

Popular cafés include: **Cafe Elite**, (1288 Dundas St. W); **Alto Basso Bar**, (718 College St); **Cervejaria Downtown Café and Bar**, (842 College St); **Bigodes Café**, (Tel. 416-588-9097, 211 Geary Ave); **Copas Café**, (Tel. 416-516-2179, 229 Geary Ave); **A Churrasqueira do Sardinha**, (Tel. 416-531-1120, 707 College St), and **Bloor Village Grill**, (Tel. 416-538-3197, 1184 Bloor St. W).

The Portuguese are known for their love of sweets, and a popular neighbourhood story is about the bakery owner who never bothered to replace his lost key because the store was busy 24 hours a day. The first Portuguese bread to be baked in Canada was at **Lisbon Bakery** in the 1950s. At **Micaelense Home Bakery**, (Tel. 416-923-6266, 498 Gilbert Ave), first opened in 1958; owner Bert Rebello specializes in Portuguese wedding cakes. Many grocery stores in the city carry Portuguese foods, one of which specializes in carrying all Portuguese products. **Tavora Supermarkets**, (Tel. 416-656-1592, 1625 St. Clair Ave. W; Tel. 416-537-9687, 15 Janet Ave; Tel. 905-949-1592, 1030 Dundas St. E, Mississauga) which sells Portuguese sardines, Sao Miguel, Sao Jorge and Sao Joao Portuguese cheese, bacalhau (dried codfish),and chourico (smoked sausage) as well as many other fine portuguese products and goods.

Other downtown stores selling Portuguese baked goods include: **Brazil Bakery & Pastry Ltd.**, (Tel. 416-531-2888, 1566 Dundas St. W); **Courense Bakery**, (Tel. 416-536-1522, 1012-1014 Bloor St. W); **Nova Onda Bakery**, (Tel. 416-656-0967, 2057 Dufferin St); **Dundas Bakery**, (Tel. 416-536-5671, 1492 Dundas St. W); **Golden Wheat Bakery**, (Tel. 416-534-1107, 652 College St); **Nova Era Bakery and Pastry**, (Tel. 416-538-8200, www.novaera.ca, 200 Geary Ave; Tel. 416-538-7700, 1172 Dundas St. W; Tel. 416-651-5000, 490 Rogers Rd; Tel. 416-516-1622, 770 College St; Tel. 416-531-1222, 980 Bloor St. W; Tel. 416-658-5000, 1492 St. Clair W); **Caldense Bakery and Pastries Inc.**, (Tel. 416-534-3847,www.caldensebakery.ca, 1298 Dundas St. W; Tel. 416-535-9993, 337 Symington Ave; Tel. 416-657-1999, 2406 Eglinton Ave; Tel. 416-245-3847, 2625-A Weston Rd. Unit 2;Tel. 416-703-3433, 802 Dundas St. West; Tel. 416-

761-9499, 3497 Dundas St. West; Tel. 905-814-0049, 5425 Creditview Rd. Unit 14, Mississauga); **Doce Mel Bakery**, (Tel. 416-537-2993, 191 Geary Ave); **Venezia Bakery**, (Tel. 416-537-2914, 114 Ossington Ave, and Tel. 416-535-1455, 951 Ossington Ave).

Papelaria Portugal, (Tel. 416-537-3730, 220 Ossington Ave), carries Portuguese books, newspapers, and magazines. The store also sells imported stationery and wallets, along with the Barcelos cocks—ceramic roosters in all sizes and colours that symbolize faith, justice, and good luck. Decorating the shelves are ceramic fruit baskets and ornamental plates decorated with crayfish. Music includes recordings by Roberto Carlos, Jose Malhoa, Roberto Leal, and Jorge Ferreira.

Portuguese Book Store, (Tel. 416-538-0330, 1331 St. Clair Ave W), is the oldest bookstore in the neighbourhood. It started 45 years ago when the Tomás family began importing newspapers and magazines from Portugal and selling them from their home. Today, the shop carries 20 papers, including daily soccer papers from Portugal that sell at a rate of 1,000 a week. Books from romance novels to the classics, as well as CDs are sold.

Gift stores include: **Ruby Jewellery**, (Tel. 416-537-5390, 735A Dufferin St); **Manata Jewellery and Electronics**, (Tel. 416-603-9572, 846 Dundas St. W).

Works by Portuguese artists are available at **Hildebrando's Studio** (Tel. 416-535-5179, 1078 Queen St. W).

On display at the Spadina North docks at the foot of Spadina Avenue is the **Feliz Viagem** (Happy Voyage). The Portuguese vessel was built near Lisbon in 1919, and was used to transport fish and other cargo to Lisbon markets and towns alone the River Tagus. Its colourful paintwork is in the tradition of the canoa (boat)—it is decorated with a mixture of motifs native to the province of Ribatejo. Canoas are no longer used for commercial sailing, and when the vessel was displayed at the Marine Plaza of Expo '86 in Vancouver, it attracted over a million visitors.

Religious Centres, Schools and Other Institutions

The Portuguese are predominantly Roman Catholic, but some belong to other Christian denominations, such as the Pentecostal, Baptist, and Seventh Day Adventist.

◆ ST. MARY'S CHURCH, (Tel. 416-703-2326, 589 Adelaide St. W), is located at Portugal Square. The church holds four Sunday services as well as weekday services at 9:00 a.m. and 6:30 p.m. daily.

◆ ST. MARY'S OF THE ANGELS CHURCH, (Tel. 416-532-4779, 1481 Dufferin St).

◆ OLIVET BAPTIST CHURCH, (Tel. 416-535-1357, 36 Margueretta St). The church was first organized in 1890 and now includes many Portuguese-speaking people from Portugal, Angola, Brazil, and other parts of the world.

◆ PORTUGUESE SEVENTH DAY ADVENTIST CHURCH, (Tel. 416-923-5285, 506 College St).

◆ SANTA CRUZ CATHOLIC CHURCH, (Tel. 416-533-8425, 142 Argyle St).

◆ SCARBOROUGH BAPTIST CHURCH, (Tel. 416-698-1973, 1597 Kingston Rd).

◆ ST. AGNES CHURCH, (Tel. 416-603-1715, 15 Grace St).

◆ ST. ANTHONY'S CHURCH, (Tel. 416-536-3333, 1041 Bloor St. W).

◆ ST. HELEN'S CHURCH, (Tel. 416-531-8188, 1680 Dundas St. W).

◆ ST. PETER'S CHURCH, (Tel. 416-534-4219, 659 Markham St).

Portuguese schools in Toronto include:

◆ THE FIRST PORTUGUESE CANADIAN CULTURAL CENTRE, (Tel. 416-531-9971, 722 College St), operates a school with approximately 750 students.

◆ ESCOLA COMUNITARIA DO CLUBE PORTUGUESE TRANSMONTANO, (Tel. 905-279-2257, 2381 Old Pheasant Rd., Mississauga). Contact: Mr Damião Costa.

◆ TERRA NOVA (NEW-FOUND LAND), (Tel. 416-588-3847, 1289 Dundas St. W), is a 149-suite senior citizens residence for Toronto's Portuguese. The complex has a library, as well as games and crafts rooms.

Among the community's financial institutions are:

◆ BANCO ESPIRITO SANTO, (Tel. 416-530-1700, 860C College St).

◆ BCA—BANCO COMERCIAL DOS ACORES, (Tel. 416-603-0802, 836 Dundas St. W).

◆ BANCO TOTTA ACORES, (Tel. 416-538-7111, 1110 Dundas St. W).

◆ PORTUGUESE CANADIAN (TORONTO) CREDIT UNION, (Tel. 416-533-2578, 722 College St).

Holidays and Celebrations

◆ SANTO CRISTO, celebrated on the fifth Sunday after Easter, is high-lighted by the festival of Senhor Santo Cristo dos Milagres (Christ of Miracles). The outside of **St. Mary's Church** is decorated with flowers, and during a ceremony, worshippers crawl on their knees around the church courtyard. A statue of Christ is carried in a procession along Adelaide Avenue to **Portugal Square**. The clergy, marching bands, and the faithful carry large candles as they follow the statue to a park for an outdoor mass. After mass, a festival takes place with games and food. A musical tradition from the Azores Islands is Cantigas ao desafio, where two musicians skillfully debate an issue by singing impromptu replies.

- THE FESTIVAL OF THE HOLY SPIRIT is held in spring, commemorating the coming of the Holy Spirit. Festivals are held at Portuguese Catholic churches.
- THE DAY OF PORTUGAL, June 10, has been expanded to the **Week of Portugal**, which celebrates Portuguese communities around the world. The event also commemorates the death of national poet Luis de Camões. In tribute, flowers are placed at the Portuguese monument in High Park, and the Portuguese flag is raised at Toronto's City Hall.
- NOSSA SENHORA DO MONTE (OUR LADY OF THE MOUNTAIN), is celebrated every summer by Toronto's Portuguese from Madeira Island. The festival is held in **Madeira Park**, near Sutton, Ontario, in honour of the spiritual protectress of the island. A shrine on the site is decorated with lights and flowers, and an outdoor mass is held.
- SENHOR DA PEDRA. On the first Sunday in August, St. Agnes Roman Catholic Church holds Senhor Da Pedra, a religious festival that includes a procession from the church to a nearby park for a mass.

The author joining the largest Portuguese community parade in North America. It takes place every first week in June.

The procession is led by marchers carrying a statue of Christ sitting on a rock, which is returned to the church after mass. Portuguese come from across Canada and the U.S. to attend the festival, which also includes picnics, games, and folk dancing.

◆ AMALIA RODRIGUES DAY. In 1985, October 5 was declared Amalia Rodrigues Day by the City of Toronto on behalf of the most popular Portuguese fado and folk singer of the 20th century. Rodrigues has appeared at **Roy Thomson Hall**, and her farewell performance was held in Toronto in 1989. Amalia has since passed away on October 6, 1999 (aged 79).

See Holidays and Celebrations in Glossary.

Folklore group "Rancho Folklorico" of the Portuguese community at city hall.

Media

◆ ASAS DO ATLANTICO, CPWA 90.5 FM, (Tel. 416-596-1566, 62 Nassau St). Provides 24 hours of Portuguese radio. Owner: Frank Nunes.

◆ FESTIVAL PORTUGUES, FPTV, (Tel. 416-537-1088, 1087 Dundas St. W).

◆ BLUE PAGES PORTUGUESE DIRECTORY, (Tel. 416-531-1000, 1079 College St). Editor: Jorge Ribeiro.

◆ CORREIO PORTUGUES (PORTUGUESE MAIL), (Tel. 416-532-9894, 793 Ossington Ave). Established in 1963; the oldest Portuguese newspaper in the city. Editor: Maria Alice Ribeiro.

◆ GUIA COMERCIAL PORTUGUES (PORTUGUESE TELEPHONE DIRECTORY), (Tel. 416-532-3167, 1278 Dundas St. W).

◆ JOURNAL "POSTMILÉNIO," (Tel. 905-822-8111), a weekly Portuguese newspaper. Editor. Alexandre Franco.

The Banda do Senhor Santo Christo at Santa Maria Catholic Church.

- ◆ **PORTUGUESE SUN**, (Tel. 416-538-1788, 977 College St). Published by **Sol Portuguese Publishing Inc**. Editor: Alice Perinu.
- ◆ **VOICE-LUSO CANADIAN NEWSPAPER LTD.**, (Tel. 416-534-3177, 428 Ossington Ave). Director: Joaquim R. Batista.
- ◆ **CIRV, 88.9 FM**, (Tel. 416-537-1088, 1087 Dundas St. W), a multicultural radio station serving 12 ethnic groups. President: Frank Alvarez.
- ◆ **OMNI-TV**, (Tel. 416-260-0047, 545 Lakeshore Blvd. W). Programs include:
  - ◆ **CANADA CONTACTO**. Sunday, 10:00 a.m. to 10:30 a.m.
  - ◆ **PORTUGUESE NOVELLA**. Monday to Friday, 4:00 p.m. to 5:00 p.m.
  - ◆ **OMNI NEWS PORTUGUESE EDITION**. Monday to Friday, 5:00 p.m. to 5:30 p.m.
  - ◆ **QUINAS MAGASINE**. (Tel. 416-533-1375, Fax 416-533-8658). Editor: Teresa Botelho.
- ◆ **CHIN 100.7 FM**, (Tel. 416-531-9991, 622 College St). Portuguese programs are aired Monday to Friday, 5:00 a.m. to 9:00 a.m. and Saturday 6:00 a.m. to 12:00 p.m.
- ◆ **GENTE DA NOSSA**. City TV, (Tel. 416-516-9225, 1284A Dundas St. W.,). Saturday 8:00 a.m. to 9:00 a.m. Host: Christine Costa.

Organizations

- ◆ **THE FIRST PORTUGUESE CANADIAN CULTURAL CENTRE**, (722 College St). Incorporated in 1956 and originally located in Kensington Market on Nassau Street. Organizes cultural, educational, and sports programs, including folk dancing. The club's soccer and cycling teams have won many trophies, including **National Soccer League** titles and the **Grand Road Race** in Montreal. President: Valter Lopes.

♦ ALLIANCE OF PORTUGUESE CLUBS AND ASSOCIATIONS OF ONTARIO, (Tel. 416-536-5961, 722 College St., Suite 306). The members of this cultural umbrella organization are sports, regional, and cultural clubs. The alliance organizes the festivities and events for the Week of Portugal.

♦ CASA DO ALENTEJO, (Tel. 416-537-7766, 1130 Dupont St). Represents a region in Portugal and sponsors a week-long festival, usually held in February, that features Portuguese food, fado, and folklore, as well as art exhibits, films, and speakers.

♦ FEDERATION OF PORTUGUESE-CANADIAN BUSINESS & PROFESSIONALS OF TORONTO, (Tel. 416-537-8874, www.fpcbp.com, 722 College St., Suite 301). A non-profit organization set-up to help business and professional persons, merchants, and manufacturers of Portuguese origin and descent to develop professional, commercial, and cultural ties within the Portuguese communities of Ontario. President: Paul Silva.

♦ PENICHE COMMUNITY CLUB OF TORONTO INC., (Tel. 416-536-7063, Fax 416-536-4347, 1264 College St). President: Luis Filipe.

There are many Portuguese social clubs, which hold dances and picnics throughout the year, as well as sports clubs. They include:

♦ ARSENAL DO MINHO-S.C. BRAGA OF TORONTO, (Tel. 416-532-2328, 1166 Dundas St. W). Winners of the 1988 **Ontario Soccer Cup**.

♦ ASSOCIACAO CULTURAL DO MINHO, (Tel. 416-781-9290, 165 Dynevor Rd).

♦ CANADIAN MADEIRA CLUB, (Tel. 416-533-2401, 1621 Dupont St). Home to the **Rancho Folklorico Madeirense** and a soccer team.

♦ SPORT CLUB ANGRENSE, (Tel. 416-537-1555, 1195 Bloor St. W).

♦ SPORT CLUB OF LUSITANIA, (Tel. 416-532-3501, 103 Ossington Ave).

♦ SPORTING CLUB PORTUGUES DE TORONTO, (Tel. 416-763-1707, 1650 Dupont St).

♦ AMOR DA PATRIA , (Tel. 416-535-2696, 865 College St).

♦ VASCO DA GAMA COMMUNITY CENTRE OF BRAMPTON, (Tel. 905-840-6061, 20 Fisherman Dr. Unit 20, Brampton).

Consulates, Trade Commissions and Tourist Bureaus

♦ CONSULATE GENERAL OF PORTUGAL, (Tel. 416-217-0966, 438 University Ave., Suite 1400, Box 41) Consul General: Dr. Júlio Vilela.

- ◆ **PORTUGAL TRADE AND TOURISM COMMISSION**, (Tel. 416-921-4925, 60 Bloor St. W., Suite 1005, Tourist Information, Tel. 416-921-7376).
- ◆ **PORTUGUESE CANADIAN NATIONAL CONGRESS**, (Tel. 416-532-3233, Fax 416-532-8703,www.congresso.ca, 1081 Bloor St. W., Suite 300). President: Emanuel Linhares.

Prominent Torontonians

Frank Alvarez, broadcaster and TV personality; Bento de Sao Jose, community leader; Carlos Botelho, recipient, Queen Elizabeth II Golden Jubilee Medal; John Diaz, recipient, Queen Elizabeth II Golden Jubilee Medal; Jose Eustaquio, President of the Alliance of Portuguese Clubs & Associations of Ontario; Dr. Thomas Ferreira, renowned physician; Avelino Fonseca, recipient of the Queen Elizabeth II Golden Jubilee Medal, former Vice-President of Portuguese Canadian Businesses and Professionals, Treasurer of the Portuguese Cultural Centre of Mississauga; Tony Letra, first elected Portuguese-Canadian separate school trustee; Jack Prazeres, recipient, Queen Elizabeth II Golden Jubilee Medal; Mariano Rego, guitarist, introduced the festivities of Santo Cristo to Toronto; John Santos, former member Assessment

Avelino Fonseca
recipient of the Queen Elizabeth II Golden Jubilee Medal, former vice-president of Portuguese Canadian Businesses and Professionals, Treasurer of the Portuguese Cultural Centre of Mississauga, President of Trican Masonary Contractors Inc.

Review Board; Armindo Silva, President, Villa Corte Real; Ezequial Silva, first Portuguese citizenship court judge; Lamartine Silva, Citizenship Court Judge; Mario Silva, MP; Tony Dionisio, labour leader; Peter Fonseca, MPP and Minister of Labour; Armando Viega, Prominent community leader and President of Casa do Alentejo; Charles Sousa, MPP; Mr. Jack Carvalho, owner of Jack's Bakery; John Santos, founder and musical director of the Amateur Singing Contest; Ana Bailão, City Councillor.

Contributors: Alexandre Franco, Editor of MillenioPost; Antonio Alves, Director, Friends of Lisbon Cultural Association; Rui Ruivo, Kevin Ferreira, Carla Lemos; Manuel Depaulos, European Catering.

The Romanian Community

Romanians began arriving in Canada in the last quarter of the 19th-century. Most of them came from the provinces of Transylvania and Bukovina which belonged to the Austro-Hungarian Empire. They first settled in the prairie provinces and in Quebec. More Romanians immigrated to Canada in the 1920s. A large group of refugees arrived following the Second World War, settling primarily in Ontario and Quebec. Included in this group were a number of officers and military personnel who had been in German camps after the war and others who had fled Romania's new Communist regime. They found jobs as farmers, tailors, gardeners, cleaners, and in meat slaughterhouses.

One of the first organizations was the **Romanian Cultural Society** on Dewson Street, formed to help newcomers find employment. The organization started *Tribuna Romana*, a newspaper published for three years. Cultural events were held at a Ukrainian church hall on Bathurst Street.

In 1954, the community established **St. George**, which is affiliated with the **Romanian Orthodox Episcopate of America and Canada**. The church was located on Broadview Avenue, the former home of the **German Club**. As the parish grew, it was necessary to move to a larger location, and the present church was purchased at 247 Rosethorn Avenue. The church was decorated with icons, brass inlaid chandeliers, crosses, tableclothes, wood carving, textiles, pottery, and other decorative art. Works by Romanian artists are often exhibited in the newly renovated church hall.

Places to Go

St. George Romanian Orthodox Church, (Tel. 416-651-1321, 247 Rosethorn Ave). The church operates a library and Sunday school, and serves as the site for banquets celebrating religious or national holidays. The schedule of events is published in the parish bulletin and in **The Ban's Guide to Toronto** home page at www.thebans.com. Parish Priest: Rev. Fr. Ioan Bunea.

Romanian cuisine includes a number of hearty dishes, including pork, chicken, and smoked sausage accompanied by mamaliga (corn meal cooked until firm). Typical dishes are sarmalute in foi de vita (ground meat wrapped in vine leaves and served with yogurt or sour cream), pui la ceaun (chicken cooked in a garlic sauce), baked carp, tchorba (a stew of meat and vegetables), and ghiveci calugaresc (vegetables cooked in oil). Most dishes are accompanied by vegetables or yogurt. Desserts include cheese pancakes and plum puddings. Two popular drinks are tuica (plum brandy) and mastika (grape brandy). Some restaurants and stores where you can find typical Romanian fishes and products:

Melody Restaurant, (Tel. 416-740-1718, 9 Milvan Dr); **Transilvania Restaurant**, (Tel. 416-932-9915, 2579 Yonge St); **Break Time Restaurant**, (Tel. 905-673-6989, 7305 Bramalea Rd., Mississauga); **Cindrelul Restaurant**, (Tel. 416-693-6964, 2013 Danforth Ave).

Religious Centres, Schools and Other Institutions

Most of Toronto's Romanians belong to the Romanian Orthodox Church.

◆ CORUL BIZANTIN (AGNI PARTHENE), (Tel. 416-725-7039, 3267 Havenwood Dr., Mississiuga). The **Agni Parthene choir** was founded on a single motivation: God-praising. Contact: Gavriliu Nicolae.

◆ ST. GEORGE ROMANIAN ORTHODOX CHURCH, (Tel. 416-651-1321, 247 Rosethorn Avenue).

◆ ST. JOHN'S EVANGELIST ROMANIAN CHRISTIAN ORTHODOX CHURCH, (Tel. 416-614-1942, 217 La Rose Ave.). Contact: The Very Reverend Father Ionel Cudritescu.

Several organizations are affiliated with the church, including:

◆ THE LADIES' AUXILIARY.

◆ SENIORS' ORGANIZATION.

◆ YOUTH ORGANIZATION.

◆ DACIA ROMANIAN CULTURAL ASSOCIATION.

◆ ROMANIAN SCHOOL, **Milne Valley Public School**, (Tel. 416-225-5279, 100 Underhill Dr). Saturday, 9:30 a.m. to 12:00 p.m. Contact: Marcel Ban.

◆ SAINT DUMITRU CHURCH, (Tel. 416-398-5095, www.st-dimitru.org, 5801 Leslie St).

◆ SAINT ANDREW CHURCH, (Tel. 905-282-9481, 4030 Dixie Rd., Mississauga).

◆ JOHN THE EVANGELIST CHURCH, (Tel. 416-614-1942, 100 Old Orchard Grove).

◆ BUNA VESTIRE CHURCH, (Tel. 416-686-0300, 78 Clifton Rd).

◆ ALL SAINTS ROMAN ORTHODOX PARISH, (Tel. 416-444-9095, 545 Danforth Rd).

Holidays and Celebrations

- ◆ THE UNION OF PRINCIPALITIES of 1859 is celebrated on January 24. It was the day Muntenia and Moldova were united to form the single state of Romania with Bucharest as the capital city. Special church services are held with a program to recall Romanian history and its present state in world affairs. Poems are recited as part of the celebration, along with songs and folk dancing.

- ◆ BESSARABIA AND BUCOVINA DAY on March 27 commemorates the 1919 reunification of Bessarabia and Bucovina with Romania. Religious and community programs are held with dances and poetry recitals.

- ◆ INDEPENDENCE DAY, May 10, honours the day in 1877 that Romania gained its independence from the Ottoman Empire. Celebrations are held on the nearest weekend, with religious services, speeches, dances, and cultural programs.

- ◆ MARTYRS' DAY is held the Thursday before Ascension Day or 40 days after Easter. A religious and national ceremony takes place at the martyrs' cross on the Romanian camp grounds near Hamilton.

- ◆ CAMP. Every year in the first week of August, there is a week-long Romanian camp featuring literature and cultural seminars in addition to recreational activities. It is held at the Romanian camp retreat near Hamilton and is organized by Nae Ionescu, the **Romanian Cultural Association of Hamilton**. **St. Mary's Chapel** is located on the campgrounds along with a modern pavilion with a hall, library, and meeting rooms.

- ◆ BANAT FESTIVAL. In September, during Labour Day Weekend, the Romanian Banat Festival draws Romanians from across North America to Kitchener, Ontario.

- ◆ NATIONAL DAY IN ROMANIA. Cultural and religious programs on December 1st celebrate the union of Transylvania with Romania.

- ◆ CHRISTMAS celebrations include a children's Christmas party and Colinda, a celebration in which carollers dressed in traditional Romanian costumes carry a star decorated with the nativity scene and share good cheer with their neighbours.

See Holidays and Celebrations in Glossary.

Media

- ◆ FAPTU DIVERS NEWSPAPER, Rari Press, (Tel. 416-287-6626, or 416-287-6924, www.faptudivers.com, 23 Whiterock Dr).

- ◆ OBSERVATORUL, (Tel. 416-483-5154, www.observatorul.com, 149 South Dr., #1). Director: Dumitru Popescu.
- ◆ ROMANIAN SHOW, CHIN 1540 AM, 622 College St., M6G 1B6, Tel. 416-531-9991. Saturday, 6:00 a.m. to 6:30 a.m. Host: Maria Cojocaru.
- ◆ THEBANS.COM Romanian website which presents a comprehensive step-by-step guide to the city of Toronto, targeted to people that are moving here.

Organizations

- ◆ CONSULATE GENERAL OF ROMANIA, (Tel. 416-585-5802, 555 Richmond St. W, Suite 1108) Consul General: Valentin Naumescre
- ◆ ASSOCIATION OF ROMANIAN ENGINEERS IN CANADA, (Tel. 416-663-2029, www.arec.ca, 55 Henry Welsh Dr). President: Vlad Siperco.
- ◆ ALLIANCE OF ROMANIAN CANADIANS, (Tel. 416-283-9241, www.arcweb.ca, 5795 Yonge St). Preserve, enhance, and promote the cultural and spiritual heritage of the members of the Romanian-Canadian community and pass them to the younger generations.
- ◆ ROMANIAN BUSINESS NETWORK SOCIETY (RBNS), (Tel. 416-732-8886, www.rbn-society.com).
- ◆ TORO ARTS GROUP, (www.toroartsgroup.com) President: Andrei Tanasescu.

Prominent Torontonians

Georgiana Dana Balanica, talented piano player; George Balasu, pharmacist; Tudor Bompa, professor; Dan Chirtu, industrialist; Kathy Dumitrascu Dell-Arnold, pop folk singer, and President of the Canadian Cultural Society; Elena Dumitru, event organizer; Martha Horvath, owner of a ballet school; Augustine Medan, Professor of Music; Maria Micsia, cosmetologist, owner of Nouvelle Maria; Dumitru Popesov, manager of Observatorul; Mr. Vlad Siperco, President, Association of Romanian Engineers in Canada; Marta Teodosiu, President, Apollo Travel; Eugene Roventa, Founding President of the Association of Canadian-Romanian University Professors; Michaela Moisin, architect; Petre Nica, sculptor; Jean Mazare, founder of L'Express de Toronto and Observatorul; Florin Zamfirescu, painter.

Contributors: Corneliu Chisu; George Hojbota, DACIA Romanian Cultural Association; Rev. Fr. Ioan Bunea, St. George Romanian Orthodox Church; Lawrence Dafinescu; Luca Viorel; Vlad Sipercu.

Mrs Ida Ruprecht (centre) with two of her friends, posing in authentic 19th century Romanian clothing from the area of Iassi.

The Russian Community

A theatre at the University of Toronto bears the name of Russian-born George Ignatieff, once chancellor of the University of Toronto and Canada's former Ambassador to the United Nations. His father, Count Paul Ignatieff, a minister of education to Tsar Nicholas II, gave lectures at what is now the **University of Toronto Bookroom** and his son, Michael is the current leader of the **Liberal Party of Canada**. The five sons of Count Paul Ignatieff contributed to Canadian engineering and civil service, adding to the list of accomplishments by Toronto's Russian community, whose members include scholars, ballet dancers, and musicians, among others.

The first Russians to arrive in Canada were fur traders, in the 1790s, and several officers who served with the British navy in Halifax. In the 1870s, German Mennonite colonists from southern Russia settled in Western Canada, followed by some 7,500 Doukhobors, religious dissidents who arrived in 1899.

Beginning in the 1890s, several thousand Russian Jews emigrated from Western Russia. Many found work in Canada's industries, or as farm labourers, loggers, and miners. Among the professionals was Leonid I. Strakhovsky, who pioneered Slavic studies at the **University of Toronto**. Some Russians joined Canada's **MacKenzie-Papineau battalion** which fought for the Republican side during the Spanish Civil War.

The first Russian Orthodox church services in Toronto were held in 1915, and a church building was later purchased on Dupont Street. Some of the Russian faithful attended the **Bulgarian Macedonian Church** on Trinity Street. After the Russian October revolution of 1917, Canada saw the wave of so-called "White Russian" emigration.

In 1930, the **Christ the Saviour Russian Orthodox Cathedral** (now on Manning Avenue) was established on Glen Morris Street. The church was home to choirs, dance groups, cultural groups, and a library of Russian classic books. Cadets and hussar officers from the Russian Imperial Guard of old Russia organized balls, and the woman's auxiliary held bazaars offering folk crafts and Russian foods. In 1948, Grand-Duchess Olga Alexandrovna, the sister of Tsar Nicholas II, arrived from Denmark and became a member of the parish. A parish Sunday school was established bearing her name.

Much of the cultural life of the 62,000 Russian-speaking Torontonians centres around the city's Russian Orthodox churches and organizations. Following the Second World War, Russian refugees came to Toronto from camps in Europe. They helped establish **Holy Trinity Russian Orthodox Church**, which included a parochial Sunday school and the **Sisterhood of Myrrh-Bearing Women**.

The **Federation of Russian Canadians**, with 15 branches across Canada, was established in 1942 by the descendants of pre-revolutionary settlers. It publishes a left-wing Russian newspaper called *Vestnik* (Herald). The 1950s saw the founding of the **Russian Canadian Cultural Aid Society**, which published the literary magazine **Russian Word** in Canada for many years and still operates a centre for social and cultural activities.

It was only in the mid-1970s that the Russian community of Toronto started to expand again due to considerable Jewish immigration from the Former Soviet Union. After the collapse of the USSR a community of ethnic Russians united by several Russian Orthodox churches (parishes) of Toronto grew considerably. However, ethnic Russians still constitute a minority of Russian speakers in the city. At present Russian-speaking immigrants can be found all over Greater Toronto. There are several areas densely populated by Russian speakers: North York, Vaughan, Thornhill, Richmond Hill, and High Park. North of Toronto—previously populated predominantly by Russian Jews—is presently home to numerous ethnic groups from the Former Soviet Union. Recent years have witnessed quick growth of Russian-speaking communities throughout Greater Toronto. Contrary to preconceived ideas voiced by the Canadian mass media, the community is in no way dominated by notorious "Russian Mafia." Districts populated by Russian speakers are still among the safest in Toronto.

Places to Go

Christ the Saviour Russian Orthodox Cathedral, (Tel. 416-534-1763, 823 Manning Ave), has a library of more than 2,000 volumes of Russian literature and non-fiction. The **Holy Trinity Church**, (Tel. 416-979-2990, 23 Henry St), has a library of children's literature and religious books. Every Sunday, following the Divine Liturgy at 10:00 p.m., parishioners at **Holy Trinity Church** participate in a meal of Russian delicacies and Russian tea. Pelmeni (Siberian dumplings filled with chopped beef served in meat broth with sour cream), pirozhki (meat or cabbage-filled pastries), and other delights can be bought frozen to take home. Books in Russian and English are sold, along with artifacts and icons. Russian foods can also be purchased after the Sunday Divine Liturgy at the **Russian Orthodox Church of the Holy Resurrection**, (Tel. 416-651-3226, 213 Winona Dr).

Basic Russian breads and cereals include dark whole-grain rye and coarse wheat breads, and kasha (grains, usually buckwheat, cooked as porridge). Zakuski (appetizers) include eggplant, pickled herring, and ikra (caviar). Hearty entrées are beef stroganoff, blinchiki (crepes filled with cottage cheese or preserves and served with sour cream), chakhombili (chicken casserole with tomatoes and onions), and charlottka (Charlotte Russe). The dessert list may include kissel (a fruit purée served with cream) and strawberries Romanoff (cointreau and whipped cream). Popular drinks are Russian tea and ice-cold vodka.

Amber European Restaurant, (Tel. 416-763-6164, 2372 Bloor St. W), is a tiny, cosy nook in Bloor West Village, offering Russian menu staples such as borsch and pelmeni as well as other European delicacies. Some other restaurants and Russian food stores include: **National**, (Tel. 416-650-0019, 1118 Finch Ave. W); **International Discount Food**, (Tel. 416-739-6651, 2777 Steeles Ave. W.).

Several shops in the Jewish commercial district along Bathurst Street and Lawrence Avenue West carry Russian canned goods, including caviar.

For nearly 40 years, **Troyka Ltd.**, (Tel. 416-535-6693, 2777 Steels Ave W Unit 11), has been selling Russian literature, cookbooks, dictionaries, magazines, and newspapers. The store also carries handicrafts and souvenirs imported from Russia, including matroshki (stacking dolls), porcelain, hockey sticks autographed by Russian players, icons, folk music recordings, amber and stone carvings, embroidered blouses, and intricate lacquered boxes with scenes from Russian fairy tales. Gifts and books can be purchased at **West Arka Gift Store**, (Tel. 416-762-8751, 2282 Bloor St. W); and **Russian Gift and Book Store**, (Tel. 416-636-8888, 616 Sheppard Ave. W).

Religious Centres, Schools and Other Institutions

Most Russians belong to the Russian Orthodox Church, founded in A.D. 988 by Vladimir the Great. Other Russians follow the Baptist, Lutheran, and Roman Catholic faiths.

◆ RUSSIAN ORTHODOX CHRIST THE SAVIOUR CATHEDRAL AND HALL,
(Tel. 416-534-1763, 823 Manning Ave). Affiliated with the Orthodox Church in America. Originally an Anglican church built in 1894, the church is decorated with stained glass windows and contains icons painted by the the Grand Duchess Olga in the 1940s. The altar

contains icons of saints, including St. Herman, the first saint to be canonized in North America (1970). Vesper services are held each Saturday night and the Divine Liturgy takes place Sunday mornings.

Groups at the church include a women's auxiliary, the **Volga Dance Group**, **Beryozka Dancers**, and the acclaimed **Christ the Saviour choir**. The **Grand Duchess Olga Russian School** holds language and history classes in the adjoining hall. Orthodox Sunday school and Orthodox bible study classes are also taught. The parish publishes a bimonthly newsletter.

◆ RUSSIAN ORTHODOX HOLY TRINITY CHURCH, (Tel. 416-979-2990, 23 Henry St). The parish belongs to the Russian Orthodox Church Outside of Russia. Holy Trinity has a children's Sunday school (held on Saturday), where Russian language and literature, history, religion, singing, and folk dancing lessons are taught. The children perform at concerts and at the annual Christmas pageant. The parish also has a school choir, and services are sung in Slavonic by the church choir. Vesper services are held Saturdays from 7:00 p.m. to 9:00 p.m., and the Sunday Liturgy is held from 10:00 a.m. to 12:00 p.m. The parish publishes its own bulletin. The **Sisterhood of the Holy Trinity Church** holds a bazaar once a year to help raise money for convents and monasteries.

Other religious sites include:

◆ A RUSSIAN SUMMER CHAPEL dedicated to Our Lady of Smolensk (a Russian city), has been built at Beryoski, the Russian cottage site at Jackson's Point, Lake Simcoe. Regular Sunday liturgies as well as picnics, celebrations, and campfires are held throughout the summer at Beryoski.

◆ RUSSIAN ORTHODOX CHURCH OF THE HOLY RESURRECTION, (Tel. 416-651-3226, 213 Winona Dr). Father John Hrihosrik.

◆ RUSSIAN UKRAINIAN CHURCH OF EVANGELICAL CHRISTIANS, (Tel. 416-504-5155, 24 Carr St).

◆ JEWISH RUSSIAN COMMUNITY CENTRE, (Tel. 416-222-7105, www.jrcc.org, 5987 Bathurst St., Suite 3).

Holidays and Celebrations

◆ RUSSIAN ORTHODOX NEW YEAR is celebrated on January 13 with festivities at church halls.

- MASLYANITSA (BUTTER WEEK) is celebrated the week preceding Lent. On this occasion, it is customary to serve blini (pancakes).
- EASTER, the greatest feast day for Russians, is celebrated seven weeks after Butter Week. The Russian Easter table is noted for its beauty and variety.
- THE DAY OF MOURNING, July 17, is held in memory of Tsar Nicholas and his family, who were executed in 1918.
- ST. VLADIMIR'S DAY on July 28 honours the saint who brought Christianity to Russia in the 10th century.
- THE ICON OF POKROV (THE MOTHER OF GOD) is venerated on October 14 by Russian Cossacks as their patron saint.
- ST. NICHOLAS DAY, held on December 19, honours the saint renowned for his kindness and charitable deeds, particularly to children. Icons of St. Nicholas are placed in Russian homes.
- CHRISTMAS. December 25 is Christmas for Russian Protestants, while members of the Orthodox churches celebrate according to the Julian calendar on January 7. The highlight of the festive season is a holy supper of 12 meatless dishes in honour of the apostles. The supper begins when the children see the first star in the evening sky. Yolka (Christmas Tree) is the custom of singing and circle-dancing around the Christmas tree as Grandfather Frost (Santa Claus) arrives bearing gifts.
- FEAST DAYS. Each Orthodox church celebrates a feast day in honour of its patron saint.

See Holidays and Celebrations in Glossary.

Media

- NORTHSTAR COMPASS, (Tel. 416-593-0781, www.northstarcompass.org, 280 Queen St. W., 2nd floor), a monthly magazine, prints news about the present situation in former Soviet Union which is not dealt with in the local news media. This NSC goes to 69 countries of the world. It published news that is in opposition to the present course of events. Videos are available of the history, culture, economy and sports.
- RUSSIAN CANADIAN INFO, a weekly newspaper, (Tel. 416-226-4777, 5987 Bathurst St., Suite 108).
- CANADIAN COURIER, a weekly newspaper, (Tel. 416-398-5011, 4400 Bathurst St., Suite 12).
- RUSSIAN EXPRESS, a weekly newspaper, (Tel. 416-663-3999, 1881 Steeles Ave. W., Suite 207A).

Opening the best Volga Pavillion at International Caravan. Here, the Mayor and Princess of the pavillion are being congratulated by M.P.P. Tony Ruprecht, at the time Minister of Citizenship with Responsibilities for Multiculturalism.

- ◆ RUSSIAN WAVES, OMNI-TV, (Tel. 416-260-3621, 545 Lakeshore Blvd. W). Saturday 11:00 p.m. to 11:30 p.m.
- ◆ RUSSIAN CANADIAN BROADCASTING, MIX TV, (Tel. 905-738-1109, 592 Champagne Dr).

Organizations

- ◆ CANADIAN FRIENDS OF SOVIET PEOPLE, (Tel. 416-977-5819, Fax 416-593-0787, 280 Queen St. W), shows Russian films, holds lectures, and publishes books and magazines. President: M. Lucas.
- ◆ FEDERATION OF RUSSIAN CANADIANS, (Tel. 416-504-8404, 6 Denison Ave). Owns a building and a hall, where concerts are performed by its own choir and visiting Russian musicians. The centre also teaches dance lessons. Contact: Helen Klukach.
- ◆ RUSSIAN CANADIAN CULTURAL AID SOCIETY, (Tel. 416-653-1361, 91 Kersdale Ave). Established in 1950 to preserve the Russian heritage in Canada and assist newcomers with settlement. Sponsors cultural

evenings, dinner dances, afternoon recitals, and lectures on topics such as Russian literature, art, and history. Affiliated performing groups include the **Polyanka Dancers**. The **Literary Circle**, founded in 1949, and the **Drama Circle** are also affiliated with the society. An annual charity ball is held in January. The society belongs to the **Canadian Ethnocultural Council**, the **Ontario Folk Arts Council**, and **Easter Table**, and **Christmas Around the World**. It also maintains a library of Russian books. President: Maria Blagoveshchensky.

◆ RUSSIAN ORTHODOX IMMIGRANT SERVICES OF CANADA (ROIS), (Tel. 416-653-1361, 91 Kersdale Ave, "Russian Hot Line." ROIS was founded in 1993 and combines the efforts of the **Holy Trinity parish** of the **Russian Church Abroad** and of the **Christ the Saviour parish** of the **Orthodox Church in America** to help newly arrived people from the former Soviet Union. Since its beginning its volunteers have found accommodation, assisted with job searches, located furnishings, clothes, assisted with schooling issues, medical services, family counselling, orientation to the community and status issues. It received charitable status from **Revenue Canada** in 1999.

Consulates, Trade Commissions and Tourist Bureaus

◆ CONSULATE GENERAL OF RUSSIA, (Tel. 416-962-9911, Fax 416-962-6611, 130 Bloor St. E, Suite 807). Consul General: Mr. Andrey Veklenko.

Prominent Torontonians

George Berns, Professor of Chemistry at the University of Toronto; S.O. Boldireff, choirmaster and singer; Paraskeva Clark, artist; Michael Ignatieff, writer, MP, Leader of Her Majesty's Loyal Opposition; T. N. Kulikowsky, nephew of the last emperor of Russia, Nicholas II; Boris Lebedinski, architect; Nadia Potts, former dancer with the National Ballet of Canada; M.S. Shevtsov, choirmaster and singer, graduate of the Moscow Conservatory; I.P. Suhacev, artist and iconographer, painted icons for Slovak Cathedral in Unionville.

Contributors: Maria Blagoveshchensky, President, Russian Canadian Cultural Aid Society; Vladimir I. Handera; Richard F. Piotrovsky; Victor Popov.

The Scottish Community

In a 1985 ceremony, kilted pipers and drummers of the **48th Highlanders of Canada Regiment** assembled in **Allan Gardens** near Sherbourne Street to re-dedicate a statue to 18th-century Scottish poet Robbie Burns. The Burns memorial (first unveiled in 1902) and an annual banquet featuring the toasting of the haggis celebrate the author of "Auld Lang Syne" and the Scottish tradition in Toronto.

A strong Scottish legacy has shaped Toronto's cultural, religious, political, and economic history. Toronto's oldest church, **Little Trinity Church** on King Street East, was built in 1842 under the patronage of Scotsman John Strachan, the first Anglican bishop of Toronto and founder of **King's College**. On the lawns of **Queen's Park** sits a bronze bust of the city's first mayor, Scotsman William Lyon Mackenzie (1795–1861), along with a statue of George Brown (1818–1880), founder of *The Globe* newspaper. And at Queen and Yonge streets, a plaque at the former **Simpsons**' building (now **The Bay**) is a reminder of the achievements of Robert Simpson, a dry-goods merchant who opened the city's first highrise department store in 1881.

The Scots have been in Canada since 1621, when the Kingdom of Scotland established one of its earliest colonies—New Scotland (Nova Scotia). The first wave of settlers were groups of men from Orkney who arrived in 1720, recruited by the **Hudson's Bay Company**.

In the late 1700s, Scottish merchants—many of them United Empire Loyalists—settled in Quebec, where they dominated commercial life and the fur trade. Scottish settlements emerged in Ontario in the 1820s, including Perth, MacNab Township, and Guelph—founded by Scottish novelist John Galt, who also helped found Galt, Ontario.

Scotsman Sir John A. Macdonald was Canada's first Prime Minister, and Toronto's first mayor, William Lyon Mackenzie, began the **Colonial Advocate** newspaper in 1820 and led the Rebellion of 1837 against the city's oligarchic government. His grandson, William Lyon Mackenzie King, served as prime minister of Canada for 27 years.

From 1871 to 1901, 80,000 Scots entered Canada seeking new economic opportunities, primarily in Ontario. More than 240,000 Scots arrived in Canada just prior to the First World War, followed by 200,000 more between 1919 and 1930 and another 147,000 between 1946 and 1960.

More than half a million Scots live in Ontario. The community's cultural activities are centred around the **St. Andrew's Society**, the **Royal Scottish Country Dance Society**, the **Caledonia Society**, and a large number of clan societies connected with world-wide organizations. The societies hold local ceilidhs (gatherings) and publish newsletters containing historical information. One of the most important organizations is the **School of Scottish Studies**, established at the **University of Guelph** in 1966. It is composed of professional academics and laymen and publishes the semi-annual journal, **Scottish Traditions**, containing articles on Scottish culture, history, and literature.

The sport of curling was brought to Canada by the Scots; the **Granite Club**, a Toronto sports and social club was established by early Scot settlers. In the 1700s, many Scottish Highlanders helped protect British territory from American sieges. Today, the Highland military dress, Gaelic mottoes, piping and dance performances can be spotted at many of the city's parades and are featured at the **Highland Games** held across Ontario in July and August. The annual kirin' o' the tartans (blessing) is held every June with a procession from **Queen's Park** to **St. Andrew's Presbyterian Church** on Simcoe Street, the oldest Scottish church in the city.

Places to Go

Lucy Maud Montgomery Park, Riverside Drive, was named in honour of the Canadian author of Scottish descent who created **Anne of Green Gables** and lived the remaining years of her life in Toronto.

Mackenzie House, (Tel. 416-392-6915, 82 Bond St), is the former home of William Lyon Mackenzie, built in 1850. The house and Mackenzie's print shop have been made into a museum. Open Tuesday to Sunday, 12:00 p.m. to 5:00 p.m. Closed Monday.

The **Campbell House**, (Tel. 416-597-0227, 160 Queen St. W), was built in 1822 for Scottish-born Chief Justice William Campbell. The neo-classical Georgian manor house contains a model of the town of York as it existed in 1834. Open year round, Monday to Friday, 9:30 a.m. to 4:30 p.m.; weekends, 12:00 p.m. to 4:30 p.m.

Hearty soups, meat pies, fish and beef dishes, and a variety of breads and cakes characterize Scottish cuisine. Among the staples of the Scottish diet is oatmeal, used in cooking and as a popular breakfast dish. Cheese is a main ingredient in dishes such as rarebit (a thick sauce of melted cheese with beer or ale, seasoned with mustard and served on toast) and hattit kit (a Scottish version of cream cheese). Haggis (a pudding made with kidneys, liver, and heart cooked in a sheeps stomach) is eaten on special occasions. Accompanying most meals are tea breads, baps, bannocks, scones, tarts, buns, and biscuits served with jellies, jams, marmalades, and preserves. Butterscotch and taffy are famous Scottish sweets. Scotch whisky, beer, and tea are among the most popular beverages.

Mary Macleod's Short Bread, (Tel. 416-461-4576, 639 Queen St. E), carries Scotch shortbread, pies, and other pastries. Other Scottish butchers and bakeries include **But' N' Ben Butchers**, (Tel. 416- 438-4214, 1601 Ellesmere Rd).

Richardson Tartan Shop, 3435 Yonge St), has been open for business for more than 60 years. The shop offers kilt outfits with over 350 tartans in stock, along with Scottish tapes, books, prints, ties, sweaters, scarves, hats, T-shirts, and jewellery.

Hector Russell Scottish Imports, (Tel. 416-782-5227, 1825 Avenue Rd), features Scottish Highland dress rentals and sells tartans, kilts, and jewellery.

Religious Centres, Schools and Other Institutions

The city's Scots belong to the Presbyterian and Roman Catholic churches. Some of the oldest churches in the city include:

- ◆ KNOX PRESBYTERIAN CHURCH, (Tel. 416-921-8993, 630 Spadina Ave).
- ◆ LITTLE TRINITY CHURCH, (Tel. 416-367-0272, 425 King St. E).
- ◆ ST. ANDREW'S PRESBYTERIAN CHURCH, (Tel. 416-593-5600, 73 Simcoe St), was built in 1872 in the revival Norman Romanesque style borrowed from Scotland.
- ◆ ST. ANDREW'S UNITED CHURCH, (Tel. 416-929-0811, 117 Bloor St. E).
- ◆ ST. JOHN'S PRESBYTERIAN CHURCH, (Tel. 416-466-7476, 415 Broadview Ave).
- ◆ VICTORIA PARK FREE PRESBYTERIAN CHURCH, (Tel. 416-491-9778, 2712 Victoria Park Ave).

Holidays and Celebrations

- ◆ ROBBIE BURNS DAY, January 25, honours Scotland's beloved poet, born in 1759. Commemorative dinner festivities begin with piping in the haggis. A piper in Scottish dress plays bagpipes followed by a procession around the banquet hall with the haggis, which is then placed on a table in front of the master of ceremonies. During the dinner poems are read and speeches are given in tribute to Burns. Dances and songs follow.

- KIRKIN' O' THE TARTAN is celebrated in June when Scots take their tartans to **St. Andrew's Church** to be blessed by the minister.
- THE HIGHLAND GAMES take place across Ontario during the summer months. The events include tug-of-war, Highland dancing, tossing the caber, and sheep-dog trials.
- ST. ANDREW'S DAY, November 30, is held in recognition of the patron saint of Scotland and one of the 12 apostles. Scots hold religious services as well as secular festivities.
- HOGMANAY, December 31, is a day of conviviality and merriment. Parties are held and festive food is served.

See Holidays and Celebrations in Glossary.

Organizations

- CLAN FRASER SOCIETY OF CANADA, (www.clanfraser.ca, 71 Charles St. E., Suite 1101). Chair: W. Neil Fraser. Clan Fraser Society of Canada is one of the national societies operating worldwide under the authority of The Rt. Hon. The Lady Saltoun, Chief of the Name and Arms of Fraser; and The Rt. Hon. The Lord Lovat, Chief of Clan Fraser of Lovat, a major branch of Clan Fraser. Their goal is

Traditional Scottish garments.

to provide accurate information on the origins, history, and accomplishments of Frasers and the surnames associated with Clan Fraser and Clan Fraser of Lovat.

◆ **SCOTTISH STUDIES FOUNDATION**, (www.scottishstudies.ca, 2482 Yonge St., P.O. Box 45069). The Scottish Studies Foundation is a Canadian charitable organization based in Toronto. Currently the **Scottish Studies Programme**, under the auspices of the **Department of History**, supports graduate research into Scottish and Scottish-Canadian history at MA and Ph.D. levels. Director: Dr. Paul Thomson.

Consulates, Trade Commissions and Tourist Bureaus

◆ **BRITISH CONSULATE-GENERAL**, (Tel. 416-593-1290, 777 Bay St., Suite 2800). Consul General: Geoffrey Berg.

◆ **BRITISH TOURIST BOARD**, (Tel. 905-405-1720, 5915 Airport Rd., Suite 120, Mississauga).

Prominent Torontonians

David Crombie, popular former mayor of Toronto; Alastair Lawrie, jazz musician and journalist; Pauline McGibbon, former Lieutenant-Governor of Ontario.

Contributor: Neil Fraser, Secretary Treasurer, Clans and Scottish Societies of Canada.

The Serbian Community

On the evening of January 6, Christmas Eve for Orthodox Serbs, an old Serbian custom is carried out by Toronto's Serbian community. The "badnjak" (an oak tree that's the equivalent of the Yule log) is decorated with fruits, nuts and ribbons and carried into each of the Serbian Orthodox churches in the city. The branches are blessed by the priests and given to each parishioner to take home, a symbol of bringing Christ into their lives. Events such as this, along with other customs and religious observances that take place at the city's parishes, exemplify the spiritual and cultural presence of Toronto's 75,000-member Serbian community.

Toronto's Serbs trace their roots to Serbia and all regions of the former Yugoslavia. Approximately 200 Serbs settled in the Toronto area around 1912. Mostly men, these early settlers worked in Ontario's factories, industries, mines, farms, and lumber towns. These newcomers established several businesses in Toronto's East End, including the **Belgrade Coffee House** on King Street East, a popular gathering place. In 1916, the newcomers formed their first organization, the **Serbian National Shield Society of Canada**, an affiliate of the New York–based organization that was established for the purposes of providing humanitarian assistance during the First World War. A second wave of Serbian settlers arrived between 1924 and 1928. This group immediately set about organizing a performing arts group that staged concerts. The **Circle of Serbian Sisters**, **Queen Alexandra**, founded in 1934, hosted cultural events, raised money to build a church, and assisted in the Allied war effort.

Toronto's first Serbian Orthodox Church parish was formed in 1948, and the first church, **St. Sava**, named after the patron saint of the Serbian people, was built in 1953 at the corner of River and Gerrard streets. The second Serbian Orthodox parish, **St. Michael the Archangel**, purchased a church on Delaware Avenue in 1965. The parishes became the focus of religious and cultural activities in the community.

Following the Second World War, students, professionals, political refugees, labourers, and academics were among those who settled in the city. The late 1960s and early 1970s brought a wave of highly skilled Serbs to the city. Thousands more Serbs have made Toronto their new home following the civil war and break-up of the former Yugoslavia in 1991.

Among these recent immigrants were many professionals, including computer programmers, engineers, actors, writers, and artists.

Over the years, a number of prominent members of the community have contributed to the city's cultural and sports scenes. In the arts, Dr. Luigi Von Kunits (1860 to 1931), a composer, violist, and conductor, laid the foundations for the **Toronto Symphony Orchestra** and started the **Canadian Music Journal**. Momo Markovich was an artist for the Ontario Government whose murals depict many of the province's construction and works sites in the 1960s. Composer and music professor Marinko Michael Pepa has helped promote Canadian musicians, and Dusan Petricic is a well-known illustrator and artist whose works have appeared in the **New York Times**, **Washington Post**, and **Toronto Star** newspapers. Hockey star Peter Zezel, and former **Canadian Football League** players Srecko and Ljubo Zizakovic, and Mike Jovanovic have all made a contribution to Canadian sports.

Places to Go

In the Hall of Fame at the **University of Toronto's** Medical Faculty, a bronze plaque commemorates the humanitarian work of a group of Canadian physicians and nurses who volunteered their services to the sick and wounded in Allied Serbia and Greece during the First World War. The plaque was donated by the **Serbian Heritage Academy** and **Wintario**, and displays the special bond that continues to exist between Canadians and Serbs.

Serbian cuisine can be sampled at cultural celebrations and dinners at the church parish halls. A number of the city's restaurants and delicatessens carry Serbian foods. Favourite Serbian cuisine includes roast lamb or pork, gibanica (filo pastry filled with cheese and eggs), burek, kajmak, cevapcici (ground spiced meat sausages), and raznjicic (pork tenderloin kebobs), and for dessert palacinke (crepes), tortes, and Serbian coffee.

Restaurants serving Serbian cuisine include: **Skadarlija Restaurant**, (Tel. 416-539-0378, 1608 Queen St. W); and **Zam Restaurant and Bar**, (Tel. 416-252-0170, 1340 The Queensway).

For desserts, **Sweet Gallery Exclusive Pastry** has several locations: (Tel. 416-232-1539, 350 Bering Ave,; Tel. 416-766-0289, 2312 Bloor St. W,; and Tel. 416-484-9622, 694 Mount Pleasant Rd).

Serbica Books, (Tel. 416-539-0476, 2465 Dundas St. W), is the first and only Serbian bookstore in Canada. For more than 40 years its proprietors, Zivko and Olga Apic have been selling Serbian literature, history, geography, and reference books. **North American Distribution Centre**, (Tel. 416-537-7167, C/o 747 Travel, 2182 Dundas St. W), has been carrying Serbian newspapers, music, and souvenirs and providing information on Serbia and Yugoslavia for over 25 years.

Red Violin Restaurant, (Tel. 416-465-0969, 95 Danforth Ave); **Old Town Tavern**, (Tel. 905-501-8997, 151 Brunel Rd., Mississauga); **McAdam Place Restaurant**, (Tel. 905-890-0681, 5659 McAdam Rd., Mississauga); **Jolly Café Bar**, (Tel. 416-538-3662, 165 Dufferin St); **Peter's Cajun Creole Pizza**, (Tel. 416-368-8099, 181 Parliament St); **Three Brothers Restaurant**, (Tel. 416-253-8809, 657 The Queensway); **Pastries & Delicatessen**, (Tel. 416-626-9329, 290 The West Mall).

Religious Centres, Schools and Other Institutions

◆ ST. SAVA SERBIAN ORTHODOX CHURCH AND CHURCH HALL, (Tel. 416-944-3297, 203 River St). Part of the Serbian Orthodox Diocese of Canada. The church-school organization includes the St. Sava folklore group **Oplenac**, and Sunday and Serbian schools where children are taught the Serbian language, history, culture, heritage, and religion at 2520 Dixie Rd. S., Mississauga. The St. Sava Church Choir, **Queen Alexandra Circle of Serbian Sisters**, also play a major role at the St. Sava parish. The church publishes a quarterly bulletin for its members.

◆ ST. ARCHANGEL MICHAEL SERBIAN ORTHODOX CHURCH AND CHURCH HALL, (Tel. 416-536-8565, 212 Delaware Ave). Part of the **New Gracanica Metropolitante Diocese of America and Canada**, the church is also home to the **St. Michael the Archangel Church Choir**, **Hajduk Veljko Folkdance Group**, the **Circle of Serbian Sisters**, **Duchess Zorka**, **Sunday school**, and a weekly school teaching children the Serbian language, history, singing, and dancing. The church congregation publishes a bulletin.

◆ THE SERBIAN ORTHODOX DIOCESE OF CANADA, (Tel. 905-878-0043, 7470 McNiven Rd), the first Serbian Orthodox monastery in Canada (built in 1994), and the Episcopal residence. The bishop for Canada is Right Reverend Bishop Georgije. The Episcopal Dean for New Gracanica Metropolitante Diocese of America and Canada is Very Reverend Miodrag Popovic, (212 Delaware Ave).

◆ ALL SAINTS SERBIAN ORTHODOX CHURCH AND SERBIAN CENTRE, (Tel. 905-272-5944, 2520 Dixie Rd., Mississauga).

Holidays and Celebrations

Serbs of the Orthodox faith celebrate all the traditional holidays and feasts of the Eastern Orthodox Church according to the Julian Calendar.

◆ ALL SOULS' DAY (PARASTOS AND POMEN) is the universal commemoration of the souls of the deceased. It is customary to visit the graves of deceased family and friends during this religious observance. Individual memorial services are also held throughout the year.

◆ BADNJE VECE (CHRISTMAS EVE), January 6, Serbians celebrate the old custom of bringing in the badnjak, or yule log. Family members place the badnjak in the fireplace for good fortune in the coming year. Straw is scattered on the floor of the house as a reminder of Christ's birth in a manger.

◆ BOZIC (CHRISTMAS) on January 7th is celebrated with a midnight matins, followed by a morning liturgy. The Christmas dinner includes roast pork, cabbage rolls, hot tea, and plum brandy, called Shumadiski Caj. The cesnica (bread cake), containing a silver coin wrapped in tinfoil, is broken among family members. It is believed the recipient of the coin will receive good fortune in the coming year.

◆ DICESAN DAY, held in the summer in Milton and Binbrook, Ontario, is commemorated with an outdoor church service and a picnic.

◆ ST. SAVA DAY is celebrated on January 27th in memory of the Serbian prince who entered monastic life to serve God and his people. As the first Serbian Archbishop, he was instrumental in creating an independent, autocephalic Orthodox Church in the Kingdom of Serbia in 1219. Along with his father, King Stephen Nemanya, he built numerous churches, promoted education, and laid the foundation for the Serbian Orthodox Church. Serbians, particularly children, honour his birthdate with an evening of song, dance, and poetry recitals at their local church hall. St. Sava is the patron saint of the Serbian Nation.

◆ THE FEAST OF ST. LAZARUS (VIDOVDAN) is celebrated on June 28th in memory of the great martyr and prince of Serbia. In 1389, at the Battle of Kosovo, Tsar Lazar led the outnumbered Serbian army against the Turks but lost. Serbia was placed under 500 years of Ottoman Turkish rule. Despite this, Serbs never lost their identity or their religion. A two-day observance of the battle was first held in Canada in 1945. On the closest weekend to the date, a Saturday night dance is followed by a church liturgy and memorial service on the next day. The afternoon picnics attract some 15,000 Serbs from across

North America for a cultural program, outdoor dancing, and singing. The event is held annually with celebrations in both Niagara Falls and Binbrook, Ontario.

◆ **DAY OF REMEMBRANCE.** On the closest Sunday to July 17th, remembrance services are held at local churches for General Draza Mihailovich, the Serbian national hero who organized the first guerrilla movement of Serbian nationalists resisting Nazi and Communist takeover attempts during the Second World War. After the war, Mihailovich was captured by the Communists and executed. Traditional picnics are also held at two picnic grounds owned by Serbian organizations in southern Ontario.

◆ **REMEMBRANCE FOR KING PETER II.** On the first Sunday nearest September 6, Serbs remember the birthday of the exiled King Peter II of Yugoslavia, who died in 1970.

◆ **REMEMBRANCE FOR KING ALEXANDER I.** On October 9, a memorial service is held to commemorate the assassination of King Peter II's father, King Alexander I, who was killed in Marseilles where he was to propose a mutual defence treaty against Hitler's forces.

◆ **PATRON SAINT DAY (KRSNA SLAVA)** is one of the holiest days of the year for any Serbian family. The Krsna Slava is passed down from father to son and commemorates the day the family's ancestors were baptized into Christianity. Each Serbian home has an icon of their family patron saint. Slavas are celebrated with church services and a festive household celebration, where relatives and friends gather for a special meal that includes breaking the traditional bread (Slavski Kolac) and serving cooked wheat (zito). Serbian Orthodox churches also celebrate their respective patron saint's day.

◆ **SERBIAN MOTHER'S DAY FATHER'S DAY** are celebrated on the three last Sundays before Christmas. The tradition of gift giving is practised during this time, symbolic of Jesus Christ's gift to humankind.

See Holidays and Celebrations in Glossary.

Media

◆ **SERBIAN TELEVISION TORONTO**, Informative & Entertaining TV program, since 2000, Rogers TV, Channels 10, 63, 84, (Tel. 416-503-3300, www.stvt.ca, 3265 Wharton Way, Unit 17, Mississauga). Alternate Saturdays, 9:00 a.m. to 9:30 a.m. Alternate Tuesdays, 7:00 a.m. to 7:30 a.m. Producer: Balgoja Ristic.

- BRATSTVO (FRATERNITY), (Tel. 416-663-3409, 1 Secroft Cres). A monthly publication established in 1954. Editor: Milenko Durovic.
- GLAS KANADSKIH SRBA (VOICE OF CANADIAN SERBS), (Tel. 416-496-7881, 1900 Sheppard Ave. E., P.O. Box 303). Established in 1934; published monthly and sponsored by the **Serbian National Shield Society of Canada**. Editor: Bora Dragasevic.
- ISTOCNIK, 7470 McNiven Rd., Milton). The official quarterly publication of the **Serbian Orthodox Diocese of Canada**.
- KANADSKI SRBOBRAN (CANADIAN SRBOBRAN), (Tel. 905-549-4079, 335 Britannia Ave., Hamilton). Established in 1951; a bi-weekly newspaper sponsored by the **Serbian League of Canada**.
- NEZAVISNE NOVINE, (Tel. 416-466-0888, www.nezavisnenovine.com, 429 Danforth Ave., Suite 357). A bi-weekly newspaper.
- CHIN 100.7 FM, (Tel. 416-531-9991, 622 College St). Programs include:
  - RADIO SUMADIJA, (Tel. 416-496-7881), Saturday, 7:00 p.m. to 8:00 p.m. Director: Boro Dragasevic.
  - RAVNA GORA, (Tel. 416-663-3409), Sunday, 5:00 p.m. to 6:00 p.m. Program Director: Milenko Djurovic.
  - SUMADIJA, Saturday, 7:30 p.m. to 8:30 p.m. Director: Boro Dragasevic.
  - VOJVODINA CABARET BLAGOVESNIK, Saturday, 10:00 p.m. to 10:30 p.m. A religious program of the Canadian Serbian Diocese.
  - ZVUCI RODNOG KRAJA, Sunday, 6:00 p.m. to 7:00 p.m. Program Director: Mike Milicevic.
- ASSOCIATION OF POETS AND WRITERS "DESANKA MAKSIMOVIC," (Tel. 416-767-5779, 93 Lavinia Ave). President: Katerina Kostic.
- SRPSKI KORENI, Saturday, 9:00 a.m. to 10:00 a.m. WTOR 770 AM, (Tel. (716) 754-9514). Program Editor: Mike Milicevic.

Organizations

- ASSOCIATION OF SERBIAN WOMEN, The Hudson's Bay Centre, (P.O. Box 75008, 20 Bloor St. E).
- CANADIAN SERBIAN CLUB OF TORONTO, (Tel. 416-496-7881, 1900 Sheppard Ave. E., P.O. Box 303). Established in 1970 to enhance the Serbian contribution to the Canadian mosaic. Director: Bora Dragasevic. President: Milan Markovich.
- CANADIAN SERBIAN NATIONAL COMMITTEE, (Tel. 416-663-3409, 1 Secroft Cres). Established in 1960 as an umbrella organization for several other Serbian organizations. Contact: Milenko Durovic.

- **CANADIAN-YUGOSLAV RADIO AND TV CLUB (KOLO)**, (Tel. 416-537-7167, 2182 Dundas St. W). A Serbian cultural association established in 1972 to maintain and enhance Serbian traditions in Canadian society.
- **MONTENEGRIAN CULTURAL SOCIETY "VLADIKA DANILO."** (Tel. 416-534-4365), President: Rado Aleksic.
- **SERBIAN ASSOCIATION AT THE UNIVERSITY OF TORONTO**, (Tel. 416-443-0963). Sponsors lectures and dances.
- **SERBIAN CENTRE "ST. SAVA,"** (Tel. 905-272-5944, 2520 Dixie Rd., Mississauga).
- **SERBIAN LEAGUE OF CANADA (NATIONAL ORGANIZATION)**, (335 Britannia Ave., Hamilton). A patriotic organization; the Toronto chapter is named Gavrilo Princip. National President: Cedomir Asanin.
- **SERBIAN HERITAGE ACADEMY**, (Tel. 416-588-8550, 2381 Dundas St. W).
- **SERBIAN NATIONAL FEDERATION (NORTH AMERICAN ORGANIZATION)**, (203 River St). Originally established in 1901 to provide Serbian immigrants with moral and financial support. The Toronto chapter, Plavi Jadran, was established in 1927.
- **SERBIAN NATIONAL SHIELD SOCIETY OF CANADA**, (1900 Sheppard Ave. E., P.O. Box 303). A patriotic organization. The Toronto chapter, Karadjordie, was established in 1916. National President: Bora Dragasevic.
- **ERINDALE COLLEGE SERBIAN ASSOCIATION (ECSA)**, (3359 Mississauga Rd., Mississauga).
- **MOVEMENT OF SERBIAN CHETNIKS "RAVNA GORA" IN THE FREE WORLD**, (203 River St). A war veteran's association, established in 1953 to aid veterans from the Second World War. Toronto President: Milorad Uzelac.
- **SERBIAN CENTRE FOR NEWCOMERS IN ONTARIO**, (Tel. 416-588-8550, 2381 Dundas St. W). Provides settlement and orientation services in English and Serbian language to newcomers to Ontario.
- **SERBIAN YOUTH LEAGUE**, (Tel. 647-866-5688, www.serbianyouthleague.org), Largest organization for Serbian students and youth in Canada, established in 2008.

Consulates, Trade Commissions and Tourist Bureaus

- **CONSULATE GENERAL OF SERBIA**, (Tel. 416-487-5776, 377 Spadina Rd). Consul General: Mr. Dragan Grkovic.

Prominent Torontonians

Igor Divljan, junior chess champion of Canada; Bora Dragasevic, radio personality; Dr. Milutin Drobac, Professor at the University of Toronto, and head of non-invasive cardiology lab at Women's College Hospital; Danny Mijovic, professional golfer and former Canadian Amateur Golfing champion; Lilana Novakovich, columnist and soap opera personality promoter; Nikola Pasic, lawyer and grandson of the former prime minister of Serbia; Dr. Svetislav Popovic, specialist in internal medicine; Dragomir Radojkovic, nuclear engineer; Zoran Churchin, President, St. Sava Church; Gordon Kuzmanovic, First Serbian to receive the "Order of St. Sava" from the Holy Synod and recipient of the Canada Confederation Medal.

Contributors: Mike Milicevic, President, North American Marketing Inc; Bojan Ratovic, Proprietor of Sweet Galleries.

The Sikh Community

Wherever they settle, the Sikhs' first communal activity is to build a gurdwara (house of the Guru). Since founding their first gurdwara on Eglinton Avenue West in the 1960s, a familiar Toronto scene is Sikh followers entering one of the city's many temples. Uncut hair and beards and protective turbans are symbols of their religious identity.

Sikhs are the disciples of a world religion that arose from the teachings of Guru Nanak (1469–1538) in Punjab, India. The first Sikh temple in Canada was established in Goldney, British Columbia, in 1908. Other Sikhs came to Canada in 1902 as part of a Hong Kong military contingent travelling to the coronation of Edward VII; they later returned and settled along the west coast of British Columbia.

One of the first Sikhs in Ontario was Jamait Singh Gill, who arrived from British Columbia in 1938. Until the late 1950s there were only about 10 sikh families living in Toronto. Sikhs began arriving in large numbers from the late 1950s to the 1970s, mainly via Great Britain and former British Indian trading colonies in Africa, such as Uganda.

A few of the Toronto community's founders were Dr. Biant Singh, Dr. Jarnail Singh, and Dr. R.S. Khanna, who established the city's first Sikh temple in 1968 in a rented hall on Eglinton Avenue West. Businesses that opened in the 1960s included **Gill's Grocery Store** and the **Sher-E-Punjab** on Danforth Avenue, Toronto's oldest Sikh restaurant.

The early 1970s saw the first major influx of Sikhs to Toronto; many found jobs as labourers, taxi drivers, real-estate agents, and insurance salesmen, or started businesses such as grocery stores and restaurants. The major concentration of Sikh businesses was the **Indian Bazaar** in the Pape Avenue and Gerrard Street area.

There are now approximately 80,000 Sikhs living in and around Toronto. Early newcomers were often farmers and ex-soldiers, but the more recent settlers are from the professional classes and include engineers, doctors, and teachers.

Sikhs have contributed to Toronto's cultural life with art exhibits and Indian classical music. The first Sikh Conference was held in 1979, and a heritage conference in 1981 featured an exhibition of lithographs and pictures depicting the history of the Sikhs. Sikh athletes are among the members of Canada's national field hockey team.

Places to Go

Toronto's Sikh-owned restaurants serve Punjabi specialties such as goat, chicken and egg curries, tandoori (baked in a clay oven) dishes, and breads such as chapatis. **Indian Rice Factory**, (Tel. 416-961-3472, 414 Dupont St), is popular for its curries, poori chole (chickpeas in a sauce with tomatoes), and eggplant served with ginger, tomatoes, green pepper, and coriander. **Sher-E-Punjab**, (Tel. 416-465-2125, 351 Danforth Ave), features curry dishes, lamb saag (spinach), palak and mattar paneer (cottage cheese cooked with peas, yogurt, and spices), and a variety of breads including chapatis and puri.

Religious Centres, Schools and Other Institutions

Community life centres around the gurdwara. There are celebrations for births, marriages, holy days, and to honour the dead. The gurdwara also serves as a language school, as well as a social and recreational centre. The langar (communal kitchen) offers a free meal to all visitors who respect the temple.

Gurdwara is an open place of worship where all are welcome. The Granth (sacred scriptures of the Sikhs) occupies the central place, and is wrapped in silk cloth with a canopy overhead. During the service, an attendant stands by the Granth, which embodies the physical presence of the ten gurus (Sikh masters) and the other saints who speak to the congregation through the person who recites the hymns.

◆ ONTARIO KHALSA DARBAR, (Tel. 905-670-3311, 7080 Dixie Rd., Mississauga).

◆ GURSIKH SABHA SCARBOROUGH, (Tel. 416-299-4800, 905 Middlefield Rd).

◆ RAMGARHIA SIKH SOCIETY, (Tel. 416-748-9442, 140 Rivalda Rd).

◆ REXDALE SIKH SABHA, (Tel. 416-746-6666, 9 Carrier Dr).

◆ SHRI GURU RAVIDAS SABHA, (Tel. 905-333-1924, 2266 Queensway Dr).

◆ SHIROMANI SIKH SOCIETY PAPE, (Tel. 416-463-3132, 269 Pape Ave).

◆ SHIROMANI SIKH SANGAT MISSISSAUGA, (Tel. 905-828-2710, 2377 Dunwin Dr, Mississauga).

◆ SRI GURU SINGH SABHA WESTON, (Tel. 416-656-5699, 331 Old Weston Rd).

Holidays and Celebrations

On religious occasions and at ceremonies, Sikhs recite the hymns of the holy Granth, the scriptures composed by the gurus (teacher prophets) and 23 of the other saints from the Hindu and Muslim religions. The Granth is the source of spiritual knowledge and the complete recitation from beginning to end takes 48 hours. The scripture is read continuously by changing readers every two hours. On the last day of reading, the congregation grows in number. The Ragi Jatha (groups of three or four persons) sing the relevant hymns on special occasions. Poets and Dhadis (professional singers who sing about historical events and the brave deeds of martyrs) take part in the function. The celebration ends with a communal meal, Langar.

The Sikh Holy Scriptures arrive in Toronto on the 400th anniversary of the Revelation of Guru Granth Sahib.

- ◆ THE BIRTHDAY OF GURU GOBIND SINGH JI (1666–1708), the tenth guru and spiritual master, is celebrated in the first week of January.
- ◆ BAISAKHI (NEW YEAR'S DAY) is celebrated on April 13. For Sikhs, the day has an added significance, as it was on this day in 1699 that the community was organized by Guru Gobind Singh. Toronto's Sikh community usually celebrates with a procession starting at Queen's Park. Cans of food are donated to the hungry, and blood donations are made on this day.
- ◆ THE BIRTHDAY OF GURU NANAK, the 15th-century founder of Sikhism, is celebrated in October or November/December.

Media

- ◆ EYE ON ASIA, City TV, (Tel. 416-531-9991, ℅ CHIN Radio/TV International, 622 College St). Saturday, 10:00 a.m. to 11:00 a.m. Hindi/English.

◆ **PUNJABI PROGRAM**, CHIN 1320 CJMR/AM, (Tel. 416-531-9991, 622 College St). Monday to Friday, 9:30 p.m. to 10:00 p.m. Contact: Darshan Sahota.

◆ **CHARDI KALAA**, OMNI-TV, (Tel. 416-260-0047, 545 Lakeshore Blvd. W). Sunday, 12:00 p.m. to 1:00 p.m. Punjabi.

◆ **AJJ DE AWAZ**, 1320 CJMR AM, Monday to Saturday, 6:00 a.m. to 6:30 p.m.; 9:30 p.m. to 10:00 p.m. Punjabi.

◆ **RADIO INDIA**, 530 CJAO AM, Monday to Friday, 6:00 p.m. to 8:00 p.m.

◆ **RADIO ASIA**, 100.7 CHIN FM, Monday to Friday, 10:30 p.m. to 11:00 p.m. Sri Lankan.

◆ **ASIAN HORIZONS**, OMNI News: South Asian Edition, Monday to Friday, 8:00 p.m. to 9:00 p.m.

Organizations

◆ **SIKH TEMPLE SHROMANI SIKH SOCIETY**, (Tel. 416-463-3132, 269 Pape Ave).

◆ **SRI-GURU-SINGH SABHA**, (Tel. 905-671-1662, 7280 Airport Rd., Mississauga).

◆ **THE SIKH FOUNDATION**, (Tel. 416-777-6697, 40 King St. W., Suite 4900). Co-ordinator: Kawal Kohli.

Prominent Torontonians

Mr. Chandhoke, justice of the peace; Gurjit Singh Grewal, executive; Surjit Hans, furniture retailer; Dr. Gurcharan Jauhal, teacher and businessman; Mr. Kholi, entrepreneur, import and export business; Kuldev Singh Sandhu, businessman; Avtar Singh, owner of Singh Farms; Fulel Singh, owner of gas stations; Hardev Singh, artist; Gurbax Singh Malhi, first Sikh Member of Parliament; Raminder Gill, first Sikh Member of Provincial Parliament; Gary Singh, stock broker; Sarabjit Singh Marwah, VP, Bank of Nova Scotia; Tiger Jeet Singh, wrestler; Monita Rajpal, CNN; T. Sher Singh, lawyer and columnist; Harinder Jeet Singh Takhar, MPP and Minister of Government Services; Dr. Kuldip Singh Kular, MPP; Harbhajan Singh Pandori, Ontario Gurdwaras Committee; Rajinder Sidhu, Metro Toronto Police; Steve Nijjar, film producer, actor, professional boxer, professional soccer team coach; Rajinder Singh Sidhu Onkar, travel industry; Kesar Singh, Bombay Palace Restaurants; Ravi S. Juneja, EIPROC; Irvinderpal Singh Babra, journalist/Sikh Press; Harbhajan Singh Pandari; Vic Dhillon, MPP; Amrit Mangat, MPP.

Contributors: Gurdip Singh Chauhan, Jagjar Singh Mann.

The Slovak Community

On Sundays, the sound of the world's largest triad of bells rises above the golden domes of the **Cathedral of the Transfiguration** at Woodbine Avenue and Major Mackenzie Road in Unionville. Built in 1984, the Slovak cathedral was blessed by Pope John Paul II the same year. Inside, a mammoth 60-foot by 40-foot mosaic made from five million pieces of glass and ceramic tiles towers above the altar of the Roman Catholic cathedral of the Byzantine Rite. The late Stephan B. Roman, a mining magnate often called the Uranium King, was benefactor of the cathedral. The prominent Torontonian immigrated to Canada in 1937 and established **Denison Mines**, one of the country's leading uranium companies. Roman was also the founding President of the **Slovak World Congress**.

Toronto's early community dates back to 1870, when Joseph Bellon arrived from Slovakia and set up a flower shop. The first known Slovak in Canada, Bellon served in the Canadian Expedition sent to quell the Riel Rebellion. He and his brother later established a wireworks factory.

Slovaks, who were first directed by the Canadian government to settle in Western Canada, eventually made the trek to Toronto, Hamilton, and the Niagara region. Following the First World War, Latin and Byzantine rite Roman Catholic and Lutheran Slovak parishes emerged in the downtown area. By 1927, the community was large enough to organize its own associations and branches of three main fraternal societies: the **First Catholic Slovak Union**, the **Slovak Catholic Sokol**, and **Assembly 418 of the American Slovak League**, which later became the **Canadian Slovak League and Canadian Slovak Benefit Society**.

Between 1934 and 1941, Latin Rite Roman Catholics held mass at the Jesuit Seminary on Wellington Street, now the site of the **Globe and Mail**. In 1941, a sod-turning ceremony at Robinson and Claremont streets marked the future location of the first Slovak Catholic church in Toronto. In 1942, Slovak Lutherans formed **St. Paul's Evangelical Lutheran parish**, moving to their present quarters at 1444 Davenport Road in 1973. And by the 1950s, Byzantine rite Catholics owned their own church, **St. Mary's**, on Shaw Street.

During the Second World War, Canadian Slovaks fought in the Canadian Armed Forces in Europe, while those at home lent their support through efforts such as providing ambulances for the **Canadian Red Cross Society**. A group of doctors, professors, engineers, and skilled tradesmen were among those fleeing the Communist takeover of Czechoslovakia in 1948. A similar wave occurred after the Soviet Union and its satellites invaded Czechoslovakia in 1968.

The growth of the Slovak population in the Greater Toronto area led to the construction of a new **Sts. Cyril and Methodius Slovak Roman Catholic Church of the Latin Rite** in Mississauga (near Highway 10 and Eglinton), to which the old parish moved from its downtown location.

Torontonians of Slovak origin were thrilled when Slovakia gained independence on January 1, 1993. For many, a life-long desire to have their own self-governing country had been realized.

Slovaks have contributed to Toronto in the fields of politics, business, and sports. Brothers Peter and Miroslav Ihnacak and Marian Stastny have all played for the **Toronto Maple Leafs**. Tennis professional Helen Kelesi, swimmer Marcel Gery, and rhythmic gymnast Jana Lazor have also brought honours to the city and community.

Places to Go

The **George Ben Park** in Parkdale honours the memory of George Ben, Q.C., a spirited and admired politician who served on Toronto's city council and was a member of the Ontario legislature.

Hearty Slovak foods include bryndza (a pure sheep's milk cheese similar to Greek feta), wiener schnitzel, and steak tartare. Favourite dishes are smoked meat sausages and cabbage rolls filled with rice and meat. Various Slovakian treats, such as poppy seed and nut rolls, crêpes, and apple strudel, can be found in Toronto's European-style delis.

Religious Centres, Schools and Other Institutions.

◆ NATIVITY OF THE BLESSED VIRGIN MARY CATHEDRAL, (Tel. 416-531-4836, 257 Shaw St). This dignified Cathedral is attended by Slovaks of the Byzantine Rite of the Roman Catholic Church. There is also a youth dance group.

◆ STS. CYRIL AND METHODIUS ROMAN CATHOLIC CHURCH, (Tel. 905-712-1200, 5255 Thornwood Dr., Mississauga). For more than half a century, Slovaks have attended this parish. It contains a meeting place and a Slovak language school. The parish hall is often used for cultural and benevolent purposes.

◆ ST. PAUL SLOVAK EVANGELICAL LUTHERAN CHURCH, (1444 Davenport Rd). Headquarters for the religious and charitable Slovak Lutheran Union; Maria Martha, a women's benevolent group; and the Luther League, a youth organization.

◆ SLOVAK LUTHERIAN, (3200 Bayview Ave), a strongly mission oriented ministry, developing outreach ministry among Slovak communities around the world.

Media

◆ CANADIAN SLOVAK, (Tel. 905-507-8004), weekly publication, published by the Canadian Slovak League.

Holidays and Celebrations

◆ SLOVAK INDEPENDENCE DAY is celebrated on January 1.

◆ FIRST SLOVAK REPUBLIC INDEPENDENCE DAY, on March 14, remembers the day in 1939 when the Slovak nation attained statehood.

◆ SLOVAK AWARENESS DAY is June 21.

◆ PILGRIMAGE. On the first Sunday in July, a pilgrimage to the **Martyr's Shrine** near Midland is made by Latin rite Catholics.

◆ SLOVAK DAY, the second Sunday in July, is held at various sites in Southern Ontario by the **First District Assembly of the Canadian Slovak League**.

◆ ODPUST. On the first Sunday in August, Odpust is held at the Cathedral and on the second Sunday Family Day is sponsored by **Jednota** and **Sts. Cyril and Methodius parish**. On the first Sunday in September, Odpust is held at the Jesuits in Cambridge.

◆ SLOVAK CONSTITUTION DAY is September 1.

◆ OUR LADY OF SORROWS DAY is held in honour of the patron of Slovakia on September 15.

◆ REFORMATION. On the last Sunday in October, Lutherans recognize Reformation Sunday.

See Holidays and Celebrations in Glossary.

Organizations

- ◆ FIRST CATHOLIC SLOVAK UNION (JEDNOTA), (Tel (416) 231-4006, 19 Tromley Dr). Director: Michael Dobis Jr.
- ◆ SLOVAK CANADIAN WOMEN'S ASSOCIATION, (Tel. (519) 940-4603).
- ◆ THE SLOVAK SINGERS OF TORONTO, (Tel. 905-712-1200, 5255 Thornwood Dr, Mississauga). Director: Miro Letko.

Consulates, Trade Commissions and Tourist Bureaus

- ◆ CONSULATE OF THE SLOVAK REPUBLIC, (Tel. 416-862-1270, Fax 416-363-3528, 1 King St. W, 12th Floor). Honorary Consul: Mr. Michael Martincek.

Prominent Torontonians

Charles Dobias, violinist; Peter Kovalik, artist; Helen Roman-Barber, CEO, Roman Corporation; Helen Kelesi, tennis player; Drs. Otto and Anna Sirek, professors at the University of Toronto, Banting and Best Institute; Paul Szabo, MP; Thomas Sramek, ballet artist; John Voitech Stephens Q.C., Former honourary council and former Chairman, York Region Board of Education; Rudy Toth, musician; Dusan Miklas, entrepreneur; Josef Hoffman, entrepreneur.

Contributors: Frank and Ann Novorlsky; Dusan Doric, Director, Slovak Dancers; John V. Stephens Q.C; Ondro Mihal, President, Slovak Cultural and Information Centre.

The Slovenian Community

For Slovenians, the linden tree with its fragrant yellow blossoms represents both the home and their homeland, once a republic in the former Yugoslavia and now a small, independent free country bordering Austria, Italy, Hungary, and Croatia. In Etobicoke, the modern **"Dom" Lipa Linden Foundation for the Aged and Disabled**, beautified by a large linden tree on its front lawn, was built by Toronto's Slovenian community. The linden tree is also celebrated in folk songs sung on Slovenian Day and appears in the names of Toronto Slovenian organizations and businesses.

The history of Slovenians in Canada dates back to 1830 when Rev. Frederick Baraga, a missionary and later the first bishop of **Sault Ste. Marie and Marquette**, came to work among the native community of the Upper Great Lakes. He was called the "Father of Indian literature" for his dictionary of the "Otchipwe" language. Written in 1853, the dictionary is still the definitive reference to the Otchipwe language. Among his other literary works, Baraga published prayer books and hymnals for the native community and sermons for missionaries.

Intrigued by Father Baraga's reports, a large group of Slovenians began arriving in North America between 1875 and 1900. Those who settled in Canada worked primarily in mines, forestry, and road construction. During another period of immigration in the 1920s and 1930s, Slovenians settled in three Ontario communities: Timmins, Kirkland Lake, and the farming area of the Niagara Peninsula.

Slovenian immigration increased substantially after the Second World War, following the establishment of the Communist regime in Yugoslavia. Some 25,000 Slovenians arrived in Canada from neighbouring European countries and started new lives as farm labourers, domestics, and railway construction workers. In the 1950s, Slovenians began settling in Toronto's west-central neighbourhoods. The community organized mutual benefit societies which served as social and cultural centres. A number of post-war immigrants included professionals; others were craftsmen who initiated home-building enterprises and construction projects.

Today, there are approximately 20,000 Slovenians living in Toronto. Centres for the community's cultural, religious, and social activities are the two Slovenian Roman Catholic parishes founded by Rev. John Kopac and Rev. Jakob Kolaric in the 1950s and '60s, respectively. Toronto Slovenians also own two credit unions and spacious properties used for camping, hunting, and community events.

Prominent Slovenians who have furthered arts and sciences in the city include the late Dr. Vojko Bratina, former professor of metallurgy at the **University of Toronto**, whose research essays and papers can be found in the University library, and the late Ludmila Dolar-Mantuani, internationally renowned geologist and author of **The Handbook of Concrete Aggregates**. In the field of the arts, the following names come to mind. Artist Ted Kramolc has works on permanent display in the **National Gallery** and the **Art Gallery of Ontario**. Music is an integral part of every Slovenian's life, both choral and instrumental, and the following individuals brought this gift to the Slovenian community: the late Jurij Erzen, organist; choral director, Rev. Anton Zrnec; conductor and teacher, Rev. Franc Sodja; the late Joze Osana, organist, pianist and composer; and choir director, Ignac Krizman, whose career as choir director started in the late 1940s in the railyards of Smiths Falls, and has continued right up to the present day.

Places to Go

Soups, meats, and sweets are some of the popular courses of a Slovenian meal. Specialties include: golaz (beef and pork sauce similar to goulash), vampe (potato and tripe soup), krvavice pecenice (sausages made of pork meat and rice), dunajski zrezki (breaded veal cutlets), rizota (giblets and rice or chicken wings and rice casserole), divjacina (wild game meat), polenta (corn meal with sauerkraut), bujta repa (turnips and pork hock soup), and kranjske klobase (home-made smoked sausages). Desserts include palacinke (crepes filled with either cottage cheese or fruit jams and preserves), potica (walnut roll), cespljevi cmoki (plum dumplings), orehovi struklji (cooked walnut rolls), krem snite (puff pastry with vanilla custard), strudelj (apple or cheese strudel), and krofi (deep fried whole doughnuts with or without jam).

At present, there are no restaurants in the city serving authentic Slovenian cuisine. Slovenian-owned restaurants include: the **Fresh Grind Cafe**, (Tel. 905-271-5385, 714 Lakeshore Rd. E., Mississauga); and **Captain John's Harbourboat Restaurant**, (Tel. 416-363-6062, 1 Queen's Quay W), located aboard a large Slovenian ship, the **Jadran** (Adriatic), docked at **Harbourfront** (foot of Yonge St.).

Slovenian delicatessens stock shelves with imported products such as jams, teas, cookies, candies, and pickled and jarred fruits and vegetables.

They include: **Slovenija Meat Delicatessen**, (Tel. 416-535-8946, 2409 Dundas St. W).

Religious Centres, Schools and Other Institutions

Slovenians are predominantly Roman Catholic and the parishes are centres for religious, cultural, and social activities. Slovenian classes are held at the church cultural centres, as well as meetings and practices by choirs, dance ensembles, scouting groups, and drama societies. Inside, churches and community halls are adorned with magnificent works of art. Parishioners of both parishes have purchased a plot of land at **Assumption Catholic Cemetery** in Mississauga. A statue of Our Lady of the Miraculous Medal bears the inscription: "Here Slovenians wait for Resurrection."

◆ OUR LADY HELP OF CHRISTIANS CHURCH, (Tel. 416-531-2316, 611 Manning Ave). The first Slovenian church in Canada, it was built in 1953. A 1927 painting of Mary the Blessed Mother hangs in the sanctuary. This beautiful masterpiece was painted by Blaz Farcnik, donated by Pater Bernard Ambrozic, uncle of His Emminence Cardinal Aloysius Ambrozic. The painting is a replica of the original art work that hangs inside the **Shrine Church of Brezje**, in Slovenia. Statues of Mary and Joseph feature the art of Ted Kramolc, and the stations of the cross, statues, and reliefs were sculpted by Slovenian artist Franc Gorse. A memorial plaque in the church's entrance was erected by anti-Communist fighters as a reminder of Communist atrocities perpetrated in Slovenia during and after the Second World War.

◆ OUR LADY OF THE MIRACULOUS MEDAL PARISH, (Tel. 416-255-2721, 739 Browns Line). Dedicated in 1961, under the pastorship of Rev. John Kopac, it has become the largest Slovenian parish in Canada. The church's statues and stations of the cross were sculpted by Franc Gorse. The **24th Lakeshore Scouting Group** (formed in 1962) is located at the parish, and the founding missionaries of **St. Vincent** and the sisters of **St. Mary** have residences adjacent to the church.

◆ SLOVENIAN LINDEN FOUNDATION (DOM LIPA), (Tel. 416-621-3820, 52 Neilson Dr), maintains a Slovenian senior citizens' home that tends to the medical, social, and recreational needs of its residents. A chronic care wing was added in 2000. Director: Gisela Styka. President: Darko Medved.

◆ SLOVENIAN SCHOOL OF OUR LADY OF THE MIRACULOUS MEDAL, (Tel. 416-233-8311), was established in 1961 under the principalship of the late Frank Cerar and now the current principal Sonya Kulinko.

Current enrolment is between 80–100 students; classes are offered on Saturday mornings from 9:00 to 12:30 p.m. Slovenian language courses for adults are being offered three times weekly. Contact: Sonya Kulinko.

◆ SLOVENIA HALL (SLOVENSKI DOM), (Tel. 905-669-2365, 864 Pape Ave). Dedicated to Slovenian heritage, culture and charitable activities. President: Oscar Koren.

Financial institutions include:

◆ SLOVENIA PARISHES (TORONTO) CREDIT UNION, (Tel. 416-255-1742, 725 Browns Line, and Tel. 416-531-8475, 618 Manning Ave).

◆ JOHN E. KREK CREDIT UNION LTD., (Tel. 416-532-4746, 611 Manning Ave, and Tel. 416-252-6527, 747 Browns Line).

Holidays and Celebrations

◆ CORPUS CHRISTI. Slovenians dressed in their national costumes or scouting uniforms, hunting uniforms, and young girls in white First Communion dresses attend a religious observance of Corpus Christi held on a Sunday in late May or early June. A mass said by priests with the cooperation of a musical choir from both Slovenian parishes in Toronto, is followed by a procession to four prayer stations situated on the grounds of the **Slovenian Summer Camp**, near Bolton.

◆ A MEMORIAL SERVICE is held on a Saturday in the first week of June for Slovenians killed during and after the Second World War.

◆ SLOVENIAN PILGRIMAGE. A religious pilgrimage and memorial service are held on the second Sunday in September at **Martyr's Shrine** in Midland, Ontario. Slovenian victims of the Second World War are honoured at the **Slovenian Memorial Cross** erected at the site. This cross was designed by architect Vilko Cekuta and erected in 1975 by War Veterans Association "**Tabor**." The Stations of the Cross follow the memorial service after which a High Mass is celebrated within the Shrine itself.

◆ CATHOLIC DAY (KATOLISKI DAN) is held on the first Sunday in July. A morning mass is followed by a religious and cultural program held at the **Slovenian Summer Camp** near Bolton.

◆ SLOVENIAN DAY (SLOVENSKI DAN) is held on a Sunday at the end of June or beginning of July, corresponding with Slovenian Independence Day, June 26. The day's festivities include a morning mass followed by a program of folk dances, choral selections, traditional displays, and international guest speakers. Slovenians who have made unique contributions to Slovenian culture are recognized on this day. Slovenian Day is organized by the **Slovenian Canadian Council** in cooperation with the **Canadian Slovenian Community**.

◆ BISHOP FREDERICK BARAGA DAY (BARAGOV DAN) is now celebrated on the third Sunday in January, a day closest to his date of death, January 19, 1868, in Marquette, Wisconsin. Known as the "Snowshoe Missionary" among the Indians of the Upper Great Lakes, a process is in place to have him beatified by the Pope. He lived from 1797 to 1868.

◆ BISHOP ANTON MARTIN SLOMSEK DAY (SLOMSKOVA NEDELJA) is celebrated on a Sunday, as close to September 19 as possible, the day of his beatification by the Pope in Maribor, Slovenia. Bishop Slomsek is the patron of Slovenian language and culture. He lived from 1800 to 1862.

◆ CULTURAL DAY (PRESERNOV PRAZNIK) is celebrated at the end of February, honouring one of Slovenia's greatest poets and the author of the lyrics to the National Anthem of Slovenia—**Zdravljica**.

◆ DR. FRANCE PRESEREN'S DAY is sponsored by the Slovenian embassy in Ottawa, Ontario. The ambassador also sponsors Slovenia's Independence Day at the end of June with a celebration of Slovenian culture and language in Toronto. In 1999, a celebration was held in the newly opened Consulate for the Republic of Slovenia, in Mississauga.

See Holidays and Celebrations in Glossary.

Media

◆ BOZJA BESEDA (THE WORD OF GOD), (Tel. 416-255-2721, 739 Browns Line). A religious bi-monthly magazine published since 1950 by the Slovenian Vincentian fathers. Editor: Rev. Anthony Zrnec.

◆ DOM LIPA NOVICE (DOM LIPA NEWS), (Tel. 416-621-3820, 52 Neilson Dr). This newsletter is published quarterly by the members of the Board of Directors. Information found within this newsletter includes special announcements and events for and about the residents of **Dom Lipa** (Linden Foundation).

◆ CANADIAN SLOVENIAN BUSINESS DIRECTORY, (Tel. 416-251-8456), published by the **Canadian Slovenian Chamber of Commerce** every three years, contains a directory of businesses operated by Slovenians, as well as a personal directory of telephone numbers. Editor: Frank Brence Sr.

◆ UPDATE, (Tel. 416-251-8456), a bi-monthly newsletter published by the **Canadian Slovenian Chamber of Commerce**, informs the members of upcoming meetings and special events. Editor: Frank Brence Sr.

◆ GLAS KANADSKIH SLOVENCEV (VOICE OF CANADIAN SLOVENIANS), CHIN 100.7 FM, (Tel. 905-277-8358, 622 College St). A radio program heard on Sundays between the hours of 9:00 a.m. and 10:00 a.m. (summer hours) and 11:00 a.m. and 12:00 p.m. (September to May), is hosted by the members of the **All Slovenian Cultural Committee**, which was founded in 1991. Contact person: Florian Markun.

◆ KREK'S SLOVENIAN CREDIT UNION NEWSLETTER. (Tel. 416-252-6527), This quarterly newsletter provides information on new products and services as well as community events and member features. Contact person: Joe Cestnik.

◆ PLANICA NEWS, (Tel. 416-281-6794), a newsletter published by the **Planica Hunting and Fishing Club** (www.planica.org) for its members, reports on Club activities and newsworthy happenings within its membership. Contact person: Frank Brence Sr.

◆ STZ NEWSLETTER (SLOVENIAN SPORTS FEDERATION), an environmental newsletter hoping to raise awareness among the members of the Slovenian community and to educate them in the different facets of recycling. Contact person: Frank Gormek,; Oscar Koren.

Organizations

◆ CANADIAN SLOVENIAN HISTORICAL SOCIETY (CSHS), The CSHS is an independent society with its own constitution and by-laws. Its sole objective is to acquire, organize, and preserve the history of Slovenians in Canada. Its logo combines the linden and the maple leaf, both strong symbols. The documents, art, and artifacts of Slovenians in Canada will be stored in the **Slovenian Senior Citizens Centre** (Dom Lipa), (52 Neilson Dr). All Slovenians are invited to help preserve their rich history in Canada. President: Stan Kranyk.

◆ THE SLOVENIAN CULTURAL ASSOCIATION "SIMON GREGORCIC," (Tel. 416-248-0530), founded in 1949, is named after one of Slovenia's greatest poets and writers. A statue of Simon Gregorcic is found on the grounds of the association's summer camp west of Newmarket. Each year the association holds Gregorcic Day, which is celebrated with a cultural program attended by Slovenians from across Canada. Contact: Joe Kanalec.

- **ALL-SLOVENIAN CULTURAL COMMITTEE**(Tel. 905-277-0273, 770 Browns Line). Contact: Florian Markun, President.
- **SLOVENIA HOME ASSOCIATION (SLOVENSKI DOM)**(864 Pape Ave). Established in 1960 by a group of Slovenian-Canadian shareholders to preserve the Slovenian language and heritage. The association purchased a building on Pape Avenue in 1962 which served as a club-house and home base for the **Slovenian Sports Federation** (STZ). The building has also been used for exhibitions of art by Slovenian artists. Contact: Oscar Koren.
- **SLOVENSKA IGRALSKA SKUPINA (SLOVENIAN THEATRE CLUB ENSEMBLE)**, (Tel. 416-251-9428, 5 Dunning Cres). Established in 1988, the group puts on theatrical productions throughout Southern Ontario and the northern United States. Contact: Mrs. N. Cemas.
- **SLOVENSKA TELOVADNA ZVEZA (SLOVENIAN SPORTS FEDERATION)**, (Tel. 905-473-6632). Established in 1948, Frank Gormek and members of STZ have competed as gymnasts on the Canadian Gymnastics team. The organization also owns approximately 1,000 acres of hunting land near Bancroft. Contact: Frank Gormek.
- **SLOVENSKI-KANADSKI SVET (SLOVENIAN-CANADIAN COUNCIL)**, (Tel. 416-489-8331, 57 Anderson Ave), was formed in 1978 to speak for the community in affairs concerning Slovenians in Canada and to coordinate visiting groups from Slovenia. Contact: Emma Pogacar.
- **SLOVENSKO GLEDALISCE (SLOVENIAN PLAYHOUSE)**, (Tel. 416-654-4066). This theatre ensemble has staged more than 125 productions over the last four decades. Productions include comedies, dramas, and light operettas held in Slovenian community centres throughout Ontario and the United States. Producer and Director: Vilko Cekuta.
- **SLOVENSKO LOVSKO DRUSTVO (THE SLOVENIAN HUNTERS AND ANGLERS CLUB)**, (770 Browns Line). Established in 1971 by individuals inter-ested in continuing a sport that was part of their everyday life in their homeland of Slovenia. The club has a lodge near Everett, Ontario, with an in-ground swimming pool, a soccer field, campsites, and trapshooting facilities. They also sponsor chess tournaments, card (Tarok) tournaments, hunting and fishing expeditions, picnics with live music, barbecues, and publishes an annual review which also acts as a directory of Slovenian businesses and members phone numbers. President: Rudy Mihelic; Contact: Louis Kocjancic; Miro Rak.
- **VECERNI ZVON (EVENING BELL)**, (Tel. 905-625-5485), founded in 1956, is one of the oldest Slovenian societies, which assists its members in times of illness and hardship and fosters a sense of community among

Slovenians in North America. It holds an annual cultural day, named "**Proscenje**" (Polish Fair) or "**Pomurski Dan**," at its summer campgrounds near Tottenham, Ontario. Contact: Joe Hozjan.

◆ HOLIDAY GARDENS, (Tel. 905-686-0782, www.holidaygardens.ca, 3315 Balsam Rd). A Slovenian country club association established in 1964 by Slovenians from the Oshawa and East Toronto communities. The grounds incorporate a large hall, swimming pool, camping sites, and sports facilities. The association arranges picnics and cultural and sporting events for its members and other Slovenians. President: Tony Cernivc.

◆ DANCE ENSEMBLE NAGELJ (CARNATION), (Tel. 905-276-7258). A folk-dance company, established in 1959, which has toured Canada, the United States, as well as Slovenia and Austria. Choreographer: Ciril Sorsak.

◆ PLANICA HUNTING AND FISHING CLUB, (Tel. 416-281-6794, Fax 416-281-4287, www.planica.org). Slovenian hunters and anglers own 1000 acres of land with a clubhouse and two lodges with 47 private rooms near Bancroft.

◆ SLOVENSKI SPORTNI KLUB (SLOVENIAN SPORTS CLUB), (Tel. 905-274-8730), was founded in 1959. This club takes part in provincial hockey, soccer, and volleyball tournaments. Both female and male divisions of the volleyball team have attended Canadian championships. The women's teams have claimed a number of Ontario titles in women's volleyball. All three divisions have attended European tournaments. Contact: John Kavcic Jr; President: Paul Zabukovec Jr.

◆ SLOVENSKO LETOVISCE (SLOVENIAN SUMMER CAMP), (Tel. 905-880-4850, www.sloveniansummercamp.com, 17196 Mount Wolfe Rd., Palgrave). The grounds are located near Tottenham, and are owned by the **missionary order of St. Vincent**, the religious order to which the priests of both Slovenian parishes belong. Several annual events take place on the grounds, including Corpus Christi procession, Slovenian Day, Thanksgiving, and Closing Day. Facilities include an open-air chapel, a large hall, camping sites, a swimming pool and a wading pool. The camp sponsors sporting activities throughout the year. President: John Kuri Jr.

◆ DANCE ENSEMBLE—MLADI GLAS (VOICE OF YOUTH).(Tel. 905-812-3735). This dance troupe was molded into a folklore dance ensemble in 1974, during the early years of Metro International Caravan. It evolved from a mini theatre presentation to a full fledged dance group that has performed throughout North America and Europe during its 35-year existence. Contact: Nada Petrovic.

◆ SLOVENIAN CULTURAL COMMITTEE (VSESLOVENSKI ODBOR).(Tel. (519) 884-9413), After Slovenia had won its independence in 1991, a committee of patriots formed a cultural organization whose statement reads as follows: "this association's aim is to be a forum to link, inform and to coordinate the activities of the various Slovenian organizations." It also sponsors and plans tours for performing groups coming from Slovenia. This newly formed organization works in close association with the Ministry of Culture in Slovenia, an organization held over from the previous regime. Contact: Ivan Plut.

◆ CANADIAN SLOVENIAN CONGRESS (KANADSKI SLOVENSKI KONGRES), (770 Browns Line). A voluntary non-profit organization of Slovenian origin, regardless of member's affiliation or political persuasion, this council is formed by 15 members who are voted in for a mandate of two years. The organization has branches in Vancouver, Winnipeg, Windsor, Hamilton, and Ottawa. Its main focus is cultural aspirations, defending rights and interests of Slovenians, and acting on behalf of Slovenian individuals in the community at all government levels. The organization is also a member of the **World Slovenian Congress**. President: Dr. Frank Habjan.

◆ BELOKRANJSKI KLUB, (Tel. 905-238-9258) an association of Slovenians from the Belokrajina region of Slovenia, this club organizes an annual banquet to raise funds for their charitable activities. Members come from all over North America to reminisce and at the same time support worthy causes such as **Dom Lipa**, **Folklore Dance Ensembles**, **Slovenian Radio Club**, and other such activities. President: Janko Bubas.

◆ JUNIOR CHOIR—NOVI ROD (NEW GROWTH) is a choir of junior members of the Slovenian community. Their main focus is to learn Slovenian folk songs as well as Canadian folk songs to be sung at various events and during their concerts. They like to perform for the residents of senior citizen homes, they become carollers during the Christmas season, and they perform at religious ceremonies. Contact: Kristina Krizan, Tel. 905-949-9668, or Laurie Ulcar, Tel. 416-626-1755.

It's a Slovenian tradition on Palm Sunday: branches of pussy willows and greenery (called butare) are taken to the church for blessing.

Consulates, Trade Commissions and Tourist Bureaus

◆ REPUBLIC OF SLOVENIA CONSULAR OFFICE, (Tel. 905-804-9310, Fax (905) 804-9313, 4300 Village Centre Court, Main Floor, Mississauga). Honourary Consul: Mr. Joseph Slobodnik.

◆ EMBASSY OF SLOVENIA, (Tel. (613) 565-5781, 150 Metcalfe St., Suite 2101, Ottawa). Ambassador: Veronika Stabej.

◆ CANADIAN SLOVENIAN CHAMBER OF COMMERCE, (Tel. 416-251-8456, www.cdnslocc.ca, 747 Browns Line). Established in 1990, the chamber boasts 90 members and promotes international trade.

Prominent Torontonians

Cardinal Aloysius Ambrozic, Former Cardinal of the Catholic Archdiocese of Toronto; Judy Brunsek, Publisher of Quill and Quire; Aggie Cekuta-Elliot, actress and vocalist at Stratford Festival Theatres; Ben (Blago) Cekuta, theatre arts teacher, transport coordinator in the movie industry; Rev. Martin Dimnik, Superior of the Pontifical Institute for Medieval Studies; Anton Jemec, sculptor and artist; Joseph Kastelic, prominent builder who received recognition from the Mayor of Mississauga; Marion Mozetich, internationally renown classical and contemporary composer with the CBC and professor of music at Queen's University (Kingston, ON); Joe Petric, recording and concert classical accordionist performing on the world's stages; Rev. Dr. Joseph Plevnik, Director of Advanced Degree Studies at Toronto School of Theology; Joseph Slobodnik, Honourary Consul for the Republic of Slovenia; Elvis Stojko, three-time World Figure Skating Champion and Olympic medalist; Joe Mihevc, City of Toronto Councillor.

Contributors: Frank Brence Sr; Dr. Augustin Kuk; Andrej Pahulje, B.A. (Mus.); Carla M. Pahulje R.T.R; Ciril Plesko, P.Eng; Ema Pogacar; Marta Jamnik-Sousa; Oscar Koren; Frank Gormek; Bernarda Cemas; Frank Osredkar, Architect.

The Somali Community

In 1975, the first 13 Somali newcomers to the city came together and began a tradition of meeting three times a year. These early pioneers have helped Toronto's Somali community flourish over the years. Today, Toronto's 70,000 Somalis have added a new flavour and diversity to the city's multicultural make-up.

The first wave of settlers were refugees who arrived following the Ethiopian–Somali war in 1988. More than 3,000 Somali political refugees arrived in Canada following the civil war in Somalia. Many settled in Parkdale and the Lawrence Avenue West–Caledonia Road area. From 1989 to 1992, over 15,000 Somalis sought refuge in Canada from the drought, war, and hardships that overcame their homeland in Northeast Africa. A majority settled in Toronto. The largest group of Somalis immigrated to Toronto in the 1990s.

Today, Somali neighborhoods are found in Northern Etobicoke, Don Mills, Scarborough, Weston, the Dundas Street West–Bloor Street area, and the Annex. Many Somali professionals have settled in the city, including engineers, teachers, doctors, and business people. Somalis are known for their love of soccer and have been instrumental in the organization of several soccer tournaments in the city.

Places to Go

Somali shops and businesses can be found in several areas of Toronto: Weston Road and Lawrence Avenue West; Dundas Street West and Bloor Street West; Kipling Avenue and Dixon Road; and Dundas Street West and Keele Street.

Subhan Halal Superstore Inc., (Tel. 416-633-4474, 3296 Keele St); **Somali Halal Supermarket**, (Tel. 416-244-8248, 2371 Weston Rd); **Alif Supermarket**, (Tel. 416-247-3232, 2011 Lawrence Ave. W); **Somali Hall Fame Store**, (Tel. 416-244-9998, 2070 Lawrence Ave. W); **Buwe Halal Meat & Foods**, (Tel. 416-248-4880, 1834 Weston Rd); **Dixon Halal Meat**, (Tel. 416-249-7515, 1735 Kipling Ave).

Somali restaurants include, **Hamar Weyne Restaurant**, (Tel. 416-744-0447, 296 Rexdale Blvd); **Hamdi Restaurant**, (Tel. 416-745-7888, 18A

Rexdale Blvd); **Al-Aruba Restaurant**, (Tel. 416-746-4089, 383 Albion Rd); **Gal Restaurant**, (Tel. 416-242-7058, 2007 Lawrence Ave. W); **Banadir Restaurant**, (Tel. 416-703-8815, 272 Parliament St); **Etobicoke Restaurant**, (Tel. 416-746-9703, 379 Albion Rd); **Sahara Restaurant**, (Tel. 416-203-2593, 134 Dundas St. E).

Iman Beauty Supply, (Tel. 416-241-4541, 2083 Lawrence Ave. W), **Hudda Book Store and Audio**, (Tel. 416-245-3733, 962 Scarlett Rd).

Religious Centres, Schools and Other Institutions

Somalis are devout Muslims who worship at the city's mosques, where they share in religious and cultural activities.

◆ KHALID BINAL-WALID MASUE, MOSQUE, (Tel. 416-745-2888, 16 Bethridge Rd).

Holidays and Celebrations

Somalis celebrate the following as well as all Muslim holidays.

◆ NATIONAL HOLIDAY is June 26.
◆ INDEPENDENCE DAY is July 1.

See Holidays and Celebrations in Glossary.

Media

◆ DHAMBAAL SOMALI NEWSPAPER, (Tel. 416-743-3335, 1987 Kipling Ave). Editor: Liban Bashir.
◆ MUUQAALKA SOOMAALIDA (EYE ON SOMALIA), OMNI TV, (Tel. 416-260-3621, 545 Lakeshore Blvd. W). Saturday, 9:00 a.m. to 9:30 a.m.
◆ SOMALI PRESS(Tel. 416-242-7777, 1776 Weston Rd). Editor: Ahmed Barkhadle.

Organizations

◆ DEJINTA BEESHA, (Tel. 416-743-1286, 8 Taber Rd).
◆ SOMALI CANADIAN COMMUNITY CLUB, (Tel. 416-249-6742, 1680 Jane St).
◆ MIDAYNTA, (Tel. 416-544-1992, Fax 416-440-3379, www.midaynta.com, 1992 Yonge St., Suite 203). The Midaynta Youth sports club was established in October 15, 1997. Midaynta sponsors and runs sports

programs such as basketball, soccer, hockey, table tennis, football. The programs are run throughout the year, indoors during winter and outdoors in summer. Dozens of youth sports club participate in the programs which are designed to promote healthy lifestyles, mental and physical fitness, and safe neighbourhoods.

- ◆ SOMALI CANADIAN ASSOCIATION OF ETOBICOKE, (Tel. 416-742-4601, 925 Albion Rd., Room 202). Executive Director: Osman Ali.
- ◆ SOMALI YOUTH ASSOCIATION OF TORONTO (SOYAT), (Tel. 416-247-6333, www.soyat.org, 2304 Islington Ave., Suite 101).
- ◆ SIWA-SOMALI IMMIGRANT WOMEN'S ASSOCIATION, (Tel. 416-741-7492, 1735 Kipling Ave).
- ◆ YORK COMMUNITY SERVICES, (Tel. 416-653-5400. ext. 226), Abukar Mohamed.
- ◆ SOMALILAND WOMEN'S ORGANIZATION OF METRO TORONTO, (Tel. 416-293-6585, 67 Commander Blvd).

Prominent Torontonians

Samsam Ismail, Somaliland Women Organization; Mohamed Ismail (Bergeel), founder of Somaliland Canadian Association and member of elder committee; Ahmed Samatar, member of Somaliland Canadian Association, activist against war crimes; Shiek Shakir Hussien, Beder Islamic Association; Kinzi Ismail, community member.

Contributor: Abdulahi I. Ali.

The Spanish and Latin American Communities

A number of the large events in the community are celebrations of Latin American folklore shows at **Nathan Phillips Square** and **Mel Lastman Square**, where thousands of people gather together to share the variety and richness of the Latin American culture. Every fall, the Arts and Crafts Building at the **Canadian National Exhibition** also vibrates with the Latin rhythms of the three-day **International Hispanic Fiesta**. The Fiesta features the food, art, and music of 20 different countries. Mariachi bands, flamenco shows, Mexican ballets, folklore exhibitions, and tango shows coalesce to demonstrate the spirit of Toronto's Hispanic community.

The 270,000-member community is made up of Spanish-speaking people primarily from North, Central, and South America, the Caribbean, and Spain. The Chileans and the Ecuadorians, with more than 45,000 people, are the two largest groups in the Hispanic community. Newcomers include Uruguayans and Argentinians.

Significant Spanish settlement did not occur in Canada until the 20th century. By 1914, approximately 2,000 Spaniards had arrived in Canada, followed by a small group that settled here between the two World Wars. The largest group of settlers included Latin Americans, who arrived between 1968 and 1975, boosting the population of Hispanics in Canada to 50,000.

Although the arrival of Hispanics can be traced to the post-war years, in the last three decades three main waves of immigrants from different historical-spatial roots have settled in Canada. They are the Andean wave (1971–1975), the Coup wave (1973–1979), and the Central American wave (since 1981). The causes of these waves are both economic and political. The amnesty legislation of 1973 resulted in an inflow of nearly 50,000 individual regularizations (most from Ecuador and Colombia). At the same time, the military coup in Chile displaced thousands of Chilean professionals and labourers, leaving them to seek political asylum. The Central American wave of the 1980s was caused by socio-political shocks in Nicaragua, the escalation of the civil war in El Salvador, and repressive policies in Guatemala.

An early area of settlement was College Street between Bathurst Street and Spadina Avenue. Today, many Hispanics have left this neighbourhood to live in the Keele and Finch area of North York. Members of the Chilean community reside primarily in Etobicoke and Don Mills.

Regional clubs, soccer leagues, community centres, and other institutions preserve Hispanic culture in the city. The **Spanish Tourist Office** was established in 1958, and **Banco Central of Canada**—a direct affiliate with **Banco Central de Espana**—opened its first branch on Bay Street in 1982. **First Canadian Place** houses the offices of **Banco Nacional De Mexico** and consulates of more than 10 Latin American countries.

To commemorate the 200th anniversary of the birthday of Simon Bolivar —liberator of six Latin American countries—a bronze bust was sculpted by artist Armando Sorondo. The monument was presented by the Consul General of Venezuela as a gesture of friendship to Torontonians and placed on the lawns of **Trinity Bellwoods Park** in the heart of the city's Hispanic district.

Places to Go

In the area bounded by Dundas, Spadina, Ossington, and Bloor, the names of restaurants, stores, and offices are evidence of the prevailing Hispanic influence in the neighbourhood.

Latin American cultural exhibitions, sporting events, and plays are presented at cultural centres and parks, while the sounds of salsa, cumbia, and merengue can be enjoyed at the city's increasingly popular Hispanic night spots. Relaxing neighbourhood restaurants provide the forum for guitarists, colourful flamenco dancers, and traditional Spanish and Latin American cuisine.

Peruvian cuisine is served in the distinctive South American setting of the **Boulevard Cafe**, (Tel. 416-961-7676, 161 Harbord St). The restaurant features a huge outdoor patio decorated with potted flowers. Inside, handmade tapestries, wood and stucco walls, and shutters are part of the decor. Appetizers include ostras (oysters with lime and hot sauce), and fresh warm cornbread is served with every meal. Peruvian specialties include empanadas (spicy chicken or beef in pastry), anticuchos (marinated and charbroiled brochettes with a choice of sea bass, shrimp, beef tenderloin, or chicken), and the Peruvian Plate (a salad with steamed vegetables) served with huancaina (a spicy cheese sauce). On Peruvian Independence Day, celebrated on July 28, owner Lirio Peck presents a traditional menu of seafood salad, lamb stew, and fish.

South American cuisine is available at **Plaza Flamingo**, (Tel. 416-921-2752, 430 College St), which features cumbia and salsa dancing in the adjoining **Borinquen Night Club**. **El Palenque**, (Tel. 416-653-5593, 816 St. Clair Ave. W), serves Mexican cuisine. **Babalu'u**, (Tel. 416-515-0587, 136 Yorkville Ave), serves many tasty tapas platters, including chicken, seafood, and salsas.

Flavourful Spanish seafood dishes include paella (saffron-flavoured rice with chicken and shellfish) and zarzuela (seafood with sauce). Tapas (appetizers), gazpacho (chilled soup made with tomatoes, oil, garlic, and lemon), and calamares (deep-fried squid) are popular starters to a meal and can be enjoyed with sangria (red wine mixed with soda and fruit) and cerveza (light beer).

Casa Barcelona, (Tel. 416-234-5858, 2980 Bloor St. W); **La Cucina de Dona Luz**, (Tel. 416-652-7430, 807 St. Clair Ave. W); **Rancho Relaxo**, (Tel. 416-920-0366, 300 College St); **Mario's Latin Video**, (Tel. 416-537-3449, 616 Bloor St. W).

Around Toronto:

Peruvian cuisine can be found at: **El Bodegon**, (Tel. 416-944-8297, 537 College St); **Restaurant Tipico Ecuatoriano**, (Tel. 416-614-1136, 2312 Keele St).

Seafood, authentic decor and guitar music heighten the coziness of **Segovia**, (Tel. 416-960-1010, 5 Saint Nicholas St). Spanish specialties include paella for two, gazpacho, fresh hake, garlic shrimp, and mussels in a tomato-based sauce.

The staples of a Mexican diet include tortillas (flat, pancake-like bread), chilies, frijoles (refried beans), and chorizo (pork sausage with seasonings). One of the city's first Mexican restaurants, **Elsewhere**, (Tel. 416-489-8482, 2468 Yonge St), serves traditional tacos, enchiladas, and burritos. The menu also includes pollo veracruz (grilled chicken topped with a purée of fresh tomatoes, cilantro, and jalapenos), camarones al mesquite (grilled shrimp with garlic butter), and fajitas (grilled strips of steak, chicken, or shrimp, served in a sizzling hot skillet with green peppers, onions, and tomatoes). The bar carries the largest selection of Mexican beer in Ontario.

Other restaurants serving Mexican foods include: **Coyote Willie**, (Tel. 416-778-4578, 689 Queen St. E); **Margaritas**, (Tel. 416-929-6284, 229 Carlton St, and Tel. 416-977-5525, 14 Baldwin St); **Rio Grande**, (Tel. 416-536-8452, 1661 Bloor St. W); **Tacos El Asador**, (Tel. 416-538-9747, 690 Bloor St. W); **The Willow**, (Tel. 416-469-5315, 193 Danforth Ave); **Tortilla**

Flats, (Tel. 416-593-9870, 429 Queen St. W); **Hernando's Hideaway**, (Tel. 416-929-3629, 545 Yonge St, and Tel. 416-366-6394, 52 Wellington St. E); **La Mexicana Restaurant**, (Tel. 416-783-9452, 3337 Bathurst St); and **La Rosa Chilena**, Bakery, (Tel. 416-398-6393, 788 Wilson Ave; Restaurant, (Tel. 416-635-1837, 760 Wilson Ave).

Spanish and Latin American foods, as well as books and magazines, are available at **El Eden Equatorino Importers**, (Tel. 416-923-8879, 396 College St), carries food products imported from Ecuador and South America, including the exotic naranyilla (jungle juice) and tarnarindo juice.

Other shops carrying fruits, canned products, Sidra Mayador (imported sparkling apple cider), records, magazines, and books include **Pepes Mexican Foods Inc.**, (Tel. 416-674-0882, 122 Carrier Dr). **Marisel's Bakery and Delicatessen**, (Tel. 416-248-8806, 1742 Jane St), is a Latin-American bakery.

Religious Centres, Schools and Other Institutions

Approximately 25 churches in the city are attended by Hispanics belonging to Roman Catholic, Baptist, Pentecostal, and Evangelist congregations. The largest churches are:

◆ HISPANIC BAPTIST CHURCH, (Tel. 416-654-8936, 9 Boon Ave).
◆ ST. JOHN THE BAPTIST, (Tel. 416-603-2266, 941A Dundas St. W).
◆ ST. PETER'S CATHOLIC CHURCH, (Tel. 416-534-4219, 659 Markham St).
◆ ST. PHILIP NERI, (Tel. 416-241-3101, 2100 Jane St).
◆ ST. WENCESLAUS, (Tel. 416-532-5272, 496 Gladstone Ave).

Spanish is taught at the city's universities and high schools. Other institutions preserving Hispanic culture include:

◆ CENTRO DEL BAILE ESPANOL (CENTRE FOR SPANISH DANCE), (Tel. 416-924-6991, 103 Avenue Rd., Suite 511).
◆ ACADEMY OF SPANISH DANCE, (Tel. 416-595-5753, 401 Richmond St. W).

Holidays and Celebrations

◆ EPIPHANY, January 6. On this day the Centre for Spanish-Speaking Peoples sponsors a special party for children. Instead of Santa Claus, the three kings present gifts to the children.
◆ GOOD FRIDAY is celebrated by Toronto's Ecuadorians as a feast day to symbolize the continuation of life. Fanesca soup, made from blending

vegetables, corns, beans, and peas with dry corn, is eaten on this day only.

◆ FESTIVALS. In May, the **Spanish Centre** holds a festival on a weekend at the end of the month with dance performances. Spanish regional groups hold festivals in the city throughout the year. In mid-May the **Madrid Festival** is celebrated with theatrical presentations, and in July a dinner dance and performance mark the **Basque Festival**.

◆ BATALLA DE PICHINCHA is celebrated with speeches and a cultural program on May 24, 1822, for the day Ecuador won its freedom from Spain.

◆ INDEPENDENCE DAY (VENEZUELA). On July 5th, a reception is held by the Toronto Venezuelan Consulate to commemorate the day in 1811 the country proclaimed its independence from Spain.

◆ FIESTA DE SAN FERMIN. On July 6, the city of Pamplona, Spain, celebrates the feast of its patron saint by holding bullfights. In Toronto, the Fiesta de San Fermin takes the form of a week-long celebration with dancing and singing.

◆ INDEPENDENCE DAY (ARGENTINA). July 9 marks Argentina's formal Declaration of Independence, signed in 1816. This day is celebrated with a cultural program.

◆ INDEPENDENCE DAY (COLOMBIA). On July 20th, Colombians celebrate their independence from Spain, achieved in 1810. On the nearest weekend to the date, the Colombian community holds a social and cultural evening.

◆ CUBAN HOLIDAY. Cubans hold a celebration on the nearest weekend to July 26 in recognition of the 26 of July Movement in 1953 when Fidel Castro led an attack on the Moncada Barracks at Santiago. The revolt against the Batista government was unsuccessful but was the first step to the revolution that led to Castro's overtaking the government in 1959.

◆ INDEPENDENCE DAY (PERU). July 28 recognizes the day in 1821 that Peru proclaimed its independence. The Toronto Peruvian community celebrates the event on the weekend nearest the date.

◆ INDEPENDENCE DAY (BOLIVIA). August 6 marks the day Bolivia (known as Upper Peru) defeated the occupying Spanish forces and became a separate nation. The community celebrates the occasion with a reception, speeches, and a cultural program.

◆ ECUADOR'S INDEPENDENCE DAY is celebrated on August 10, on the anniversary of the first uprising and declaration of independence that took place in Quito in 1809. The celebrations include receptions, speeches, dinners, dances, and contests. A Miss Pichincha is chosen to preside over the festivities.

◆ INDEPENDENCE DAY (URUGUAY). August 25 marks the day in 1825 that Uruguay achieved its independence from Spain, Argentina, and Brazil. It is celebrated the weekend nearest to the date with a two-day program of sporting events, singing, and dancing.

◆ INDEPENDENCE DAY (GUATEMALA). September 15 is National Day, when Guatemala received its independence from Spain in 1821. The community celebrates with a social and cultural evening.

◆ INDEPENDENCE DAY (MEXICO). September 16 marks the day in 1810 that a priest, Miguel Hidalgo, demanded Mexico's independence from Spanish rule. Celebrations are held on the closest weekend to the day.

◆ INDEPENDENCE DAY (CHILE). September 18 celebrates the day in 1810 when Chile established a governing junta. The Chilean community celebrates the event on the weekend nearest to the date in various places around Toronto.

◆ INDEPENDENCE DAY (GUAYAQUIL). October 9 recognizes the Independence of Guayaquil, the Ecuadorian city that attained self-government in 1820. Former residents celebrate with a program of music, singing, and dancing.

◆ DIA DE LA RAZA is held on October 12, commemorating the discovery of America by Christopher Columbus in 1492. The day is remembered with a dinner, speeches, and a cultural program.

◆ INDEPENDENCE DAY (COMMONWEALTH OF DOMINICA). On November 3, Dominicans hold a dance and social evening to celebrate Discovery and Independence Day, the day Dominica was discovered by Christopher Columbus in 1492. In 1978, Dominica received its independence from Great Britain and became the Republic of the Commonwealth of Dominica.

◆ INDEPENDENCE DAY (DOMINICAN REPUBLIC). On February 27, Dominicans celebrate their independence from Haiti (1844) and on August 16 their restoration from Spain (1865).

See Holidays and Celebrations in Glossary.

Media

◆ CORREO CANADIENSE, (Tel. 416-785-4300, www.elcorreo.ca, 101 Wingold Ave).

- EL POPULAR (SPANISH DAILY), (Tel. 416-531-2495, www.diarioelpopular.com, 2413 Dundas St. W).
- EBEN-EZER INTERNACIONAL (WEEKLY NEWSPAPER), (Tel. 416-635-1558, 1110 Wilson Ave., Suite 202, Downsview). Editor: Oscar Ortiz.
- PAGINA AMARILLA (SPANISH WEEKLY), (Tel. 416-533-7225, 599 Bloor St. W). Editor: Manuel Guerra.
- EL MUNDO LATINO NEWS LTD. (Tel. (905)306-7929, 3050 Kirwin Ave, Mississauga).
- AQUI NUESTRA AMERICA. Sunday, 10:30 a.m. to 11:30 a.m. Contact: Neri Espinoza.
- VENTANA AL BARRIO. Friday, 7:00 p.m. to 9:00 p.m. Contact: Maria Elena Escobar.
- LATIN LIFE NEWS, (Tel. 416-480-1668, 4646 Dufferin St., Unit 2,).

Other radio / TV programs include:
- ONDAS HISPANAS, CIRV Radio International, (Tel. 416-537-1088, 1087 Dundas St. W). Monday to Friday, 5:00 a.m. to 8:00 a.m. Producer: Alberto Elmir; Media Consultant: Arturo Gutiérrez.

Organizations

- ALIANZA CULTURAL HISPANO CANADIENSE is a theatre group, formed in 1978 by newcomers from Spain, along with some Canadians. It has been active in spreading Spanish culture in Toronto by organizing conferences, art exhibitions, musical programs, poetry workshops, and dramas. The group also performs plays by Spanish dramatists such as Federico Garcia Lorca.
- CANADIAN HISPANIC CHAMBER OF COMMERCE, (Tel. 416-480-1668, 2327 Dufferin St., Unit 103). Promotes and helps to expand the Hispanic culture by assisting artists, painters, singers and bands to increase their exposure and the marketing of their art within the Canadian market. Contact Roberto Hausman
- CENTRO NUEVA VIDA (NEW LIFE CENTRE), (Tel. 416-699-4527, 1774 Queen St. E). A community agency that offers an immigrant settlement adjustment program.
- CENTRO PARA GENTE DE HABLA HISPANA (THE CENTRE FOR SPANISH-SPEAKING PEOPLES), (Tel. 416-533-8545, www.spanishservices.org, 2141 Jane St). Provides programs ranging from counselling and orientation services to handicraft workshops and legal clinics. English

classes are available for adults and Spanish classes for adults. Contact: Gerard Ratsech.

◆ CLUB HISPANO, (SPANISH CENTRE), (Tel. 416-760-7210, 3465 Dundas St. W). Formed in 1964 to assist fellow countrymen in need, the club provides a social and cultural contact for the Spanish-speaking community of Toronto. President: Josephina Torre. At the same address: Casa De Espana, Spanish Centre Dancers.

◆ HISPANIC DEVELOPMENT COUNCIL, (Tel. 416-516-0851, 179 John St). Contact: Duberlis Ramos. A social planning council.

◆ LATIN AMERICAN CULTURAL CENTRE OF CANADA, (Tel. 905-507-6479, www.centrolationcanadiensc.com, 801 Ashprior Ave). Director: David Palmer.

◆ PERUVIAN-CANADIAN CHAMBER OF COMMERCE, (Tel. 905-825-8001, www.perucanadacc.com, 66 Wellington Street W, PO Box 1151). President: Jose Zlatar.

◆ THE PERUVIAN COMMUNITY RESOURCE CENTRE IN CANADA, (Tel. 647-341-4092).

◆ PLAZA COMMUNITARIA, (65 Samor Rd) was created to promote, manage and provide education services for adults.

◆ SCHOOL FOR SPANISH DANCE, (Tel. 416-924-6991). Contact: Paula Moreno.

◆ SPANISH CLUB, Glendon College, York University, (Tel. 416-487-6787, 2275 Bayview Ave). Contact: Margarita Feliciano.

◆ SPANISH TRADE COMMISSION, (Tel. 416-967-0488, 8 Bloor St. E).

◆ YORK HISPANIC CENTRE, (Tel. 416-651-9166, 2696 Eglinton Ave. W). A centre for Spanish speaking people. Organizes social activities and offers social services. President: Javier Cepeda.

Other organizations include:

◆ ACADEMY OF SPANISH DANCE, (Tel. 416-595-5753, 401 Richmond St. W., Suite B104). Director: Esmeralda Enrique.

◆ CHAMBER OF COMMERCE ECUADOR-CANADA, (Tel. 416-861-0733; Fax 416-861-8183, 33 Harbour Sq). President: Cesar Tello.

◆ CLUB HISPANO, (Tel. 416-760-7210, 3465 Dundas St. W).

◆ FOLKLORE INCA, (100 Alexander St., Apt. 901). President: Alberto Herrera.

◆ GRUPO AMAZON, (30 Gloucester St). Director: Yasmina Ramzy.

◆ GRUPO AZTECA DE MEXICO, (5 St. Pietro Way). Director: Ramon Franco.

◆ GRUPO DE DANZAS CLUB DEPORTIVO COLOMBIA, (2 Prestwick Ave., Maple). Director: Karen Trujillo.

- GRUPO FOLKLÓRICO "TRADIÓN ARGENTINA", (85 Emmett Ave., Apt. 2012). Coordinator: Hilda Diaz.
- GRUPO FOLKLÓRICO PICHINCHA, (1130 Wilson Ave., Apt. 411). Director: Nancy Supo.
- GRUPO FOLKLÓRICO CHILE, (29 Radwinter Dr.) Director: Patricia Medina.
- GRUPO INSTRUMENTAL "PERU LLACTA", (5 Wales Ave), Director: Ernesto Cardenas.
- HERMANOS HISPANOS FAMILY HELP CLUB, (Tel. 416-658-1818, 129 Day Ave).
- PAULA MORENO SPANISH DANCE, (Tel. 416-924-6991).

Consulates, Trade Commissions and Tourist Bureaus

- CONSULATE GENERAL OF ARGENTINA, (Tel. 416-955-9075, 5001 Yonge St., Suite 201). Consul General: Mr. Julio Miller.
- CONSULATE GENERAL OF CHILE, TRADE COMMISSION OF CHILE, Tel. 416-924-0106, Fax 416-924-2627, 2 Bloor St. W., Suite 1801). Consul General: Mr. Patricio F. Powell Osorio.
- CONSULATE OF COLOMBIA, (Tel. 416-977-0098, Fax 416-977-1025, 1 Dundas St. W., Suite 2108). Consul General: Ms. Gloria Cecilia Rodriguez Varon.
- CONSULATE GENERAL OF COSTA RICA, (Tel. 416-961-6773, 164 Avenue Rd). Honorary Consul General: Peter A. Kircher.
- CONSULATE OF CUBA, (Tel. 416-234-8181, Fax 416-234-2754, 5353 Dundas St. W., Suite 401). Consul General: Mr. Jorge Soberón.
- CUBA TOURIST BOARD, (Tel. 416-362-0700, www.gocuba.ca, 1200 Bay St., Suite 305).
- CONSULATE OF THE DOMINICAN REPUBLIC, (Tel. 416-739-1237, 2727 Steeles Ave. W).
- CONSULATE OF ECUADOR, (Tel. 416-968-2077, 151 Bloor St. W., Suite 450). Consul General: Ms. Mirian Esparza Jacome.
- CONSULATE GENERAL OF EL SALVADOR, (Tel. 416-975-0812, 151 Bloor St. W., Suite 320). Consul General: Dr. Guillermo Iglesias.
- CONSULATE GENERAL OF MEXICO, (Tel. 416-368-2875, Fax. (416) 368-2875, www.consulmex.com, 199 Bay St., Suite 4440). Consul General: Mauricio Toussaint
- CONSULATE GENERAL OF PANAMA, (Tel. 416-651-2350, 2788 Bathurst St. Suite 211). Consul General: Mr. Bosco R. Vallarino M.

Ancient Peruvian culture finds expression in these glorious costumes.

- ◆ CONSULATE GENERAL OF PERU, (Tel. 416-963-9696, www.conperutoronto.com, 10 St. Mary St., Suite 301). Consul General: Mr. Benjamin A. Ruiz Sobero.
- ◆ CONSULATE GENERAL OF SPAIN, (Tel. 416-977-1661). Consul General: Mr. Julio Fernández Torrejón.
- ◆ CONSULATE GENERAL OF URUGUAY, (Tel. 416-730-1289, 300 Sheppard Ave. W., Suite 302). Consul General: Mr. Fernando Lopez Fabregat.
- ◆ CONSULATE GENERAL OF VENEZUELA, (Tel. 416-960-6070, Fax 416-960-6077, 365 Bloor St. E., Suite 1904). Consul General: Mrs. Mirna Quero de Peña.

Prominent Torontonians

Esmeralda Enrique, Dance & Ballet Producer; Guillermo Silva-Marin, Opera Director; Johnny Campuzano, Police Official; Margarita Feliciano, Literature; Mario Guilombo, Human Rights Activist; Glenda del Soto, Concertista; Amanda Martinez, Latin Jazz; Gabriela Montero, International Pianist; Luis Jacob, Art Painter; Maria de Herrera, Harvard University, Papa récipes; Julio Chuquihura, Community Organizer; Roberto Hausman, President Latin American Chamber of Commerce and TV personality; Cesar Palacio, City Councillor.

Contributors: Ana Maria Salaverry, publisher and founder of Latin American Culture House; Juan Reece, Consul General of Ecuador.

Sources: Dr. Oscar Millones; Gary Motta; Henry Ackerman; Julio Chuquihuara; Alex Zisman; Orlando Raucatti.

The Swedish Community

Every December, a young woman wearing a crown of candles appears on the steps of **Queen's Park**, followed by an entourage of white-clad attendants called tarnor (maids) and stjamgossar (star boys). The woman represents Saint Lucia, who died a Martyr's death in 304 A.D., and according to legend, reappeared in Sweden with food for the starving during a great famine. Toronto's Lucia is chosen by the Swedish Church, which then arranges the annual entourage that also appears at the Swedish Christmas Fair at Harbourfront and various sites around the city. The celebration of Saint Lucia's Day reveals the presence of a Swedish community estimated to number 5,000. Toronto is home to the largest concentration of Swedish and Swedish-affiliated companies in North America, reflecting the thriving trade relationship between Sweden and Canada.

During the latter part of the 19th century, Swedes were attracted to North America for its land opportunities. As early as the 1870s, a number of Swedes migrated to the Canadian West. Some moved to British Columbia for its milder climate and job opportunities, while others settled in Northwestern Ontario, working as farmers or in the lumber industry. Following the Second World War, a large number of Swedish businessmen, engineers, and representatives of Swedish export industries came to settle in Toronto.

Swedish cultural activities are centred around the **Swedish Canadian Chamber of Commerce**, the **Swedish Lutheran Church**, and the **Swedish Women's Educational Association (SWEA Toronto)**. An annual event arranged by **SWEA Toronto** is the Swedish Christmas Fair at **Harbourfront**. The fair is held during one weekend in late November and features Swedish Christmas music and carols, handmade Swedish crafts and Christmas decorations, a children's Christmas workshop, and Swedish delicacies such as open-faced sandwiches and glogg (hot mulled wine), as well as the **Saint Lucia Pageant** with folk dancers and children's tableau.

Several interest groups are organized by **SWEA**, including weavers and other craft artists and a folk-dancing troupe which performs regularly in Toronto. Proceeds from traditional events hosted by the organization are used to promote Swedish culture and education, such as a scholarship fund which provides financial support for a student/teacher exchange program between Ontario universities and universities in Sweden.

Places to Go

In **Earl Bales Park** in North York, the main thoroughfare bears the name of Raoul Wallenberg, the Swedish hero who helped thousands of European Jews during the Second World War. A bust of Wallenberg sculpted by Ernest Raab was unveiled in the park in September 1996.

Swedes are famous for their smorgasbord, a table made up of many sliced cheese and meat dishes, herring, pickles, and fish. Popular foods include kottbullar (meatballs accompanied by lingonberry sauce), and a delicacy is gravlax (dill-cured salmon). Traditional dishes include Janssons fretstelse (a dish of anchovies, potatoes, and onions), and arter med flask (pea soup with pork). Swedes enjoy knackebrod (crispbread), and a number of breads including the sweet-tasting limpa bread. Coffee and yeast breads are often served to guests. The traditional drink with smorgasbord is ice-cold akvavit (an aperitif distilled from potatoes or grain and flavoured with caraway seed). The ritual of "skoal" is to look your companion in the eye, say "skoal" and drink the akvavit in one gulp, ending with a final nod to each other.

Milbree Viking, (Tel. 416-425-7200, 133 Laird Dr), carries a variety of Swedish food products, including crispbread, fish products, herring, preserves, and candies. The store welcomes pre-Christmas ordering of the traditional Swedish Christmas ham. **Elizabeth's Deli and Meat Market**, (Tel. 416-921-8644, 410 Bloor St. W), also carries Swedish food products.

IKEA, (Tel. 416-222-4532, 15 Provost Dr, Tel. 416-646-4532, 1475 The Queensway, and Tel. 905-695-5075, 200 Interchange Way, Concord), carries a large line of furniture, house and giftware, and textiles of Swedish design. A Swedish restaurant and cafe serves full meals and light snacks including Swedish open-faced sandwiches. The gourmet shop sells typical Swedish foods such as coffee, jams, soups, cookies, and candies.

Religious Centres, Schools and Other Institutions

Most Torontonians of Swedish descent are Lutheran.

♦ THE SWEDISH LUTHERAN CHURCH OF TORONTO, (Tel. 416-486-0466, 25 Old York Mills Rd), is located at the **Agricola Lutheran Church**. In addition to its Sunday services in Swedish, it arranges many events throughout the year: **Easter Fair**, **National Day** and midsummer celebrations, **Christmas Bazaar** and **Lucia Pageant**. An open house is held once a week for parents and their children (up to 5 years of age).

♦ Swedish magazines and books can be borrowed from the small but well-stocked library.

There are two Swedish schools, in Toronto and Halton. They receive grants from the Swedish government as well as from the **Canadian Heritage Language Program**. The schools are run by parents' associations. Lessons at the Swedish school in Toronto take place on Saturdays between 9:30 a.m. and 12:00 p.m. at **Gateway Public School**, (Tel. 416-397-2970, www.swedishschool.ca, 55 Gateway Blvd).

Holidays and Celebrations

◆ WALPURGIS, April 30, is a joyful festival marking the arrival of spring. In Sweden, the day is celebrated with parties, bonfires, dancing, and traditional singing.

◆ THE OFFICIAL NATIONAL DAY OF SWEDEN is June 6. The holiday was formerly called **Flag Day**, commemorating Sweden's official flag, which was created in 1663. For Swedes living in Toronto, National Day is celebrated with a reception hosted by the Swedish, in addition to a special service and reception held at the **Swedish Lutheran Church**.

◆ MIDSUMMER DAY, celebrated on the third Friday in June, is the festival of the summer solstice. In Sweden, families gather to pick flowers and summer foliage for the decoration of the traditional midsummer pole (Maypole), around which musicians lead dancing, singing, and children's games. In Toronto, festivities are organized by the **Swedish Lutheran Church**.

◆ WINTER SOLSTICE. Since prehistoric times, Swedes have celebrated the winter solstice. According to the Julian calendar, this date was December 13, which later became the name day of the Catholic Saint Lucia. The celebration of the return of light to a northern country now coincides with the commemoration of Lucia, who suffered a martyr's death in 300 A.D. for her Christian beliefs. Before being pierced by a soldier's sword, she miraculously withstood the flames of the pyre where she was sentenced to burn to death. Lucia is believed to appear every December 13 in the early morning, dressed in virginal white, with a blood-red sash, the mark of her martyr's death, and wearing a crown of candles, symbolizing the flames that did not touch her. Lucia celebrations take place in Swedish homes, schools, and workplaces. Women dressed as Lucia serve coffee and traditional breads baked with saffron and raisins, and traditional songs are performed. The **Swedish Canadian Chamber of Commerce** arranges an annual **Lucia Luncheon** for its members and Canadian guests.

♦ CHRISTMAS. Family Christmas celebrations take place on December 24 on Julafton (Christmas Eve). Christmas dinner consists of Lutfisk (dried cod, soaked in lye, cooked, and served with mustard and white sauce), ham (cured in salt and sugar and then boiled or cured), red cabbage, dip-in-the-pot (an ancient tradition of dipping bread in the broth from the ham), and rice porridge (tradition says that singles who get the blanched almond hidden in the dish will be married within a year). Following dinner, the family awaits the arrival of Jultomten, the Christmas gnome who brings gifts. Carrying a big sack, he knocks on the front door and awaits the answer to, "Are there any nice children around?" On Christmas day, there is the Julotta, the traditional morning church service.

See Holidays and Celebrations in Glossary.

Media

♦ KYRKONYTT NEWS (Tel. 416-486-0466, 25 Old York Mills Rd), and calendar of events published quarterly by the **Swedish Lutheran Church**.

Swedish Christmas Fair at Harbourfront Centre.

Organizations

◆ SWEA TORONTO (SWEDISH WOMEN'S EDUCATIONAL ASSOCIATION INTER-
NATIONAL), (Tel. 416-922-8152, www.swea.org/toronto). The
Canadian chapter of an international cultural and networking organi-
zation; promotes Swedish culture, history, language, education, and
heritage. Its largest annual event is the **Christmas Fair** at **Harbourfront
Centre**.

◆ TORONTO SWEDISH FOLK DANCERS AND SINGERS, (www.tsts.ca).

Consulates, Trade Commissions and Tourist Bureaus

◆ CONSULATE OF SWEDEN, (Tel. 416-963-8768, 2 Bloor St. W., Suite 504).
Honorary Consul: Mr. Lars Henriksson.

At the same address:

◆ SWEDISH TRADE COUNCIL INC., (Tel. 416-922-8152;
www.tradewithsweden.com, 2 Bloor St W Suite 2120).

◆ SWEDISH CANADIAN CHAMBER OF COMMERCE, (Tel. 416-925-8661;
www.sccc.ca).

Contributors:Lars Henricksson; Maude M. Vännman.

The Swiss Community

At 4 a.m. on a cold winter morning, a thousand-year-old Swiss tradition is brought to life as masked revellers parade through city streets with fifers and noisy drums to wake the neighbourhood. The **Basel Carnivale**, held on the Sunday closest to February 28, originally celebrated the departure of mercenary soldiers from Switzerland. Toronto's participants, members of the **Canadysli** carnival group, warm up from the brisk morning parade in Etobicoke by eating quiche and a traditional hearty soup.

Although they are a small community in Toronto, with only 3,500 members, the Swiss have played a role in Canada's history. Swiss soldiers served in Acadia in 1604, and pioneer Sebastian Fryfogel (1791–1873) is credited with opening the Huron Tract east of Lake Huron. The Swiss are one of the oldest ethnic communities in Ontario, dating back to 1786 when a group of Swiss-born Mennonites left Pennsylvania and moved into York, Niagara, and Waterloo counties. Other early settlements included Zurich, Ontario, named after the Swiss city and founded in 1856 by a group of farmers from Berne.

Most of the early settlers who came to Toronto and the surrounding areas were agricultural workers and dairy farmers. In 1918, the **Swiss Club of Toronto** was formed to provide cultural, social, and recreational activities for special-interest groups. Today, members of the **Swiss Rifle Club** still practise traditional Swiss shooting exercises using single-shot rifles.

A wave of immigration between 1960 and 1974 brought Swiss professionals to Canada, many contributing to trade, industry, and banking. In Toronto, hotel administrators and chefs have bolstered the reputation of the city's hospitality and tourism industry. Swiss-born academics and professors lecture at the city's universities, and in the towers of Toronto's financial centres, world-renowned Swiss banks have established offices.

Places to Go

A monument to Sir Frederick Haldimand (1718–1791) can be found in a park at the **University of Toronto**. The Swiss-born Haldimand was the

Governor of Quebec and was later responsible for establishing the Loyalist refugees in Ontario at the end of the American Revolution.

Toronto's Swiss restaurants offer traditional veal dishes cooked in cream sauces, or popular fondues and raclettes made with Swiss Emmenthal and gruyère cheeses. Swiss cuisine unites three cultures: French, German, and Italian. Bread and rosti (coarsely shredded potatoes cooked in butter) are the staples of a Swiss meal. Kirsch (a cherry spirit) is a popular drink enjoyed with fondue, while cafe au lait (coffee mixed with hot milk) is appropriate anytime.

Part of a 50-year-old Swiss chain, The **Academy of Culinary Arts**, (Tel. 416-486-1859, 1703 Bayview Ave), sells imported Swiss products and accessories. **Swissmar Imports Ltd.**, (Tel. 905-764-1121, 35 East Beaver Creek Rd., Richmond Hill), imports products from Switzerland. **Swiss Herbal Remedies Ltd.**, (Tel. 905-886-9500, 35 Leek Cr., Richmond Hill), carries Swiss health and beauty products.

Precision Swiss watches and clocks by **Omega**, **Tissot**, **Girard-Perregaux**, **Rolex**, and **Bretling** are available at various Toronto stores, including the 70-year-old **Swiss Watchmakers**, (Tel. 416-922-2622, 512 Yonge St). Swiss watches of high calibre can also be found at The **Royal de Versailles**, (Tel. 416-967-7201, 101 Bloor St. W).

Religious Centres, Schools and Other Institutions

The Swiss belong to many denominations, although they are predominantly Roman Catholic and Protestant.

Two Swiss financial institutions are:
- ◆ CREDIT SUISSE FIRST BOSTON, (Tel. 416-352-4600, 100 King St. W).
- ◆ UBS BANK (CANADA), (Tel. 416-343-1800, 154 University Ave., Suite 800).

Holidays and Celebrations

- ◆ NATIONAL DAY. Cultural events, speeches, dancing, and singing highlight the celebrations on National Day, August 1. Switzerland existed as a confederation as early as 1291, although it was not officially named until 1803. In 1988, on the 70th anniversary of the **Swiss Club of Toronto**, joint festivities were held with National Day that included a barbecue in the countryside as well as a huge celebration in the **CNE**.
- ◆ GRUEMPELTOURNIER (SOCCER TOURNAMENT) is held every summer for members of the **Swiss Club** and their family and friends.

See Holidays and Celebrations in Glossary.

Media

◆ SWISS RADIO, CHIN 100.7 FM, (Tel. 416-531-9991, 622 College St). Saturday, 6:30 a.m. to 7:00 a.m. Host: Markus Rickli.

◆ TELL TALE, (Tel. 416-733-1827, Fax 416-733-7663, 238 Willowdale Ave), is delivered free to the members of the **Swiss Club**. Publisher: Heidy Lawrance.

Organizations

◆ THE SWISS CLUB TORONTO, which meets in various locations, is the largest and oldest Swiss organization in the city, with more than 500 members. President: Erika Tiéche, (Tel. 416-424-4661).

Groups that belong to the Swiss Club include:

◆ AMICALE ROMANDE, (Tel. 416-488-6493). Contact: Jean-Marc Velen.

◆ BOWLING, (Tel. 905-634-3824). Contact: Doug Gross.

◆ FIVE-PIN BOWLING, (Tel. 905-837-0455). Contact: Erika Roth.

◆ GYMNASTICS, (Tel. 416-534-5141). Contact: Suzi Hubler.

◆ JASS SECTION, (Tel. 905-513-1825). Contact: Albert Lenz.

◆ MEN'S GROUP, (Tel. 416-493-8025). Contact: Arno Sigrist.

◆ SWISS RIFLE CLUB, (Tel. 905-707-0243). Contact: Heinz Vollenweider.

◆ WOMEN'S SECTION, (Tel. 416-223-7257). Contact: Elizabeth Walder.

◆ YOUNG SWISS, (Tel. 416-593-4323). Contact: Daniel Kobler.

◆ YODEL CHOIR, (Tel. 416-249-2076). Contact: Urs Doerig.

Consulates, Trade Commissions and Tourist Bureaus

◆ SWISS CONSULATE GENERAL, (Tel. 416-593-5371, 154 University Ave., Suite 601). Consul General: Mrs. Bernadette Hunkeler Brown.

◆ SWISS CANADIAN CHAMBER OF COMMERCE (ONTARIO), (Tel. 416-278-1779, 154 University Ave., Suite 601). The chamber holds monthly business luncheon meetings with speakers from the business community. President: Tom Grohmann.

Contributors: Sonia Evans; Ernest Keller; Dr. Alexander Lang; Claude Duboulet, Consul General; Ursula Sigrist; Arno Sigrist.

The Tamil Community

In 1983, there were fewer than 5,000 Tamils living in Toronto. Today, the community is one of the city's largest with 150,000 members. Serving the needs of Tamils are 19 publications, four business directories, more than 100 restaurants and caterers, and five Canadian Tamil Broadcasting Corporations, which provides 24 hours a day of radio programming.

Back in the early 1960s, there were only a few Tamil families living in Canada. Large-scale immigration began in the early 1980s, when thousands fled Sri Lanka after riots in the capital city. By 1988, there were more Tamils living in Canada than in Australia, New Zealand, or any country in Europe.

The community formed its first organization in 1976. It is now the **Tamil Eelam Society**, an organization that helps members adjust to life in Canada. Tamil restaurants and businesses are located at most major intersections in Toronto's east end.

Places to Go

◆ **Hopper Hut Restaurant**, (Tel. 416-299-4311, 880 Ellesmere Rd). Serves hoppers (French crabs), rice, rotis, curries, and string hoppers (crab noodles).

Other restaurants in the city include **Can-Cey Restaurant**, (Tel. 416-265-5555, 2817 Eglinton Ave. E); **Rashnaa Restaurant**, (Tel. 416-929-2099, 307 Wellesley St. E);**Royal Palace Banquet Hall**, (Tel. 416-265-3360, 3150 Eglinton Ave. E); **Tastay Restaurant**, (Tel. 416-538-7912, 1222 King St. W); **Masala Bites Restaurant**, (Tel. 416-743-5400, 827 Albion Rd); **Madras Mahal Restaurant**, (Tel. 416-269-3666, 286 Markham Rd); **Vinushun Restaurant**, (Tel. 416-752-5760, 2398 Eglinton Ave. E).

Religious Centres, Schools and other Institutions

Among Tamils, Hinduism is the predominant religion. During European rule, some converted to Christianity. Some Tamils became Muslims when Islam spread across Asia.

- **CANADA SRI AYYAPPAN TEMPLE**, (Tel. 416-321-6104, 635 Middlefield Rd).
- **HARE KRISHNA TEMPLE**, (Tel. 416-922-5415, 243 Avenue Rd).
- **HINDU MISSION OF MISSISSAUGA**, (Tel. 905-612-1856, 1808 Drew Rd., Mississauga).
- **OUR LADY OF LOURDES**, (Tel. 416-924-6257, 41 Earl St), Tamil Services, Sunday 5 p.m.
- **PERIYA SIVAN TEMPLE**, (Tel. 416-907-7434, 1960 Ellesmere Rd., Unit 10).
- **SRIDURKA HINDU TEMPLE**, (Tel. 416-759-9648, 30 Carnforth Rd).
- **SRI VARASITHI VINAYAGAR TEMPLE**, (Tel. 416-291-8500, 3025 Kennedy Rd., Unit #10).
- **SRI MEENAKSHI AMMAN TEMPLE**, (Tel. 416-535-6560, 3354 Kingston Rd).
- **SRI SHAKTHI DURGA DEVI TEMPLE**, (Tel. 416-439-9483, 750 Markham Rd).
- **SRI NAGAPOOSHANI AMMAN TEMPLE**, (Tel. 416-412-1289, 5637 Finch Ave. E., Unit 5A).
- **ST. MARIA GORETTI CHURCH**, (717 Kennedy Rd), Tamil Services (Catholic). Sunday and Monday at 4:30 p.m.
- **SRI MUTHU MAARI AMAN TEMPLE**, (Tel. 905-602-2068, 3057 Universal Dr., Mississauga).
- **SRI MUTHU VINAYAGAR TEMPLE**, (Tel. 416-413-7747, 435 Parliament St).
- **SIVAN TEMPLE**, (Tel. 416-742-8484, 80 Brydon Dr).
- **TAMIL CHRISTIAN CHURCH OF CANADA**, (Tel. 416-449-4802, 37 Marchington Circ).
- **THE HINDU TEMPLE OF CANADA**, (Tel. 905-883-9109, 10865 Bayview Ave., Richmond Hill).
- **TAMIL CO-OP HOMES**, (Tel. 416-538-6015, 20 Wade Ave), offers Saturday language classes. Tamil language classes are offered during the school year by the Toronto Board of Education.
- **THIRUCHENTHUR MURUGAN TEMPLE**, (Tel. 416-744-9568, 2500 Finch Ave. W., Unit 10).

Holidays and Celebrations

Christian and Muslim religious days are celebrated by some Tamils.
- **NEW YEAR'S**, January 1, is celebrated with midnight prayers in Hindu temples. However, Tamil New Year falls on April 14 each year and their first obligation is to visit temples and renew their vows and make New Year resolutions which guide them to achieve their goals in life.

◆ HINDU FESTIVAL DAYS are Thai-Pongal, Tamil New Year, and Deepavali.

See Holidays and Celebrations.

Media

◆ CANADIAN TAMIL BROADCASTING CORPORATION, (Tel. 416-429-2822, www.ctbc.com, 86 Laird Dr). Provides 24 hours of radio programming. Contact: Kandi Sivasothy.

◆ CANADIAN TAMIL RADIO, (CTR-24hrs)(Tel. 416-264-0699, 2401 Eglinton Ave. E).

◆ CANADIAN THAMIL OSAI RADIO, (Tel. 416-292-2262, 30 Loggerhead Grv).

◆ POTHIKAI, (Tel. 416-961-4691, 2347 Eglinton Ave. E). Editor: Nirupa Thangavetpillai.

◆ TAMILS' GUIDE, (Tel. 416-615-4646, www.tamilguide.com, 2390 Eglinton Ave. E., Suite 203).

◆ TVI TAMIL TELEVISION, (Tel. 416-593-9300, 501 Passmore Ave., Unit 34).

◆ WORLD TAMIL, CJMR 1320, (Tel. 416-461-5991, 64 Eaton Ave). Everyday, 7:00 p.m. to 8:00 p.m.

◆ VOICE OF TAMILS, ℅ World Tamil Movement, (Tel. 416-335-0622, 39 Cosentino Dr). A bi-weekly newspaper published by the World Tamil Movement. Editor: Kamal Vasan.

Organizations

◆ ACADEMY OF TAMIL ARTS AND TECHNOLOGY, (Tel. 416-757-9601, 2130 Lawrence Ave. E., Suite 200B).

◆ CANADIAN MOVEMENT FOR TAMIL CULTURE, (Tel. 905-848-5633).

◆ FEDERATION OF ASSOCIATIONS OF CANADIAN TAMILS, (Tel. 416-498-3228, 2191 Warden Ave., No. 202).

◆ SOUTH ASIAN WOMEN'S CENTRE, (Tel. 416-537-2276, 1332 Bloor St. W). Provides counselling to South Asian women.

◆ TAMIL EELAM SOCIETY OF CANADA, (Tel. 416-265-0514, 3150 Eglinton Ave. E., Unit 6; and Tel. 416-536-5678, 1212 Bloor St. W). An organization helping Tamils with immigration, the **Language Instruction for Newcomers to Canada** program, counselling workshops, seminars, and other matters. President: Mr. Thambipillai Puvananathan.

◆ TORONTO TAMIL SENIORS ASSOCIATION, (Tel. 416-323-9086, 275 Bleecker St).

◆ **WORLD TAMIL MOVEMENT**, (Tel. 416-335-0622, 39 Cosentino Dr).

Consulates, Trade Commissions and Tourist Bureaus

◆ **CANADIAN TAMILS' CHAMBER OF COMMERCE**, (Tel. 416-335-9791, www.ctcc.ca, 5200 Finch Ave. E., Suite 301). President: Mr. Mano Thillainathan.

The Thai Community

Every April 13, diners at the **Bangkok Garden Restaurant** take aim at each other with water pistols supplied by the restaurant. The tradition of splashing one's friends with water is considered a gesture of goodwill and is practised widely in Thailand on this day as a way to celebrate the New Year.

Thailand, a constitutional monarchy in Southeast Asia, was formerly the Kingdom of Siam and is often associated with the romance of exotic lands depicted in fairy tales. Today, Thailand has become an important trading partner with Canada. Shelves in Toronto's supermarkets and Chinatown's shops carry canned tuna, shrimp, pineapple, rice, noodles, peppers, vegetables, and spices imported from Thailand. Thai silk, considered the best in the world, along with silk flowers and jewelry, can be found in boutiques throughout the city.

The first Thai people in Toronto were a handful of students who came to study in the early 1950s and returned home after their education was completed. Few others came to settle here until the mid-1960s when the Canadian Embassy was established in Bangkok. Many of these early immigrants were former students who were sponsored by their Canadian spouses, while others arrived to work as domestics. The city's Thai are employed as professionals, technicians, and tradespeople. Chefs have brought exotic Thai cuisine and the famed satay sauce—the heart of Thai cooking—to Toronto.

In 1982, Raphi Kanchanaraphi and a group of friends formed **Toronto's Thai Association**. The association organizes two events for the community: an annual New Year's Eve dance with traditional music, dance, and food; and an annual barbecue held on August 7. Several less formal gatherings throughout the year are held at the homes of members.

The **Thai Buddhist Organization** carries out services and wedding ceremonies at Thai temples and at the homes of members. These services are often performed by resident monks or visiting monks from Chicago, Texas, California, or Thailand.

In 1989, Thailand was the featured country at the **Canadian National Exhibition**, with 80 exhibitors in the **International Pavilion**. In 1997, the Canadian Government hosted "**Canada Year of Asia Pacific**," a project intended to promote and enrich multiculturalism in Canada. The **Thai Society of Ontario**, sponsored by the Canadian Government, along with the **Thai Tourist Authority**, held a Thai cultural exhibition at **Scarborough Town Centre**. Thai classical dance, Muay Thai, food, and silk products highlighted the show.

Places to Go

Thai satay dishes (meat and seafood grilled and served with spicy peanut sauce) have become popular among Toronto's restaurant patrons. Thai cuisine is known for its spicy combinations and hot chili peppers. Food is curried with different sauces, but not all Thai food is hot—it can be sweet, sour, salty, or neutral. Rice is served with every meal. National dishes include pla too (fried and salted mackerel), mee krob (sweet crisp noodles with shrimp and banana flower), and tom yam (hot and sour soup).

At **Bangkok Garden**, (Tel. 416-977-6748, 18 Elm St), owner Sherrie Brydson has brought chefs from Thailand to prepare authentic cuisine like phad thai (rice noodles, minced meats, shrimps, and peanuts), seafood dishes, curries, soups, grilled chicken with coconut milk, and barbecued and stir-fried dishes. Decorated with stained glass and wood, statues of Thai dancers, teak, plants, and a flowing brook, the restaurant also features a shop that carries Thai ceramics and crafts. Bangkok Garden also publishes a monthly newsletter outlining Thai festivals celebrated at the restaurant. The **Royal Barge Festival**, a week-long celebration in October, marks the end of a retreat by Buddhist monks during the rainy season. The restaurant offers a menu drawn from an 1809 ceremony at which King Rama I offered food to 2,000 monks. The food was prepared at the royal palace and carried by a gilded royal barge to the temple. Other festivals celebrated at the restaurant include an annual **Elephant Festival** and **Thai New Year**. In November, on **Loy Kratong**, floating offerings are launched on Thailand's waterways. Bangkok Gardens celebrates by offering a festival menu and activities on the restaurant's "river."

Other restaurants include: **Golden Thai Restaurant**, (Tel. 416-868-6668, 105 Church St); **Young Thailand Restaurant**, (Tel. 416-368-1368, 81 Church St), (owner and manager Wandee Young also publishes two famous Thai cookbooks); **Bangkok Paradise Restaurant**, (Tel. 416-504-3210, 506 Queen St. W); **Thai Princess Restaurant**, (Tel. 416-977-8222, 387 King St. W); **Bangkok Thai Restaurant**, (Tel. 416-599-8308, 112 Dundas St. W); **Thailand Restaurant**, (Tel. 905-780-0780, 10088 Yonge St., Richmond Hill); **Vanipha Restaurant**, (Tel. 416-654-8068, 863 St. Clair Ave. W). **Thai Shan**

Inn Restaurant, (Tel. 416-784-1491, 2039 Eglinton Ave. W), serves spiced shrimp, crab claws, po tak (mushroom soup), marinated chicken satay with homemade peanut sauce, mango salad, and phad thai. **Thai Bangkok**, (Tel. 416-598-4701, 412 Spadina Ave); **Sala Thai Restaurant**, (Tel. 416-785-1727, 1100 Eglinton Ave. W).

Food stores in Toronto's Chinatown carry a wide variety of imported canned and dry goods, world famous Thai rice, tropical fruits, and vegetables from Thailand. **Vientiane Trading**, (Tel. 416-743-2911, 2 Bradstock Rd), specializes in Thai products.

Vieng Ratry Night Club and Karaoke, (Tel. 416-744-5067, 295 Eddystone Ave), offers Thai entertainment.

Religious Centres, Schools and Other Institutions

Most members of the Thai community are Theravata Buddhists who worship at the city's temples.

◆ YANVIRIYA TEMPLE II, (Tel. 905-884-8786, 166 Cedar Ave., Richmond Hill), was established in 1993.

◆ RATCHADHAM VIRIYARAM BUDDHIST TEMPLE II, (Tel. 905-374-8849, 4694 Morrison St., Niagara Falls), displays the world's largest Jade stone, weighing 16 tonnes. The temple is a popular attraction.

Both temples often hold daily practices, with morning and evening chanting followed by 30 minutes of meditation. Members of the Thai community often bring their friends and families to group meditation retreats at the temples. The congregation includes Laotians, Cambodians, Vietnamese, Chinese, and Canadians.

◆ THAI-BUDDHIST ORGANIZATION, (5 Devin Rd., Aurora). Contact: Mr. or Mrs. Salayajivin.

◆ THAI STUDENTS' ASSOCIATION OF THE UNIVERSITY OF TORONTO, (thaiu-toronto@yahoo.com).

Holidays and Celebrations

The following religious holidays are commemorated:

◆ MAKHA PUJHA DAY remembers the **First Council of Buddhist Monks**, led by the Buddha in India in 659 B.C.

◆ VESAK DAY celebrates the Buddha's birthday in 624 B.C.

◆ KHAOPUNSA DAY is a day when people offer requisites to the monks.

- **CANADA AND WORLD PEACE PARADE.** On the first weekend in June, both temples join with 34 temples and organizations to celebrate the Canada and World Peace Parade that moves from **Toronto City Hall** to **Queen's Park**.
- **QUEEN'S BIRTHDAY.** Thai communities across Canada celebrate Her Majesty Queen Sirikit's birthday on April 12.
- **SONGKRAN (THAI NEW YEAR)** is held on April 13 according to the Lunar calendar. It is also the water festival, featuring the blessing of waters. The day is celebrated in temples with religious and family celebrations.
- **KING BHUMIPOL'S BIRTHDAY** is celebrated on December 5. In Thailand, the long reigning King Bhumipol and Queen Sirikit are well-respected figures. The **Thai Society of Ontario** often organizes a trip to the Thai Embassy in Ottawa for a weekend of ceremonies, speeches, and dinners to toast the health of the popular king.
- **NEW YEAR'S EVE.** Every December 31, the **Thai Association** organizes a New Year's Eve party, complete with authentic Thai cuisine, dancing, and music.

See Holidays and Celebrations in Glossary.

Media

- **FAIRCHILD RADIO,** AM 1430, (Tel. 905-889-1430, 135 East Beaver Creek Rd., Richmond Hill). Saturday 10:00 p.m. to 12:00 a.m. Producer: Prasert Budsinghkhon.

Consulates, Trade Commissions and Tourist Bureaus

- **ROYAL THAI CONSULATE GENERAL,** (Tel. 416-367-6750, 40 King St. W., 41st floor). Consul General: Richard Meech. Consul: Bill Dickinson.

Prominent Torontonians

Sarit Buracond, President, Thai Society of Ontario; Prasert Budsinghkhon, radio producer; Raphi Kanchanaraphi, Canadian Badminton Team trainer; Wandee Young, restaurant owner and author of two Thai cookbooks; Dr. Nitas Kongkam, physician; Arunee Mandlsohn, Mr. and Mrs. M. Salayajivin, Theravard Buddhist Centre.

Contributors: Bill Dickinson, Thai Consul; Pramunan Dickinson; Kove Dusit Kow.

The Turkish Community

Throughout the year, 10,000 Turkish-speaking members celebrate their culture with a Turkish theatre troupe and heritage classes.

There were Turks in Canada as early as the 1880s, but the first large group was made up of students and visitors who applied to stay in the country permanently in the 1950s. The last decade has seen the largest wave, with immigrants coming from Turkey and Cyprus, as well as from the neighbouring countries of Yugoslavia, Greece, Bulgaria, and Middle East countries.

One of the first Turkish organizations in the city was the **Turkish-Canadian Friendship Association**, founded in 1964 by a group of Turkish workers from Germany. Located in the **Kensington Market** area, it was a social club and information centre for new immigrants. In the 1970s, the Turkish community helped reconstruct a mosque on Annette Street. Today, the community owns its own mosque at Pape Avenue and Gerrard Street.

In the mid-1990s, **Turkish Canadian Social Services** was established to help orientate Canadian Turks to their new country. It provides economic and social support, as well as family services.

Mississauga is home to a large number of Turkish Cypriots. Other members of the community are scattered across Toronto with areas of concentration in Don Mills, Thorncliffe Park, and Downsview. Skilled or semi-skilled tradespeople have furthered industry in the city and Turkish professionals include engineers, doctors, dentists, accountants, and teachers.

Turkish folklore groups participate in various cultural activities in Canada.

Places to Go

Popular Turkish foods such as dried apricots, beans, tomato paste, olives, fish products, Turkish pizza, Turkish shish kebab, Turkish delight, halva, coffee, pistachios, raisins, and figs are available at various Turkish markets including: **Marhce Istanbul**, (Tel. 416-782-8668, 3220 Dufferin St., Unit 10A). Imported leather goods and fashions from Turkey are available at **Janan Boutique**, (Tel. 416-222-4742, 2901 Bayview Ave).

Turkish restaurants include: **Anatolia Restaurant**, (Tel. 416-207-0596, 5112 Dundas St. W); **Istanbul Turkish Delights**, (Tel. 416-788-8912, 5112 Dundas St); **Club OV's**, (Tel. 416-533-9588, 1302 Queen St. W); **Turkuyem Restaurant**, (Tel. 416-621-4860, 290 The West Mall); **Pizza Memo** (three locations) (Tel. 416-654-3654, 1216 St. Clair Ave. W, Tel. 416-516-3030, 551 Bloor St. W, and Tel. 416-531-3400, 1407 Queen St. W).

Ankara Library, (Tel. 416-489-9371, 501 Eglinton Ave. E). Small community library that contains mostly books on Turkish history and literature.

Religious Centres, Schools and Other Institutions

Turks are Muslims with a secularized approach to religion.

◆ THE TURKISH MOSQUE, (Tel. 416-469-2610, at 336 Pape Ave), was established in 1984.

◆ FATIH MOSQUE, (Tel. 416-462-1401, 182 Rhodes Ave).

◆ MELVANA MOSQUE, (Tel. 416-784-2013, 65 Wingold Ave).

Another group of Turks are more fundamental in their approach to religion.

◆ ANATOLIA ISLAMIC CENTRE, (Tel. 905-629-4764, 5280 Maingate Dr., Mississauga), is the main community centre. President: Remzi Mete.

Turkish language classes are held in five different language schools in the GTA, in North York, Mississauga, Toronto, Richmond Hill, and Brampton.

◆ TURKISH LANGUAGE INTERPRETERS AND TRANSLATOR: (Tel. 416-226-9610), Hulya Oyman.

Holidays and Celebrations

◆ THE ANNUAL ANATOLIA BALL with a dinner and dance is organized by the **Turkish Culture and Folklore Society of Canada** in March.

◆ AN ANNUAL PICNIC is organized by the **Turkish Canadian Islamic Heritage Association**.

◆ THE GREAT FESTIVAL (KURBAN BAYRAMI) is an important religious event.

◆ NOAH'S PUDDING, Turkish communities world-wide commemorate this event in January each year by the sharing of Noah's Pudding with neighbours, community groups and the poor. The sharing of Noah's Pudding reminds us that we must all help each other, regardless of differences in cultural or religious beliefs, because we are all part of one community. Noah's Pudding is a symbol for different cultures living together in harmony while each preserves their original identities.

See Holidays and Celebrations in Glossary.

National Days for Turkish-speaking people:
- CHILDREN'S DAY, April 23.
- VICTORY DAY, August 30.
- REPUBLIC DAY, October 28, 29.

Media

- BIZIM ANADOLU, (www.bizimanadolu.com), newspaper published twice a month.
- CANADATURK, (www.canadaturk.ca), newspaper, based in Hamilton.
- TURKUAZ TV, OMNI TV, 545 Lakeshore Blvd. W., Saturdays, 9:30 a.m to 10:00 a.m. and Mondays, 11:30 a.m. to 12:00 p.m. Host: Haber Bulteni.

Organizations

- CANADIAN TURKMEN CENTRE, (29 Tinton Cres).
- CANADIAN TURKISH COMMUNITY CENTRE, (51 Lillac Ave).
- CANADIAN TURKISH BUSINESS COUNCIL, (Tel. 905-568-8300 ext. 288, Fax (905) 568-8330, www.ctbc.ca, 5995 Avebury Rd., Suite 900, Mississauga). Promotes and facilitates the flow of bilateral trade between Canada and Turkey.
- ITU ALUMNI ASSOCIATION, (www.itu.ca, P.O. Box 925, Station F).
- THE FEDERATION OF CANADIAN TURKISH ASSOCIATIONS, (Tel. 416-915-2331, Fax 416-369-0515, www.cnturkfed.org, 1 Yonge St., Suite 1801). Contact: Ozdemir Asli
- TORONTO TURKISH FESTIVAL, (Tel. 416-787-2300, Fax 416-787-2344, 2488 Dufferin St., 2nd Floor, Toronto). .
- TURKISH CANADIAN ISLAMIC HERITAGE ASSOCIATION, (Tel. 416-793-9107, Fax 416-469-2610, 336 Pape Ave). Maintains religious ties between the mosque and the community. President: M. Okem.
- THE TURKISH CULTURE AND FOLKLORE SOCIETY OF CANADA, (660 Eglinton Ave. E., P.O. Box 50001). Founded in 1976 as a non-profit organization to promote an understanding of Turkish culture and folklore among Turks and Canadians; its Turkish theatre group is the only one in North America. Although it generally performs plays in Turkish, in recent years, the group has performed in English with Canadian-Turkish born members. President: Mutlu Aycan.

A colourful performance by the Ottoman Military Band at Queen's Park.

- ◆ SOLIDARITY OF TURKS FROM BULGARIA, (Tel. 905-949-9309, Fax (905) 949-6970, 4101 Westminster Pl., Unit 47). Contact: I. Vataner.
- ◆ IRAQI TURKOMAN ASSOCIATION OF TORONTO, (1306 Bloor St. W).
- ◆ CANADIAN INTERCULTURAL DIALOGUE CENTRE, (Tel. 416-787-2300, www.canadianintercultural.ca, 777 Supertest Rd), Canadian Intercultural Dialogue Centre (CIDC) sponsored by **Canadian Turkish Friendship Community**) has an annual Noah's Pudding Campaign. CIDC promotes free Noah's Pudding across the GTA in churches, hospitals, Police Headquarter, City Hall, Universities and Colleges, senior homes, shelters, and more between the months of January and February.

Consulates, Trade Commissions and Tourist Bureaus

- ◆ CONSULATE GENERAL OF THE REPUBLIC OF TURKEY (10 Lower Spadina Ave, Unit 300), Consul General: Mr. M. Levent Bilgen.

Prominent Torontonians

Dr. Mehmet Bor, President, The Federation Of Canadian Turkish Associations; Ismail Vataner, President, Turkish Federation Community Foundation; Yusuf Sertpolat, President, Canadian Turkish Heritage Association Inc; Celal Ucar, President, Turkish Culture & Folklore Society Of Canada; Ahmer Gokgoz, President, Istanbul Technical University Alumni Association

Of Canada, Ayfer Samancioglu, President, Ankara Library Toronto Inc; M. Fatih Yegul, Executive Director, Anatolian Heritage Federation; Varol Soyler.

Contributors: Faruk Arslan, Journalist, Writer; Filiz Tumer, former Executive Director, Turkish Federation; Al Bukey, ABCO Engineering and founding member of the Canadian Turkish Business Council; Demir Delen, partner, Morrison Hershfield Consulting Engineers; Yaman Uzumeri, Former Chief Building Official, Toronto.

Serving coffee to visitors at the Turkish festival.

The Ukrainian Community

Throughout Toronto, parks, monuments, and the brilliant cupolas and domes of Ukrainian churches reflect Ukrainian culture and tradition in the city. A statue of St. Volodymyr was erected in front of **St. Vladimir Institute** to mark the 1988 millennium of Christianity in Ukraine. Dedicated to freedom, a beautiful monument to the poetess Lesya Ukrainka is found in **High Park**, while the bravery of Ukrainian Canadian soldiers who fought in four wars is commemorated by the **Ukrainian Canadian Memorial Park** at Scarlett Road and Eglinton Avenue West.

In 1991, Metro Toronto's 105,000-member Ukrainian community celebrated the centennial anniversary of its immigration to Canada. Toronto's first known settler of Ukrainian ancestry was Charles George Horetzky, who built a house at 88 Bedford Street in 1891.

Early Ukrainian settlers left the mines and forests of Northern Ontario and the farms of Western Canada to find employment in Toronto's construction, manufacturing, and shipping industries, as well as in factories, hotels, and restaurants. Large numbers of Ukrainians seeking a better life began to arrive in the 1900s and settled in Toronto's downtown St. John's Ward. Another Ukrainian neighbourhood formed in the West Toronto Junction where new industries offered jobs. Erected in 1914, **St. Josaphat's Ukrainian Catholic Church** on Franklin Avenue was the community's first building. It became the centre of community activity with a choir, orchestra, drama circle, and school.

From 1920 to 1950, the Ukrainian language could be heard along Queen Street between Bathurst Street and Spadina Avenue, where boarding houses, parishes, and businesses began to flourish. The area is still home to some Ukrainian Torontonians and holds special memories for those who come back to visit the neighbourhood churches and shops. Ukraine, once a powerful nation in Eastern Europe, lost its independence after a four-year struggle and was absorbed into the USSR in 1922. To provide assistance to those in their war-torn homeland, the Toronto community organized the **Ukrainian Red Cross**.

Between 1918 and 1939, the community continued to grow, as a second wave of Ukrainians arrived. Several branches of Ukrainian national cultural organizations were formed in Toronto. The community expanded to include settlement in the Mimico–New Toronto area and in Scarborough. In 1958, **St. Demetrius Ukrainian Orthodox Church** was established in Etobicoke.

Today, the Toronto Ukrainian community is held in high esteem by Ukrainians all over the world who are conscious of preserving their heritage. The first Ukrainian bookstore and printing office opened on York Street around 1910. At present, the **University of Toronto Press** has published more books on Ukrainian subjects than any publisher outside Ukraine, and the headquarters for the **Ukrainian World Congress** is located in the city.

The strong professional and commercial presence of the community is exemplified by the number of members of the **Ukrainian Professional and Business Association**. Ukrainian credit unions are found throughout the city, and the community has its own trust company, **Community Trust**, on Bloor Street West.

Since the 1960s, Ukrainians from the Prairies have moved east to settle in Toronto, primarily in Bloor West Village. The Village is a vibrant neighbourhood for the Ukrainian community, with art and ceramic exhibits, specialty shops, and stores that carry imported foods.

Places to Go

More than any other street in the city, Bloor Street West between High Park and Jane Street is Ukrainian. The aroma of smoked ham and kobasa blends with the redolence of fresh kolach and poppyseed pastries. Pastry shops and meat markets are family-owned, and the tradition of smoking and curing meat on the premises is still carried on. Bloor West Village contains Ukrainian art exhibits, handicraft displays, and Ukrainian literature. Potted plants along a tree-lined avenue—evidence of a conscientious merchants' association—make the street one of the most pleasant strolls in the city.

The finest collection of works by Ukrainian Canadian artists in the country is showcased at **The Ukrainian Canadian Art Foundation**, (Tel. 416-766-6802, 2118A Bloor St. W). The founders, Mykhailo and Yaroslava Szafraniuk, donated the first books and works of art. The permanent collection includes more than 500 works by four generations of Ukrainian artists, including Holovatsky, Magdenko, Gamula, Hnizdovsky, Kozak, Kurelek, Shostak, Babytsch, Mol, and Krushelnycky. Traditional works embrace classical themes such as King Volodymyr the Great's acceptance of Christianity in 988 A.D., while new works depict Canadian life, such as a model of Leo Mol's bronze statue of prime minister John Diefenbaker. Other talents to arrive from Ukraine are Vitaly Lytvyn and Ivan Ostafiychuk. Close to 20 exhibitions are held annually. Open every day except Monday, from 12:00 p.m. to 6:00 p.m. and Sunday, 1:00 p.m. to 5:00 p.m. Admission is free.

Since 1964, **West Arka Gift Store**, (Tel. 416-762-8751, 2282 Bloor St. W), has specialized in imported handicrafts such as pysanky (decorated Easter eggs), patterned ceramics, richly embroidered tablecloths, and the guitar-like bandura. Ukrainian music plays while customers browse through hundreds of books, including folktales by Ivan Franko, guides for decorating eggs, and children's stories illustrated by renowned artist William Kurelek. Owners Andrew and Olga Chorny offer jewelry with the trident, the Ukrainian national emblem, and records and tapes of artists such as the Bandura Ensemble Choir, Toronto's Burlaka Choir, and the Vesnivka Women's Choir.

Ukrainian cuisine is very robust with smoked meats, wheat dishes, hearty vegetables dishes such as holubtsi (cabbage rolls stuffed with rice and sometimes ground meat), with beets and potatoes being staple foods. A typical meal starts with borsch (beet soup), and may include sausages, pork and beef on a stick, and the popular perohy (fluffy dumplings stuffed with potato, cabbage, and cheese) usually topped with sour cream, butter, and onions. Desserts include cake and fruit preserves, and "makivnyk" (poppy-seed cake roll). Horilka remains the most popular alcoholic beverage.

An old neighbourhood gathering place for the Ukrainian community is the **Future Bakery & Café**, (Tel. 416-922-5875, 483 Bloor St. W, and Tel. 416-266-7259, 95 Front St. E). The Wrzesnewskyj family bakes korovai (wedding bread), Ukrainian paska, kolach, babka, poppy-seed rolls and breads, and syrnyk (cheesecake). Recipes were handed down from grandfather Wrzesnewsky, who baked for Czar Nicholas II's St. Peterburg court until 1915. Following the Second World War, the family fled to Canada and opened a bakery called Future, to symbolize their hope for success in their new country. Today, the bakery includes an attractive cafe offering a menu of Ukrainian delicacies.

Two Ukrainian delis that sell homemade Ukrainian kobasa (sausage), blood pudding, kholodets (jellied pig's knuckles), and head cheese are **Jerry Czarniecki's Astra Meat Market**, (Tel. 416-763-1093, 2238 Bloor St. W), and **Durie Meat Products**, (Tel. 416-762-4956, 2302 Bloor St. W), owned by the Mociak family for more than 25 years. Labels from around the world decorate the Mociak's homey deli, which also offers homemade varenyky, cabbage rolls, pickles, herring, and borsch.

Around Toronto:

The **Ukrainian Museum of Canada**, (Tel. 416-923-3318, 620 Spadina Ave). The Ontario Branch, of the St. Vladimir Institute, displays Ukrainian crafts, such as decorated easter eggs, embroidered regional costumes, icons, heirlooms, ceramic art, and wood carvings. Open Monday to Friday, 10:00 a.m. to 4:00 p.m.

The **Ukrainian Catholic Women's League Museum**, (Tel. 416-762-2066, 2118A Bloor St. W), is maintained by the women's organization to preserve religious, national, and cultural traditions. Open Saturday by appointment.

Ukrainian Shevchenko Museum of Toronto, (Tel. 416-534-8662, www.infoukes.com/shevchenkomuseum, 1614 Bloor St. W). Opened in 1995, it has numerous paintings by and about Taras Shevchenko (1814–1861), as well as various editions of the poet's works. Open Monday, Tuesday, and Friday 10:00 a.m. to 1:00 p.m., and Wednesday and Thursday 1:00 p.m. to 4:00 p.m.

Ukrainian cultural centres are home to many Ukrainian dance and folklore groups that perform at concerts and festivals. Dance groups perform prev'tania, the dance of welcome, which offers the traditional Ukrainian greeting of bread (hospitality) and salt (friendship). Other dances include the high-spirited hopak, tropotianka, and arkan. Many of the centres also maintain libraries.

St. Vladimir Institute, (Tel. 416-923-3318, 620 Spadina Ave), is a community centre that contains an art gallery, library, the **Ukrainian Museum of Canada (Ontario Branch)**, a theatre, and a bookstore. The St. Vladimir Library has a collection of 20,000 books, periodicals, and special holdings that serve as a resource for Ukrainian studies. It includes a music collection, photo archives, posters, and historical maps. The **Ukrainian Canadian Research and Documentation Centre** museum is located on the second floor. Hours are Monday to Friday, 10:00 a.m. to 4:00 p.m.

The **Ukrainian Cultural Centre**, (Tel. 416-531-3610, 83 Christie St), contains a 3,000-volume collection in the **Ukrainian Research and Information Library**. **Plast Ukrainian Youth Association of Canada**, (Tel. 416-769-9998 and (416) 763-2186, 2199 Bloor St. W., 2nd floor). The Plast Library holds 2,000 volumes of Ukrainian literature.

The Robarts Library of the University of Toronto has Canada's largest collection of Ukrainica. The **Peter Jacyk Research Centre** is located here, at 130 St. George St., Room 8002 (Tel. 416-978-0588). Open Monday to

Friday, 10:00 a.m. to 6:00 p.m. **York University**, (Tel. 416-736-2100, 4700 Keele St), also has Ukrainian Studies and a Ukrainica library. Other cultural centres include: **The Ukrainian Orthodox Cathedral of St. Vladimir**, (Tel. 416-603-3224, 406 Bathurst St); and **Ukrainian Community Centre**, (Tel. 416-255-6249, 482 Horner Ave).

Religious Centres, Schools and Other Institutions

In 1988, Ukrainian Canadians held celebrations across the country to mark the millennium of Christianity, adopted by King Volodymyr (Vladimir) in 988 A.D. More than half of Ukrainian Canadians belong to the Ukrainian Orthodox and Ukrainian Catholic churches.

◆ ST. DEMETRIUS THE GREAT MARTYR UKRAINIAN CATHOLIC CHURCH, (Tel. 416-244-5333, 135 La Rose Ave). The church is crowned by an eight-foot-wide dome skylight decorated with depictions of Christ and seven angels, and a traditional resurrection scene glows through a 17-foot-high stained glass window. An adjacent 259-unit senior citizen apartment building, cultural centre, and school form a miniature village around the church (Tel. 416-246-7979, 123 La Rose Ave). The church is home to the **Yavir Dance Ensemble** (formerly called the **Kolomaya Dancers**).

◆ ST. JOSAPHAT'S UKRAINIAN CATHOLIC CATHEDRAL, (Tel. 416-535-9192, 143 Franklin Ave). The community's oldest church, it has a historic altar imported from Lviv and decorated with eight large religious paintings.

◆ HOLY EUCHARIST UKRAINIAN CATHOLIC CHURCH, (Tel. 416-465-5836, 515 Broadview Ave).

◆ ST. ANDREW UKRAINIAN ORTHODOX CHURCH, (Tel. 416-766-7511, 1630 Dupont St).

◆ ST. ANNE'S UKRAINIAN ORTHODOX CHURCH, (Tel. 416-284-9642 or 416-282-9427, 525 Morrish Rd).

◆ ST. BASIL THE GREAT UKRAINIAN CATHOLIC CHURCH AND HALL, (Tel. 416-656-3772, 449 Vaughan Rd).

◆ ST. DEMETRIUS UKRAINIAN ORTHODOX CHURCH, (Tel. 416-255-7506, 3338 Lakeshore Blvd. W).

◆ ST. MARY'S UKRAINIAN CATHOLIC CHURCH, (Tel. 416-531-9944, 18 Leeds St).

◆ ST. MARY'S DORMITION UKRAINIAN CATHOLIC CHURCH, (Tel. 416-603-8049, 276 Bathurst St), was the second Ukrainian Catholic parish building.

◆ ST. NICHOLAS UKRAINIAN CATHOLIC CHURCH HALL & SCHOOL, (Tel. 416-504-4774, 4 Bellwoods Ave).

◆ ST. PETER & PAUL UKRAINIAN CATHOLIC CHURCH, (Tel. 416-291-7401, 231 Milner Ave).

◆ ST. VLADIMIR'S UKRAINIAN ORTHODOX CATHEDRAL, (Tel. 416-603-3224, 406 Bathurst St).

◆ THE FIRST UKRAINIAN PENTECOSTAL CHURCH, (Tel. 416-922-2038, 557 Bathurst St.,).

◆ UKRAINIAN EVANGELICAL BAPTIST CHURCH, (Tel. 416-504-3744, 148 Tecumseth St).

◆ UKRAINIAN SEVENTH-DAY ADVENTIST CHURCH, (Tel. 416-636-2471, 535 Finch Ave. W).

Toronto is an important centre for Ukrainian research and scholarship; a chair of Ukrainian Studies has been established at the **University of Toronto**, and there is a Ukrainian Studies program at **York University**.

The community has three senior citizens' homes:

◆ THE UKRAINIAN HOME FOR THE AGED, (Tel. 416-239-7364, 767 Royal York Rd).

◆ ST. PETER AND PAUL UKRAINIAN COMMUNITY HOME, (Tel. 416-291-3900, 221 Milner Ave).

◆ UKRAINIAN CANADIAN CARE CENTRE, (Tel. 416-243-7653, 60 Richview Rd).

Financial institutions include:

◆ BUDUCHNIST (TORONTO) CREDIT UNION, West Toronto Branch, (2280 Bloor St. W); Mississauga Branch, (Tel. 905-238-1273, 1891 Rathburn Rd. E.); and Scarborough Branch, (Tel. 416-299-7291, 221 Milner Ave.).

◆ COMMUNITY TRUST, (Tel. 416-763-2291, 2271 Bloor St. W).

◆ ST. MARY'S (TORONTO) CREDIT UNION LTD., (Tel. 416-537-2163, 832 Bloor St. W).

◆ SO-USE CREDIT UNION LTD. (HEAD OFFICE), (Tel. 416-763-5575, 2265 Bloor St. W).

◆ UKRAINIAN CREDIT UNION, is Canada's largest Ukrainian credit union: Head Office, (Tel. 416-922-1402, 295 College St); West Toronto Branch, (Tel. 416-762-6961, 2397 Bloor St. W); Etobicoke Branch, (Tel. 416-233-1254, 225 The East Mall); Mississauga Branch, (Tel. 905-272-0468, 3635 Cawthra Rd).

Holidays and Celebrations

◆ BLOOR WEST VILLAGE UKRAINIAN FESTIVAL. This festival runs during the weekend closest to Ukrainian Independence Day, August 24. The weekend celebrations include a parade, cultural events, Ukrainian food, Ukrainian dances, Ukrainian arts and crafts, children's corner plus a pavilion called "It's Fun to be Ukrainian." The event is sponsored by the **Ukrainian Canadian Congress**, Toronto Branch, and the Ukrainian TV Network, "**Kontakt**."

◆ CHRISTMAS. The majority of Ukrainians celebrate Christmas on January 7, with the highlight being the eve, January 6. A Holy Supper of 12 meatless dishes is served in memory of the 12 apostles, and begins when the children see the first star in the evening sky. The father offers a prayer which is followed by the traditional Christmas greeting, "Christ is born." The family responds with, "Let us glorify Him." The traditional meal starts with kutya (boiled wheat mixed with poppy seeds, honey, and sometimes nuts), meant to symbolize family unity and prosperity.

◆ NEW YEAR'S EVE. On January 13, Ukrainians celebrate New Year's Eve with the singing of carols and dances at halls and university youth clubs.

◆ JORDAN DAY, sometimes called "little Christmas," January 19, celebrates the baptism of Christ and Epiphany.

◆ THE BIRTHDAY OF THE GREAT POET AND ARTIST TARAS SHEVCHENKO (1814–1861) is always celebrated on March 9 with poetry readings and a concert.

◆ EASTER sees Ukrainians prepare ornamental eggs or "pysanky." The Easter egg is associated with early Christian ceremonies. Before decorating eggs, they make the sign of the cross and whisper "God, help me," in hope that the religious meanings symbolized in the designs will come true on Easter morning. A decorative ribbon around the egg represents the endless line of eternity; a ladder suggests prayer; leaves or flowers mean life and growth; and the butterfly is a symbol of resurrection. Easter church service begins at midnight and may last until dawn. Another ceremony is the blessing of Easter food baskets in church.

◆ SAINT VLADIMIR (VOLODYMYR) DAY, July 28, recognizes the day in 988 A.D. that King Volodymyr accepted Christianity for his people.

◆ INDEPENDENCE DAY. Since 1991, August 24, Ukrainian Independence Day, has been the year's major holiday. It was previously celebrated on

January 22 to mark the Declaration of Ukrainian Independence in 1918 and the 1919 re-establishment of a united Ukrainian National Republic. Flag-raising ceremonies at **Toronto City Hall**, and dinners, speeches, and a musical performance highlight the festivities.

◆ UKRAINIAN INDEPENDENCE DAY, celebrated on the closest Sunday to August 24, is sponsored by **Ukrainian Canadian Congress, Toronto Branch**.

◆ REMEMBRANCE DAY, November 11, sees Toronto Ukrainians and veterans gather at the **Ukrainian Canadian Memorial Park** in Etobicoke.

◆ SAINT ANDREW'S DAY. On December 13, Ukrainians recognize their patron saint, Saint Andrew, who is said to have erected a cross on the mount where Kiev, the capital of Ukraine, stands. The slanting bar on the cross of many Ukrainian churches signifies the X-shaped cross on which St. Andrew was crucified.

See Holidays and Celebrations in Glossary.

Media

There are over 50 Ukrainian newspapers, magazines, and bulletins published in Toronto. The major ones are:

◆ MEEST (WEEKLY NEWSPAPER), (Tel. 416-236-2007, Fax 416-236-0321, www.meest.net, 99 Six Point Rd).

◆ HOMIN UKRAINY (UKRAINIAN ECHO), (Tel. 416-516-2443, Fax 416-516-4033, 83 Christie St). A weekly newspaper with a readership of over 10,000. Publisher: W. Okipniuk.

◆ NOVY SHLIAKH (NEW PATHWAY), (Tel. 416-960-3424. 145 Evans Ave). A Ukrainian weekly since 1930, with a readership of 7,000. Editor: Ms. Lesia Panko.

◆ SVITLO (THE LIGHT), (Tel. 416-234-1212, 265 Bering Ave). A monthly Catholic magazine with a readership of 3,000, published by the Basilian Fathers in Canada. Editor: Rev. Basil Cembalsta.

◆ KONTAKT UKRAINIAN TV NETWORK, OMNI-TV, (Tel. 416-260-0047, 545 Lakeshore Blvd., W), Saturday 1:00 p.m to 2:00 p.m. Executive Producer: Jurij Klufas.

◆ UKRAINIAN CANADIAN HERALD (MONTHLY NEWSPAPER), (Tel. 416-534-8635, 962 Bloor St. W). Editor: Lari Prokop.

- UKRAINIAN SVITOHLIAD TELEVISION PROGRAM, OMNI-TV, (Tel. 416-260-0047, 545 Lakeshore Blvd. W). Monday, 6:00 a.m. to 7:00 a.m. and Saturday, 8:00 p.m. to 9:00 p.m.
- VISNYK, a quarterly newspaper published by the Ukrainian World Congress, (Tel. 416-323-3020, 145 Evans Ave). Editor: Dr. Wasyl Veryha.
- YUNAK MAGAZINE (YOUTH), (Tel. 416-763-2186, 2199 Bloor St. W). Published six times a year with a circulation of 2,000. Editor: O. Zakydalska.
- ON LINE, (Tel. 416-925-1256, 620 Spadina Ave). A newsletter published by the **Ukrainian Canadian Professional and Business Association of Toronto**.
- PROMETHEUS. CHIN 100.7 FM, (Tel. 416-531-9991, 622 College St). Monday to Friday, 1:30 p.m. to 2:00 p.m.

Organizations

There are more than 200 Ukrainian organizations, societies, and institutions to fill the educational, social, cultural, economic, intellectual, and political needs of the community. The **Ukrainian Canadian Committee** provides the co-ordination needed for such a large community.

- UKRAINIAN CANADIAN CONGRESS, (Tel. 416-323-4772, Fax 416-323-6772, 145 Evans Ave). Established in 1940 as the central coordinating body for the community to protect, enhance, and promote the cultural identity of Ukrainians. This umbrella group includes cultural, religious, and social groups. President: Maria Szkambara. At the same address:
- UKRAINIAN WORLD CONGRESS, (Tel. 416-323-3020, Fax 416-323-3250). Promotes and defends the rights of Ukrainians in the international arena, including human, cultural, and political rights. President: Askold Lozynsky.
- THE UKRAINIAN PROFESSIONAL AND BUSINESS ASSOCIATION OF TORONTO, (Tel. 416-925-1256, 620 Spadina Ave). Publishes a directory of business and professional people, as well as a monthly newsletter. President: Bohdan Chwyl.
- UKRAINIAN CANADIAN SOCIAL SERVICES, (Tel. 416-763-4982, 2445 Bloor St. W). Operates an information bureau to assist the needy, elderly, and immigrants. Volunteers visit the elderly and disabled in their homes, hospitals, and care centres. Weekly discussion groups and seminars are held to promote interest in politics, social services and

health issues. President: Merion Barszczyk. Executive Director: George Mujej.

◆ **UKRAINIAN CANADIAN ART FOUNDATION**, (Tel. 416-766-6802, 2118A Bloor St. W).

◆ **UKRAINIAN CANADIAN RESEARCH & DOCUMENTATION CENTRE**, (Tel. 416-966-1819, Fax 416-966-1820, 620 Spadina Ave). Includes Ukrainian exhibits on pioneers, famine and famous Ukrainians. Monday to Friday, 10:00 a.m. to 4:00 p.m. President: Prof. Wsevolod Isajiw.

◆ **CANADIAN FOUNDATION FOR UKRAINIAN STUDIES**, (Tel. 416-766-9639, Fax 416-766-0599, www.cfus.ca, 2336A Bloor St. W., Suite 205). President: Olya Kuplowska.

◆ **ROYAL CANADIAN LEGION (UKRAINIAN BRANCH)**, (Tel. 416-593-0840, #360, 326 Queen St. W). President: J.B. Gregorovich.

◆ **CANADIAN FRIENDS OF UKRAINE**, (Tel. 416-964-6644, 620 Spadina Ave).

◆ **CANADIAN SHEVCHENKO CULTURAL SOCIETY**, (Tel. 416-480-2440, 39 Castle Knock Rd). President: Andrew Gregorovich.

◆ **CANADIAN UKRAINE CHAMBER OF COMMERCE**, (Tel. 416-234-5334, 302 The East Mall, Unit 609).

◆ **CANADIAN UKRAINIAN IMMIGRANT AID SOCIETY**, (Tel. 416-767-4595, 2150 Bloor St. W., Suite 96).

◆ **CIVIL LIBERTIES COMMISSION, UKRAINIAN CANADIAN COMMITTEE**, (Tel. 416-767-4595, 2150 Bloor St. W., Suite 96). Chair: John Gregorovich.

◆ **PLAST UKRAINIAN YOUTH ASSOCIATION OF CANADA**, Toronto Branch, (Tel. 416-769-9998, 2199 Bloor St. W., 2nd floor). Established in 1936, it is an organization similar to the Scouts.

◆ **SHEVCHENKO UKRAINIAN COMMUNITY CENTRE**, (Tel. 416-255-6249, 482 Horner Ave). Same address: **Ukrainian Opera Choir**.

◆ **ST. VLADIMIR UKRAINIAN INSTITUTE**, (Tel. 416-923-3318, 620 Spadina Ave). Home to: **Slovo Ukrainian Canadian Writers' Association**; **Ukrainian-Canadian Community Women's Council**; the **Ukrainian Librarians Association of Canada**. The institute publishes Visti News quarterly.

◆ **THE UKRAINIAN ACADEMY OF DANCE**, Stefura Dance Studios, (Tel. 416-255-8577, 80 Park Lawn Rd., Suite 221).

◆ **THE UKRAINIAN CULTURAL CENTRE**, (Tel. 416-531-3610, 83 Christie St). Member groups include: **League of Ukrainian Canadians**, National Executive; **League of Ukrainian Women of Canada**, National Executive, (Tel. 416-516-8223); **Ukrainian Youth Association of Canada**, National Executive, (Tel. 416-537-2007); **League of Ukrainian Canadians**, Toronto Branch, (Tel. 416-533-0244); **Ukrainian Youth**

Association, Toronto Branch, (Tel. 416-533-9014); **Dibrova Women's Choir**; **Prometheus Male Choir**; and **Baturyn Marching Band of the Ukrainian Youth Association**.

◆ BARVINOK UKRAINIAN DANCE ENSEMBLE. Practices held at **St. Mary Dormition Church**, (Tel. 905-279-9387, 3625 Cawthra Rd., Mississauga). Artistic Director: Fedir Danylak.

Bloor West Village Ukrainian Festival.

◆ THE UKRAINIAN ORTHODOX CATHEDRAL OF ST. VLADIMIR, (Tel. 416-603-3224, 406 Bathurst St). Organizations at St. Vladimir include: **Ukrainian Self-Reliance Association**, Toronto Branch, founded in 1927; **Ukrainian War Veterans' League**; **Ukrainian Democratic Youth Association of Canada**; **Vesnianka Dance Ensemble**; **Iiarion Dance Ensemble**; and **Desna Dance Company**. **The Ukrainian Canadian Women's Association**, Toronto Branch, founded in 1927, focuses on cultural, educational, and charitable work.

◆ YAVIR SCHOOL OF UKRAINIAN DANCE, (Tel. 416-243-3072, 125 La Rose Ave). Artistic Director: Alexander Nebesnyj.

◆ UKRAINIAN HISTORICAL ASSOCIATION, Toronto Branch, (Tel. 416-536-0402, 215 Grenadier Rd). Contact: Wasyl Veryha.

◆ UKRAINIAN LABOUR TEMPLE (AUUC), (Tel. 416-588-1639, 1604 Bloor St. W).

Consulates, Trade Commissions and Tourist Bureaus

◆ CONSULATE GENERAL OF UKRAINE, (Tel. 416-763-3114, Fax 416-763-2323, 2120 Bloor St. W). Consul General: Mr. Oleksandr Danyleiko.

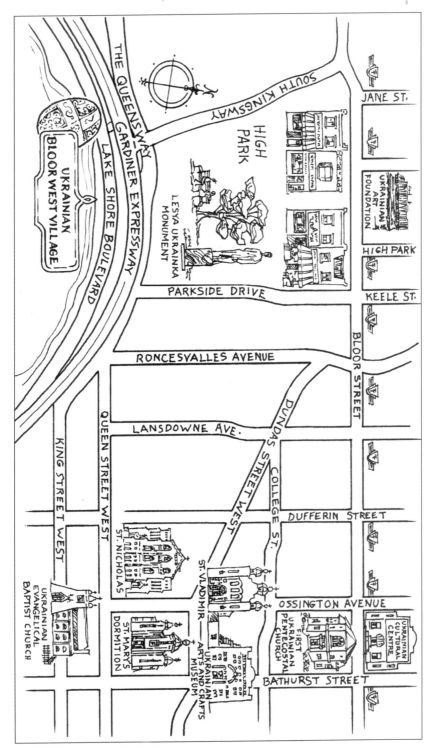

Prominent Torontonians

Oksana Borowik, documentary producer and director; Roman Borys, cellist, member of Gryphon Trio; Daria Darewych, York University art historian; Jurij Darewych, York University physicist; Ivan Fecan, President & CEO, CTVglobemedia; Andrew Gregorovich, librarian, researcher and author; Luba Goy, radio and TV actress; Ihor Ihnatowycz, President & CEO, Acuity Funds and philanthropist; Nadia Jacyk, President, Prombank Investments and philanthropist; Wasyl Janischewskyj, University of Toronto physicist; Alicia Kay-Markson, CTV reporter; Slawko Klymkiw, Canadian Film Centre Executive Director; Gary Kulesha, composer and conductor; Mimi Kuzyk, film and TV actress; Gloria Lindsay Luby, City of Toronto Councillor; Ihor Macijiwsky, documentary producer and photographer; Victor Malarek, CTV reporter, journalist and author; Myroslava Oleksiuk, activist, producer and director; Christina Pochmursky, CBC host and business reporter; Yuri Shymko, former federal and provincial politician; Frank Sysyn, Ukrainian historian and researcher; James Temerty, President, Northland Power and philanthropist; Tanya Tkachenko, pianist, RCM examiner and pedagogue; Ted Woloshyn, radio personality and newspaper columnist; Borys Wrzesnewskyj, federal politician and businessman; John Yaremko, former Ontario Solicitor General; Donna Cansfield, MPP; Walter Petryshyn, lawyer.

Contributors: Andrew Gregorovich, President, Canadian Shevchenko Cultural Society, and editor of Forum: A Ukrainian Review; Mary Szkambara, former President, Ukrainian Canadian Congress, Toronto Branch; Mary Lopata, Ukrainian Canadian Congress; Bob Myndiuk, Canadian Ukraine Chamber of Commerce.

The Vietnamese Community

Throughout the city, Vietnamese-owned jewelry stores, printing shops, real estate agencies, and auto collision companies mirror a sprouting community. Intermingled with the fruit markets and restaurants of Toronto's Chinatown, Vietnamese restaurants have added to the pleasure of dining out, with the exotic new flavour of fish sauce and the adventure of drinking specially filtered and prepared Vietnamese coffee. More than 60 Vietnamese-owned restaurants, cafes, and specialty stores have opened since 1981.

Many Vietnamese immigrated to Canada after Saigon (now Ho Chi Minh City) fell to the North Vietnamese in 1975. About 45,000 Vietnamese have made Toronto their home. The first newcomers were students who attended the city's universities during the 1950s and '60s. Professionals, bureaucrats, and military personnel were among the few thousand refugees who settled in Toronto in the late 1970s. In the early 1980s, 120,000 Vietnamese immigrated to Canada. Toronto became the welcoming city for some 18,000 South Vietnamese "boat people"—so named for fleeing their homeland in tiny boats for refugee camps in Hong Kong, Malaysia, Indonesia, Thailand, and the Philippines.

Members of the community have been successful in adapting to a new life. Vietnamese now own homes in Mississauga, Etobicoke, Scarborough, and other areas close to the manufacturing industries where many are employed.

The Vietnamese value education and the pursuit of excellence in their chosen professions. This is reflected by the numerous Vietnamese dentists, doctors, and pharmacists practicing in the city, and by students who excel in computer science programs.

Places to Go

The Vietnamese are coffee connoisseurs who enjoy strong blends. The preparation is a ritual which allows coffee to slowly drip through a filter and into a cup containing milk. Coffee is enjoyed three ways: cafe Sua is made with condensed milk; cafe Da is served with ice; and cafe Sua Da contains both milk and ice. The Vietnamese believe that ice brings out the coffee's richest flavour. Various Vietnamese coffee houses are located throughout the downtown area, including: **Café Lang Van**, (Tel. 416-536-5482, 70 Ossington Ave); **Anh Dào**, (Tel. 416-598-4514, 383 Spadina Ave); **Cafe Dong Phuong**, (Tel. 416-534-5939, 1532 Dundas St. W); and **DaLat Coffee**, (Tel. 416-537-0769, 182 Ossington Ave).

Vietnamese cuisine consists mainly of fish and vegetable dishes. Popular meals include pho (rice noodle in chicken or beef soup), cha gio (deep-fried rolls with meat, shrimp, and mushrooms), and chao tom (shrimp paste wrapped with sugar cane and barbecued). Noodles are rice-based and fresh spices like cilantro, dill, and mint are used in cooking. Known for its lightness and subtlety, Vietnamese cuisine is closely related to Chinese cooking. The main difference is that the Vietnamese use nuoc mam (fish sauce) instead of soya bean sauce for flavouring.

At **Anh Dao**, (Tel. 416-598-4514, 383 Spadina Ave), owned by Luu Vinh Phu and his wife Ngo, who came to Canada in 1979, the menu items include shrimp and pork rolls, shredded pork, spareribs, banh cuon cha lua (Vietnamese meat lasagna), and barbecued beef coupled with a basket of beansprouts, mint leaves, lettuce, and coriander that can be rolled in thin rice pancakes. Popular beverages are mango and jack fruit juice. The room is adorned with small Buddhist shrines and watched over by Oriental fighting fish.

Indochine Thai Vietnamese Restaurant, (Tel. 416-922-5840, 4 Collier St), serves French-style Vietnamese and Chinese cuisine in an elegant candlelit atmosphere. No M.S.G. is used in the cooking, which includes a seafood firepot, beef fondue, barbecued oyster in a garlic citron sauce, spareribs, asparagus soup, and cornish hen spiced with five seasonings.

Other restaurants that serve Vietnamese cuisine include: **Bun Saigon**, (Tel. 416-504-2188, 252 Spadina Ave); **Gia Phung**, (Tel. 416-658-3993, 1768 St. Clair Ave. W); **Kim Vietnamese Restaurant**, (Tel. 416-596-8589, 546 Dundas St. W); **Pho Hoa**, (Tel. 416-597-8395, 393 Dundas St. W., #8); **Golden Turtle**, (Tel. 416-656-1549, 1776 St. Clair Ave. W); **Saigon Flower Restaurant**, (Tel. 416-533-6629, 1138 Queen St. W); and **Vietnamese Garden Restaurant**, (Tel. 416-609-9796, 4188 Finch Ave. E).

Vietnamese groceries are available at **Lawrence Supermarket**, (Tel. 416-248-8078, 1635 Lawrence Ave. W); **Tai Kong Supermarket**, (Tel. 416-581-0129, 310 Spadina Ave); **Tuong Phàt 1 Supermarket**, (Tel. 416-249-4302, 1611 Wilson Ave); and **Hung Phàt Supermarket**, (Tel. 416-604-4918, 604 Runnymede Rd).

The **Vietnam Bookstore**, (Tel. 416-595-5199, 415 Spadina Ave), carries a wide selection of Vietnamese books, novels, and dictionaries as well as videos and cassettes. Artists include Khanhy Ly, Elvis Phuong, Ngoc Minh, and Duy Quang. Hoang Oanh is a popular singer of traditional music. **Hanh Phuc Video**, (Tel. 416-536-1311, 210 Ossington Ave), rents and sells Vietnamese videos.

Religious Centres, Schools and Other Institutions

The community's dominant religions are Christianity and Buddhism. The faithful attend churches and temples located throughout the city.

◆ MISSION OF THE VIETNAMESE MARTYRS, (Tel. 416-769-8104, 161 Annette St).

◆ TORONTO VIETNAMESE ALLIANCE CHURCH, (Tel. 416-658-1620, 9 Boon Ave).

◆ VIETNAMESE EVANGELICAL CHURCH, (Tel. 905-274-4636, 1015 Alexandra Ave., Mississauga).

Holidays and Celebrations

The Vietnamese follow the lunar calendar and as a result holidays fall on different dates from year to year.

◆ NEW YEAR'S DAY, celebrated in January or February, is one of the

Young Vietnamese dancer.

most important events. Celebrations organized by various groups include cultural activities such as music, dancing, fashion shows, food displays, poetry, and Vietnamese art exhibitions. Families visit each other to exchange gifts and share in a New Year's meal. It is regarded as a time to forget past mistakes and plan a better future.

◆ WOMEN'S DAY falls in March and pays tribute to the Trung Sisters, two heroines who fought the invading Chinese in the year 40 A.D. One of the sisters, Trung Trac, reigned as Queen of Vietnam for three years. On this day, women's groups meet for a ceremony, refreshments, and entertainment.

◆ FATHERLAND FOUNDER'S DAY is celebrated in March or April in honour of the First Dynasty, which ruled the nation more than 4,000 years ago.

- BLACK APRIL, on April 30, commemorates the collapse of the Saigon government in 1975.
- A MID-AUTUMN CHILDREN'S FESTIVAL is held in September.

See Holidays and Celebrations in Glossary.

Media

- THOI BAO (THE VIETNAMESE NEWSPAPER), (Tel. 416-925-8607, www.thoibao.com, 1114 College St). Publisher: Dave Nguyen.
- BAN VIET, (Tel. 416-536-3611, 1364 Dundas St. W). A monthly magazine.

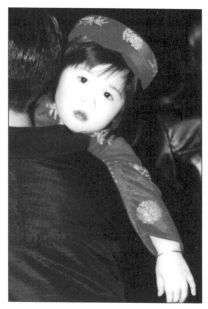

The face of today's Vietnamese-Canadians.

- SAIGON CANADA WEEKLY MAGAZINE, (Tel. 416-534-0989, 851 College St).

Organizations

- THE VIETNAMESE ASSOCIATION OF TORONTO, (Tel. 416-536-3611, Fax 416-536-8364, www.vatoronto.ca, 1364 Dundas St. W). Founded in 1972 by a group of students, it is the main social and cultural focus for the community. Provides employment counselling, translations, and seniors' services, and publishes a Vietnamese monthly magazine, a newsletter named **Ban Viet**, and an English bi-monthly newsletter. President/Chair: Dr. Terry Ho.
- VIETNAMESE ELDERLY ASSOCIATION OF ONTARIO, (Tel. 416-588-8532, 2001 Dundas St. W). President: Lam Nguyen.
- VIETNAMESE YOUTH AND WOMEN'S CENTRE OF TORONTO, (Tel. 416-534-8842, 1313 Queen St. W).
- VIETNAMESE WRITERS ABROAD P.E.N. CENTRE, ONTARIO CHAPTER. An association of Vietnamese poets, playwrights, essayists, editors, and novelists, (Tel. 905-607-8010, P.O. Box 218, Station U). President: Cung Vu.
- THE VIETNAMESE PROFESSIONALS' ASSOCIATION, (Tel. 416-784-5660, 85 Varna Dr).

Prominent Torontonians

Nguyen Van Truong Quang, P.Eng., President, Vietnamese Association of Toronto; Ho Van Thua, Ph.D., Past President, Vietnamese Association of Toronto; Dr. Nguyen Hoanh Khoi, board member, Vietnamese Association of Toronto; Nguyen Dat, P.Eng., publisher, *Thoi Bao* newspaper; Nguyen Ngoc Ngan, MC, international performer, writer; Tran Gia Phung, historian, writer; Do Ky Anh, CA, Past President, Vietnamese Association of Toronto; Tran Trung Luong, writer; Phung Quang Tuan, educator, professor; Nguyen Tang, artist; Do Khanh Hoan, authors, writers; Huynh Thien, writer.

Richard Nguyen
Philanthropist and proprietor of
successful Nice One Nails franchise.

Contributors: Ban Viet; Bich N. Pham, Vietnamese Association of Toronto; Do Trong Chu; Nguyen Huu Nghia; Publisher Lang Van; Henry Thuan, *Thoi Bao* newspaper; Trac Bang Do, prominent entrepeneur.

The Welsh Community

On St. David's Day (Dydd Gwyl Dewi), Toronto's Welsh community gathers together to sing "Hen Wlad Fy Nhadau" ("Land of My Fathers"), the Welsh national anthem, and drink a toast to St. David, the 6th-century Welsh monk and patron saint of Wales. The annual event is held on the weekend closest to March 1st. It's organized by the century-old **St. David's Society** and features a formal dinner and a speaker at a downtown hotel. The **Dewi Sant Welsh United Church**, holds a dinner and a "Noson Lawen" (Merry Evening) at the church.

Wales has been politically united with Britain since 1536, yet the Welsh have retained their distinct culture and language. Welsh sailors joined John Cabot on his 1497 voyage to the coast of Newfoundland over 500 years ago. Other Welsh explorers included Sir Thomas Button, who commanded an expedition in search of the Northwest Passage in 1612, and David Thompson, a trader and explorer with the North West Company.

Among the early pioneers in the city was Welsh-born Elizabeth Gwillim, the wife of Lieutenant Governor John Graves Simcoe. A diarist and an artist, she chronicled the events and scenes of Toronto's settlement in the late 1700s. Another Welsh native was Augustus Jones, the provincial land surveyor and road engineer of Upper Canada, who marked out the site of York and graded Yonge Street from York to Holland River in 1796. Jenkin Williams was the first secretary of the Council of Lower Canada, and lawyer William Dummer Powell became Chief Justice of Upper Canada in 1816.

Three Welsh regiments served in Canada and played a major role in the American Revolution, the War of 1812, and the Rebellion of 1837. Some of these soldiers stayed on after the wars and settled in Canada. In the 1880s and '90s, Welsh settlers arrived in Canada from Wales and the United States. Many were Presbyterians who helped establish Protestant churches in Canada. In Toronto, the early community formed its first organization in 1887, when a group of Welshmen gathered at a house for the first elections of the **St. David's Society**. **Dewi Sant Welsh Church** was established 20 years later and Sunday prayer meetings and a bible class were held in a room on Wellington Street.

In 1908, a Welsh Sunday school and choir were formed and the groups moved to **Temperance Hall** on Bathurst Street. The church rented the Christian Workers' church building on Clinton Street, and purchased it two years later in 1917. The **Dewi Sant Church**, located in North Toronto, was built by the congregation in 1969 under the direction of Reverend John Humphreys Jones. Since 1946 all ministers have come from Wales.

From 1900 to 1950, more than 50,000 Welsh came to Canada in four waves of immigration: in 1906, following the First World War, following the Second World War, and in 1957. From the 1960s to the present, few Welsh have moved to Canada. The largest groups of Welsh settlers are located in Ontario, particularly Toronto.

Notable Welsh Canadians include Sir Charles G.D. Roberts, an animated-story writer and member of the Poets of Confederation, who was knighted in 1935; the Most Reverend Derwyn Trevor Owen, the Anglican Primate of Canada and the Archbishop of Toronto; and George Brett, former Chairman of the Philosophy Department at the **University of Toronto** and author of several books. Leonard Brockington, a speech writer for Prime Minister Mackenzie King, was the first chairman of the **CBC**. Senator Rupert Davies, former publisher of the **Kingston Whig Standard**, was given the honourary Welsh title, High Sheriff of the County of Meirioneth, in recognition of his service to Canada. His son, Robertson Davies, became a celebrated author and Master of **Massey College** at the **University of Toronto**.

Today, the city's Welsh express their love of rugby, singing, dancing, and poetry through tournaments and annual festivals. Visiting choirs from Wales often perform concerts at **Roy Thomson Hall**. Every year, the **St. David's Society** presents a goat to the **Fort Henry** detachment in memory of the mascot of Welsh military regiments stationed in Kingston, Ontario, during the 1800s.

Places to Go

Many Welsh attend local and provincial Celtic fairs. Welsh singing, dancing, cooking, and storytelling take place at these events. Welsh food includes leek soup, meat pies, sausage rolls, and sponge cakes.

Religious Centres, Schools and Other Institutions

Many Welsh in the city are Methodists and Presbyterians and frequent their own church:

◆ DEWI SANT WELSH UNITED CHURCH, (Tel. 416-485-7583, www.dewisant.com, 33 Melrose Ave).

Lessons in the Welsh language (Cymraeg) are given by John Otley.

Holidays and Celebrations

◆ ST. DAVID'S DAY is celebrated on the closest weekend to March 1 in honour of the patron saint of Wales who preached Christianity and comforted the sick and the poor. According to legend, daffodils burst into bloom on this day. Another legend says that the Welsh won a victory over the Saxons by wearing leeks in their hats, which prevented the accidental killing of their own men. Every year on St. David's Day, the Welsh place leeks in their hats and attend a ball and dinner, followed by a church celebration.

◆ GYMANFA GANU (FESTIVAL OF SACRED SONGS) is held annually, just after Easter, at local, provincial, national, and international levels. The aim of the festival is to promote hymn-singing and Welsh unity. The Welsh church in Toronto holds its own Gymanfa on Good Friday evening with people attending from all over Toronto. Every few years the Gymanfa Ganu of North America is held in Toronto, hosted by the church or the **St. David's Society**.

◆ EISTEDDFOD, a national arts festival featuring choral and solo singing, poetry, and crafts, is held in Wales in the winter.

See Holidays and Celebrations in Glossary.

Organizations

◆ ST. DAVID'S SOCIETY, (Tel. 416-485-7583, 33 Melrose Ave). One of the Loyal Societies, St. David's is a Welsh cultural club that was started in 1887, with affiliates across Canada. Meets monthly at the **Dewi Sant Welsh United Church**. President: Myfanwy Bajaj.

Prominent Torontonians

Myfanwy Bajaj, President of St. David's Society; Anne Johnston, Former Toronto Councillor; Tom Jones, Richmond Hill Town Crier; Frank Jones, newspaper columnist for the Toronto Star; Gaynor Jones Low, professor of music at University of Toronto and opera singer; Dave (Tiger) Williams, former NHL hockey player; Jason Howard, opera singer; Shannon Mercer, opera singer; Peter Williams, entrepeneur/businessman; Gwyndaf Jones, professional opera singer; Geraint Wyn Davies, actor; Lynette Jenkins, Volunteer with 'Sleeping Children Around the World.'

Sources: Tom Jones, Harold Woodey, Myfanwy Bajaj.

Glossary of Holidays & Celebrations

Members of Toronto's cultural communities are predominantly Christians, Jews, Muslims, Hindus, Sikhs, Buddhists, Zoroastrians, and Jains. Depending on the group, holidays and feast days are calculated according to lunar (Buddhist, Muslim), lunisolar (Chinese, Hindu, Jewish), and solar (Gregorian, Julian) calendars. Christian churches celebrate the feast day of their patron saint, usually on the day the saint died.

Holidays

New Year's Day is an event celebrated by cultural groups around the world. The highlight of festivities is New Year's Eve when parties are held to usher out the old and welcome in the New Year. The day has many traditions and for some it is a religious observance devoted to spiritual preparation. While the public holiday is celebrated on January 1, followers of the Julian calendar celebrate on January 14. Others such as the Hindus, Sikhs, Jains, and Buddhists, celebrate Baisakhi (meaning the first day of that month) on April 13. The Chinese celebrate Chinese New Year according to the lunar calendar in January or February.

Buddhist Holidays (celebrated according to the lunar calendar)

The basic element of the calendar year is the lunar month, which is divided into periods of the waxing and waning moon. The 8th and 15th days of the waxing moon and the 8th day and the final day of the waning moon are sacred Buddhist days. During the 8th and 15th days of the waxing moon, the laity go to the pagoda to hear scriptural readings, and a strict fast is observed. On the 8th day and the final day of the waning moon, joyous festivities take place.

Buddhists celebrate the Birth, Enlightenment, and Parinirvana (final demise) of Buddha, the founder of Buddhism. In addition to observing religious practices in the home or in the temple, Buddhists light lanterns in the evening.

See Chinese and Laos chapters for more Buddhist holidays.

Christian Feast Days

January 6 is Epiphany, a festival celebrating the arrival of the three Magi who bore gifts for the Christ child in Bethlehem. Some Christians also link this celebration with Christ's birth and baptism. Those who follow the Julian calendar celebrate Theophany (the baptism of Christ) on January 20.

On February 2, Candlemas Day commemorates the presentation of Christ in the temple, which occurred 40 days after Christ's birth. In the Orthodox Church, this event is honoured on February 16.

On February 14, Sts. Cyril and Methody Day is held in honour of the brothers who influenced the religious development of the Slavic people in the ninth century A.D., and created a new Slavonic alphabet (Cyrillic). It is celebrated as a day of piety and remembrance in honour of their work. Followers of the Julian calendar generally celebrate on February 26, while the Bulgarians and Macedonians commemorate the saints on May 24, and the Czech and Slovak communities hold a celebration on the first Sunday in July.

In February or March, Shrove Tuesday (also known as Pancake Tuesday) is a movable feast commemorating the last day before the beginning of Lent and is associated with confessing sins. Butter Week, which precedes Lent, is a joyous occasion where pancakes with butter are served. On the weekend before Lent, many communities hold a Mardi Gras festival with masquerade balls.

Ash Wednesday, in February or March, follows Shrove Tuesday and marks the first day of Lent. It is observed to teach humility. In Roman Catholic and Anglican churches, ashes are used to trace the sign of the cross on the forehead of worshipers. On the first Monday of Lent (called Clean Monday), the Eastern Orthodox fast by consuming only vegetables or shellfish. The following 40 days of the Lenten season are marked by fasting and prayers (Wednesdays and Fridays are also fast days in the Orthodox calendar).

In March, April, or May, Christians celebrate Holy Week. It starts on Palm Sunday, held the Sunday before Easter, which commemorates Christ's triumphant entry into Jerusalem, when palm branches were strewn in His path. Churches distribute palm leaves or pussy willows to parishioners. On Maundy Thursday, church services commemorate the Last Supper when Christ instituted the Eucharist. Good Friday, held the Friday preceding Easter Sunday, is a day of fasting, abstinence, and penance commemorating the suffering and crucifixion of Christ. The culmination of Holy Week is Easter Sunday, signifying Christ's resurrection from the dead. Easter is a movable feast (as are all Holy Week feast days) held on the Sunday following the first full moon that occurs on or after March 21. New clothes are worn and parades are held. Orthodox Christians celebrate Easter with a candlelight procession that circles the edifice three times after evening prayers. They greet each other with "Christ is risen" and respond with "He has risen indeed." Coloured hard-boiled eggs, which represent the empty tomb and signify new life, are given out after the church service. Easter Monday is celebrated with church services.

Forty days after Easter is Ascension Day, commemorating the appearance of Christ before His apostles for the last time. Fifty days after Easter, Christians celebrate Pentecost, which signifies the coming of the Holy Spirit to Christ's followers after His resurrection and ascension. Orthodox Christians celebrate the Feast of the Holy Trinity (Pentecost). Green leaves and new grass are scattered on the floor of the church, as a reminder that Christ's spirit lives on.

Saint George's Day is celebrated on April 23 (and on May 6 according to the Julian calendar). Church services and secular festivities are held on this day.

In June, the Feast of St. Peter and St. Paul is celebrated by the Catholic Church with special services.

On September 14 (and on September 28 according to the Julian calendar) Christians celebrate the Feast Day of the Holy Cross, commemorating the finding of the Holy Cross by the Byzantine Empress, St. Helena.

At the end of November, Christians celebrate Advent, in preparation for Christmas. In Western churches, Advent (Christmas Lenten) begins on the Sunday nearest November 30 and includes the four Sundays before Christmas. In the Eastern Orthodox Church, Advent begins on November 28, and in the Coptic Orthodox Church on November 25.

St. Nicholas Day is celebrated on December 6, and on December 19 by Orthodox Christians. St. Nicholas was a bishop who was renowned for his kindness and charitable deeds, particularly to children. Gifts are given to children in honour of the Saint.

In December or January, Christmas celebrates the birth of Christ. For most, the celebration takes place on December 24 or 25, while Eastern Church followers celebrate on January 6 or 7. Gifts are exchanged.

Hindu Observances

March is the month of Holi, a joyous festival when friends sprinkle coloured water on each other for good fortune. Special foods are prepared and the celebration includes dancing and singing.

Jamashtami is a festival in honour of the birth of Lord Krishna celebrated with devotional singing and dancing, and all-night prayer vigils.

Homes are decorated with lights on Diwali (Deepawali), the Hindu Festival of Lights. It is celebrated on the weekend nearest the date with prayers, festivities, and gifts of new clothing.

Hindus celebrate Durga Puja and Dussehra in October. These festivals recognize the triumph of good over evil and are celebrated with religious festivities.

See East Indian chapter for more Hindu Observances.

Jewish Holidays

See pages 266–68.

Muslim Holidays

Dates are calculated according to the lunar calendar. Muharram is the beginning of the New Year and is marked by a community or family dinner.

The Birth of the Prophet Mohammed (570–632 A.D.) is celebrated on the 12th day of Rabi'l. This religious celebration places emphasis on the Prophet's life.

Ramadan is the ninth month in the Muslim calendar, and signifies the occasion of the revelation of the Koran to Mohammed. It is observed as a month of strict fasting from sunrise to sunset.

Eid-ul-Fitr is the holy day held on the first day of Shawwal which marks the end of Ramadan. It is a joyful occasion with a reaffirmation of Muslim virtues.

On the ninth day of Dulhegga, Eid-ul-Adha (the Feast of Sacrifice) remembers Abraham's test of obedience to God. It is commemorated with traditional rites and a ceremonial dinner.

Organizations Serving Multiculturalism

- **Canada Maple Leaf Dragon Founder & Multicultural Society**, (Tel. 416-690-8067, 121 Newport Ave). President: Mr. Willy Tong. Their purpose is to bring all multicultural organizations under one umbrella in order to address their concerns in a unified manner.
- **Caribbean Cultural Committee**, (Tel. 647-777-1018, 138 Hamilton St). Organizes Caribana parade.
- **Canadian Ethnic Media Association**, (canadianethnicmedia.com, 24 Tarlton Rd). President: Dat Nguyen.
- **National Ethnic Press and Media Council of Canada**, (www.nepmcc.ca, P.O. Box 266, Station O). Has a membership of publishers and editors representing dozens of different cultures and languages across Canada, holds meetings throughout the year, and sponsors an Ethnic Press Festival at **Ontario Place**, usually held on the last Sunday in August. President: Thomas S. Saras.
- **Harbourfront**, (Tel. 416-973-3000, www.harbourfrontcentre.com, 235 Queens Quay W). Harbourfront hosts a number of multicultural events throughout the year, including: **St. Jean Baptist Day** on June 24; **World Stage** in June, featuring theatre companies from around the world; **Freedom Fest** in early July; **World Of Music arts and Dance** festival in August, featuring arts, music, and dance from five continents; **International Festival of Authors** in October, featuring readings by 40 authors; an international film and dance series; and a multicultural reading series which is held throughout the year. CEO: William Boyle.
- **Human Rights and Race Relations Centre**, (Tel. 416-487-9763, 120 Eglinton Ave. E., Suite 500). Resource centre dealing with issues of equity, multiculturism, racism, immigration, and ethnic media. It gives gold medals to individuals and institutions who excel in promotion to racial harmony. President: Hasanat Ahmad Syed
- The **Multicultural History Society of Ontario (MHSO)**, (Tel. 416-979-2973, www.mhso.ca, 901 Lawrence Avenue West, Suite 307). Formed in 1976, an important part of the MHSO's mandate is to

enhance both academic and community understanding of multicultur-alism. It preserves and records the province's immigrant and ethnic history through: supporting research programs and the collection of archival and library resources; promoting exhibits of newly gathered heritage materials and records; sponsoring international conferences; and an extensive publishing program. Its research library (which includes collections of ethnic press, manuscripts, and thousands hours of oral testimony in more than 50 languages), and editorial and administrative offices are housed at the **Multicultural History Centre** on the campus of the **University of Toronto**. The Society publishes a bulletin, **Polyphony**. A non-profit corporation, MHSO is a registered charity. Chair and CEO: Prof. Milton Israel.

- **Maytree Foundation**, (Tel. 416-944-2627, www.maytree.com, 170 Bloor St W, Suite 804). Maytree invests in leaders to build a Canada that can benefit from the skills, experience and energy of all its people. Their policy insights promote equity and prosperity. Their programs and grants create diversity in the workplace, in the boardroom, the media and in public office, changing the face of leadership in the country. President: Ratna Omidvar

- The **Community Folk Art Council of Toronto**. (Tel. 416-368-8743, 173B Front St. E). sponsors several events, including: Canada Day celebrations on July 1; **Heritage Celebrations** on Labour Day; **Christmas Trees in Setting** at the **ROM** and **Christmas Around the World** in December; **Easter Around the World**; and the **International Folk Art Fair**. Contact: Wendy Limbertie, Executive Director.

- **Heritage Toronto**, (Tel. 416-338-0684, www.heritagetoronto.org, 157 King St. E., Historical St. Lawrence Hall, 3rd floor). A charitable agency of the City of Toronto, it is responsible for presenting heritage programming with city-wide perspective.

- **Ministry of Citizenship and Immigration**, (Tel. 416-327-2422, Fax 416-314-4965, www.citizenship.gov.on.ca/english, 400 University Ave). Contact: The Honourable Dr. Eric Hoskins.

- **Ministry of Culture**, (Tel. 416-212-0644, www.culture.gov.on.ca, 99 Wellesley St. W., Room 4320, Whiney Block). Contact: The Honourable Michael Chan.

- **Ontario Multicultural Association**, (Tel. 416-979-2973, 43 Queen's Park Cres. E). Promotes multicultural education through a series of workshops, conferences, and seminars. Membership is composed of school boards, libraries, multicultural organizations, and other groups and individuals.

- **Ontario Folk Dance Association**, (Tel. 416-537-7360, www.ofda.ca). A non-profit organization established to promote international folk dancing. Sponsors events of interest to the folk-dance community, including workshops and ethnic theme evenings, and publishes a magazine, **Folk Dancer**, seven times a year. Contact: Kevin Budd.
- **Working Women Community Centre**, (Tel. 416-532-2824, 533A Gladstone Ave). Service available throughout the Greater Toronto Area in a variety of languages. Free services available to all immigrant women and their families.

Bibliography

Abu-Laban, Baha. *An Olive Branch on the Family Tree: The Arabs in Canada*. Toronto: McClelland and Stewart, 1980.

Allen, G.P. (Glyn). *Days To Remember*. Toronto: Ministry of Culture and Recreation, 1979.

Anderson, Grace M., and David Higgs. *A Future to Inherit: The Portuguese Communities of Canada*. Toronto: McClelland and Stewart, 1976.

Armenians in Ontario. Ed. Isabel Kaprielian. Polyphony, Vol. 4, No. 2. Toronto: The Multicultural History Society of Ontario, 1982.

Barer-Stein, Thelma. *You Eat What You Are: A Study of Canadian Ethnic Food Tradition*. Toronto: McClelland and Stewart, 1979.

Bonavia, George. *Maltese in Canada*. Ottawa: Multiculturalism Directorate, 1980.

Bratina, Dr. V.J. "Slovenia and Slovenians in a Nutshell" in *Lovski Vestnik* (The Slovenian Hunters and Anglers Review), 1988.

Canada, Department of the Secretary of State. Multiculturalism Directorate. *The Canadian Family Tree: Canada's People*. Don Mills, Ontario: Corpus, 1979. See entries under various cultural groups.

The Canadian Encyclopedia. Edmonton: Hurtig Publishers, 1985 ed. See entries under various cultural groups.

Chimbos, Peter D. *The Canadian Odyssey: The Greek Experience in Canada*. Toronto: McClelland and Stewart, 1980.

Froeschle, Harmut. *Die Deutschen in Kanada: Eine Volksgruppe im Wandel*. Vienna: Oesterreichische Landsmannschaft, 1987.

Gathering Place: Peoples and Neighbourhoods of Toronto, 1834–1945. Ed. Robert F. Harney. Toronto: The Multicultural History Society of Ontario, 1985.

Hill, Dan. "The Blacks in Toronto."

Nicolson, Murray W. "Peasants in an Urban Society: The Irish Catholics in Victorian Toronto."

Nipp, Dora. "The Chinese in Toronto."

Petroff, Lillian "Sojourner and Settler: the Macedonian Presence in the City, 1903–1940."

Speisman, Stephen A. "St. John's Shtetl: the Ward in 1911."

Zucchi, John E. "Italian Hometown Settlements and the Development of an Italian Community in Toronto, 1875–1935."

Gellner, John, and John Smerek. *The Czechs and Slovaks in Canada*. Toronto: University of Toronto Press, 1968.

German-Canadian Yearbook, vols. 1–10. Ed. Harmut Froeschle (vols. 1–7), Gerhard Friesen and Karin Guerttler (vols. 7–10). Toronto: Historical Society of Mecklenburg Upper Canada, 1973–1989.

Houston, C., and W.J. Smyth. "Toronto, The Belfast of Canada." Paper read at British-Canadian Symposium in Historical Geography, Danbury, May 1977.

Hungarians in Ontario. Ed. Susan M. Papp. Polyphony, Vol. 2, No. 2–3. Toronto: The Multicultural History Society of Ontario, 1980.

The Iranian Directory. Toronto: Mihan Publishing Inc., 1987.

Kazemi, M.S. *Iranians in Ontario*. Toronto: Mihan Publishing, 1986.

Kirschbaum, J.M. *Slovaks in Canada*. Toronto: Canadian Ethnic Press Association of Ontario, 1967.

Lehmann, Heinz. *The German-Canadians, 1750–1937, Immigration, Settlement and Culture*. Trans., ed. and intr. by Gerhard Bassler. St. John's Nfld.: Jesperson Press, 1986.

MaGee, Joan. *The Belgians in Ontario*. Toronto: Dundurn Press, 1987.

Marques, Domingos, and Joao Medeiros. *Portuguese Immigrants 25 Years in Canada*. Toronto: Marquis Printers, 1980.

McHugh, Patricia. *Toronto Architecture: A City Guide*. Toronto: Mercury Books, 1985.

Ritts, Morton. "The High Holidays Handbook." *Toronto Life*. October, 1986.

Sadouski, John. *A History of Byelorussians in Canada*. Belleville, Ontario: Mika Publishing, 1981.

Salute to 25 Years, 1963–1988. Toronto: The Japanese Canadian Cultural Centre, 1988.

Schmidt, Frank. *Who Are The Danube Swabians?* Toronto. (1988).

Serbs in Ontario: A Socio-Cultural Description. Eds. Sofija Skoric and George Vid Tomashevich. Islington, Ontario: The Serbian Heritage Academy of Canada, 1988.

Speisman, Stephen A. *The Jews of Toronto.* Toronto: McClelland and Stewart, 1979.

25 Years Sts. Cyril and Methodious Parish Toronto, Canada 1934–1959. Toronto: Sts. Cyril and Methodius Parish.

Toronto Civic Sculptures. Toronto: City of Toronto Planning and Development Department, 1985.

The Torontonians: Toronto's Multicultural Heritage. Toronto: Toronto Historical Board, 1982. See entries under various cultural groups.

Toronto's People. Ed. Robert F. Harney. Polyphony, Vol. 6, No. 1.

Toronto: The Multicultural History Society of Ontario, 1984.

"A Romanian Boardinghouse."

"Native People."

"The Rise of the Toronto Jewish Community, the Reminiscences of S.M. Shapiro."

"Wartime Toronto and Japanese Canadians."

Aruja, Endel. "The Estonian Presence in Toronto."

Boekelman, Mark. "The Duca Community Credit Union."

Bustamante, Rosalina E. "Filipino Canadians: A Growing Community in a Fast-Developing City."

Cumbo, Richard C. "A Brief History of the Maltese Canadian Community of Toronto."

Danys, Milda. "Lithuanian Parishes in Toronto."

Duran, Marcela S. "Characteristics of the Spanish-Speaking Latin American Community."

Edwards, Afroze. "Indian Immigrant Aid Services."

Fernandez, M., and Perez, A. "Spanish Iberian Community of Toronto."

Forde, Jean. "Jamaicans in Toronto."

Gadon, Sean. "The Syrian Religious Experience in Toronto, 1896–1920s."

Gagat, Zofia. "St. Stanislaus Parish: the Heart of Toronto Polonia."

Grubisic, Vinko. "Croatians in Toronto."

Handera, Vladimir I. "The Russian Orthodox Church in Toronto."

Harney, Robert F. "Chiaroscuro: Italians in Toronto, 1885–1915."

Jones, Rev. J. Humphreys. "A Short Story of the Dewi Sant Welsh United Church."

Kaprielian, Isabel. "Armenians in Toronto: a Survey of One Hundred Years."

Kim, Jung-Gun. "How Koreans Came to Call Toronto Their Home."

Liepins, Valdis. "The Latvian Canadian Cultural Centre."

Lindstrom-Best, Varpu. "The Finnish Immigrant Community of Toronto, 1887–1913."

Mackenzie King, William Lyon. "The French Colony."

Mah, Valerie. "Early Chinatown."

Markoff, Irene. "Persistence of Old-World Cultural Expression in the Traditional Music of Bulgarian Canadians."

Martens, Hildegard M. "The German Community of St. Patrick's Parish, 1929 to the Present."

Mavalwala, Jamshed. "The Zoroastrian Community of Ontario."

Nicolson, Murray W. "The Other Toronto: Irish Catholics in a Victorian City, 1850–1900."

Miezitis, Solveiga. "Reflections on Cultural Maintenance, Innovation and Change in the Latvian Community."

Papp, Susan M. "The Hungarian Community of Toronto: Over Fifty Years of Change."

Qureshi, M.H.K. "The South Asian Community."

Ray, Riten. "Bengali Community Life in Toronto."

Shepperd, Patrick. "Caribana."

Salloum, Habeeb. "History of the Canadian Arab Friendship Society."

Singh, Jarnail. "Sikhs."

Sugunasiri, Suwanda H.J. "Sri Lankans in Canada."

Vagners, Martin. "Latvian Settlement in the City."

Wai-Man, Lee. "Dance No More: Chinese Hand Laundries in Toronto."

Yilmazkaya, E. "Research Report for the Multicultural History Society on the Toronto Turkish Community."

Ziniak, Madeline. "Byelorussian Literature in Toronto."

Ukrainians in Ontario. Ed. Lubomyr Luciuk and Iroida Wynnyckyj. Polyphony, Vol. 10. Toronto: The Multicultural History Society of Ontario, 1988.

Gregorovich, Andrew. "The Ukrainian Community in Toronto from World War One to 1971."

Sokolsky, Zoriana Yaworsky. "The Beginnings of the Ukrainian Settlement in Toronto, 1891–1939."

Ukrainian Toronto: A Directory of Ukrainian Cultural Groups, Organizations and Institutions in Toronto. Compiled by Andrew Gregorovich. 2nd ed. Toronto: Ukrainian Canadian Committee, 1976.

Urbanc, Peter, and Eleanor Tourtel. *Slovenians in Canada.* Stoney Creek, Ontario: Slovenian Heritage Festival Committee, 1984.

Von Vulte, Manfred J. *Where Have All of Toronto's German's Gone?* Nepean, Ontario: Borealis Press Ltd., 2003